The Alabama Black McGruders

J.R. Rothstein, et al.

Redstone Publishing

New York

First Edition

For more information about white Magruders and black McGruders generally, visit www.magruderslanding.com.

ISBN: 978-1-7353986-8-6

Library of Congress Control Number: 2020923222

For the Lucilles

Credits

Cover Design

Patrice Aggs

J.R. Rothstein, Esq.

Sahar Amiri

Authors

J.R. Rothstein, Esq.

Professor Kevin McGruder

Professor Susan Tichy

Lead Editor

Professor Susan Tichy

Editors

J.R. Rothstein, Esq.

Professor Kevin McGruder

Jay Rothstein

Marie McGruder

Dr. Jill Magruder

Nikki Smith

Contributors

Catherine Gibbs-Robertson

Curtis Robertson, Jr.

Professor Kevin McGruder

Sabrina Franklin

Professor Susan Tichy

Lucille Burden Osborne

Tanya Robertson-Rothstein

Betty Shaw

Rev. Orlando McGruder

Rhea Mihalisin

Jill Magruder

Jonathan May

Kathy Miller

Ellen Fancy

Wilmar McGruder

Gwendolyn Hubbard

"What became of the black people of Sumer?"

the traveler asked the old man,

"for ancient records show

that the people of Sumer were black.

What happened to them?"

"Ah", the old man sighed.

"They lost their history,

so they died."

Chancellor Williams
The Destruction of Black Civilization

Table of Contents

Part I

Introduction

By J.R. Rothstein, Esq.

Maya Angelou once remarked that there "is no greater agony than bearing an untold story inside you." For over a century, the men and women of the black McGruders of Hale and Greene Counties, Alabama, a family I call the Alabama Black McGruders, have carried the untold story of their ancestors—Ned, Mariah, and Charles—within them.

Writing some three decades ago, Marva McGrew, an Alabama Black McGruder, observed the importance of memorializing the history of this family. She wrote:

> The [Alabama Black] McGruder legacy is rich and varied. As blacks, we tend not to write about ourselves, preferring instead to leave the chore to others. However, the significance for documenting our history cannot be overemphasized. Our history and the family land in Sawyerville are the most important things we can pass onto future generations. Family history fosters self-esteem. It serves as inspiration for future generations, challenging them to excel in their accomplishments.[1]

Likewise, Kevin McGruder, also an Alabama Black McGruder, writing around the same time, asked more specific questions about the origins of this family:

> Why did a family of former slaves adopt the surname McGruder? What is the relation between the Alabama [Black] McGruders of the mid 1800's and other McGruders that appear in census records in Augusta and Apple[ing], Georgia, Richmond, Virginia, and Muskogee, Alabama, in the late 1700's and early 1800's? What is the relation between the Alabama [Black] McGruders . . . [and other McGruders in] . . . other parts of the country?[2]

This book is a humble attempt to answer the call of Marva McGrew and the questions of Kevin McGruder by memorializing the history of the Alabama Black

---

[1] Unpublished 1992 pamphlet created for the Alabama Black McGruder family reunion.

[2] Unpublished pamphlet created for the Alabama Black McGruder family reunion. Date unknown.

McGruders. This book, at the same time, aims to share the story of the family with the "white branch" of the Alabama Black McGruders, and the people of the United States more generally.

Ned Magruder, the patriarch of the Alabama Black McGruders, was born to an enslaved black woman and Ninian Offutt Magruder, a white great-great grandson of the famed Scottish immigrant, Alexander Magruder. Upon Ninian's death, Ned, as a boy of eight years, was separated from his mother and given to Eleanor Magruder Wynne, Ninian's daughter and Ned's half-sister. Ned would marry Mariah (surname unknown), and together they would have a son, Charles Magruder. Through a series of events, to be elaborated upon in this book, Charles came to be exploited as a stud to breed enslaved people. Later, after slavery, Charles would receive reparations from his first cousin and former enslaver, Osmun Appling Wynne, often referenced throughout this book as O.A. Wynne.

Charles, in his capacity as a breeder, was sexually exploited and forced to sire a hundred children, including fifty-two sons, with numerous women. Many of these children had large families, who had large families of their own. Hundreds, if not thousands, of Charles's descendants would go on to populate Alabama and its adjacent territories during the late nineteenth and twentieth centuries. Together, they established communal and business networks and institutions to support their families and communities. Today, their descendants can be found all over the world. They have impacted the story of the United States in areas of culture, government, law, science, medicine, academia, and business.

Through memorializing this history, we honor the legacies of the ancestors of the Alabama Black McGruders—people like Ned, Mariah, and Charles. They were survivors, but they didn't just survive. Charles and his family, like so many other formerly enslaved people, built something impressive. Charles Magruder, who would come to be known in the Reconstruction era as Charles McGruder Sr., syndicated real estate deals and started businesses. He gathered and took responsibility for his many children. He zealously pursued the education of his children and grandchildren, and they, in turn, continued to build on what Charles began. These accomplishments are to be respected for any person, at any time, in any context. Even more impressive and inspiring is when they are achieved by an ambitious family emerging from enslavement and Jim Crow who had so many obstacles to overcome. It is my hope that this book and the story it contains will inspire the present generation of Alabama Black McGruders to succeed and to surpass the great accomplishments of our ancestors.

The story of the Alabama Black McGruders is also representative of the complicated racial history of the United States and has implications well beyond our family. In our country, we have a common discourse about "white" and "black" Americans; the story of the Alabama Black McGruders shows that the truth is more complex. A white descendant of Ninan O. Magruder is more closely related, genetically and historically, to the Alabama Black McGruders than to most other white descendants of Alexander Magruder, The Immigrant. Many Alabama Black McGruders are more closely related, by genetics, to the white Magruders than they are to other African-Americans.

The genetic and familial interconnectedness illustrated by white Magruders and Alabama Black McGruders is not unique. In his PBS series, *Finding Your Roots*, the eminent historian, Professor Henry Louis Gates Jr., frequently points out that almost all descendants of enslaved African-Americans are mixed with some European blood and have someone in their ancestry who fathered a mulatto child in the slavery era by rape and coerced sexual relations. According to Gates, on average, African-Americans have approximately thirty-percent European ancestry.

Yet, because of the history of the United States, and its present racial divide, some amongst the Alabama Black McGruders have overlooked their connection to the white Magruders. One might suggest that they have repressed the connection from their historical memory due to the painful knowledge of the transatlantic slave trade, enslavement, emasculation, and exploitation that such a connection evokes. Likewise, some white Magruders are unaware that they are related to black McGruders and the topic raises feelings of awkwardness, guilt, and shame. Although understandable, the instinct to bury our history is mistaken. We cannot ignore the past just because it is painful.

In order to write a justice-based future for our family, and our nation, we must first become more conscious of our history and our connections to each other. We cannot move beyond this moment in time, in which we are still caught in the currents of racism and colorism, until we first understand our past and its present consequences. The legacy of enslavement, built on the belief that one group of human beings—white skinned people—is superior to another—black skinned people—is still actively with us today. It is expressed as the legacy of disparity in wealth and income, health and education, policing and incarceration, colorism, and housing discrimination. It is present even in the best efforts of a historian who might attempt to write a history of enslavement from an African-American perspective while suffering from a lack of primary documents drafted from an enslaved perspective.

However, this injustice and its disparity will not last forever. It is by embracing the true complexity of our past—much in the way I posit that O.A. Wynne and

Charles Magruder Sr. did—that we—McGruders and Magruders of all races—can begin to take concrete actions to heal our collective pain. This is the necessary step we must take if we are to live up to the promise of this country and enter a new post-racial era, as envisioned by the Reverend Dr. Martin Luther King Jr.

The story of Charles McGruder Sr. and Osmun A. Wynne, outlined in Chapter 8, also raises a thought experiment with implications well beyond the history of the Alabama Black McGruders. What would have happened if formerly enslaved families had been compensated with 40 acres and a mule? What would have happened had Reconstruction continued and included a Truth and Reconciliation commission, rooted in Judeo-Christian values, to encourage dialogue and healing between human beings with white and black skin? The story of the Alabama Black McGruders during the Reconstruction era highlights the missed opportunity of the United States to conduct a racial reckoning. The consequences of this dream deferred are self-evident.

Yet despite our national failure during Reconstruction, due to the actions and foresight of Charles McGruder Sr. the Alabama Black McGruders attained a measure of economic independence and self-confidence rooted in land ownership that has lasted for generations. Although some of that independence was lost in the oppression and terror of the Jim Crow era, the integrity of that family ethic remains undiminished to this day. What is special about the Alabama Black McGruders is that we have used our history not as a boulder to weigh heavily upon us, but rather as a foundation from which to build something better.

The Next Chapter

Reflecting on the traumatic history of African-Americans, James Baldwin wrote, "History is not the past. It is the present. We carry our history with us. We are our history." This is true; yet the story of the Alabama Black McGruders shows us that we are not irrevocably bound to the past. A heartbreaking past does not doom us to a tragic tomorrow. History and ancestry, whether glorious or dark, can inspire us to be better in the present.

Ninian Offutt Magruder, the white father of Ned Magruder, left a contradictory legacy. On one hand, he heroically fought for freedom in the American Revolution, one of the greatest advancements of self-government in human history. On the other hand, he betrayed his oath to liberty and God's law when he enslaved other human beings, impregnated at least one of the women he enslaved, and treated his own son, Ned, as if he were common chattel. In short, he was the archetype of a Southern plantation owner of his era. His contradictory legacy is something with which both groups of his descendants, black and white, continue to struggle with as Americans.

Before the white and black descendants of Ninian Offutt Magruder, however, is a choice: do we continue as we have been, or do we begin a process that may lead to family and national healing? We cannot control the actions of our ancestors, nor are we responsible for their actions, but the type of actors we choose to be in the present will define our character. As Juan McGruder, an Alabama Black McGruder, has remarked, "what unites us is not whether we are black or white, but our [actions and] faith in God."

With this value in mind, this book brings together black and white McGruders and Magruders for the purpose of telling this painful yet inspiring story—one of perseverance, ambition, family, forgiveness, and reconciliation. The journey started by Charles McGruder Sr. is the commitment to put one foot in front of the other, believing in the possibility of shaping a better tomorrow. This determination is inspiring not just for Magruders and McGruders, but for all human beings. By sharing this story, the Alabama Black McGruders are engaging in an act of healing the compounded collective trauma of generations inherited from our ancestors. Our story offers hope for the enduring power of the human spirit to persevere and rebuild after unspeakable horrors. This makes the story of the Alabama Black McGruders not just relevant to a single Southern African-American family, but one of universal significance.

My desire and ability to reach across the racial divide to craft this book is no doubt informed by my multiracial background. My mother is an Alabama Black McGruder, a great-great granddaughter of Charles McGruder Sr., and my father descends from Jewish refugees. I am comfortable crossing "racial barriers" to serve as a bridge between "white" and "black" cultures. I did so during the preparation of this book, which includes submissions from both white and black descendants of Ninian O. Magruder. I also collected the letters, written between white Magruders and black McGruders, that are annexed to the narrative. Each of these letters is a step toward creating our own McGruder and Magruder Truth and Reconciliation endeavor.

I am conscious of the overwhelming weight of the history presented within and outwith these pages. We have a tremendous task before us. I am not naïve regarding the deep trauma and pain that exists. It will be difficult to overcome our past—although faith teaches us that it will happen one day. Let the Talmudic maxim of Rav. Tarphon guide us: "Ay, yes the work is much, and the day is long.

But we are not obligated to finish the task, but neither are we permitted to withdraw from it."[3]

Together, we are about to undertake a journey. Together, we will recount the story of Ned, Mariah, and Charles. Together, we will wrestle with how to acknowledge our painful familial and national past and use it as inspiration to fashion a better tomorrow. Together, we have now begun a multi-generational conversation about healing the divergent branches of our collective, bringing us together as one.

Methodology

Disclaimers need to be made concerning the historical accuracy of some events described herein, as this document has been compiled, in part, from oral accounts from many sources about events and people who lived well over a century ago. Much of this document results from my parsing together different oral accounts from different descendants of Charles McGruder Sr.—an arduous task which is prone to error.

If I have been successful in accurately portraying the people and events herein, then all the credit is due to G-d and the ancestors, and only the errors in judgment or interpretation are mine. Throughout this document, I note the points that need more research. I invite the reader to contribute and challenge this narrative so that we may together complete the story. Should you, the reader, have a different understanding of the people and events described, or have something to add, please do not defer to this history. Rather, contact me so we can document a differing understanding of events and amend this history accordingly.

Style & Content Notes

A few notes regarding style and content should be pointed out to the reader:

a.   The cover of this book presents a logo inspired by international artist Patrice Aggs, an Alabama Black McGruder, contemplating what a family coat of arms could look like. It adopts both African and Scottish themes. This is a recent innovation and not part of the historic identity of the Alabama Black McGruders;

b.   This book does *not* attempt to trace the familial line of all black Magruders and McGruders. It is relevant *only* to those black Magruder and McGruder families that were enslaved by the Magruder-Wynne families of Hale and Greene Counties, Alabama. Numerous other black Magruder and McGruder

---

[3]   Robert Young and Nathan, ha-Bavli, *The Ethics of the Fathers* (Edinburgh: Robert Young, 1852), 2:1.

families exist elsewhere, with their own separate histories, and share no direct connection to the Alabama Black McGruder patriarch, Ned Magruder;

c.   Although most Alabama Black McGruders today employ the *McGruder* spelling of their surname, at the beginning of the narrative I refer to the Ned and Mariah *Magruder* family, using the form of the surname used until the 1870s, when the *McGruder* spelling was adopted by the vast majority, though not all, of the family;

d.   I have included many, but not all, of what I believe are important primary historical documents in the history of this family. They have been transcribed to the best of my ability and I have not altered wording or spelling from the originals. However, I have bolded the names of the enslaved people within the documents—names which are not bolded in the original. I did this out of sensitivity to the fact that these legal documents are discussing, transacting, and trafficking in human beings, who are my ancestors, and by bolding their names we give these enslaved people a voice they did not have at the time.

e.   Sometimes, the reader may find a lack of citation to statements made in the book. This is because the narrative of the Alabama Black McGruders has been parsed together from stories, told by dozens of people, that by themselves were not significant but when put together like a puzzle formed a compelling narrative. I have faithfully relayed the original pieces of the puzzle, but the arrangement and interpretation of these pieces are entirely mine.

f.   In writing this book, I also relied on oral history accounts—scraps of paper and notes from dozens of family members circulated at family reunions. Where possible, I cite specific individuals. Unless otherwise stated, all individuals cited as sources are biological members of the Alabama Black McGruders—with the exception of Sabrina Franklin of Texas, who has studied the family in the context of her work on the black Wynne family of Texas.

g.   I have, in the preparation of this work, referenced the archive of Wilmar McGruder, a man who dedicated his life to researching the history of the Alabama Black McGruders. The snippets provided by his research and hand-written notes have enriched this manuscript. The Wilmar McGruder Archive is now in the possession of his granddaughter, Shayla McGruder, and great-grandson, Isaiah McGruder-Cruz, both of whom intend to continue Wilmar's work.

h.   I also have referenced a number of local newspaper accounts about historical events and people described herein. Select articles can be found interspersed throughout this manuscript. It must be noted, however, that many of these articles were drawn from southern white newspapers known for their racism and anti-black sentiment. Although there were numerous black newspapers during the Reconstruction era, their contents have not been digitized. For reasons beyond my control (which included, among other things, a global pandemic) I was not able to access these papers in the preparation of this book. Therefore, it will be up to those who come after me to conduct a survey of such papers to determine if there is anything of value to add to this narrative.

i. Throughout this book, I occasionally describe an individual's skin tone (e.g., from the "light skinned" Charles Magruder Sr. to the "dark-black" Curtis Robertson Sr.). I am conscious of the history of colorism in the country at large and in the black community. I am conscious of the horrendous consequences of both. My inclusion of these descriptors in no way endorses this legacy of enslavement. I have chosen to present these descriptions due to their historical value, and because it was, in all cases, my source narrator who used such descriptors when conveying the stories to me. My use of such adjectives therefore reflects the biases, limitations, and realities of the era in which we all live.

j. Finally, at the end of the book I have annexed primary historical documents, newspaper articles, and photographs. I did this so that future researchers can benefit from my labors, and so that others may question and reexamine my conclusions using the same documents I employed.

Acknowledgments

This book would have been impossible without the coming together of many people. Particular thanks must go to the following:

a. My beloved grandmother, of blessed memory, Catherine Dove Gibbs, wife of Curtis Robertson Sr. (family line: Lucille McGruder, William McGruder, Charles McGruder Sr., Ned Magruder, Ninian O. Magruder), who took the time to document a family history that was not hers, but which she entirely adopted as her own. When I was a boy of no more than nine or ten years, she took me to The Newberry Library in Chicago where she trained me in the art of genealogy and archival research. I miss and love her greatly and remain eternally indebted to her for the many gifts she provided me;

b. My parents, Tanya Robertson-Rothstein and Jay R. Rothstein, and my brothers, Joshua Rothstein and Rabbi Isaiah Rothstein, all of whom I love deeply, and who supported me in this project. I'm grateful to my mother, an Alabama Black McGruder, for this wonderful legacy and for my father's consistent support;

c.   My uncles and aunt who, with time and money, have supported my desire to learn more about my roots and have provided me with valuable feedback on this manuscript;

d.   Lucille Burden Osborne, an Alabama Black McGruder, who at 96 still has the same curiosity and passion for family history that she did as a child. I spent days with Lucille, over many years, recounting family history and stories, captivated by her sense of humor, strength, and charming personality. Lucille is an inquisitive and adventurous spirit. When I was not able to travel to her in person, she flew from California to New York in a surprise visit for my birthday, where she captivated a group of fifty people with her stories. Through our discussions, Lucille was able to provide nearly 150 years of family history and allow me to seamlessly weave together the oral history, archival records, and DNA data. This book relies on her testimony, keen analysis, and sense of duty to family. However, it must also be noted that the interpretation and *how* I arranged the pieces of the oral history puzzle that Lucille gave me are my own. In some cases, she would have arranged the pieces of the puzzle differently;

Lucille B. Osborne addresses guests at a birthday party for J.R. Rothstein, an event of the Entreprenuer Shabbat Dinner Series. From left to right: Lucille B Osborne: J.R.Rothstein, the author; and New York Times best-selling author, Dan Schawbel. New York, New York, 2016

e.   Kevin McGruder, an Alabama Black McGruder, who offered me guidance and mentorship throughout this journey. When I was about fourteen years old,

Kevin mailed me a thick packet of material, including a many-foot-long family tree containing the names of Charles McGruder Sr.'s children which he had collected over the years. Kevin is a teacher and a person of service who has given freely of his knowledge to all the members of his family. I stand on the shoulders of his research and organizational skills. Without his decades-long research this book would not have happened. His original work not only inspired me to learn more about the Alabama Black McGruders, but also inspired other McGruder historians. I am honored that Kevin has written an introductory chapter to this book, providing an overview of slavery in Maryland and the transatlantic slave trade;

f.   Susan Tichy, a member of the white Magruder family and editor of Magruder's Landing (https://magruderslanding.com), a website dedicated to the history of the Magruder family and to uniting its various branches, both black and white, as well as assisting descendants of others enslaved by Magruders. She spent many long days painstakingly editing numerous drafts of this work. She is a brilliant and hardworking scholar with tremendous attention to detail, who has greatly enhanced the quality of this manuscript. She is committed to bringing together the different branches of the Magruder and McGruder family. Her commitment to racial healing and honoring truth is moving. I am honored that she has written an introductory chapter to this book, providing an introduction to the white Magruders;

g.   Sabrina Franklin, a member of the black Wynne family, who gives true meaning to the word *genealogist*. Sabrina, who is the mother of six adopted children, spent hundreds of hours over a period of decades gathering details of the life of Ned Magruder. It was due to her research that McGruder family historians have been able to trace the life of Ned Magruder and his connection to the white Magruder family. I am honored that she adopted me as her mentee and lovingly served as an advisor to me throughout this journey;

h.   Jill Magruder-Gatwood, a member of the white Magruder family, who has been seeking links between white and black Magruders/McGruders (and other African-Americans who connect to the Magruders via slavery) for many years. She administers the African-American Magruders/McGruders Y-DNA project through Family Tree DNA (www.ftdna.com) and has financially supported DNA testing for African-American Magruders/McGruders, to help them learn more about their family histories. Jill also provided me with access to subscriptions to numerous databases during the preparation of this manuscript. Jill's commitment to genealogy and to racial healing is unparalleled. Her big heart has provided the social glue that allowed this diverse group of people to work together;

Introduction

i. Marie McGruder, an Alabama Black McGruder, who spent days with me exploring Sawyerville, Alabama and the Alabama Black McGruder family lands. Marie has established McGruder Farms LLC and is building a modern farming project on the historical Alabama Black McGruder homestead. She has been consistently loving and supportive throughout this process, and for that I am grateful;

j. Juan McGruder, an Alabama Black McGruder, who hosted me in his home in Sawyerville and whose faith in God has moved my soul. His positive spirit always gives me joy. He, like Rev. Orlando McGruder, has helped me understand the spiritual history of the Alabama Black McGruders, and for that I am grateful;

k. Betty McGruder Shaw, who was one of the first of the Alabama Black McGruder historians, along with Herman English and Wilmar McGruder, to locate the will of Eleanor Magruder Wynne. Betty spent years researching the family history, visiting research libraries, and collaborating with Kevin McGruder, Herman English, and Wilmar McGruder. It is the work of Betty and her generation of Alabama Black McGruder historians that laid the foundation for this manuscript;

l. Rev. Orlando McGruder, an Alabama Black McGruder, a man of faith, a wonderful listener, who throughout this journey offered me spiritual and practical guidance and mentorship and has helped me understand the Black McGruder story in spiritual terms. I am grateful for his thoughtful analysis and ideas about what the next chapters of our family history should look like;

m. Alice Coleman Griffin, a white descendant of Ninian O. Magruder, via his grandson, O.A. Wynne (family line: Alice Coleman, Osmund Appling Coleman, Bestor Wynne Coleman, Bestor Coleman, Laura Frances Wynne Coleman, Osmun A. Wynne, Eleanor Magruder, Ninian O. Magruder), who is excited to assist the Alabama Black McGruders in our research. Alice preserved hundreds of letters between members of the Wynne family, discovered in a relative's attic. Spanning two centuries, the letters contain numerous references to members of the Alabama Black McGruders. Alice spent years typing up these letters, and eventually established the Wynne Archives at the University of Alabama. She is the author of three books on the family of O.A. Wynne, on which I relied in the preparation of this book: *Laura's Letters* (2008); *Laura's and Her Children's Letters* (2009); and *Laura's Family's Letters* (2011). Our correspondence and her acknowledgment of the Alabama Black McGruders have meant so much to me;

n. Dr. Milton Bosch, a white descendant of Ninian Beall Magruder and a generous, humble, and empathic person, who, at the beginning of my journey, inspired me to persevere, much as he has in his life;

o. Nikki McGruder Smith, who served as an advisor and mentor in preparation of this book, and inspired me to believe, with prayer and positive thinking, that anything is possible;

p. Jonathan May, a fascinating human, and local white historian of Sawyerville, whose passion for history, human fraternity, and great ideas have greatly enriched this manuscript. I am indebted to him regarding much of the material I was able to source in Chapter 5 of this book. I am grateful for his giving spirit, pouring his heart into our story, and for his enthusiastic ideas;

q. Gwendolyn Hubbard, an Alabama Black McGruder, who generously opened her home and traveled with me on this journey. I'll never forget the many hours we shared, sitting at her kitchen table discussing the McGruder story. Gwen's passion for the story of Charles McGruder Sr. warmed my heart during my many long hours reviewing the archival record. Gwen also helped solidify the relationship I developed with Hapner Hart Media. She graciously hosted Lucille B. Osborne in her home for an extended period and provided the venue in which Lucille was interviewed for the 2021 ABC mini-documentary referenced below. Gwen played an important role in helping to bring our story to the attention of the world;

r. James Magruder, a white descendant of Ninian O. Magruder, who warmly embraced me as his long-lost cousin. Jim and I spent hours on the phone getting to know one another. Jim not only provided me with valuable insights into Magruder history, but also generously sent gifts to myself and Juan McGruder. Jim and his family also traveled to the homestead of Charles McGruder Jr. to learn about the Alabama Black McGruder family history. His openness and willingness to reach out across the great racial divide to Juan, myself, and all Alabama Black McGruders has been courageous. He is a man who stands on the right side of history and I am happy to call him a friend;

s. Rhea Mihalisin and Ellen Fancy, members of the San Diego chapter of the Daughters of the American Revolution (DAR), who assisted Lucille Burden Osborne in her historic application to the DAR. Both spent hours as researchers for this book, helping us track down key documents in the lives of the people mentioned herein. They have greatly enriched the quality of this manuscript;

t. Andrew Magruder, a white descendant of Ninian O. Magruder, who graciously shared his DNA with this project and with whom I seemingly share much in common. I hope to one day get to know him better;

Introduction

u.   Kathy Miller, a white Magruder, who spent countless hours tracing the children of Charles McGruder Sr. and who is very passionate about this story;

v.   Geneva Gibbs Wesley, an Alabama Black McGruder, a woman of faith, who provided me important oral history regarding her great-grandmother, Rachel Hill, and whose prayers have uplifted this project;

w.   All my Alabama Black McGruder cousins, who number more than I can possibly list. Each one of you played an important role in this journey. However, special additional thanks must go to Tasha Peace, Genie Adele Cooper-Ahanotu, Shayla McGruder, Isaiah McGruder-Cruz, Collette McGruder, Annie Stenmore, Ruby McGruder Wilson, Dovie Robertson-Thomas, Jimmy Thomas, Robert Brasfield, and Anita McGruder McGrew, who supported this effort with stories, DNA, love, moral support, editing, and time—I am grateful to you all;

x.   Finally, on behalf of all Magruders and McGruders, black and white, I give a special thanks to Patrick "Rafi" Murphy, Theresa Murphy, Annette Grundy, and Jimmy Haas of Hapner Hart Media; Susan Welsh, Jaz Garner of ABC News; and actors Sterling K. Brown and Marsai Martin of *Soul of a Nation* who have given us the opportunity to tell the Alabama Black McGruder story to the world.

I hope you will enjoy this book, that it will shed light on a painful part of our familial and national history, and at the same time remind us of the enduring power of the human heart. With the spirit of Ned, Mariah, and Charles behind us, I hope that together we can endeavor to make a better tomorrow.

In service,

J.R. Rothstein
New York, New York
January 1, 2022

At last, when the ship we were in had got in all her cargo, they made ready with many fearful noises, and we were all put under deck, so that we could not see how they managed the vessel... This wretched situation was again aggravated by the galling of the chains, now become insupportable; and the filth of the necessary tubs, into which the children often fell, and were almost suffocated. The shrieks of the women, and the groans of the dying, rendered the whole a scene of horror almost inconceivable.

Olaudah Equiano

The Interesting Narrative of the Life of Olaudah Equiano, or Gustavus Vassa, the African, written by Himself. London, 1789.

1 - The African Ancestry of the Alabama Black McGruders

By Kevin McGruder[4]

Ned and Mariah: their names appear in the 1848 will of Eleanor Magruder Wynne in a list of enslaved people being left to her daughter, Salina Wynne Ferrell. Born in 1795 and 1800, respectively, they are the earliest African ancestors the Alabama Black McGruders can identify by name. While a fair amount is known about the ancestry of the white Magruders, very little is known about the ancestry of the Alabama Black McGruders before the nineteenth century. It is possible, however, to peer through the veil of history to provide some focus to the early ancestry of the Alabama Black McGruders by considering the common experiences of people on the continent of Africa before European contact, and in the colony of Maryland, where Ned's mother most likely was born.

Maryland was founded by the Englishman Cecil Calvert, Lord Baltimore, who in 1632 received a charter from Charles I, King of Great Britain and Ireland, to establish a colony that would serve as a refuge for Catholics, who were severely persecuted in predominantly Protestant Britain. The area of settlement, north of the 1607 colony of Virginia, was on the Chesapeake Bay and occupied by indigenous people that included the Susquehannock, the Piscataway, the Mattapanient, and the Patuxent.

The first English settlers arrived in Maryland in early 1634.[5] A plantation system centered on tobacco was soon established, relying on labor primarily from English, Scottish, and Irish indentured servants who agreed to work for a term, typically four to seven years, in exchange for passage to the colony, after which they were entitled to 50 acres of unimproved land. While Africans did serve as laborers in Maryland, indentured servants outnumbered enslaved Africans until

---

[4] Kevin McGruder, M.B.A., Ph.D., is Associate Professor of History at Antioch College and the author or co-author of four books. His research on McGruder family history began in the early 1980s when he interviewed his grandmother, Dora Lee Coleman McGruder, who provided him with names and relationships of McGruders dating back to the early 1800s. Kevin's full biography can be found in Part 7.

[5] James McHenry, *A History of Maryland: From its Settlement in 1634 to the Year 1848* (Buffalo, Wyoming: Creative Media Partners, 2015), 26-33.

the 1690's. Indeed, between 1619 and 1697, fewer than one thousand Africans arrived in Maryland. These black men and women of Maryland's charter generation are also known as Atlantic Creoles, because, as explained by Eugene Irving McCormac, "[m]ost came from the Caribbean islands, while some were born elsewhere in the Americas. Many spoke English, practiced Christianity, and were familiar with English law and trading etiquettes."[6]

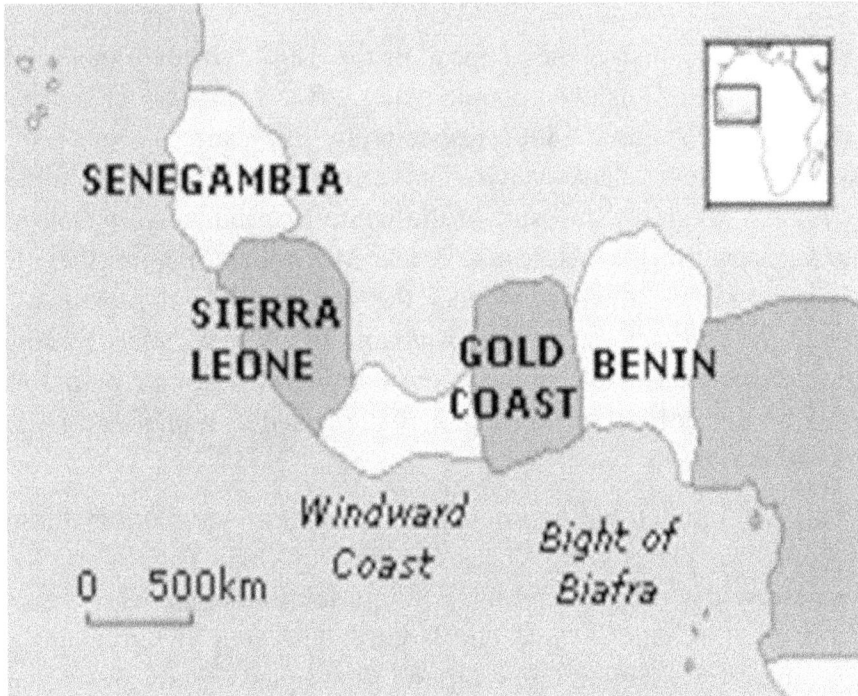

The Windward and Gold Coasts of West Africa

[7]

Following a 1689 revolt by Protestants against the Calvert family's rule, Maryland planters gained control of the colony.[8] With political power, they expanded their landholdings, which increased their need for laborers. Meanwhile,

---

[6] Eugene Irving McCormac, *White Servitude in Maryland, 1734-1820* (Baltimore: Johns Hopkins University Press, 1904), 38; *A Guide to the History of Slavery in Maryland* (Annapolis: The Maryland State Archives, 2020), 3-4.

[7] National Park Service, "African American Heritage and Ethnography: Africans in the Low Country," *Park Ethnography Program* (https://www.nps.gov/ethnography/aah/aaheritage/lowCountryA.htm : accessed 19 Nov 2020).

[8] A previous Protestant revolt, in 1645, plunged the colony into a two-year civil war, after which the Calverts resumed control.

as improvements in England's economy made indentured servitude in North America less attractive to the English poor,

African slavery for life was legalized in Maryland through a series of laws in the 1660s.[9] Additionally, in 1698, when England's Royal African Company's slave-trade monopoly ended, it became easier for Maryland planters to obtain enslaved Africans. Thus, between 1700 and 1775, 100,000 Africans arrived in Maryland, and by 1755, one third of the colony's population was African, primarily from the Windward and Gold Coasts of West Africa.[10]

Montgomery County in 1790, Map of Maryland[11]

Ned's mother was most likely born into this slave culture in the final years of colonial Maryland. Chapter 3 notes that it is believed that Ned's father was Ninian Offutt Magruder, of Scottish descent, the owner of Ned's mother. J.R. Rothstein asserts that in the 1780s, Ninian began a multi-year migration from Maryland through the Carolinas to eventually settle in Columbia County, Georgia. The 1790, 1800, and 1810 census records for Georgia were destroyed, so they cannot be used to determine when Ninian Offutt Magruder arrived there. Two Ninian Magruders do appear in the first census of the United States—conducted in 1790, in accordance with the provisions of the new Constitution of the nation—both in

---

[9] Prior to this period, some Africans who had begun life in Maryland enslaved had been able to gain their freedom.

[10] A Guide to the History of Slavery in Maryland, 4-5.

[11] John W. O'Neal Jr., "Maryland County Formation Maps," at *The O'Neal Website* (http://www.onealwebsite.com/MdCoMaps.htm : accessed 24 Jan 2021).

Montgomery County, Maryland. One of the households consists of four free white males and four free white females and eleven enslaved people.

The other 1790 entry for a Ninian Magruder names Ninian as the head of household and notes four enslaved people. Ninian was a common name in the white Magruder family. Because the 1790 census did not capture additional demographic information such as age, birthplace of the heads of households, or middle initials, it is not always possible to distinguish among them.[12] If Ninian Offutt Magruder was still in Maryland in 1790, these entries could represent him and his first cousin, Ninian Beall Magruder (1735-1810), who migrated to Georgia along with him.[13] Assuming that one of these men is the Ninian Magruder of our interest, his daughter Eleanor Magruder, whose 1848 will noted Ned and Mariah, would have been one of the free white females in the household, five years old in 1790.[14]

Columbia County, Georgia

15

We don't know the name of Ned's mother, or the role she played in the Magruder household. Perhaps she was a cook, a common role for enslaved women. In the household, she would have been defenseless against sexual assault by Ninian. While slaveholders occasionally freed the biracial children born of

[12] See Chapter 2 and Chapter 4 for further discussion of this matter.

[13] A further search of the Magruder-Wynne family archive and estate records, located at the University of Alabama, may solve the question of when the two Ninians migrated.

[14] 1790 U.S. Census, Montgomery County, Maryland, p.43, Ninian Magruder household; digital image, *FamilySearch* (https://www.familysearch.org : accessed 17 Jan 2021); citing NARA microfilm M637, roll 3; FHL microfilm 568,143.

1790 U.S. Census, Montgomery County, Maryland, p.242, Ninian Magruder household; digital image, *FamilySearch* (https://www.familysearch.org : accessed 17 Jan 2021); citing NARA microfilm M637, roll 3; FHL microfilm 568,143.

[15] Location maps, Columbia County, Georgia, Genealogy, *Family Search* (https://www.familysearch.org/wiki/en/Columbia_County,_Georgia_Genealogy : accessed 17 Jan 2021).

liaisons with enslaved women, Ned, the son of Ninian and an enslaved woman, remained enslaved. If Ninian Magruder's wife, Mary, knew that Ninian was the father of Ned, it is unlikely that she acknowledged it. Both the English writer Fanny Kemble, traveling in the south, and the formerly enslaved woman Harriet Jacobs wrote about the prevalence of sexual assault of enslaved women and the powerlessness of the slaveholders' wives to intervene. According to law, women ceased to exist as separate people upon their marriages; therefore a conflict that might lead to a separation or divorce could be financially devastating for a slaveholder's wife.[16]

The African Ancestry of the Mother of Ned Magruder

It is unlikely that we will ever definitively know the African ancestry of the mother of Ned Magruder, but assuming that she was born in Maryland, we can narrow the possibilities by considering the common ethnic characteristics of enslaved people in Maryland in the 1700s. If the parents of Ned's mother traced their roots to the charter generation of the enslaved in Maryland, the one thousand people who arrived between 1619 and 1697, those ancestors most likely arrived in Maryland from the Caribbean. Over the course of the Trans-Atlantic slave trade, only approximately ten percent of enslaved people were shipped directly to North America; the majority disembarked in the Caribbean. That location became known as the site where enslaved Africans were "seasoned," learning a European language, agricultural practices, and/or other skills that would increase their value. Many were then sold and taken to other areas in the Americas, such as Maryland.

In "A Brief Overview of the Trans-Atlantic Slave Trade," David Eltis notes:

> The trans-Atlantic slave trade was the largest long-distance coerced movement of people in history and, prior to the mid-nineteenth century, formed the major demographic well-spring for the re-peopling of the Americas following the collapse of the Amerindian population. Cumulatively, as late as 1820, nearly four Africans had crossed the Atlantic for every European, and, given the differences in the sex ratios between European and African migrant streams, about four out of every five females that traversed

---

[16] John David Cox, *Traveling South: Travel Narratives and the Construction of American Identity* (Athens: University of Georgia Press, 2005), 129-131; Kathryn Cullen-Dupont, *Encyclopedia of Women's History in America,* 2nd ed. (New York: Facts on File, 2000), 87.

the Atlantic were from Africa.[17]

If ancestors of Ned's mother arrived in Maryland after 1700, when direct slave trade with Africa grew dramatically, they could well have been from the Windward or Gold Coasts and, if so, potentially from the Igbo ethnic group that came to dominate the enslaved population in Maryland. Igboland, the home of the Igbo people, covers most of what is now southeastern Nigeria. It is divided by the Niger River into two unequal sections——the midwestern region and the larger eastern region. In "The Ibo People——Origins and History," Katherine Slattery notes that:

> [a]nalysis of the sources that are available (fragmentary oral traditions and correlation of cultural traits) have led to the belief that there exists a core area of Igboland, and that waves of immigrant communities from the north and west planted themselves on the border of this core area as early as the ninth century. This core area——Owerri, Orlu, and Okigwi——forms a belt, and the people in this area have no tradition of coming from anywhere else. Migration from this area in the recent past tended to be in all directions, and in this way, the Igbo culture gradually became homogenized. In addition to this pattern of migration from this core area, other people also entered the Igbo territory in about the fourteenth or fifteenth centuries.[18]

Also, according to Slattery:

> The first contact between Igboland and Europe came in the mid-fifteenth century with the arrival of the Portuguese. From 1434-1807, the Niger coast acted as a contact point between African and European traders, beginning with the Portuguese, then the Dutch, and finally the English. At this stage, there was an emphasis on trade rather than empire building. In this case, the trade consisting primarily of Igbo slaves.

---

[17] David Eltis, "A Brief Overview of the Trans-Atlantic Slave Trade," *Slave Voyages* (https://www.slavevoyages.org/voyage/essays#interpretation/a-brief-overview-of-the-trans-atlantic-slave-trade/introduction/0/en/ : accessed 20 Nov 2020).

[18] Katherine Slattery, "Igbo People: Origins and History," at *Discoveries in Natural History and Exploration* (https://faculty.ucr.edu/~legneref/igbo/igbo1.htm : accessed 19 Nov 2020).

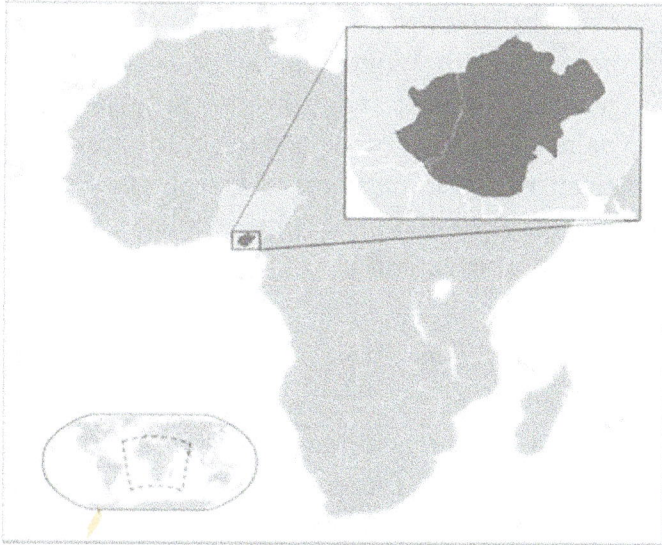

Location of the Igbo homeland (dark gray) in Nigeria (light gray) [19]

In "Igbo Culture and History," Don C. Ohadike describes Igbo culture:

> Igbo people have smelted and forged iron for centuries, and their oral traditions are rich with accounts of iron working and iron use… The widespread use of iron tools enabled the Igbo people to make better use of the forest. With iron tools they grew yams (their principal staple food), cocoyams, bananas, and plantains… At its fully developed stage, the Igbo agricultural system was based on shifting cultivation, a type of rotating cultivation where the same fields were planted for several years in succession and then left fallow to regain their fertility… A striking feature of Igbo society was the lack of centralized political structures. The Igbo lived in autonomous villages and towns, ruled by their elders. With few exceptions, they organized themselves in patrilineages—lineage groups organized along lines of descent from father to son.[20]

Slavery has existed in most societies of the world at various points. Slavery in Africa existed long before European contact. Warfare was the main factor contributing to enslavement, with a standard practice in Africa of enslaving prisoners of war. Africans identified with their ethnic group and not with a common African identity. Before sustained European contact in the fifteenth

---

[19] Igbo People, *Wikipedia* (https://en.wikipedia.org/wiki/Igbo_people : accessed 15:13, 24 Nov 2020).

[20] Don C. Ohadike, "Igbo Culture and History," in Chinua Achebe, *Things Fall Apart* (Portsmouth, NH: Heinemann Educational Publishers, 1996), xxii-xxiii.

century, the concept of Blackness or a black race was irrelevant in the absence of white people and the concept of Whiteness. Africans typically enslaved people from other ethnic groups. The enslaved were not necessarily enslaved for life. They often worked as household servants, and in some cases administrators, such as the Ethiopian eunuch who was treasurer to Queen Candace of Ethiopia, who encountered Philip in Acts 8:26-40 of the Bible. Enslaved Africans retained their humanity within African cultures, and in some cases married into the families of the slaveholders.[21]

Although African slavery differed from what would become Trans-Atlantic slavery, African slaves could be bought and sold. As Europeans began to make contact with Africa, and as the demand for slave labor grew with the colonization of the Americas after the 1490s, the enslaved became another trade category among those managed by African leaders. European slave traders typically worked through African middlemen working at the behest of African leaders, who assembled enslaved Africans in the interior of the continent and walked them to the coast. On the coast, they were imprisoned in factories or forts, really warehouses, until enough were assembled to fill a ship. They then boarded ships for the Americas.

The journey to the Americas has become known as the Middle Passage. Firsthand accounts, such as those by Dr. Alexander Falconbridge and Olaudah Equiano, describe extreme trauma. The enslaved were chained and packed below deck, where for most of the weeks-long journey, they lay in their own excrement receiving little food. Occasionally, they would be taken on deck for fresh air and exercise, and it was common for some to take advantage of the opportunity and jump overboard. According to David Eltis, from the growth of the Trans-Atlantic slave trade after 1500 until its end in the 1860s, "some 12.5 million slaves [were] shipped from Africa and 10.7 million had arrived in the Americas, likely the most costly in human life of all of the long-distance global migrations."[22] The ancestors of the mother of Ned Magruder survived, and arrived in the Americas through a journey like this.

---

[21] S. Pearl Sharp and Virginia Schomp, *The Slave Trade and the Middle Passage* (Tarrytown, NY: Marshall Cavendish Benchmark, 2007), 43-51; Sean D. Burke, *Queering the Ethiopian Eunuch* (Minneapolis: Fortress Press, 2013), 98.

[22] David Eltis, "The Ending of the Trans-Atlantic Slave Trade," *Slave Voyages* https://www.slavevoyages.org/voyage/essays#interpretation/a-brief-overview-of-the-trans-atlantic-slave-trade/the-ending-of-the-slave-trade/7/en/ : accessed 20 Nov 2020.

By oppression's woes and pains

By your sons in servile chains

We will drain our dearest veins

But they shall be free!

Lay the proud usurpers low

Tyrants fall in every foe

Liberty's in every blow

Let us do or die!

Roberts Burns

"Scots Wha Hae" (1789)

A poem imagining a speech given by Robert the Bruce, later King of Scots, to his army, before the Battle of Bannockburn *in 1314.*

2 – Who Were the White Magruders?

By Susan Tichy[23]

Alexander Magruder, "The Immigrant," (1610-1677) was the first of his name in America. Born at the small estate of Belliclone (now Nether Belliclone farm) in Madderty Parish, Perthshire, in Scotland's Central Highlands. Alexander was the son of Alexander McGruder, the elder, and Margaret Campbell of Keithick.[24] He is believed to have arrived in Maryland in January 1652 as a prisoner of war, having been captured during Cromwell's invasion of Scotland late in the civil wars that attended the Protestant Reformation.[25] Upon arrival, Alexander was sold into indentured servitude.

In the malaria-ridden Chesapeake, half of all indentured servants died within a year. Those who survived five years received their freedom and a "headright" to 50 acres of unimproved land—which they first had to pay a surveyor to find, survey, and register. Alexander received his first of two headrights in October 1653, indicating that he served a remarkably short indenture.

At that time, twenty years after the founding of the colony, more than 300 crude plantations were strung up and down the Patuxent River, growing tobacco for export and subsistence crops for survival. Buildings were of log or mud-wattle and livestock roamed free. Labor-saving methods for clearing and farming the

---

[23] Susan Tichy, Professor Emerita of English at George Mason University, is the author of six poetry collections and *Trafficke* (Ahsahta Press, 2015), a mixed-genre investigation of family, race, and language spanning from Reformation Scotland to the abolition of slavery in Maryland. Her work has been published in the US, UK, and Australia, and recognized by numerous awards, including a fellowship from the National Endowment for the Arts. Her website, *Magruder's Landing*, includes the history and legacy of both black and white Magruders. She serves on the Editorial Board of *Poetry Daily* (https://poems.com). More at https://SusanTichy.com.

[24] John MacGregor, "The McGrouthers of Meigor in Glenartney," *The Genealogist* XXXV (Jan 1919): 65-81; digital image, *Magruder's Landing* (https://magruderslanding.com/bibliographies/magruders/); Charles G. Kurz, "McGruder Lineage in Scotland to Magruder Family in America," *Yearbook of the American Clan Gregor Society* LXII (1979): 53-72 [gathering of 1978]; Don McGruther, *Wha's Like Us? MacGrouthers in Scotland before 1855* (Privately printed, 2007), 14-17, 46-53, 73-86.

[25] Though the proprietors of the Maryland colony were Catholic, most settlers were Protestant. The original McGruders/Magruders were Protestants in both Scotland and Maryland.

wet, wooded riverbanks were learned from the Yoacomoco, Mattapanient, Piscataway, and Patuxent people whose land the colony had purchased. White women were scarce, men worked their own fields (with or without the help of indentured labor), and married late. Perhaps half the children born lived to their twentieth birthday.[26]

For indentured men and women who survived, the colony in its early years offered opportunities most would not have enjoyed in England or Scotland, and, though few in number, people of African descent lived under the same laws that governed Europeans. Mathias de Sousa, an indentured mulatto, is the most famous person of African descent in the early days of the colony.[27] He arrived in Maryland with the first colonists in 1634, obtained his freedom by 1638, and in 1641 was elected to the Maryland Assembly. After 1643 he disappears from the record.[28] The first two slaves documented in the colony arrived in 1644. Twenty years later the Assembly passed the first chattel slavery laws.

Alexander was married at least twice in Maryland, and his will names six living children, three times the average in extant wills. Four of his sons also reproduced and their descendants spread throughout the colonies and states along the general patterns and migrations of white settlers. With few exceptions, the many thousands of white Magruders and McGruders in the United States descend from this one man. At least eighteen spellings of the name survive in Maryland records—including Magruther, McGruder, Magrowder, and Magruda—and forty or more in Scotland. The *Magruder* spelling, with which Alexander signed his will, is uniquely American.

Alexander was one of the largest landowners of his generation. Historian Russell R. Menard, who studied men who arrived as indentured servants from 1648-1652, identifies him as one of only three who owned more than 1,000 acres when they died.[29]

We cannot document how Alexander became so successful. We do know that in Scotland his family had close ties to the titled and powerful Drummond family, whom they had served as clerks, scribes, and chamberlains for several

---

[26] Russell R. Menard, *Economy and Society in Early Colonial Maryland* (New York & London: Garland Publishing, 1985), 144.

[27] Some historians believe that de Sousa was also Jewish.

[28] "Mathias de Sousa," at *Exploring Maryland's Roots: Library* (https://mdroots.thinkport.org/library/mathiasdesousa.asp : accessed 24 Jan 21).

[29] Russell R. Menard, *Economy and Society in Early Colonial Maryland*, 174-75.

generations. Alexander's father was Chamberlain to James Drummond, the first Lord Madderty, and his older brother, James McGruder, rose to be chamberlain to Lord Madderty's nephew, the Earl of Perth. It is probable that through these connections, Alexander was able to buy out his indenture and begin acquiring land at an early date. He also built or acquired Magruder's Landing—a tobacco shipping point on the Patuxent River—for the export of tobacco to Europe. This gave him a steady source of income not tied to the unstable price of tobacco itself. The inventory of his estate shows that in addition to a few books, some old furniture, clothing, farm implements, livestock, and of course tobacco, he owned several parcels of land, four indentured servants, and "one man negro named Sambo."[30]

This inventory reflects the changing patterns of labor in Colonial Maryland, where slavery at first existed alongside indentured servitude, not fully replacing it until the start of the 19th century. Land without labor was worthless—in the 17th century, a good cow was worth more than 50 acres of uncleared land—so the economic factors driving the transition to enslaved labor are easy to analyze. Astonishingly, however, not a single document has survived from 17th century Maryland that records an attitude, a thought, or a reflection on the new concept of chattel slavery or the emerging ideology of race.

Maryland's first census, in 1790, shows 45 Magruder households in three counties, of which 41 owned slaves. Clearly, in the century between the recording of Sambo's name and the new State of Maryland's first census, Magruders had fully embraced the practice of slavery.

Alexander's children and grandchildren achieved various levels of prosperity. Nathaniel, his youngest son, lived on an unproductive remnant of Alexander's home plantation, Anchovie Hills, where tobacco cultivation had exhausted the soil.[31] Unable even to repair the house, Nathaniel's son, George, and his wife

---

[30] Maryland State Archives, Prerogative Court (Inventories and Accounts) 1674-1718, Calvert County, Liber 4, Folio 606, estate inventory of Alexander Magruder, 1677; digital images, Huntington Collection of Maryland State Archives Security Microfilm 1945-1946, images 627-28 (http://mdhistory.msa.maryland.gov/msaref10/msa_te_1_063/html/msa_te_1_063-0627.html : accessed 10 Feb 2021). Historians have observed that in the 17th century Chesapeake, the name *Sambo* seems to attach to people brought from the Caribbean. Atlantic Creoles were sought after for their knowledge of tobacco cultivation.

[31] Lord Madderty's estate in Perthshire was Inchaffray Abbey—pronounced anchAFFray, comically degraded in America to *Anchovie*. This and other local Perthshire names among Alexander's properties help to confirm his origins. Some American Magruders have been taught that the McGruders/McGruthers in Scotland were part of Clan Gregor—a belief still cherished by The American Clan Gregor Society, founded by Magruders in 1909. This claim

Sarah were at times forced to live in their tobacco barn. Their four slaves shared a ten-foot cabin. After George's death, in the winter of 1799-1800, Sarah contracted with the slaves to free them on a future date, provided they gave good service—a tactic widows in Maryland often employed to avoid financial ruin if slaves ran away.[32] Such term-slavery agreements also provided protection of a kind to the enslaved because Maryland law prohibited the out-of-state sale of a term slave.

By contrast, Alexander's eldest son, Samuel—from whom Ninian Offutt Magruder and Ned Magruder descended—was a wealthy owner of land, slaves, town lots, and diverse business interests in Prince George's County. He held numerous public offices and twice served in the Maryland House of Burgesses. His wife, Sarah, outlived him by 24 years. In her 1734 will, she left one slave each to nine named heirs in eight households—a stinging example of the division of enslaved families in the interest of building wealth. This number also reminds us that even Maryland's wealthiest rarely owned a large number of people, or plantations extensive enough to create their own insular worlds.

Ned Magruder's descent from Alexander Magruder can be traced thus: 1) Alexander the Immigrant + Sarah [surname debated] > 2) Samuel Magruder + Sarah [surname debated] > 3) Ninian Beall Magruder + Elizabeth Brewer > 4) John Magruder + Jane Offutt > 5) Ninian Offutt Maguder + unknown enslaved woman > 6) Ned Magruder.[33]

---

has been disproved by Don McGruther's research in Scottish records and by DNA comparison.

[32] Steve Sarson, "Yeoman Farmers in a Planters' Republic: Socioeconomic Conditions and Relations in Early National Prince George's County, Maryland," *Journal of the Early Republic* 29:1 (Spring 2009): 63-99.

[33] It was once believed that Ninian Offutt Magruder descended from a different son of Ninian Beall Magruder and Elizabeth Brewer, namely their son Ninian (designated by genealogists Ninian II), who married Mary Offutt. Their son, Ninian III, was assumed to be one and the same with Ninian Offutt Magruder. In the 1940s and 50s, Martha Sprigg Poole and Regina Magruder Hill showed, through extensive research in Maryland land and court records, that all of that family's "three Ninians" remained in Maryland. Poole and Hill were the first to propose John Magruder as Ninian Offut Magruder's father, a lineage that has been widely accepted since, though not definitively proven. See Martha Sprigg Poole, "Three Ninian Magruders," *Yearbook of the American Clan Gregor Society* XXXVIII (1954): 17-24 [gathering of 1953]. Offutt genealogists trace their family from Nathaniel Offutt (1720-1775) who married a Sarah Magruder (possibly John Magruder's first cousin, d/o James Magruder and Martha Coombs) and accept Jane Offutt and John Magruder as Ninian Offutt Magruder's parents. *The Offutt Family Genealogy* (http://offutt.rocks/p12.html: accessed 31 Jan 2021). The many Ninians, and intermarriages, can lead researchers on a merry dance.

Who were the White McGruders?

The slave-owning practices of Maryland Magruders occasionally reached the public record in the form of runaway ads and court proceedings. In 1738, fourteen slaves were convicted of conspiring to poison John Beall, husband of Samuel and Sarah's daughter, Verlinda Magruder. John and Verlinda—who were Ninian Offutt Magruder's great-aunt and uncle—owned four of the conspirators, including Beall's Bess, the only person hanged.[34] Slaves could not testify, and the court record does not hint of a catalyst for this revolt. Magruders in Prince George's County also were distinguished by their use of anti-miscegenation laws to hold mixed-race descendants of white indentured women in perpetual servitude, a practice that extended from 1690 until Emancipation.[35]

Through the 18th and early 19th centuries, Alexander's descendants spread beyond Maryland, into frontier Virginia, Georgia, and the Carolinas, sometimes migrating in extended family groups. By the last decades of slavery, Magruders owned farms, businesses, and plantations from Maryland through the deep South, the hill country of Kentucky, and west to Arkansas and Texas.[36]

An unknown number of white Magruder men sexually exploited enslaved women, some of whom bore children with the Magruder/McGruder surname,

---

[34] Allan Kulikoff, *Tobacco and Slaves: The Development of Southern Cultures in the Cheasapeake, 1680-1800* (Chapel Hill & London: University of North Carolina Press, 1986), 329.

[35] In Prince George's County, in the first forty years of laws against "mulatto bastardy," 26 women were convicted for 42 births. A third of those women were bound to Sarah and Samuel Magruder, their heirs, and a few close neighbors with whom they had intermarried. It is particularly notable that most women convicted multiple times were bound to Magruders and their kin. Allan Kulikoff, *Tobacco and Slaves*, 386-87; Susan Tichy, "Priscilla Gray and Descendants," at *Magruder's Landing: Slavery's Legacy* (https://magruderslanding.com/slavery/priscilla-gray-descendants/).

[36] A small number of Magruders freed all their slaves, in their wills or in their lifetimes, and many more manumitted individuals. Magruder men served on both sides in the Civil War, with most serving the Confederacy. Throughout the history of American slavery, a majority of those manumitted were of mixed race. Of special interest is Catherine Fleming Magruder (1747-1821), widow of Revolutionary War patriot Captain Joseph Magruder (1742-1793), who directed her son, John Burgess Magruder (1782-1850), a Methodist minister, to free five of her slaves—all but the most elderly—after her death. He is said to have removed from Maryland to Ohio, whereupon he manumitted all of his enslaved people, though I have not been able to confirm that he did so. Roberta Julia (Magruder) Bukey, "The Magruder Family in its Religious Affiliations," *Yearbook of the American Clan Gregor Society* V (1916): 48-58, esp 55 [gathering of 1915]; Maryland, Montgomery County, Orphans' Court, Probate records 1777-1916. Will of Catherine Magruder, Liber N, 90-93, digital images *Family Search* (https://www.familysearch.org/ark:/61903/3:1:33SQ-GTYR-8Y6?i=71&cc=1803986&cat=51655 : accessed 17 Feb 2021) images 72-73.

while others preferred their mother's surname or that of their mother's husband. Other former enslaved people adopted the Magruder/McGruder name after Emancipation, whether or not they were related to white Magruders. Families of many surnames are related, by blood or by history, to slave communities on and around Magruder plantations. Tracing those relationships through scant archival records is frustratingly difficult.

Several factors make it especially difficult to trace black Maryland families back through the barrier of slavery. First, bondage in the Chesapeake extended for more than 200 years, during which families were repeatedly broken up and individuals sold or bequeathed, passing through numerous plantations, farms, and owners, carrying their family names with them, and forming new families in new situations. Second, most slave-owners in Maryland owned only a few—by 1860, half of all slave-owners in Maryland owned just one or two people, three-quarters owned fewer than eight, and only 10% owned fifteen or more. Even on a larger plantation, it was common for the enslaved to seek a "broad marriage" with someone elsewhere in the neighborhood.[37] Slaves were also rented out to businesses in and around Baltimore, Annapolis, and Washington, D.C., as skilled or unskilled labor—including carpenters, blacksmiths, masons, pastry chefs, waiters, seamstresses, sailmakers, longshoremen, and coachmen—increasing their social circulation and, potentially, their prospects for family formation. The third complication for researchers is manumission—by 1850, nearly half of all blacks in Maryland were free, many intermarried with those still enslaved for life or for a term. Census records of free black households often show a missing parent or child, who may appear ten years later, having gained freedom in the interim. In many families, the first freed later purchased and freed their family members. This necessity drastically slowed the economic progress of free blacks.[38] Adding to the difficulty of tracing some families, those descended from a white woman generally held onto her surname, as white maternal descent was a thin thread sometimes leading to freedom.

Unsurprisingly, both manumission papers and records created after Emancipation show that it was the exception, not the rule, for the surname of a newly free person in Maryland to match that of the last slave owner. It is likely that in many cases people with various surnames, enslaved and then freed at the

[37] Barbara Jean Fields, *Slavery & Freedom on the Middle Ground: Maryland during the 19th Century* (New Haven: Yale University Press, 1985), 24-25.

[38] T. Stephen White, *The Price of Freedom: Slavery and Manumission in Baltimore and Early National Maryland* (Lexington: University Press of Kentucky, 1997), 119-139, esp. 122-124.

same location, were related to each other through maternal lines.

Against this background, it is all the more remarkable that the Alabama Black McGruders have both passed down and documented such a wealth of information about their origins and retained their distinct family identity.

Biological races do not exist—and never have. This view is shared by all scientists who study variation in human populations. Yet prejudice and intolerance based on the myth of race remain deeply ingrained.

Robert Wald Sussman

The Myth of Race: The Troubling Persistence of an Unscientific Idea

3 – DNA Analysis of the Alabama Black McGruders

By J.R. Rothstein, Esq.

Ninian Offutt Magruder was born in Prince George's County, Maryland, in 1744. Ninian married Mary Harris, daughter of Thomas Harris and Sarah Offutt, both of Maryland. At his death, in 1803, he left an extensive estate with many enslaved people—with at least one of whom he had a child. Ninian had two daughters, Sarah Magruder (1779-1833) and Eleanor Magruder (1785-1849), and five sons: (1) Zadok (1766-1820); (2) George (1772-1836); (3) Basil (1774-1801); (4) John (1778-1826); and (5) Archibald (1780-1826).

In 1848 Eleanor Magruder Wynne produced a Last Will and Testament which has been the subject of interest to historians, including Alabama Black McGruders, for generations. In her will, Eleanor outlined the genealogy of the family of one of her enslaved people, Ned Magruder, the patriarch of the Alabama Black McGruder family. Until the advent of DNA technology, and specifically the Y-Chromosome testing offered by Family Tree DNA (www.familytreedna.com), Eleanor's actions remained a matter of speculation.

However, six years ago, I began conducting DNA studies on white Magruders and Alabama Black McGruders to test whether the two families were genetically related. The answer proved to be an unequivocal affirmative.

The first DNA test was administered to one male descendant of Charles McGruder Sr. The test revealed Y-Chromosome Haplotype R-CTS11722, mutation M-269, indicating direct patrilineal European ancestry, likely to be extracted from the British Isles, the haplotype of the white Magruder line. The test was not administered through the Family Tree DNA platform, and therefore, due to the ineffective nature of the testing platform and its database reference points, no further information could be gleaned.

A second DNA test was an autosomal test conducted on Dovie Robertson (family line: Lucille McGruder, William McGruder, Charles McGruder Sr., Ned Magruder, Ninian Offutt Magruder) through Family Tree DNA, which autosomally matched with three white Magruder families descended from Ninian O. Magruder and three black McGruder families descended from Charles McGruder Sr. in the familytreedna.com database. However, due to the imprecise nature of autosomal DNA, these results, though interesting, were not conclusive as to how these families were related.

In 2018, Alice Coleman Griffin, a white descendant of Ninian Offutt Magruder via his daughter Eleanor Magruder (family line: Alice Coleman, Osmund Appling Coleman, Bestor Wynne Coleman, Bestor Coleman, Laura Frances Wynne Coleman, Osmun A. Wynne, Eleanor Magruder, Ninian O. Magruder), took an autosomal DNA test. She matched with Dovie Robertson, an Alabama Black McGruder, as a second to fourth cousin with 67 cM shared blocks. Alice matched closer genetically with Dovie Robertson than the latter did with most of her African-American DNA matches. The two also closely matched autosomally with three other white Magruder relatives, including Dr. Milton Bosch, referenced in the introduction.

Autosomal DNA results connecting with white Magruders.

Autosomal-DNA results connecting Dovie Robertson,
an Alabama black McGruder, with white Magruders.

The third DNA test, a Y-Chromosome and autosomal test, administered to Juan McGruder (family line: William "Mack" McGruder, Charles McGruder Jr., Charles McGruder Sr. via his wife Mary May, Ned Magruder, Ninian O. Magruder) matched autosomal DNA and Y-Chromosome DNA with numerous other white Magruders and black McGruders in the familytreedna.com database. Among them were Lucille Burden Osborne (family line: Queen Mary Burge, Minerva McGruder, Charles McGruder Sr., Ned Magruder, Ninian O. Magruder) and James Magruder, a white descendant of Ninian O. Magruder (family line: James Magruder, Lawson Magruder, Cephas Bailey Magruder, George Magruder, Ninian O. Magruder).

Y-DNA results connecting with white Magruders.

This test reveals a connection not only to white descendants of Ninian O. Magruder, but also numerous other white Magruder lines that descend from Alexander Magruder, the Immigrant. The Y-Chromosome markers, tested at the highest possible resolution of 111-markers, indicate a common paternal ancestor within the past few generations shared by James Magruder and Juan McGruder.

A fourth Y-Chromosome test, administered on Wilmar McGruder (family line: Darmon McGruder, Robert McGruder, Amos McGruder, Charles McGruder Sr. via his wife Rachel, Ned Magruder, Ninian O. Magruder), produced the same results and matched all 111 markers with both Juan McGruder, a black descendant of Ninian O. Magruder, and James Magruder, a white descendant of Ninian O. Magruder.

DNA results connecting black McGruders with white Magruders.

A fifth DNA test was administered to Andrew Marshall Magruder, a white Magruder (family line: Richard L. Magruder Jr., Richard L. Magruder Sr., George Milton Magruder, Lafayette L. Magruder, George Milton Magruder, George Magruder, Ninian O. Magruder). The markers matched identically with Juan McGruder and Wilmar McGruder, as well as with numerous white Magruders.

DNA Analysis of the Alabama Black McGruders

Y-DNA results connecting black McGruders with white Magruders.

Y-Chromosome 37 test results

A sixth DNA test, conducted on Gloria Franklin, a descendant of a black Texas family enslaved by the white Wynnes (who were related to the white Magruders), reveals no genetic connection between the black Wynne family of Texas and the Alabama Black McGruders, nor between them and the white Magruders.

Interpretation

These DNA results, along with the evidence outlined in the following chapters, conclusively demonstrate the Alabama Black McGruders' genetic connection to white descendants of Ninian O. Magruder. They confirm a European heritage with haplotype sub-mutations to indicate direct male origins in the British Isles, and match perfectly with other members of the white Magruder extended family. The results confirm that a descendant of Alexander Magruder, The Immigrant, sired a male child with a female ancestor of Ned Magruder at some point within a generation of Ned's lifetime.

Based on the information presented thus far, a single question arises: which white Magruder fathered the progenitor of the Alabama Black McGruders? Marshalling the genetic, written, and oral evidence at hand, the author believes that the Ned-Charles connection put forth by other Alabama Black McGruder historians, such as Betty Shaw, Kevin McGruder, Wilmar McGruder, and Herman English, viewed in conjunction with the will of Eleanor Magruder Wynne and related documents, is conclusive.[39] Further, the author believes that Ned Magruder was the son of the white slave owner, Ninian O. Magruder (1744-1803), and an unknown enslaved woman.

Ned was born between 1795 and 1800. This means that, based on their dates of birth and death, any of the men in the nuclear family of Ninian O. Magruder could have been Ned's father—Ninian or one of his sons.[40] At the moment, this question of parentage is impossible to answer with absolute certainty from a strictly genetic perspective. Future researchers might be able to give more educated guesses when more precise DNA technology develops and as we learn more about the individual lives of these Magruder men.

However, when existing genetic evidence is read in conjunction with the archival record and oral history, one discerns an overwhelming likelihood that

---

[39] A single individual of the Alabama Black McGruder family has questioned the specific Ned-Charles connection altogether, based on oral history that specifically states that Charles Magruder's father, not grandfather, was white. This position, however, is rejected by the author. Moreover, the will of Eleanor Magruder Wynne explicitly provides that Ned was the father of Charles. It is more likely that *grandfather* was replaced with *father* in the oral history tradition inherited by this individual. It is more likely that Ned was the father of Charles and that the white Magruder who fathered the Alabama Black McGruder line was the father of Ned, not Charles.

[40] If Ned was fathered by Ninian, he was Eleanor's half-brother. Alternatively, if in fact Ned was fathered by one of Ninian's sons, he was Eleanor's nephew.

Ned was fathered by Ninian. Information in that record includes: (1) the migration patterns and other biographical details of these white Magruder men; (2) that Ned was a enslaved person who belonged to Ninian, as per Ned's mother's status—*partus sequitur ventrem* ("that which is brought forth follows the belly"); (3) that after Ninian's death, his estate transferred ownership of Ned to his daughter, Eleanor Magruder, and not to any of his sons. These facts, in addition to the genetic distance between the great-grandchildren of Charles McGruder Sr. and white descendants of Ninian O. Magruder, point to Ninian as Ned's father, the white Magruder we seek. The author's proposal fits neatly with the oral history, genetic evidence, and historical documentation set forth in the following chapters.

"No pen can give an adequate description of the all-pervading corruption produced by slavery."

Harriet Ann Jacobs

Incidents in the Life of a Slave Girl (1861)

4 - The Roots of Ned & Mariah Magruder

By J.R. Rothstein, Esq.

To write a history of the lives of Ned and Mariah Magruder[41] we are forced to explore the lives of the people who enslaved them. This is because of the paucity of records regarding enslaved people generally, and specifically about Ned and Mariah. Sabrina Franklin, a historian of the Alabama Black McGruders, puts this challenge in context:

> Enslaved African-Americans prior to 1865 were considered property. They were not human beings. They were legally no different than farm animals and household utensils. They had no legal rights or privileges as individuals. Their marriages were not legal marriages, their children did not legally belong to them, they were not paid wages, and were forbidden to educate themselves."[42]

For the most part, enslavers recorded personal details about the enslaved only when it served their interests—in runaway ads, for example, or compensation claims for the value of enslaved people who joined or were drafted into the Union army. Other records are few, and enslaved people, who were forbidden to read or write, could not keep their own.

Ned Magruder was enslaved by Ninian Offutt Magruder. Therefore, we must first turn to the life of Ninian Offutt Magruder, not to suggest that the Alabama Black McGruder history begins with him—it does not—but rather to provide a larger context for the origins of the Ned and Mariah Magruder family with the information that we have before us.

Ninian Offutt Magruder

Ninian Offutt Magruder, son of John Magruder and Mary Offutt,[43] was born in 1744, into a Presbyterian family in Prince George's County, in Colonial Maryland

---

[41] A timeline of events in the lives of Ned, Mariah, and their son Charles McGruder Sr. may be found in Part VIII.

[42] Sabrina Franklin, unpublished 2005 pamphlet created for the McGruder family reunion.

[43] There are two schools of thought regarding the parentage of Ninian Offutt Magruder: (1) the traditionalist camp; and (2) the modern camp, to which Susan Tichy and the vast majority of modern researchers belong. The moderns, whose argument Tichy adopts in Chapter Two, rely on Martha Sprigg Poole's article "Three Ninian Magruders" in the *Yearbook of the American Clan Gregor Society* XXXVIII (1954): 19-24 [gathering of 1953]. It has often been

of the British Empire.[44] Ninian was born one-hundred and twenty-five years after "20 and odd Negroes"—the first record of enslaved Africans in British North America—were brought ashore from the White Lion, a Dutch man-o-war, and into the Colony of Virginia. Ninian was a great-great-grandson of Alexander Magruder, The Immigrant, via Alexander's eldest son, Samuel Magruder.

Ninian bore the name (and perhaps the appearance) of another Scottish immigrant ancestor, Ninian Beall (1625-1717), who was reported to have "fierce red hair" and to have been six feet seven inches tall. While fighting against Cromwell's invasion of Scotland, Beall was taken prisoner at the Battle of Dunbar and landed in a London prison. Shortly after, he and 149 others were transported to the island of Barbados in the West Indies to live as indentured servants.

In 1652, Beall entered into another indenture and migrated to Maryland. Like Alexander Magruder, he seems to have served a short indenture, acquiring the first of several tracts of land by 1655. He became a member of the Maryland House of Burgesses and held a high position in Maryland's Provincial Forces. Having become fluent in several Native American languages, he served on a committee to "investigate Indian affairs," and in 1699, was appointed Commander of a troop of Rangers organized to respond to disturbances in the colony. For these "Signall Services and Laborious Endeavours," the Burgesses awarded him "three good Serviceable Negro Slaves," named in the receipt as John, Sarah, and Elizabeth. A fourth slave, Alce [Alice?] was named in his will. Beall and his sons

---

alleged by traditionalists that "Ninian III" Magruder (son of "Ninian II" Magruder, and grandson of the first Ninian Beall Magruder) is in fact Ninian Offutt Magruder, who migrated to the Augusta, Georgia, area following military service in the Revolutionary War. See the "Heraldry Notes" column of *The Baltimore Sun*, Sunday, 25th October 1908; Robert Lee Magruder, Jr., "Ninian Offutt Magruder," *Yearbook of The American Clan Gregory Society* XII (1928): 133-35 [gathering of 1927]. This understanding of the lineage is also referenced on pp. 57, 80, and 114 of the same yearbook. In the article, the "Three Ninian Magruders," Poole cites numerous land records and court cases demonstrating that "Ninian III" Magruder lived and died in Maryland, while Ninian Offutt Magruder migrated from Maryland to Georgia, where he died. There are, however, two questions which need resolution before the debate can be fully resolved in Poole's favor: (1) Is it possible that Ninian III migrated back and forth between the two states for the remainder of his life?; (2) What does a researcher do with a possible oral history component to the traditionalist camp, from geographically disparate descendants of Ninian O. Magruder? These questions, in the view of the author, need further research and therefore force the question of his parentage to remain open. However, for the purposes of this book and my narrative regarding Ninian O. Magruder, I adopt the view of the modern camp.

[44] Roberta Julia (Magruder) Bukey, "The Magruder Family in its Religious Affiliations," 55.

also were among the first settlers of Georgetown—now part of Washington, D.C., but originally a Potomac River port town in Maryland—owning nearly 800 acres of land.[45] A close associate of Alexander Magruder, the Immigrant, Beall was one of the executors of Magruder's estate and gave land to some of his grandchildren. In Maryland, the two families remained close, frequently intermarrying at least into the 20th century.

On April 19, 1775 a rebellion began with the exchange of gunfire between British troops and colonists at Lexington and Concord in the British Colony of Massachusetts. On July 4, 1776, a Declaration of Independence was adopted by thirteen British North American colonies, demanding independence from the British Empire, condemning monarchial rule, and asserting "that all men are created equal, that they are endowed by their Creator with certain unalienable Rights."

That summer, the military forces of the British Empire mobilized to crush the colonial rebellion and commence invasion of the newly formed nation calling itself the United States of America. A little more than a year later, as British military efforts developed, Ninian Offutt Magruder took the Patriot's Oath in Montgomery County, Maryland. With him was his first cousin and friend, Ninian Beall Magruder (1735-1810).[46] Also joining him in revolt against British rule were many other Magruder patriots, distant and close cousins, and his sons Basil, Archibald, John, and Zadok. During the war, Ninian served as a Sergeant in the 29th Battalion, Montgomery County Militia.

By the end of the war, Ninian and his wife, Mary Harris (1738-1820), had the following children:

1. Zadok (1770-1820);

2. George (1772-1836);

3. Basil (1774-1801);

---

[45] Caleb Clarke Magruder, *Colonel Ninian Beall* (Washington, DC: The Society of Colonial Wars, 1911) [pamphlet]; James Hadden, *Genealogical and Personal History of Fayette County, Pennsylvania*, Vol.2 (Heritage Books, 2007); Ruth Beall Gelders, "Colonel Ninian Beall," *Kim Beall's Beall History Pages* (http://www.krystalrose.com/kim/BEALL/ninian1.html : accessed 14 Jan 2021). The portrait below, believed to be that of Ninian Beall, is courtesy the Historical Society of Washington, D.C.

[46] Ninian Beall Magruder's descent is accepted as Alexander Magruder + Sarah (maiden name debated) > Ninian Beall Magruder + Elizabeth Brewer > Capt. Samuel Burton Magruder + Margaret Beall Jackson.

4. John (1778-1827);

5. Sarah (1779-1833); and

6. Archibald (1780-1839).

Both during and after the war, the new United States government offered grants of land in the public domain as an incentive to serve and a reward for national service to country, and Ninian O. Magruder took advantage of these land bounties to build a legacy for his family. During the war, in 1782, Ninian received a Bounty Warrant for land in Georgia—an act which signaled his future not in Maryland but in Georgia. On September 3, 1783, Benjamin Franklin, representing the British Colonies, signed the Treaty of Paris, ending the rebellion that is now known as the American Revolution. As a result of the treaty, the British Empire recognized the new nation, the United States of America, the first Republic formed in over two-thousand years.

Around that time, Ninian began a journey from Mayland to Georgia. According to Robert Lee Magruder Jr., writing in the 1928 *Yearbook of the American Clan Gregor Society*, Ninian's journey, undertaken with his cousin Ninian Beall Magruder, was "made by horseback and wagons, and one can truly imagine the great trials and hardships endured while traveling in those early times."[47] In Georgia, Ninian, perhaps to distinguish himself from his cousin, adopted Offutt, his mother's maiden name, as his middle name.[48] Both families presumably took their enslaved people with them.

One of the first acts of Ninian as an American and a Georgian was, in 1784, to petition as a "citizen of Georgia," for 250 acres in Washington County. The land was surveyed and recorded in March of that year.[49] I posit that it was during, or after, this period that Ninian enslaved an unknown woman who would one day give birth to Ned Magruder, the patriarch of the Alabama Black McGruders

By 1785, Ninian O. Magruder and his family had settled in the part of Richmond County now known as Columbia County, which was carved out of

---

[47] Robert Lee Magruder, "Ninian Beall Magruder," *Yearbook of the American Clan Gregory Society* XV (1928) 67 [gathering of 1927].

[48] "Address of Caleb Clarke Magruder at Rockville, Maryland, October 22, 1926," *Yearbook of The American Clan Gregory Society* XV (1928): 34 [gathering of 1927].

[49] Earlier, a great-aunt and uncle of the two Ninians, Eleanor Magruder Wade (c.1805-1765) and Nehemiah Wade (c.1805-1774), had migrated to Burke County, Georgia. Further research is needed to establish connections among both black and white descendants of these two migrations. Black McGruders from Crisp and other parts of Georgia may be related to the Alabama Black McGruders.

Richmond County in 1790.[50] Ninian established a plantation and sired one more child with Mary Harris, his youngest daughter, (7) Eleanor (1785-1849),[51] whom they called "Nelly" or "Elly." It was Eleanor who played a defining role in the life of Ned and therefore in the history of the Alabama Black McGruders.

Georgia records demonstrate that Ninian engaged in extensive land acquisition from 1785 to 1789—during which his need for slave labor increased drastically. In the spring of 1787, as Ninian concerned himself with the acquisition of more land and the building of a plantation, the new nation debated the future of slavery.

In Philadelphia, the Constitutional Convention met with delegates from the thirteen states to draft a constitution to govern the new nation. The delegates were divided between Northern and Southern states over slavery. As the spring passed, the divisions of the convention appeared to threaten the experiment of self-government embodied by the new republic. In July of 1787, Charles Pinckney of South Carolina proposed what would come to be known as the infamous Three-Fifths Compromise. The compromise provided that three-fifths of each state's enslaved population would count towards that state's total population for the purpose of apportioning the House of Representatives. The compromise was adopted by the majority of the delegates, thus enshrining the outsized power of slave states in U.S. politics. Built into the constitution was a compromise that abolitionists believed would, overtime, end the institution of slavery—the prohibition of importation of new enslaved people from Africa after 1808.

Records demonstrate that Ninian Offutt Magruder was successful in acquiring both land and enslaved people during this period. However, the absence of Georgia census records for 1790 and 1800 leave the precise state of his slave holdings during the period in which Ned Magruder, the patriarch of the Alabama Black McGruders, was born unknown. What we know for certain, as a result of DNA testing, is that in approximately 1795 Ninian Offutt Magruder fathered at least one child, Ned, with one of the women whom he enslaved.[52]

---

[50] According to research conducted by Betty McGruder Shaw, the Ninian O. Magruder family settled in the town of Appling, in Columbia County, Georgia. The Magruder family also was associated with Harlem, Georgia, nearby.

[51] Sue Emerson, a Magruder genealogist, gives Eleanor's birthplace as Alabama, but this is an error. She moved to Alabama after her marriage.

[52] No oral history survives elaborating upon the precise nature of the relationship between Ninian and Ned's mother. Due to the inherent power imbalance between an enslaver and an enslaved person, there can be no question of consent. We can therefore assume, though without any specific oral tradition, that Ned was a product of rape and/or of coerced concubinage.

Should Ninian have considered freeing Ned, or any other enslaved person on his plantation, the laws of Georgia would have made such an act difficult. Beginning in 1801, Georgia had prohibited slaveholders from independently freeing their slaves absent a court order.

During the same period, when Ned was approximately six years old, an enslaved young man named Ambrose ran away from the plantation of Ned's master and father. A runaway advertisement in the *Augusta Chronicle and Gazette of the State*, dated August 24, 1801, and republished on October 17, indicates that Ambrose remained at large for at least two months.[53] Ambrose, age 18, described as of "yellow" complexion—indicating a mulatto ancestry—had taken a horse and small bag and galloped towards freedom. The historical record is silent as to Ambrose's fate and whether he, like Ned, may have had a biological relationship with the white Magruder family.

Ninian's son, Basil, died in 1801. Two years later, in 1803, Ninian Offutt Magruder died and was buried in a family graveyard close to his home near Dearing and Grovetown, in Harlem, Columbia County, Georgia.[54] Years later, a monument was placed over his alleged gravesite.

---

[53] Magruder Runaway Ad, *Augusta Chronicle and Gazette of the State*, 17 Oct 1801, p. 4, col. 2; digital image Georgia Historic Newspapers database, Digital Library of Georgia (https://gahistoricnewspapers.galileo.usg.edu/lccn/sn82015220/1801-10-17/ed-1/seq-4/print/image_477x817_from_1115,5709_to_2170,7514/ : accessed 27 Dec 2021).

[54] Robert Lee Magruder, Jr., "The Georgia Magruders," *Year Book of the American Clan Gregor Society* I (1912): 50-54. [gatherings of 1909 & 1910].

The alleged gravesite of Ninian Offutt Magruder. Columbia County, Georgia. Photo courtesy of findagrave.com

COLONEL NINIAN BEALL

Ten Dollars Reward.

RUN-AWAY on Wednefday laft, from the fubfcriber living in Colunbia county, a negro fellow named AMBORS, or Ambrofe, about 18 years old, about 5 feet 7 or 8 inches high, yellow complected, had on a ftriped homefpun fhirt, and brown overalls, and an old hat; he took with him a fmall bag, horfe and a bridle. The above reward will be given to any perfon who will deliver faid fellow to me, or fecure him in any jail, and fend me information thereof.

N. O. MAGRUDER,

Auguft 24, 1801.

Runaway slave advertisement
placed by Ninian O. Magruder

The Last Will & Testament of Ninian O. Magruder & Inventory of Assets

Ninians's Last Will and Testament offers some details regarding his slave-holding assets at the end of his life. It allows us to peek backwards into the timeframe of Ned's childhood and analyze potential relationships among enslaved people on the plantation and thereby gain some insight into Ned's origins.

Before we look at the details of the will, it is important to first put the documents we will be analyzing in historical context. In *Tobacco and Slaves*, historian Allan Kulikoff provides some insight into the typical dynamics around estate distributions during this era. First, as enslaved people were born and died, and as enslavers sold or bequeathed their slaves, the households of enslaved people were broken and created. Husbands and wives, parents and children, were frequently separated by the transfer of enslaved family members from one generation to another, typically when children inherited slaves from their parents. Second, if economic disaster did not intervene, holdings of enslaved people grew through natural increase, enslaved families were reestablished, and extended family networks developed. When an enslaver died, enslaved people were again divided among heirs, and the process began again.

Before turning to Ninian's will, it is useful to begin an analysis by looking first at the inventory of his estate listing all the property in his possession. The inventory includes cattle, horses, household items, and 21 enslaved human beings. It is important to pay attention to how the enslaved people are grouped in the inventory, as these groupings may provide clues regarding relationships.

The following is how the enslaved people are grouped in the Inventory:

Enslaved Person(s)	Valuation
Fan,[55] Han, Bob, Will and Dave	$1,300
Nancy, Tom, Mariah, Charity, Cofy,[56] [illegible name], Mider	$1,400
Charlotte	$350

---

[55] Tan or Fan. Fan would be short for Fanny

[56] Hard to read, possibly Cofy—a common name among the enslaved—derived from the West African name Kofi.

Harry, Kate, Jim,[57] and Ned	$900
Prince, Pat, Henny, Matilda	$800
Daniel	$375

In the will, the assignments are:

Enslaved Person(s) Name(s)	White Magruder Given To	Notes
One negro girl named Charlotte	Zadok	"to be by him received out of my estate after the death" of Ninian's wife, Mary.
One Negro boy named Daniel	George	To be given to George after death of Mary
One Negro woman named Pat and her increase	John	"to be delivered over *immediately* after my death."
One Negro named Prince	John	To be given to John after death of Mary
One Negro girl named Henny	Polly Magruder, daughter of John Magruder	-
One Negro girl named Matilda	Eliza Magruder, daughter of John Magruder	-

---

57 Possibly read as Ben.

Tom, Nancy, Mariah, and Charity	Archibald	"my four negroes to be delivered over as soon as convenient"
Middleton (Mider)	Archibald	To be given to Archibald after death of Mary
Fan, Han,[58] and Dave	Sarah	"to be delivered as soon as convenient after my death"
Bob and Will	Sarah	To be given to Sarah upon the death of Mary
Ned and Jim	Eleanor	To be delivered "as soon as convenient after my death"
Harry and Cate (Kate)	Eleanor	To be given to Eleanor after the death of Mary

Who was Ned's Mother?

Although it is impossible to determine whose Ned mother was with certainty, based on current information, I offer two possibilities: that she was the Kate or the Charlotte mentioned in the will. This theory is premised on three assumptions: (1) that Ned's mother was not previously sold or deceased; (2) that in his will, Ninian grouped the slaves by their most intimate relationships; and (3) that unless enslavers had a specific economic or social interest to the contrary, they preferred to keep enslaved families together—especially in cases where they themselves were the father or grandfather of an enslaved person, or where it involved a mother and a small child, such as a Ned.

[58] Could be read as Hen, which would be short for Henny or Henrietta.

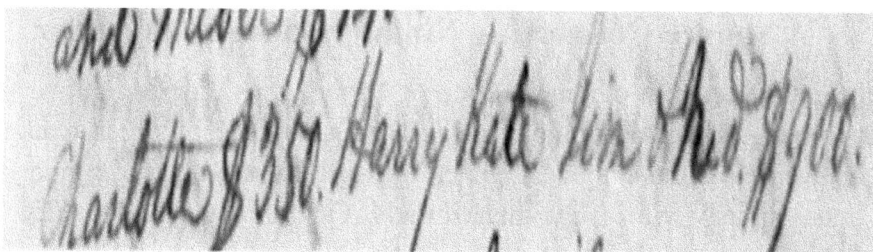

An excerpt from the will of Ninian O. Magruder.
Columbia County, Georgia. Circa 1803.

The reader can see in the inventory that groupings of people were allocated identically and in parallel to Ninian's bequests to his children in the will, with one notable exception. As shown in this image from the will, Charlotte is grouped along with Harry, Kate, Jim,[59] and Ned. She is valued at $350, which makes her one of the highest-assessed human beings in the group. Charlotte's value, when compared against these four, who had a collective value of $900 (an average of $225 each), shows that she was in a different and higher category of valuation. This number tells us that Charlotte was a young, healthy woman in her child-bearing years and that she was therefore more valuable to Ninian than any of these individuals listed to her right. Moreover, Charlotte is grouped together with Harry, Kate, Jim, and Ned, the latter of whom we know was under the age of ten. Considering the mortality rate of slaves, and their groupings within the estate documents, we can deduce that these three people were likely children of different ages and therefore would sell for less than Charlotte. For these reasons, I suggest that Charlotte was the mother of the four persons listed, including Ned. [60]

---

[59] Possibly read as Ben.

[60] Sabrina Franklin and Susan Tichy both question this analysis. Franklin argues that the grouping was not according to family relationships but rather by valuation. Franklin believes the will was crafted to achieve equal distribution among Ninian O. Magruder's heirs. Tichy agrees that this is one of several possibilities and observes that throughout the will all the females are categorized as "girl" except Pat, who is described as a "woman," implying that she had previously given birth and was a mother—possibly to Ned. Further, Tichy suggests that Charlotte may have been a house servant or possessed a unique skill set that made her more valuable.

Other less likely possibilities debated by Rothstein and Tichy are as follows:

(1) It is plausible that Pat was the mother of Ned. Perhaps Pat was pregnant to Ninian, and, sensitive to how his wife might feel retaining ownership of a woman whom he had impregnated, he was eager to get Pat out of the household, therefore mandating in his will that she be "immediately" given over to his son. However, the will provides Pat "and her increase" (i.e., her children) should be given over to John. Had Pat been the mother of Ned, he would have been included in that category, which he clearly was not. Susan Tichy,

A Source Connecting Ninian and Ned Magruder

An interesting account of the children of Ninian O. Magruder can be found in "Heraldry Notes," a weekly column in *The Baltimore Sun*, in which readers could ask and answer questions about the genealogy of Maryland and Virginia families, signing anonymously with only their initials. On Sunday, October 25, 1908, a reader identified as "M.W." lists ten children born to Ninian,[61] six of whom are mentioned in his 1803 will. Among the children, the last listed is *Ned*. A comparison of the two documents is as follows:

Ninian's 1803 Will	1908 Baltimore Sun, note by M.W.
George	George
Zadok	Zadok
John	John
Sarah	Sarah
Eleanor	Eleanore
Archibald	Archibald

however, rejects this argument as unfounded. According to Tichy, "willing a woman and her increase to an heir meant her future children. It did not mean no living children were being separated by the will."

(2) It is possible that Fan(ny) was Ned's mother. Fanny was a common black Magruder name during the early period. Perhaps Ned named one of his daughters in honor of his mother. However, the grouping of Fan with other slaves undermines this theory.

(3) Another theory is that Kate was the mother of Ned. This theory is based upon the fact that Kate is grouped together in the estate records with Ned and Jim, and therefore, she must be Ned's mother. Further support for this argument is that the will provides that after the death of Mary Harris Magruder, Kate was to join the plantation of Eleanor Magruder. Moreover, Kate appears in the 1829 Inventory of Assets of Williamson Wynne as "1 Negro Woman Kate" valued at $175. However, this argument is undermined by the low valuation of Kate in both documents. If Kate was a child-bearing woman, her valuation would have been much higher. It is more likely that she was a sister of Ned.

However, at this juncture, any analysis regarding the mother of Ned remains a matter of speculation.

[61] Heraldry Notes: Magruder, *The Baltimore Sun*, 25 October 1908, p. 14, cols. 3-4; digital image *Newspapers.com* (https://www.newspapers.com/image/371687351/?terms=%22Heraldry%20Notes%22%20Magruder&match=1 : accessed 17 Sept 2021).

Basil	**Absent**
Absent	Hezekiah
Absent	Mallinda who married a Beall
Absent	Eliza who married a Hicks
Ned (as an enslaved person)	Ned

MAGRUDER.—"M. D.," of Columbus, Ga., requested the names of the children and grandchil-

dren of Ninian Magruder and Elizabeth Brewer.
The children were: (1) Samuel, who married Margaret Jackson; (2) John, (3) Ninian, who married
Mary Offutt or Offord; (4) Sarah, who married ——
Beall; (5) Elizabeth, who married —— Perry; (6)
Nathaniel, who married Rebecca Offutt; (7) Rebecca, who married James Offutt; (8) Rachael, who
married —— Claggett; (9) James, (10) Anne, who
married —— Claggett; (11) Verlinda. Ninian Magruder 2d and Mary Offutt had Ninian Offutt Magruder (married Mary ——), William and possibly
other children. Ninian Offutt Magruder and Ninian
Beall Magruder moved from Maryland to Columbia
county, Georgia, about 1790. Ninian O. Magruder
and Mary —— had the following children: (1)
George, who married Susan Williams or Williamson; (2) Zadock, who married first —— and second
Tracy Rearden; (3) John, who married Sarah
Pryor; (4) Sarah, who married John Olive; (5)
Eleanore, who married William (or Williamson)
Wynne; (6) Hezekiah, (7) Malinda, who married
—— Beall; (8) Eliza, who married —— Hicks; (9)
Archibald, who died unmarried; (10) Ned. The will
of Ninian O. Magruder was made May 7, 1803, and
probated June 20, 1803. "M. D." says that John
Magruder, who married Sarah Pryor, had a sister,
Mrs. Oliver, but she is probably mistaken, as the
name was Olive. She was born September 16, 1779,
and died November 19, 1833. She is buried in Columbia county, Georgia. I should like to know the
names of the parents of Ninian Magruder's wife.
                                                    M. W.

*An account of the children of
Ninian O. Magruder,
The Baltimore Sun, "Heraldry Notes"
for October 25, 1908.*

There are a few issues with this note. First, no documents or sources are referenced. Second, absent from the list of children is Basil Magruder, a known child of Ninian and Mary. Taken in isolation, this is not surprising, considering that Basil died young and without issue. However, the fact that "M.W." lists three unknown children, not present in any other source, raises questions as to the accuracy of the information and the informant's level of intimacy with this family. In addition, both Ninian and Mary are given as the parents of all the children, including Ned. Overall, the newspaper account raises more questions than it answers, and I choose to rest my thesis of the Ned-Ninian connection on the DNA evidence and the Last Will and Testament of Ninian O. Magruder explored above.

The Life of Ned Magruder

In this context, we may begin to create a narrative of the life of Ned Magruder and construct the following picture of his life.

Ned was born in Columbia County, Georgia, in 1795, to Ninian Offutt Magruder and an enslaved woman or girl named Charlotte. Oral history suggests that Ned's parentage was known at the time. On March 17, 1803, when Ned was eight, his biological father (and enslaver) Ninian died. It was common for the death of a plantation owner to create great anxiety amongst the enslaved, as the disposition of any estate could mean that enslaved families would be separated—something the record suggests would later happen to Ned and his mother.

The question arises as to whether Ninian O. Magruder gave special consideration to Ned's future, as he drafted his will. An 1856 letter written by an unrelated plantation owner, James Henry Hammond, to his white son Harry, acknowledging having children with two enslaved women, Sally Johnson and her daughter Louisa, gives us a possible insight into Ninian's thinking regarding Ned. Hammond writes:

> My Dear Harry,
>
> In the last Will I made left to you, over & above my other children, Sally Johnson the mother of Louisa and all the children of both. Sally says Henderson is my child. It is possible, but I do not believe it. Yet act on her's rather than my opinion. Louisa's first child *may* be mine. I think not. Her second I believe is mine. Take care of her and her children who are both of your blood if not of mine & of Henderson. The services of the rest will I think compensate for indulgence to these. I cannot free these people and send them North. It would be cruelty to them. Nor would I like that any but my own blood should own as slaves my own blood or Louisa. I leave them to your charge, believing that you will best appreciate & most independently carry out my wishes in regard to them. Do not let Louisa or any of my children or possible children be the Slaves of Strangers. Slavery in the family will be their happiest earthly condition.
>
> Ever affectionately,
> **J. H. H**.[62]

---

[62] James Henry Hammond, *Secret and Sacred: The Diaries of James Henry Hammond, a Southern Slaveholder* (Oxford: Oxford University Press, 1989), 19.

The Roots of Ned and Mariah Magruder

In the subsequent distribution of Ninian's estate, "slavery in the family" was to be Ned's fate. Ned, and the white Magruder family secret he represented, was inherited by the eighteen-year-old Eleanor Magruder, and this so-called "asset"—but in reality, a moral burden—was taken into her domain. However, Ninian's will provides that Ned was also to be forcibly separated from his mother—an act that suggests Ninian's or his wife, Mary Harris's, spitefulness towards Charlotte.[63]

An excerpt from the will of Ninian O. Magruder.
Columbia County, Georgia. Circa 1803.

Just months after the death of Ninian O. Magruder, on December 17, 1803, in Columbia County, Georgia, Eleanor Magruder married Williamson Wynne (1760-1829), who was 25 years her senior.[64] Like her father, Eleanor's husband was a

---

[63] This scenario is accurate irrespective of whether Charlotte, Kate, or Pat was his mother.

[64] *Alabama Department of Archives and History* includes the following biographical sketch of Williamson Wynne, from Thomas McAdory Owen's *Revolutionary Soldiers in Alabama* (Greenville, SC: Southern Historical Press, 2019 [1911]); (https://archives.alabama.gov/al_sldrs/w_list.html : accessed 20 Jan 2021).

WYNNE, WILLIAMSON, private in First North Carolina Regiment, also in War of 1812, son of Major Joshua Wynne and his wife, Elizabeth Appling Wynne, was born in Pendleton District, South Carolina, in 1760. He lived for a time in Georgia and in North Carolina. Later, he moved to Alabama. He died on his plantation, "Wynnewood" in Greene County, Alabama, in 1829. He is buried on this plantation near the home of his descendants, the Wynne Coleman family; and Harris Magruder Coleman and his wife are the ones living nearest his grave. He served as a private in Captain Dixon's company, First North Carolina Regiment, Revolutionary War. He enlisted in 1777, and his service ended in January 1778. He also served in the War of 1812 as a private in Captain Jacob Welch's company 5th (McDonald's) Regiment of North Carolina from Chowan County. He was discharged on July 19, 1813. He is said to have re-enlisted later, but we do not have this record. By the records of Greene County, Alabama (certified by Judge B.B. Barnes and Miss Mary Dunlap), Williamson Wynne died in 1829—his son Osmond Appling Wynne qualified as administrator of his estate, April 1829. Williamson Wynne died intestate and left surviving him his widow, Eleanor Magruder Wynne, and five children viz: Osmond and Erasmus, both over 21 years, and Williamson, Robert, and Salina Ann, minors under 21 years. Eleanor Magruder Wynne,

man of contradictions. Williamson Wynne fought for liberty and freedom in the American Revolution, and yet would come to be the owner of many enslaved people. Eleanor would have been tasked with not only building and managing her new home, but also training her newly acquired enslaved people, which included her half-brother, Ned. This task of managing and disciplining enslaved children was a matter her new husband surely would have had an opinion about.

Nine months after her marriage, Eleanor's first son, Osmun Appling Wynne (1804-1877), was born. Osmun was followed by Erasmus Wynne (1807-1863) and Williamson Wynne, Jr. (1810-1895). In 1812, Williamson Wynne Sr. volunteered to fight in the War of 1812 as a private in Captain Jacob Welch's company, the 5th (McDonald's) Regiment of North Carolina, from Chowan County. During the war, Eleanor gave birth to another son, Robert Wynne (1812-1855). Williamson was discharged on July 19, 1813. Following the war, Eleanor gave birth to two more children, Adolphus (1813-1846) and Elizabeth A. Wynne (1815-1867). Assuming that Ned, as a mullato, was a domestic servant, living in the plantation house, Eleanor must have relied on him heavily during this period.

Ned & Mariah Build a Family

Up until approximately 1818, Ned would have been living in Columbia County, Georgia. We can assume that he lived in proximity to other enslaved people from the plantation of Ninian O. Magruder, who had been disbursed after the distribution of Ninian's estate among the different Magruder plantations of the area. It is possible that on occasion Ned would have crossed paths with these people—some of whom may have been family members.

It is possible that as a young man, through this close geographic proximity, Ned (re)united with Mariah (c.1800-c.1880).[65] The two had been children together

---

wife of Williamson Wynne, made her will February 14, 1848, probated November 26, 1849, everything settled, and executors resigned 1854, Folio 1144, Greene County, Alabama. Their children were: Joshua; Pattie, died unmarried; John; Osmond, m. Francis Anderson; Erasmus, b. Dec. 19, 1807, m. 1. Jane Sophronia Anderson (sister of Francis Anderson); 2. Mrs. Elizabeth Smither; Robert, b. Nov. 9, 1812, m. Elizabeth Wynne; Williamson, m. 1. Palomie (?) Smith, 2. Helen Robinson; Salina Ann, m. William Ferrell. The descendants of Osmond Appling Wynne still live in Alabama. Erasmus, Robert, and Williamson moved with their families to Texas and there many of them still live. —Information from Mrs. Marie Scovel Browder of Houston, Texas.

[65] It is reasonable to assume that the Mariah mentioned in the will of Eleanor Magruder Wynne as the wife of Ned was the same Mariah deeded by Ninian Magruder to Archibald Magruder. Though this is not known conclusively, it has been presumed by Alabama Black McGruder historians before me, and I cannot say whether they had an oral history basis for

on the Ninian O. Magruder plantation, Ned being several years Mariah's senior. However, they were apparently separated when Mariah was bequeathed to Eleanor's brother, Archibald Magruder.[66] We can assume that Mariah subsequently grew up on Archibald's plantation.

In or around 1819, Mariah and Ned, with Eleanor's assistance, married. At the time, marriage between enslaved people was not recognized by the state, nor did marriage before clergy protect the spouses from the abuses and restrictions imposed on them by enslavers. Enslaved husbands and wives, without legal recourse, could be separated or sold at their enslaver's will. However, the will of Eleanor Magruder tells us that was not Ned or Mariah's fate. Eleanor must have made some financial accommodation with Archibald to acquire Mariah, or she may have been gifted by Archibald to Eleanor, because Mariah was able to accompany Ned and the other enslaved people of the Magruder-Wynne plantation from Columbia County, Georgia, to Greene County, Alabama.

At some point between 1817 and 1819, Williamson Wynne began to consider a move to Alabama, a region which had opened up to settlement after the War of 1812 and the ethnic cleansing of its native tribes. Columbia County, Georgia, had become crowded, and moving to Alabama, where the family could receive free land grants courtesy of the United States government, offered Williamson and Eleanor new opportunities.[67] Williamson, his brother Robert, and perhaps other members of the extended Wynne family who lived near them in Columbia County, decided to move jointly west to Eutaw, Greene County, Alabama.

In 1823, shortly after the family's move to Alabama, Salina Ann Eleanor Wynne was born. The youngest child and only daughter of Eleanor Magruder and

---

such an assumption. Both spellings, *Mariah* and *Moriah,* appear in the records. Often, handwriting makes distinguishing the vowel impossible. The will of Ninian O. Magruder of 1803 and the inventory conducted of the estate of Williamson Wynne in 1829 seem to spell the name *Moriah*, while other documents use *Maria(h)*. The author believes *Moriah* to be more likely accurate. However, the *Mariah* spelling has been more popularly used by the Alabama Black McGruders, and therefore throughout this document I defer to that tradition.

[66] Ninian's son Archibald died on May 6, 1839. He left the bulk of his estate to his nieces and nephews. Some researchers have asserted that his birth was in 1772, rather than 1780. No record has been located confirming either date.

Based on oral history descriptions of Ned and Mariah's children as white-looking or light-skinned, it is likely that Mariah herself was a mulatto. Without any specific oral tradition or evidence, Archibald Magruder has been offered by some researchers of the family history as a possible father of Mariah, thereby making her a Magruder, and a niece to Ned.

[67] The records are unclear as to whether Williamson owned any land of his own in Georgia.

Williamson Wynne Sr., she was the first of the Wynne family to be born in Alabama.

The record suggests that, at some point in their marriage, Williamson may have tried to interfere with Eleanor's management of the enslaved people in her domain. This can be deduced from the painstaking efforts Eleanor would take years later to prevent the husband of her daughter, Salina Ann, from doing the same. As Sabrina Franklin, an Alabama Black McGruder historian, reminds us, "During that era, it was customary for men to take over all of the property owned by their wives." Williamson therefore became the *de facto* owner of Ned and Mariah Magruder.[68] The record suggests, however, that Eleanor resisted. This dynamic between Eleanor and Williamson must have created an awkward situation for Ned and his family. Who would come out on top in the struggle between two whites with power over them? To whom did they owe their loyalty? To their blood relative, Eleanor, or to her husband?

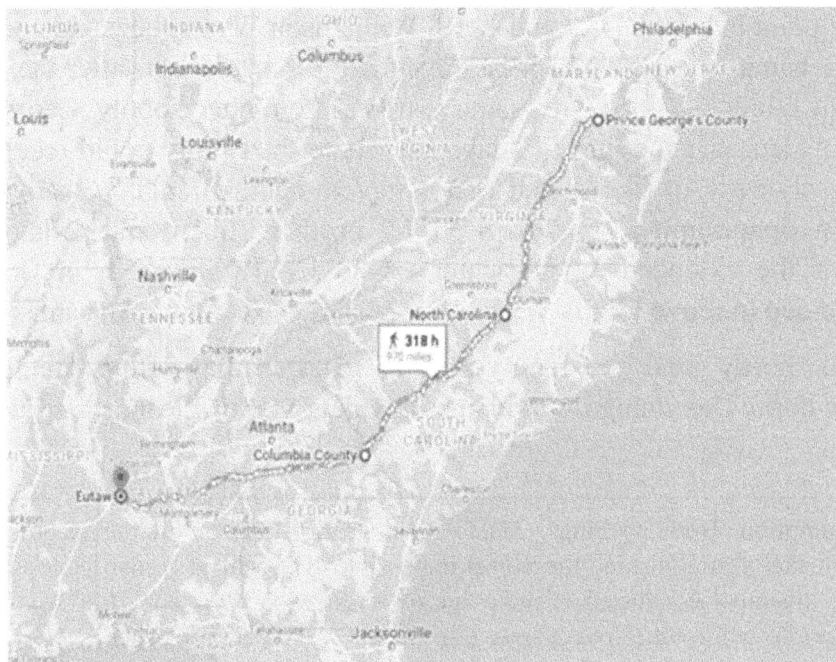

The Magruder & Wynne migrations

Around the time that Williamson began to undertake the move westward, Mariah and Ned began a family. The first-born child to Ned and Mariah was Fanny Magruder (1821-?), followed by Martha Magruder (1825-c.1869) and Charles Magruder Sr. (1829-c.1900). Some census records show that these

---

68 Sabrina Franklin, "The Alabama Black McGruders."

children were born in North or South Carolina, but the entries provided by census-takers are inconsistent with presently available information. It is possible that the Wynne family had a short hiatus in the Carolinas, where some of the children of Ned and Mariah were born prior to settling permanently in Alabama. It is also possible that the individuals themselves were uncertain of their birth location, or that census-takers gathered information from someone outside the family.[69]

Irrespective of their path of migration, and where certain individuals were born, by 1819 the black Magruders and white Wynnes were firmly established in Greene County, Alabama. The Wynnes, wielding the enslaved labor in their possession, established a plantation called Wynnewood in or around the location of what would come to be called Hollow Square.[70] The Wynnes were among the first white settlers in the area, and for the next few years Wynnewood's stabilization, mostly under the direction of Osmun A. Wynne, Eleanor and Williamson's talented eldest son, would be their highest priority.

---

[69] I posit that the consistent reference among numerous Alabama Black McGruders to origins in North Carolina more likely has its basis in the origins of Ned's mother—suggesting that Ninian O. Magruder acquired her during his migration from Maryland to Georgia. However, this matter remains unresolved.

[70] Wynnewood was said to be located near the Lea Plantation. This needs further research.

While over Alabama earth,

These words are gently spoken:

Serve—and hate will die unborn.

Love—and chains are broken.

Langston Hughes

"Alabama Earth," The Collected Works of Langston Hughes

5 – Some Notes on Hollow Square & Sawyerville, Alabama

By J.R. Rothstein, Esq.[71]

When European settlers migrated into the west-central region of what is today called Alabama they encountered a multitude of indigenous peoples, including the Chocatow, Chickawsaw and Alabama nations with whom they began to trade. One of the first trading communities in the region where the white Wynne and black Magruder families would one day settle was called Erie—located near the limestone bluff overlooking the Black Warrior River. It was less than five miles from the future site of Hollow Square and five miles southwest of present-day Sawyerville.

Over time, Erie would play a significant role in the transfer of cotton from the Alabama Black Belt, named for its dark, productive soil, to the Port of Mobile, where the cotton would be shipped around the world. Among the notable early buildings of Erie was a large cotton warehouse.[72]

On March 3, 1817, as white settlement in the region increased, the United States Congress created the Alabama Territory. Alabama was eventually admitted as the 22nd state, on December 14, 1819. Greene County was established that same year, and Erie became the county seat. Greene County was named after the Revolutionary War patriot and abolitionist, General Nathanael Greene of Rhode Island.

---

[71] Research for this chapter draws on the notes of Sawyerville historian Jonathan May. See also W. Stuart Harris, *Dead Towns of Alabama* (Tuscaloosa: University of Alabama Press, 1977); Virginia O. Foscue, *Place Names in Alabama* (Tuscaloosa: University of Alabama Press, 1989); Berenice May Fuller, *Two May Families of Hollow Square, Greene County, Alabama: Including some May-Windham-Harrison-Dargan ancestors and descendants* (Baltimore: Gateway Press, 1988); U.S. Postal Service, *Postmaster Finder: Postmasters by City* (https://webpmt.usps.gov/pmt002.cfm : accessed 16 Sept 2021).

[72] The town of Wedgeworth was adjacent to Hollow Square. Wedgeworth is named for the family of John Wedgeworth, an early settler. A post office operated under the name Greenwood from 1895 to 1904, and under the name Wedgeworth from 1904 to 1955. Wedgeworth has now become part of Sawyerville, but the two were once distinct. During the Reconstruction era, the Alabama Black McGruders held land in both towns.

The new state inspired white families to migrate to the area, including Southeastern planters like Williamson Wynne Sr. Like so many others of his class, Williamson Wynne took his enslaved people with him from the Upper South to Alabama. These enslaved people, and the cotton they produced through sweat, blood and tears, would establish the economy of the central Black Belt.

The area also drew poor, disenfranchised white people, who became subsistence farmers, and a small merchant class to which the Ferrell family, discussed in coming chapters, belonged. In 1810, Alabama, still then a territory, had an estimated population under 10,000, which increased to more than 300,000 by 1830. In that year, Congress passed the Indian Removal Act, and within a few years most Native American tribes were ethnically cleansed from the state. In 1838 the county seat was moved to Eutaw and Erie began a slow decline, most of its more distinguished citizens moving to Eutaw or Greensboro. The post office was discontinued in 1848, and after 1850 Erie no longer appeared on state maps.

As a community, Hollow Square appears to have been a later creation, although by 1848 it did have its own post office. Based on that date, a good assumption is that it replaced the discontinued office at Erie and likely served the same clientele, including the plantation-owning families of Wynne, Pickens, Sawyer, Seay, May, Kinnaird, and Kimbrough. Hollow Square was located 1.6 miles west of present-day Sawyerville, 2.7 miles east of the intersection of state highways 14 and 60, and about three miles east of the property purchased by Charles McGruder Sr. in 1877.

By 1860, the population of Alabama had increased to 964,201, of which nearly half—435,080—were enslaved Africans and their descendants, and 2,690 were free people of color. This reality generated fears amongst the white population of a slave revolt or of black political and social domination in the event of emancipation.

The Postmasters

Sawyerville was a minor hamlet in comparison with the towns of Eutaw and Greensboro, and the position of postmaster was one of the few signs of government authority.

In or around 1856, Jacob Herzfeld (Hirschfeld), an immigrant from Bavaria,[73] made his way to Sawyerville as a struggling peddler. In time, he established a modest shop and, shortly thereafter, at the sunset of the Presidency of the abolitionist Franklin Peirce, was appointed Postmaster.

Herzfeld's career, however, was short-lived. Within three years he was murdered and the small shop he established burned to the ground.[74] Herzfeld was replaced by Andrew Jackson "A.J." Mayfield, a plantation owner and slaveowner, who would play a direct role in the history of the Alabama Black McGruders by renting the labor of the black Magruders during the Civil War.

James W. Melton, the last postmaster of Hollow Square, was appointed on April 28, 1870. Prior to the Civil War, Melton had rented the Mariah Magruder family from the Estate of Salina Ann Wynne. After Melton, Enoch Sawyer, a known alcoholic, was appointed to the role on December 19, 1871. Sawyer moved the post office a mile and two-thirds east, closer to his home, to a community called Sawyer's

A Most Atrocious Murder.—Mr. Jacob Hercefield, a merchant residing at Hollow Square, in this county, was murdered last Friday night, a short distance from his residence, by some person, unknown. He boarded at Mr. C. Toberts, about half a mile from his store, and left Mr. T.'s about 10 o'clock on Friday night. His body was found on Saturday morning near a building used as a School house, located a short distance from, and West of the baptist church, situated on the greensboro' and Eutaw road. The wounds indicated that he had been shot in the head, and a severe blow inflicted upon him with an axe. As he bore the character of being a peaceable, inoffensive man, no doubt is entertained that the bloody deed was committed solely to get his money. Circumstances, we understand, also justify the belief, that an attempt was made the same night to burn his store. No clue has yet been furnished, so far as we are advised, for the detection of the murderer; but the citizens of the neighborhood are investigating the matter.

The deceased was a native of Bavaria, Germany, but had resided in this county quite a number of years. He was the Postmaster at Hollow Square, and was looked upon by the neighborhood as a worthy man.—*Greensbor Beacon*.

---

[73] Herzfeld was likely Jewish.

[74] Most Atrocious Murder, *Southern Statesman (Prattville, Alabama)*, 24 March 1860, p. 2, col. 5; digital image *Newspapers.com* (https://www.newspapers.com/image/572795463/?terms=%22Most%20Atrocious%22&match=1 : accessed 25 Sept 2021).

Depot, later known as Sawyerville.

The following is a complete list of Sawyerville postmasters during the 19th century:[75]

Name	Date Appointed
Benjamin P. Ferrell	02/18/1847
Thomas I. Anderson	08/02/1852
Samuel Beck	12/06/1854
Jacob Herzfeld	04/17/1857
Andrew J. Mayfield	05/04/1860
John G. Cox	12/27/1865
James W. Melton	04/29/1870
Enoch Sawyer	12/19/1871
Robert N. McCrory	12/15/1892
Samuel W. Walton	04/26/1893

The Civil War

In October of 1859, John Brown, a white Christian abolitionist, raided Harpers Ferry, in what was then Virginia, hoping to spark a war to free enslaved people. On November 6, 1860, Abraham Lincoln was elected President of the United States with a mandate to complete the unfinished work of the American Revolution and end the institution of slavery.

In December, Stephen F. Hale, Alabama's commissioner to Kentucky, wrote a letter to that state's governor about Alabama's justification for its forthcoming secession. Hale was an avid proponent of slavery and a committed racist. In the letter, Hale voiced support for the *Dred Scott* decision, condemned the Republican Party, and asserted that the state's secession, which would perpetuate slavery, was the only way to prevent prospective freedmen, whom Hale referred

---

[75] U.S. Postal Service, *Postmaster Finder: Postmasters by City* (https://webpmt.usps.gov/pmt002.cfm : accessed 16 Sept 2021).

to as "half-civilized Africans", from raping southern "wives and daughters." Hale wrote:

> [I]n the South, where in many places the African race largely predominates, and, as a consequence, the two races would be continually pressing together, amalgamation, or the extermination of the one or the other, would be inevitable. Can Southern men submit to such degradation and ruin? God forbid that they should. [...] [T]he election of Mr. Lincoln cannot be regarded otherwise than a solemn declaration, on the part of a great majority of the Northern people, of hostility to the South, her property and her institutions—nothing less than an open declaration of war—for the triumph of this new theory of Government destroys the property of the South, lays waste her fields, and inaugurates all the horrors of a San Domingo servile insurrection, consigning her citizens to assassinations, and her wives and daughters to pollution and violation, to gratify the lust of half-civilized Africans.[76]

On January 11, 1861, Alabama voted to secede from the United States of America. At the Alabama Secession Convention, in February, delegates from the fourteen slaveholding states joined at Montgomery for the purposes of establishing a new nation, the Confederate States of America. The convention appointed Jefferson Davis as President and Alexander H. Stephens as Vice President. A month later, in his famous "cornerstone speech," Stephens summed up the values of the new nation, declaring that the Confederacy rests "upon the great truth that the negro is not equal to the white man; that slavery,

"HOLLOW SQUARE HOME GUARDS."—We understand a Cavalry Company,—bearing the foregoing name, and composed of first rate material, has been organized in the Hollow Square neighborhood. It is armed with double-barrel guns and repeaters. The following are its officers.

E. Sawyer, Captain.

E. L. Kimbrough, 1st Lieut.

Jos. Chapman, 2nd Lieut.

J. W. Monette, O. S.

---

[76] Stephen F. Hale, letter to Gov. Beriah Magoffin, 27 December 1860, at *Teaching American History* (https://teachingamericanhistory.org/library/document/stephen-f-hale-to-governor-beriah-magoffin/ : accessed 16 Sept 2021).

subordination to the superior race, is his natural and normal condition."[77]

The majority of white Sawyerville answered the Confederate call to battle.[78] Its young men joined the newly formed militias. Its women supported their men, and its businessmen and plantation owners shifted their crop production efforts to support the Confederate cause.

In July 1862, Stephen F. Hale died of wounds received at the Battle of Gaines' Mill, in Virginia, a martyr to the Confederate cause and its ideals. His tombstone bears the epitaph "Statesman, Jurist, Patriot, Soldier & Christian Gentleman." For much of white Sawyerville, he symbolized the grief felt with the loss of their own sons, brothers, and fathers on the battlefield.

An election notice of the 38th Regiment Alabama Militia, which counted among its leaders white residents of Sawyerville, including William A. Wynne, son of Osmun A. Wynne. [79]

ELECTION NOTICE.

AN election will be held on Saturday, the 21st day of June next for
Lieutenant-Colonel in the 1st Battalion,
38th Regiment Alabama Militia, to fill
the vacancy occasioned by the resigna
tion of Lieutenant-Colonel A. C. Allen.

MANAGERS:

Havana—Geo. H. Sheldon, W. R.
Brown, P. Jones. L. L. Sexton, 'managers ; W. R. Brown, returning officer.

Hollow Square—A. J. Mayfield. W.
A. Wynne, E Sawyer, E. L. Kimbrough, managers ; W. A. Wynne, returning officer.

Five Mile—Frank Harris, W. Brown,
A. Stephens, A. Prisock, managers ; F.
Harris, returning officer.

By order of James T. Tarry, Briga-
dier-General Commanding.

A. GALLAWAY, Sheriff.

BY W. B. BRIGGS, D. S.

May 29, 1863.   20 3s 4w

After the Civil War, many white citizens of Greene County and Alabama more

[77] Alexander H. Stephens, "The Cornerstone Speech," 21 March 1861; digital text American Battlefield Trust (https://www.battlefields.org/learn/primary-sources/cornerstone-speech : accessed 28 Dec 2021).

[78] Hollow Square Home Guards, *(Greensboro) Alabama Beacon*, 5 July 1861, p. 2, col. 6; digital image *Newspapers.com* (https://www.newspapers.com/image/355740963/?terms=Hollow%20Square%20Home%20G uards&match=1 : accessed 17 Sept 2021).

[79] Election Notice, 38th Alabama Militia, *(Greensboro) Alabama Beacon*, 5 June 1863, p. 4, col. 5; digital image *Newspapers.com* (https://www.newspapers.com/image/576947992/?terms=%2238th%20Regiment%20Alabam a%20Militia%22&match=1 : accessed 17 Sept 2021).

generally, seeing themselves in the Confederate hero, named a new county in his honor—Hale County. On January 30, 1867, Greene County was split into Greene and Hale counties, with the Black Warrior River as the boundary between them. Small portions of Marengo, Perry, and Tuscaloosa counties were also incorporated into the new Hale County, with Greensboro named as county seat. Eutaw remained the county seat of Greene.

This is the region in which the Alabama Black McGruders lived from the 1820's until they dispersed from greater Sawyerville in modern times. To understand the context in which they lived, readers can review a selection of primary documents and newspaper accounts annexed to this book, providing an overview of the history of this hamlet from the 1850's until the end of the century.

Then the Lord said to Cain,

"Where is Abel, your brother?"

He said, "I do not know;

am I my brother's keeper?"

Genesis 4:9

6 - Building Wynnewood

By J.R. Rothstein, Esq.

Between 1819 and 1829, the family of Ned and Mariah Magruder and the other enslaved people of Wynnewood toiled underneath the harsh Alabama sun and its scorching heat. Together, they cleared the dense subtropical vegetation and built the plantation of Wynnewood.

In 1822 Ned and Maria gave birth to their first child, Fanny—the first of the black Magruders to be born in the new state. Two years later, in 1824, Maria gave birth to another daughter, Martha.

Under the common law legal doctrine known as *coverture*, a married woman in British North America, and later in the United States, had little legal existence apart from her husband. Her rights and obligations were subsumed under his. She could not own property, enter into contracts, or earn a salary. An unmarried woman, a *femme sole*, on the other hand, had the right to own property and make contracts in her own name. In this reality, Eleanor's enslaved people, by law, were under Williamson's control—property which included the family of Ned and Mariah Magruder.

In early 1829, Williamson died, leaving his widow, Eleanor Magruder Wynne, and three minor children. Because Williamson died intestate, the court of Greene County mandated that his estate be inventoried so it could be divided equally, ensuring each of his children a fair portion. Each minor child was appointed a guardian, to make sure the division of property was equitable.[80]

According to Alabama Black McGruder historian Sabrina Franklin, this was an extremely difficult time for the Ned and Mariah Magruder family. The death of Williamson caused distress among all the enslaved, as it created uncertainty as to whether they would remain together or be separated from family members. No doubt Ned and Mariah were relieved when Eleanor purchased them from the estate of her husband, grateful that their family would remain together.

In this context, we have an additional archival reference to the family of Ned and Mariah Magruder. In the April 1829 inventory of Williamson's property, Ned Magruder was valued at $500 and the pregnant Mariah at $350. The inventory

---

[80] Records regarding disposition of the land are complex and need further examination. Because only Osmun was over 21, each of his siblings was appointed a guardian and the estate remained open until the youngest, Salina, came of age.

also revealed that the couple had two daughters, Fanny, valued at $175, and Martha, valued at $125. Charles Magruder was born a month later in May of 1829.

When Williamson Wynne's property was sold at public auction on January 8, 1830, most, but not all, of the enslaved were repurchased by the Wynne family. According to Franklin, "there seems to have been an attempt on the part of the Wynne family to keep the [enslaved] families . . . together." Eleanor Wynne purchased Ned, Mariah, and their children—Fanny, Martha, and a new baby, Charles—for a total of $1,270. The record going forward, however, is silent as to what happened to Ned's other family members or companions. There are no further records of Jim, Harry, and Kate—the people grouped together with Ned in Ninian O. Magruder's 1803 will. As there is no mention of them in Eleanor Wynne's 1848 estate records, it is likely that between 1830 and 1848 they were traded away between Eleanor and her siblings, sold off to third parties, or died.

Eleanor never remarried. After Williamson's death, her sons, particularly Osmun A. Wynne, managed and oversaw her property. Ned and Mariah remained married and, under the control of Osmun A. Wynne, continued to grow their family at Wynnewood. In 1832 they produced another son, Jasper Magruder (1832-1881). Finally, a daughter named Lilly Magruder (1841–19??)[81] was born to Ned and Mariah in or around March 1841.

William A. Ferrell Marries Up

If Ned had accompanied Eleanor to the home of William A. Ferrell (1806-1859) and Salina Ann Wynne Ferrell, Eleanor's youngest child and only daughter, late in 1848, they would have been underwhelmed by the Ferrell's state of living. Salina Ann was sharing a homestead with another white family, who were apparently unrelated. William had brought few, if any, enslaved people into the marriage. Salina Ann appears to have been left mostly on her own, without significant help from enslaved labor, to look after Eleanor's grandchildren.

This reality, however, should not have been surprising to Eleanor. When William A. Ferrell met Salina Ann Wynne, the latter was about fifteen years old. William, born in North Carolina to a merchant family, had, by the age of 33,

---

[81] According to Sabrina Franklin, Lilly married Allen Ellis after 1870, after being a single parent to her two oldest children. She went on to have four more children with her husband. In 1880, she also took on the responsibility of caring for her mother, when Mariah was about eighty years old.

acquired little or no land, and few, if any, slaves.[82] This was in stark contrast to Salina Ann, who grew up on a large and successful plantation with a large number of enslaved people.

However, the Wynne family was not without its blemishes. In June of 1838, Salina Ann, then fourteen, had been married, though apparently the marriage quickly dissolved.[83] Still recovering from the shame of annulment or divorce, Salina Ann met William. Each seems to have overlooked the social blemishes of the other and, after a brief courtship, they married on October 14, 1839. Despite marrying into the Wynne family, William A. Ferrell would never match the success or education of the Wynne brothers or their children.

Raising the Wynnes

By 1848, the Wynne family, and particularly O.A. Wynne, were among the wealthiest landowners of Greene County, thanks to the free labor and fertility of the black Magruders and the other enslaved people of the plantation. An exceptionally competent and self-reflective administrator, Osmun, by 1850, had expanded Wynnewood from its original 320 acres and doubled his number of enslaved people to more than 60. Prior to their departure for Texas, in the early 1850's, Eleanor's other sons, Colonel Erasmus Wynne and Williamson Wynne Jr., each also enslaved approximately 44 people. Land transfers within a family were seldom recorded in the deed books, but it is likely that their land was purchased by Osmun, and perhaps some of their slaves, as well.

By 1856, O.A. Wynne owned more than 1,000 acres and the 1860 slave schedule shows him holding more than 80 human beings in bondage. Snedecor's 1856 map of Greene County also shows the respective land holdings of Osmun A. Wynne and William A. Ferrell. Osmun's wealth permitted his children to enter the highest levels of Alabama society—a world in stark contrast to the one William A. Ferrell inhabited.

---

[82] Snedecor's Map of Greene County, Alabama, published in 1856, shows that by that date William A. Ferrell owned approximately 320 acres adjoining the 360 acres Salina had inherited from her mother. The history of his land acquisitions needs further investigation. The map can be found at the Library of Congress' collection of county land ownership maps (https://www.loc.gov/item/2006626024/).

[83] A marriage license for Salina Wynne and William T. Bell was issued on 16 June 1838. Their marriage appears in indexes of Alabama marriages dated 19 June, but no further record of the marriage has been found. Greene County, Alabama, Probate Courts, Marriage Record; digital image FamilySearch.org (https://www.familysearch.org/ark:/61903/1:1:QKZ3-H3BV :accessed 28 Dec 2021).

Letters from the era, however, reveal that O.A. Wynne had two great concerns: the price of a bale of cotton and the behavior of his son, William A. "App" Wynne. Born December 7, 1831, at Wynnewood, just two years younger than Charles Magruder, he was, according to the letters discovered and preserved by Alice Coleman Griffin, the most favored son of O.A. Wynne and Francis Laura Anderson.

O.A. Wynne's highest hope was that all his children would develop well-cultivated minds. For "Master William" he hoped that he would one day become a lawyer. Osmun expressed concern that Master William was reckless in his spending habits and paying insufficient attention to his studies. Letter after letter between Master William and his parents concern the former's request for funds for some social event, or for the purchase of clothing. On numerous occasions, O.A. Wynne rebuked his son, reminding him that "it is not a fine coat nor a fine pair of boots that makes the man but [to] have your mind well cultivated."[84]

O.A. Wynne, perhaps influenced by his mother's progressive views on gender, elaborated upon below, did not distinguish between his daughters and sons in matters of education, sending both to boarding school. Master William's desire to become part of "society" was shared by his sisters, particularly Martha, who likewise at boarding school developed extravagant tastes. "I do not want you to buy anything but what you actually need," O.A. Wynne wrote on November 20, 1848. "I want you to dress neat but nothing superfluous. I do not charge so particular about spending your money because I do not want to give it to you, but it is because I don't want you to think too much about fancy dress. It is not a fine dress, or a beautiful bonnet that makes the Lady but [to] have your mind well cultivated."[85] Although O.A. Wynne himself remained conservative, his children at boarding school—influenced no doubt by their peers and wanting to express to the state's ruling class that they too were wealthy enslavers and landowners—had developed very expensive tastes.

Eleanor Magruder Wynne's Will

Perhaps O.A. Wynne's impressive success was one of the reasons that, as Eleanor Magruder Wynne drafted her will in the winter of 1848, she decided leave her sons only a symbolic inheritance of $800 each. She bequeathed the bulk of her fortune to her twenty-five-year-old daughter, Salina Ann, and her slave-and-land-poor husband, William A. Ferrell.

---

[84] Alice Coleman Griffin, *Laura's Family Letters* (Privately printed, 2009), 56.

[85] Alice Coleman Griffin, *Laura's Family Letters,* 56.

Whatever Eleanor's relationship with William had been at the beginning of his marriage with Salina, by the time Eleanor drafted her will, her distrust of her son-in-law had fully crystalized. Eleanor memorialized this sentiment when she wrote that her daughter's slaves "shall in no manner be subjected to the debts, management or control or benefit of William A. Ferrell, husband of Salina Ann Eleanor Ferrell," and that Salina Ann should otherwise exercise direct control over all the assets entrusted to her and be treated "as if she were a *Feme sole*"—a free and independent woman.[86]

Over several decades, beginning in the 1830s, statutes were enacted throughout the South that enabled women to control real and personal property, enter into contracts and lawsuits, inherit independently of their husbands, work for a salary, and write wills. These progressive statutes led southern women like Eleanor to become conscious of a woman's potential property rights—a concept she enshrined within her will for the benefit of her daughter. Yet, despite this, the patriarchal reality of the day mandated that it would be William A. Ferrell who would be tasked as an executor to oversee the distribution of Eleanor's assets, including the family of Ned and Mariah.

One may wonder whether Eleanor, in drafting her will, remembered her brother Ned. History demonstrates that economic and legal considerations usually prevailed over any sentimental feelings an enslaver may have had toward the enslaved. It is worth noting, however, that Eleanor, as her brother's keeper, did draft a will that was rare for the era. Eleanor Magruder Wynne, in contrast to her father, created legal mechanisms to keep the family of Ned and Mariah Magruder together. Eleanor left not a single enslaved black Magruder to either of her sons, giving them only a small cash gift. The family of Ned and Mariah Magruder would have been valued on the open slave market in the many thousands of dollars. Instead of dividing them, Eleanor left all the Alabama Black McGruders to her youngest child and only daughter, Salina Ann. Moreover, in stark contrast to typical wills of the era, she humanizes the Ned and Mariah Magruder family by providing the ages of all its members as well as their relationship to one another. Notably, she does this only for the family of Ned and Mariah, and not for the other enslaved people of her domain.

---

[86] In February of 1848 Eleanor purchased land from a James Ferril, likely William A. Ferrell's father, for $2,000. She later bequeathed that land to Salina. Greene County, Alabama, Probate Court, Deeds, 1802-1901, Deed Book P, p 640; digital images, *FamilySearch* (https://www.familysearch.org/ark:/61903/3:1:3Q9M-CSLX-MSBT-Z?i=868&cat=518705 : accessed 24 Jan 21).

It is impossible to say what motivated this action. Perhaps Eleanor desired to protect her brother and his children. Perhaps Eleanor, filled with compassion, was reminded of the trauma Ned experienced by being separated from his own mother. Perhaps, protective of Ned, and having witnessed the methods of enslavement employed by her father, husband, and sons felt that her daughter would be better suited to take possession of the family. Perhaps Eleanor thought little of Ned, or her other enslaved people, and was solely concerned with financial equity between her children—her sons had many slaves of their own and Salina Ann had none. Perhaps Eleanor was simply deferring to a popular southern practice of passing slaves down within a family along the female line. Perhaps Eleanor desired to free her brother but knew that even if she obtained permission from the court, the consequences for Ned would be severe, as manumitted people were required to leave the state. Under those restrictions, she may have determined that keeping Ned's family together was the better course of action.

We don't know.

Whatever happened, and whatever motivation was in Eleanor's heart, what is clear from the record is that Eleanor bequeathed to her daughter not only an entire nuclear family, but the entire extended family of Ned Magruder—grandparents, children, and grandchildren—and in the process preserved the integrity of the black Magruder family during their remaining period of enslavement.

The Death of Eleanor & Ned

Throughout the first half of 1849, the black Magruders and the Wynne family lived in fear of a cholera epidemic that was sweeping away entire families in nearby states. Letters between Wynne family members during this period express great trepidation at the arrival of the disease on the doorsteps of Wynnewood. In July 1849, Eleanor Magruder Wynne died in of dysentery, possibly as a result of cholera. Months later, Ned, Mariah, Charles, and the rest of the black Magruders came under the rule of a new master, William A. Ferrell.

It seems that the terms of Eleanor's will created controversy within the Wynne family, and an extensive probate process ensued. It took nearly four years to settle Eleanor's estate and reach a consensus on how to divide her assets. By 1852, it became apparent to the younger Wynne brothers that, whatever the outcome of the probate discussions, Greene County did not contain the future they desired. Like their father before them, Erasmus Wynne (1807-1863), Williamson Wynne Jr. (1810-1895), and Robert Wynne (1812-1855) desired a new life further west and a chance to become masters of frontier plantations of their own. The latter two left for Texas in 1852, followed by Erasmus in 1854.

At or around the same time, Ned Magruder died. Still grieving her husband, Mariah was left to say goodbye to many of her friends and extended family members as they departed from their homes in Alabama for Walker County, Texas. Mariah never saw those friends and family members again.[87]

It is unlikely that at the sunset of 1854, as Mariah nursed her wounds at the loss of her husband and friends, she could have imagined what the next chapter of her life would bring. The enslavement of the Mariah Magruder family by William A. Ferrell, followed by his and Salina's divorce, would have cataclysmic consequences for the Mariah Magruder family. These events would forever alter the life of Mariah's most favored son, Charles Magruder, and set in motion a unique series of events that would give rise to a new tribe of Magruders—one which would arise from the ashes of an epic war and come to be called the Alabama Black McGruders.

---

[87] According to initial research conducted by Sabrina Franklin of Texas, Eleanor's intention to preserve the unity of the family of Ned Magruder was not honored by her sons. A new generation with new rules prevailed and Salina Ann Wynne was unable to stop her brothers from acquiring some of her slaves. While most of Mariah's family remained in Greene County, Alabama, Fanny and Martha, two of her daughters, were taken to Texas by Erasmus Wynne. There, Martha's descendants were believed to have adopted the surname Wynne. However, Franklin's subsequent research has led her to retract this account as an inaccurate reading of the record. Franklin now believes the sisters and their children remained in Alabama with Mariah, where decades of entries for their descendants can be found in the census records.

Part II

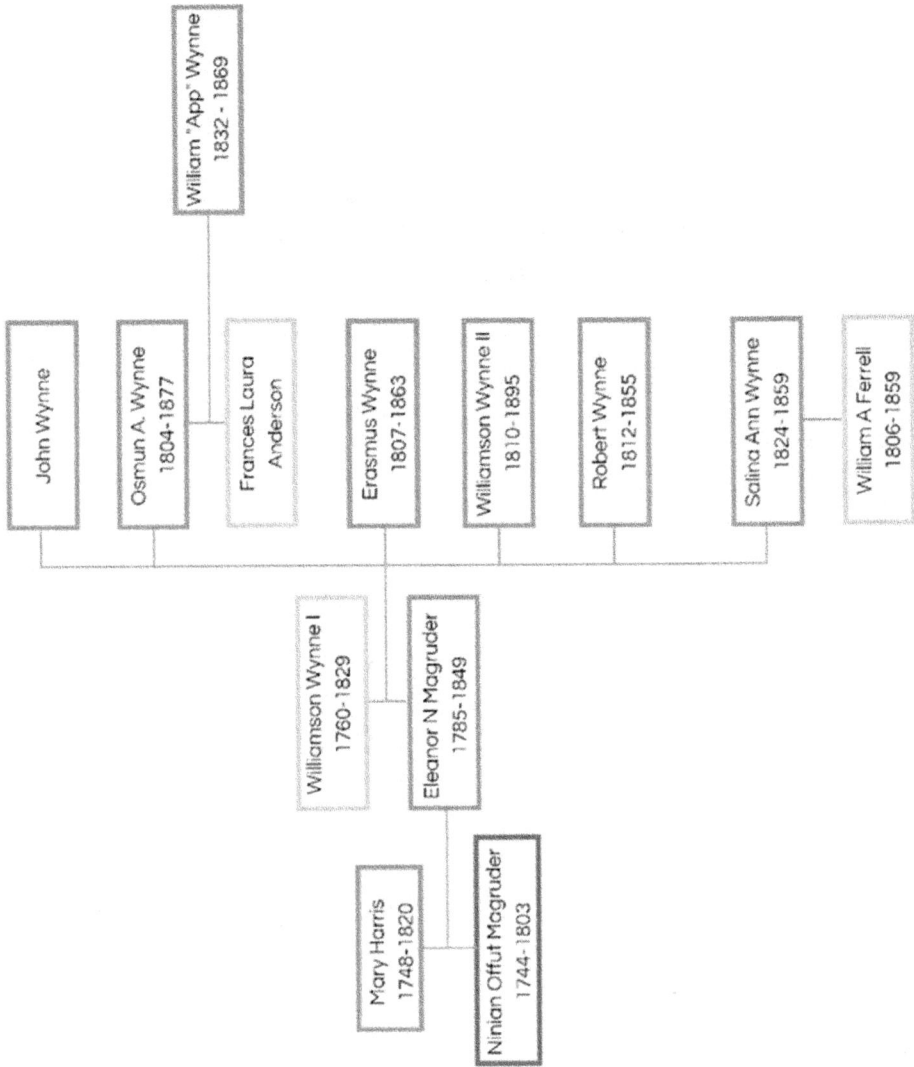

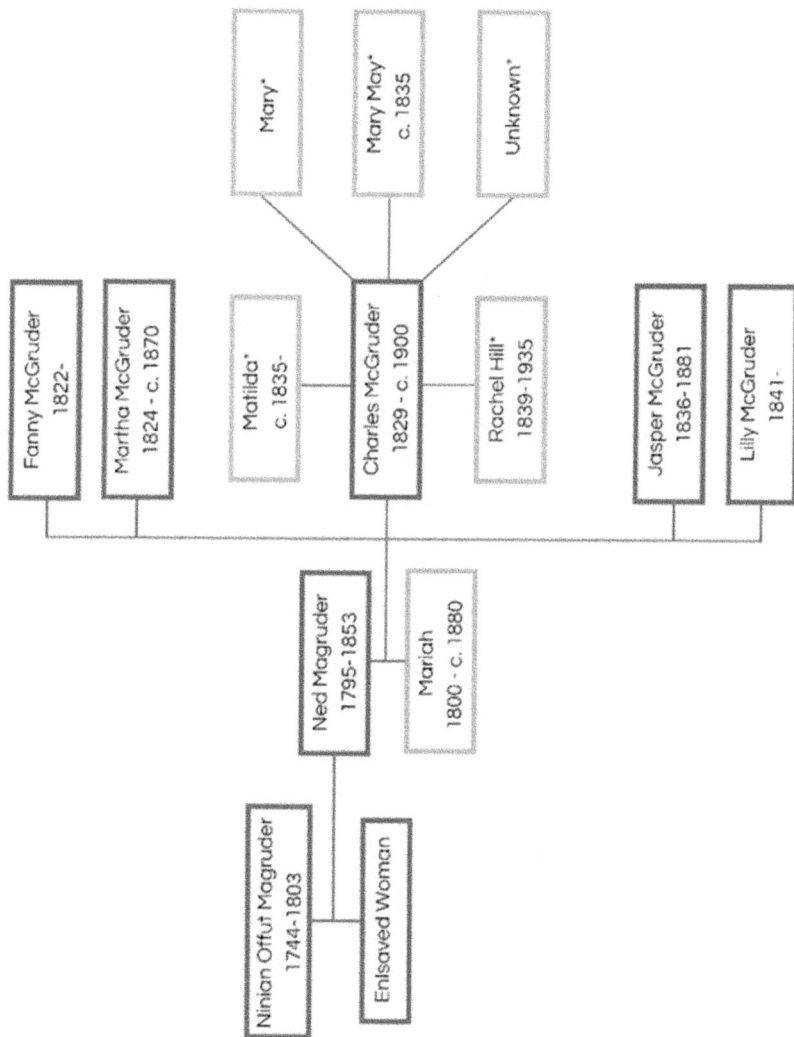

Ninian Offut Magruder
1744-1803

Enlsaved Woman

Ned Magruder
1795-1853

Mariah
1800 - c. 1880

Fanny McGruder
1822-

Martha McGruder
1824 - c. 1870

Matilda*
c. 1835-

Charles McGruder
1829 - c. 1900

Rachel Hill*
1839-1935

Jasper McGruder
1836-1881

Lilly McGruder
1841-

Mary*

Mary May*
c. 1835

Unknown*

* wife of Charles McGruder Sr.

95

So God created human beings in his own image.

In the image of God, he created them;

male and female, he created them.

Genesis 1:27

The sages ask: How did God create mankind?

The Lord God created humanity in two formations. First, he took earth from the place of the holy temple [of Jerusalem], and earth from the four corners of the world, using red, black, and white earth, the colors of mankind, and mixed it with all the waters of the world; and then God breathed into Adam's nostrils the breath of life.

Bab. Talmud, Targum Jonathan, Genesis 2

The sages ask: Why was mankind created as an individual? It was for this reason that humanity was first created as one person [Adam], to teach us that anyone who destroys a life is considered by Scripture to have destroyed an entire world; and anyone who saves a life is as if he saved an entire world. And also, to promote peace among the creations of God, so that no person would say to his fellow, "My ancestors are greater than your ancestors."

Jerusalem Talmud, Sanhedrin 4:1

7 - The Tribulations of Charles Magruder Sr.

By J.R. Rothstein, Esq.

The Early Years of Charles

Charles "Chas" Magruder[88] was born enslaved at Wynnewood, Hollow Square, Greene County, Alabama, in May 1829 to Ned and Mariah Magruder.[89] Little is known about his youth except that he was owned by a middle-aged Eleanor Magruder Wynne. Charles had a light complexion and straight red hair.[90] The author believes, based on oral history accounts and a layman's understanding of genetics, that Charles was part white from multiple family lines, possibly with two enslaved black grandmothers.

The first known known reference to Charles Magruder was recorded on January 8, 1830, when Eleanor Magruder Wynne purchased her half-brother Ned

---

[88] Charles McGruder Sr.is sometimes referenced in family records as "Chas," a nickname or abbreviation of Charles. The middle name Henry has been offered for Charles Sr. via oral history by a single informant. However, that name is not referenced in any documents and it is equally likely that the middle name was conflated with that of a descendant.

[89] Dates given for Charles's birth include 1822, May 1825, and May 1829. The will of Eleanor Magruder Wynne and other documents corroborate the May 1829 date, and some records indicate Greene County as his birthplace. The birth year of 1822 is based on the 1870 census. The 1880 census states that he was born in South Carolina, as were his parents. Anita McGruder McGrew reports that she heard that Charles (or his family?) had originally come from North Carolina.

Numerous other McGruders living at the time of the 1870 census also report that their birth location was North Carolina, such as Charles's mother, Mariah McGruder, born in 1800, and Rose McGruder born in North Carolina in 1870. These discrepancies regarding Charles's location of birth remain unresolved and need further research. The author, however, believes that Charles was born in Alabama, and that the roots of the mother of Ned Magruder prior to Georgia are not in Maryland, as Kevin McGruder asserts, but in North Carolina. The question remains unresolved and a matter of speculation. Future researchers might investigate whether Ninian Offut Magruder, or his wife, Mary Harris, had close relatives in North Carolina who might have held Ned's mother or other family members in slavery there.

[90] Many Alabama Black McGruders have asserted that Charles had red or "sandy" hair. As red hair requires a recessive gene inherited from both parents, this supports the speculation that Charles was part white from multiple lines and from recent generations. Some of Charles's children were also reported to have had red hair. However, according to Mattie Lorine Burton, Charles had a light complexion with straight or wavy black hair.

from the estate of her husband, Williamson Wynne, along with Mariah and their children, Fanny, Martha, and infant Charles, for a total of $1,270.

Alabama Black McGruder oral history provides that Charles Magruder was aware of his biological relationship to Eleanor Magruder Wynne. That relationship, along with his light complexion and red hair, seems to have distinguished Charles from others enslaved on the plantation and in his youth given him a certain level of privilege.

The 1850 Slave Schedule reveals approximately 192 enslaved people at Wynnewood. Among them, Charles enjoyed favored status as a child and later received training as a carpenter—a desired position among the enslaved. It is in this context that in late 1848, the handsome, 6'4", broad-shouldered, and light-skinned twenty-year-old Charles likely began a relationship with the fifteen-year-old Matilda (1833-?), who was also enslaved at Wynnewood.

In the summer of 1849, Charles Magruder was anxious. His pregnant wife was about to give birth and Eleanor Magruder Wynne lay dying. Ned and Mariah would have shared stories with Charles about how, twenty years earlier, when Williamson died, it was Eleanor who redeemed them from separation. Charles's thoughts no doubt turned to Osmun A. Wynne, the administrator and heir of Wynnewood. In June of 1849, as Eleanor struggled for her life, a boy named Jeremiah was born to Matilda and Charles.[91]

A month later, in July 1849, Eleanor Magruder Wynne succumbed to dysentery. Immediately after her death, controversy regarding her will initiated a probate process that lasted years. The death of Eleanor Magruder Wynne drastically altered the lives of her son-in-law, William, and her daughter, Salina Ann, making them rich in land and slaves.[92] It would come to alter the lives of

---

[91] Jeremiah Magruder is mentioned again in an 1850 record, but is absent from later records. It is possible he died as a child. According to Herman English, Charles and Matilda had four additional known children: (1) Wiley; (2) Dennis; (3) Duff; and (4) Mary. The 1880 census records a widowed Matilda Magruder (b. 1832) living in Hale County, Alabama, with four children: (1) Dennis McGruder (b. 1857); (2) Mary Ann McGruder (b. 1862); (3) Israel McGruder (b. 1869); (4) Fed McGruder (b. 1873). According to the census, Matilda and her late husband were born in North Carolina. It is noteworthy that Matilda is a neighbor to Nathan Hill—possibly the Nathan Hill who was a brother to Charles's other wife, Rachel Hill.

[92] The father of William and Benjamin was James Ferrell, who died in 1862 in Sumter County, Alabama. In his will, James Ferrell mentions sons Benjamin and Bennett, and two daughters, both married to men named Spivey. William had died prior and there is no mention of him or his children in the will.

Charles and his family too. Immediately after Eleanor's death, Charles and his family came into the possession of William A. Ferrell. The 1850 Slave Schedule provides that the family of William A. Ferrell possessed 30 enslaved people, including the black Magruders. Charles and all the other enslaved people on the plantation are listed as nameless individuals.[93]

However, Eleanor's bequest would also lead to estrangement and conflict between the Ferrell couple, the fallout of which produced consequences for Charles Magruder and his family. According to the terms of the will, Salina Ann Wynne, and therefore her husband, would inherit some three hundred and sixty acres of land and the entire family of Ned and Mariah Magruder, in addition to other enslaved people. At the same time, Erasmus Wynne (1807-1863), Williamson Wynne Jr. (1810-1895), and Robert Wynne (1812-1855) planned to leave Wynnewood for a new life on the frontier. Grieving the death of his father, Charles bid goodbye to friends and extended family as they departed for Walker County, Texas, with the younger Wynne brothers. Most likely, Charles never saw them again.[94]

William A. Ferrell and Salina Wynne Ferrell had three children: (1) twelve-year-old Martha Lavinia Ferrell (1841-?), who had just inherited Mariah's fourteen-year-old granddaughter, Sarah Ann, along with two other enslaved

---

In the 1840 Census, James Ferrell, age 65, is living next to Erasmus Wynne. Enumerated after James, in separate households, are Benjamin and Bennett Ferrell, and Jonathan and Thomas Spivey. William and Salina had married the prior year, in 1839, and may have been living with his or her parents. According to Susan Tichy, the detail that Benjamin P. Ferrell was a merchant may shed light on William's social and economic status relative to the Wynnes, especially his apparent lack of land or slaves. Merchants sometimes owned slaves, but rarely needed a great number. According to Tichy, debt or instability in the Ferrell family businesses is also a possible explanation for Eleanor's determination to keep her daughter's property separate from William's. Whatever their relative wealth, merchants generally were considered socially inferior to the land-owning class.

[93] The Slave Schedule was enumerated in Greene County in October 1850. William A. Ferrell appears in Hollow Square, 6th Precinct, as a slave owner. The first slave listed is a 54-year-old male identified as a mulatto, followed by a 51-year-old black female, a 28-year-old black female, a 26-year-old black female, and a 21-year-old black male. These ages match those of Ned, Mariah, Martha, Fanny, and Charles, based on Eleanor's will and the 1853 estate distribution (Note that the actual distribution took place in 1850 but was not recorded until 1853).

[94] Despite separations that could extend beyond 1,000 miles, some formerly enslaved families did reunite after the Civil War.

children;[95] (2) William O. Ferrell (1845-1868), then aged nine years, the heir apparent to William A. Ferrell and future soldier of the Confederate States of America's 36th Alabama Infantry Regiment; and (3) an infant girl, Eleanor Elizabeth Ferrell, named in honor of her recently deceased grandmother.[96] A fourth child, Emerette E. Ferrell, was born in February 1851.

The Rise of the Williams

In 1853, as the estate battle between the Wynne was concluded, Charles's father, Ned, died. When William A. Ferrell assumed legal control of his young wife's enslaved people, he began to take a particular interest in Charles Magruder. This interest, in the view of the author, led William A. Ferrell to exploit Charles Magruder and use him as a stud, or "stock negro," for breeding enslaved people.

The commencement of William A. Ferrell's use of Charles Magruder as a breeder paralleled his rise to power as a local white leader. Both William and his brother, Benjamin P. Ferrell, served as Justices of the Peace in Greene County. William seemingly inherited this position from Benjamin, a merchant and lawyer, who held the position from 1844 to 1853. Around the same time, William A. Ferrell began an extra-marital relationship with a woman named Torza Mary Chambers.

When traveling, William would take Charles with him, sending Salina Ann and the children to stay with her brother, O.A. Wynne. It was shortly after William's trip to Montgomery, Alabama, in November 1854,[97] that a pregnant Salina Ann initiated divorce proceedings against her husband. In the ensuing legal battle with the Wynne family, William A. Ferrell asserted ownership not only of Charles Magruder but of all his ex-wife's enslaved people. This only incited further litigation between the former couple.

As the battle between the Ferrells played out in court, William's financial success continued. Charles's breeding activities during this period were significant. On January 22, 1856, two years after Salina initiated the divorce,

---

[95] According to the estate records of Martha Lavinia Ferrell, by 1859 Sarah Ann would have a child named Nora. Greene County, Alabama Probate Court. Estate Case Files 1820-1915, Case#1546; digital images, *FamilySearch* (https://www.familysearch.org/ark:/61903/3:1:33SQ-GTW5-W4D?wc=MXR9-XPL%3A314241801%2C316387101&cc=1978117 FHL#5008479: accessed 26 Jan 2021).

[96] Eleanor Elizabeth Ferrell died before 1859, when her father wrote his will. Another infant, named for her mother, Salina, died in 1849, very close to the death of her grandmother, Eleanor Wynne.

[97] *Laura's Family Letters*, p.146.

William A. Ferrell married Torzah Mary Chambers, in Marengo, Alabama—an act which no doubt enraged Salina.

William A. Ferrell was not the only William with whom Charles had to contend during this period. Parallel to the increasing tribulations of Charles Magruder was the rise of William Appling "App" Wynne, son of Osmun A. Wynne, whom Charles had known as a child. It was upon the back of Charles and the other enslaved people of Wynnewood that O.A. Wynne acquired the financial and social means to send his son, known in the family as Master William, to the University of Alabama. At university, App Wynne joined the Alpha Delta Phi fraternity, where he mingled with sons of the state's elite, most of whom also attained their wealth upon the backs of enslaved people. Upon graduating, he went on to law school at the university, where he graduated in 1854.[98]

After law school, App Wynne returned to Sawyerville, and in Greensboro established a legal practice, Taylor & Wynne. Within short order, he made a foray into local politics, first as a Captain in the 38th Regiment of Alabama Militia in 1855 and, by 1856, Justice of the Peace of Greensboro. By 1859, he had triumphed as a significant local leader. With the support of his family and their vast wealth, Master William decided to run for Congress as a member of the Whig Party. Whigs, particularly southern "Cotton Whigs," advocated a legal regime that permitted slavery, featured written and unchanging constitutions that protected minority interests (such as the right to enslave humans as chattel property), and sought to combat majority tyranny, rebelling against abolitionism, which they saw as being arrogantly imposed on the South by Northerners.[99]

Charles Becomes a Breeder of Enslaved People

It was in this time of success for the Williams—William A. Ferrell and William A. Wynne—that, according to Alabama Black McGruder family lore, Charles Magruder was exploited as a stud to breed enslaved people.

Charles's exploitation was part of a larger effort by entrepreneurial enslavers and slave traders to breed human beings for forced labor in chattel slavery.

The constitutional prohibition of the importation of slaves from Africa after 1807 limited the supply of slaves in the United States. In the same period, the

---

[98] Around the same time, on March 19, 1853, William A. Wynne, son of O.A. Wynne, who grew up at Wynnewood with Charles, was sworn in and commissioned Justice of the Peace for Greene County, Alabama.

[99] During the Civil War, William A. Wynne served as a sergeant in a cavalry unit, Company D of the 8th Alabama Regiment. At one point, the record provides that the sergeant was absent without leave. He died a few years after the war, in early 1869.

Louisiana Purchase of 1803 doubled the size of the new republic and opened up vast new territories to settlement. The invention of the cotton gin in the 1790s had enabled expanded cultivation and increased the demand for labor in cotton-producing areas. As a result of all these factors, the domestic slave market expanded rapidly in the early 19th century. During this time, the terms "breeding slaves," "childbearing women," "breeding period," and "too old to breed" became familiar. Planters in the Upper South—Delaware, Maryland, Virginia, and North Carolina—sold slaves in large numbers to the Deep South, including Alabama, Mississippi, and Louisiana. At least a million enslaved people were trafficked from eastern states to the newer frontiers—some sold to slave traders, others forced to migrate with their owners. According to historian E. Franklin Frazier, in his book *The Negro Family*, "there were masters who, without any regard for the preferences of their slaves, mated their human chattel as they did their stock."[100] According to Alabama Black McGruder oral history, Charles Magruder was one of these "breeding slaves."

According to Lucille B. Osborne, "Charles's slave owner wanted him to have as many slave children as he possibly could so he could have more slaves, to have more money, so that he could keep the plantation going." Charles also is reported to have been hired out as a breeder, sent from plantation to plantation in order to sire children.

Jeptha Choice, a non-related former enslaved person from Texas, was also wielded as a stud to 'breed' enslaved people. His experience may provide insight into the experiences of Charles Magruder. Jeptha stated the following:

> The old Massa was mighty careful about the raisin' of healthy nigger families and used us, strong, healthy young bucks to 'stand' the healthy, young gals. You see when you was young, they took care not to strain me, an' I was a pretty good nigger, as handsome as a speckled pup, and I was much in demand for breedin'. You see in those days people seemed to know more about such things than they do now. If a young, scrawny nigger was found foolin' 'round the women, he was whyupped, and maybe sold.

> Later on, we, good strong niggers was 'lowed to marry, and the Massa and old Missus would fix the nigger and gal up in new clo'se and have the doin's in the 'Big House'. White folks would all gather round in a circle with the nigger and gal in the center.

---

[100] Edward Franklin Frazier, *The Negro Family in the United States* (Chicago: University of Chicago Press, 1966), 18.

Then old Massa would lay a broom down on the floor in front of 'em an' tell 'em to join hands and jump over the broom. That married 'em for good.

When babies were bo'n, old nigger grannies handle' most all them cases, but until they was about three years old, the children wan't 'lowed 'round our regular living quarters, but were wet nursed by nigger women who did not work in the field and kept in separate quarters. In the evenin', the mammies were let to see 'em.

We was fed good and had lots of beef and hung meat and wild game. 'Possum and sweet yams is mighty good . . . 'Course sometime they was grief, too, when some of the niggers was sold. Iffen old Massa sold a nigger man that was married, he always tried to sell the wife to the same folks so they would not be separated. Children under twelve were thrown in. But sometimes a nigger would be sold to someone, and the woman to someone else; and then they'd be carryings-on. But they was so 'fraid of getting whipped, or maybe killed, that they went peaceful-like—but mighty sorrowful. The children went with the mother . . . . I've been married eight times but haven't got any legitimate children that I know of. I've got some children from "outside" women I've had to "stand" for, but I don't know how many. You see, them old days was different from what it is now![101]

---

[101] Federal Writers' Project, *Slave Narratives: A Folk History of Slavery in the United States from Interviews with Former Slaves,* Vol.16, Texas, Part 1, Adams-Duhom, typescript, 218-19; digital images, Library of Congress Slave Narratives Project (https://www.loc.gov/resource/mesn.161/?sp=225 : accessed 10 Feb 2021).

The 1850 Slave Schedule of William A. Ferrell.

102

102 1850 U.S. Census, Greene County, Alabama, slave schedule, Hollow Square township, p43, William A. Ferrell, NARA Microform Publication M342 ;digital image Ancestry.com (https://www.ancestry.com/imageviewer/collections/8055/images/ALM432_19-0185?treeid=&personid=&hintid=&queryId=9ce0c083d151e10cd63cd23289b5d727&usePU

William A. "App" Wynne. Date and location unknown.

Erasmus Wynne. Date and location unknown.

Williamson Wynne Jr. Date and location unknown.

Another narrative, collected from an unrelated former enslaved person named Maggie Stenhouse,[103] records that:

> During slavery there were stockmen. They were weighed and tested. A man would rent the stockman and put him in a room with some young women he wanted to raise children from. Next morning when they come to let him out the man ask him what he done and he was so glad to get out. Them women nearly kill him. If he sa'd nothin' th'y wouldn't have to pay for him. Them women nearly kill him. Some of the slave owners rented these stockmen. They didn't let them work in the field and they kept them fed up good.

The experiences of Luke Blackshear parallel those of Charles Magruder in many ways. According to a slave narrative conveyed in 1938 by his descendant, Ida Blackshear, Luke, too, was wielded as a stud to breed enslaved people:

> Luke was six feet four inches tall and near two hundred fifty pounds in weight. He was what they called a double-jointed man. He was a mechanic—built houses, made keys, and did all other blacksmith work and shoemaking. He did anything in iron, wood or leather. Really he was an architect as well. He could take raw cowhide and make leather out of it and then make shoes out of the leather.

> Luke was the father of fifty-six children and was known as the GIANT BREEDER. He was bought and given to his young mistress in the same way you would give a mule or colt to a child ...

> Although he was a stock Negro, he was whipped and drove just like the other Negroes. All of the other Negroes were driven on the farm. He had to labor but he didn't have to work with the other slaves on the farm unless there was no mechanical work to do. He was given better work because he was a skilled mechanic.

> Once on the Blackshear place, they took all the fine looking boys and girls that was thirteen years old or older and put them in a big barn after they had stripped them naked. They used to strip them

---

[103] Paul D. Escott, *Slavery Remembered: A Record of Twentieth-century Slave Narratives* (Chapel Hill: University of North Carolina Press, 1979), 44-45, quoting Work Projects Administration, *Slave Narratives: A Folk History of Slavery in the United States from Interviews with Former Slaves, Arkansas Narratives*, Part 6.

naked and put them in a big barn every Sunday and leave them there until Monday morning. Out of that came sixty babies.

They was too many babies to leave in the quarters for someone to take care of during the day. When the young mothers went to work, Blackshear had them take their babies with them to the field, and it was two or three miles from the house to the field. He didn't want them to lose time walking backward and forward nursing. They built a long old trough like a great long old cradle and put all these babies in it every morning when the mother come out to the field. It was set at the end of the rows under a big old cottonwood tree.

When they were at the other end of the row, all at once a cloud no bigger than a small spot came up, and it grew fast, and it thundered and lightened as if the world were coming to an end, and the rain just came down in great sheets. And when it got so they could go to the other end of the field, that trough was filled with water and every baby in it was floating 'round in the water drownded. They never got nary a lick of labor and nary a red penny for any one of them babies.[104]

Cornelia Andrews, another unrelated formerly enslaved person from North Carolina, recounted the belief that her father may have been a breeding "stock nigger." She states:

I 'specks dat I doan know who my pappy wuz, maybe de stock nigger on de plantation. . . Yo' knows dey ain't let no little runty nigger have no chilluns. Naw sir, dey ain't, dey operate on dem lak dey does de male hog so's dat dey can't have no little runty chilluns.[105]

According to Lucille Burden Osborne, Charles was considered a "valuable piece of property" and a prized slave by his owner. Additionally, because Charles was moved and rented from place to place, from plantation to plantation, he was mandated to start a family anew in each one. Gwendolyn Hubbard reports that

[104] Federal Writers' Project, *Slave Narratives: A Folk History of Slavery in the United States from Interviews with Former Slaves,* Vol. 2, Arkansas Narratives, Part 3; digital images, Library of Congress Slave Narratives Project, (https://memory.loc.gov/mss/mesn/023/023.pdf : accessed 23 Oct 2021).

[105] Federal Writers' Project, *Slave Narratives: A Folk History of Slavery in the United States from Interviews with Former Slaves,* Vol.11, North Carolina, Part 1, Adams-Hunter, typescript, 30-31; digital images, Library of Congress Slave Narratives Project, (https://www.loc.gov/resource/mesn.111/?sp=34 : accessed 10 Feb 2021).

Charles had five different "legitimate" families during slavery. The names of just four of the women are known. Wilmar McGruder, however, asserts that only three of the wives were legitimate.

Between 1854 and 1859, William A. Ferrell managed to gain control of the black Magruder family, even after his remarriage to another woman, leaving Salina Ann Wynne enraged. The Alabama Black McGruder oral history indicates that during this period Charles cohabited with many unknown women on a variety of plantations in the region—the details of which are lost to history. Two significant relationships, however, did emerge from this time, both with women named Mary: Mary May and another Mary, for whom there are few details.

Mary May[106]

Mary May's origins are uncertain. According to one unconfirmed oral history source, she may have been associated with the Umbria Plantation.[107] Archival records, however, indicate that Mary was born in South Carolina in or around 1835 before migrating with her enslavers to Alabama.[108] Mary's parentage is also unconfirmed. According to one source, Mary's father was a white man with the surname May and "Mary was half-sister to a white man named Stephen May Sr." According to Elmer Brox, Mary also had a white half-sister named Debbie May,

---

[106] Mary May has sometimes been referenced as Mary Williams. How she acquired the surname of Williams in the oral tradition is unknown. It may have been through her coupling with a man with the surname Williams, or at some point being owned by such a man. Jonathan May, a Sawyerville historian, suggests that it is possible that Mary, or a potential unknown husband, may have been owned by Thomas Williams. Williams was one of the original trustees of the Bethel Baptist Church in Hollow Square. May suggests that Mary may have come to Alabama with the Williams family. What is more likely, however, is that Mary May was conflated with Mary Williams McGruder (1871-?), wife of James D. McGruder, one of Charles Magruder Sr. and Mary May's children. This needs further research.

[107] The Umbria Plantation was located directly east of Wynnewood, separated only by the Sawyer Plantation and within walking distance of both Wynnewood and the plantation of William Ferrell. Umbria, also known as the Samuel Pickens Plantation, was a cotton plantation noted for its Greek Revival plantation house. Samuel Pickens was born in Cabarrus County, North Carolina, in 1791. He and his brothers—one of whom was Israel Pickens, the third Governor of the State of Alabama—had all relocated to the western Black Belt of Alabama by the 1820s. Most of them established plantations near Umbria in Greene County and what is now greater Sawyerville.

[108] The 1900 Census provides her birth as April 1837 in South Carolina. The 1910 census provides her birthyear as 1833, also in South Carolina. Other records have placed her birth in 1839.

presumably a sister to Stephen May Sr.[109] Both have reported that Mary's white lineage and membership in the May family was widely known, and that Mary looked nearly white.[110]

Archival records provide that Mary was a midwife by training. Maryln Rawls, a descendant of Mary Inge,[111] says that Mary May received unwanted attention in her youth due to her almost white skin. Oral history, confirmed by DNA testing, indicates that Mary later married a man named Pleasant Inge. A marriage certificate between the two provides that Mary's maiden name was Ferrell.[112] As it was common for enslaved people to adopt the surname of their former owners, it is possible that at some point Mary was acquired by William A. Ferrell and thereafter adopted his surname.

Irrespective of her origins, Mary coupled with Charles Magruder at approximately age 19, sometime around 1854, perhaps matched by her enslaver with the intention to breed light-skinned slaves. The couple produced a child, Charles Jr., born that same year. Shortly thereafter, in October 1856, the couple had Irene Magruder,[113] followed by Emmeratte Magruder (date of birth unknown).

Census and birth data suggest that despite Charles's relationship with Mary, he continued his relationship with Matilda, his first wife, as a son, Dennis Magruder, was born in 1857. Records also provide that a child named Green Magruder was born the same year with an unknown woman. Although we know little about her, it is likely that during this period Charles coupled with a second woman named

---

[109] The 1880 Selected U.S. Federal Census Non-Population Schedules lists John May Jr. as a neighbor to Charles McGruder. The white family of Albert May is listed as a neighbor to Charles in 1900. The 1856 Snedecor Map of Greene County shows a landowner named Pleasant May. It's unclear how all these individuals connect, and this needs further research.

[110] Jonathan May, a Sawyerville historian, refers the reader to page 142 of Berenice May Fuller's *Two May Families of Hollow Square, Greene County, Alabama: including some May, Windham, Harrison, Dargan ancestors and descendants* (Baltimore: Gateway Press, 1988) to determine which May man may have been the father of Mary.

[111] It has been asserted, via oral tradition, that Mary May, Mary Ferrell, and Mary Inge are the same person. Although that position is adopted for the purposes of this book, this matter remains unresolved and requires further research.

[112] The Social Security Death Certificate index for James Daniel McGruder provides that his father was Charles McGruder and his mother Mary Ferrell.

[113] Records provide that Irene may have been born in 1857 or 1858. She married Lazarus Alexander on January 7, 1875. She is sometimes referenced in Alabama Black McGruder records as Arene or Irine.

Mary, with whom he had numerous children.[114]

The Death of the Ferrells & the War of Two Houses

Charles's life as a breeder continued from approximately 1853 to 1859. During most of this period, the courts weighed how to divide the marital assets between William Ferrell and Salina Ann Wynne. The breeding activities of Charles Magruder were disturbed, albeit temporarily, by the premature death of William A. Ferrell in early May of 1859. Despite William's access to the Wynne wealth, and his exploitation of their enslaved people during his marriage to Salina Ann, he was insolvent at the time of his death. The agent of William's estate, his friend, Andrew Jackson Mayfield, was not forthcoming or able to pay his creditors. At about the same time, the 35-year-old Salina Ann Wynne Ferrell also died.[115] The legal complications created by the divorce were now compounded by the untimely death of both Ferrells.

A property dispute between the Wynne and Ferrell estates ensued. Salina's brother Osmun A. Wynne was appointed administrator of her estate and guardian of her three children, who were minors at her death. William A. Ferrell wrote in his will that he preferred that the children remain with Torzah Mary, his second wife and widow. Since the youngest child, Emmerette, was about eight at time, the estate would not be settled for thirteen years. The courts therefore appointed the children's uncle, O.A. Wynne, as guardian *"ad litum"* to defend the estate rights of the three children. William A. Ferrell also had chosen O.A. Wynne as executor of his estate.[116]

Osmun and his wife, Frances Laura Wynne, oversaw the upbringing of Salina's three children, who probably moved to the Wynne home in late 1859. At the same time, both the estates of Salina Ann (represented by Osmun A. Wynne) and the William A. Ferrell estate (represented by Andrew J. Mayfield) attempted to assert control of Mariah, Charles, and the rest of the black Magruders. This dispute provided a legal problem for the court to resolve.

---

[114] According to research conducted by Herman English, this Mary, whose surname is unknown, was distinct from Mary May. According to his research, Charles and this second Mary had five children: (1) Mary; (2) Rose; (3) Virginia; (4) Martha Anne; (5) Wiley.

[115] The estate files of Salina Wynne Ferrell and William Ferrell contain over 500 pages and need further review.

[116] There is a contradiction in motives between the struggle over the inheritance and William A. Ferrell's choice of O.A. Wynne as his executor—which implies trust. Susan Tichy suggests that, coming from a merchant family, William A. Ferrell may have been operating other businesses, or investing in his family's businesses, actions that would have financially compromised his and his wife's estate. The matter requires further research.

As part of that process, on August 15, 1859, an appraisal of all the property of the Ferrell family, and particularly its enslaved people, was submitted to the court. Maria, aged 70 years, was valued at $150. Charles's older sister, Fanny, aged 39, was, together with her infant child, valued at $133[117.] Charles's brother, Jasper, aged 22, was valued at $1,400, Matilda, Charles's wife, age 28, was valued at $1,233, and the couple's son, Jeremiah, aged 10, was valued at $1,000. Lastly, Charles, aged 30, was valued at $1,500, identical in assessed value with a "negro man" named Creed, aged 57, making them the most valuable enslaved people in this group.[118]

To minimize expenses to the respective estates, O.A. Wynne and A.J. Mayfield agreed to submit the dispute to a panel of three arbiters. The three men chosen were charged with determining title to the enslaved, as well as "the value of the hires of said slaves" from Salina's death to December 25, 1859. The parties further agreed that should the estate of William A. Ferrell prove insufficient to cover any funds due to O.A. Wynne, as administrator of Salina's estate, those funds would "stand upon the same footing" as the estate's other debts. This clause proved prescient and ensured that tension between O.A. Wynne and A.J. Mayfield endured at least until 1867, when the court noted various sums remained unpaid.[119]

On December 13, 1859, the three arbiters submitted to the court their judgement that Osmun A. Wynne, as the administrator of Salina's Wynne Ferrell's estate, was "entitled to the following Negroes"—a list that matches almost perfectly the inventory conducted in August and includes the all of the extended Mariah Magruder family. An April 1861 court document, in which both the arbitration agreement and the judgement were recorded, states that "the said Mayfield...has delivered in compliance with said award all the slaves therein mentioned to Osman A. Wynne."[120]

---

[117] Could be read $1,433.

[118] According to Susan Tichy, to be so highly valued at that age Creed was either a house servant or a skilled tradesman—e.g. a carpenter or blacksmith—providing income and valuable work to the owner's plantation.

[119] Due to negligence, Andrew Mayfield was replaced as administrator of William Ferrell's estate in the late 1860s. The 1856 Snedecor map tells us he was a small landowner in the same district of Greene County as the Wynne and Ferrell plantations.

[120] Greene County, Alabama, Probate Court Estate Case Files, 1820-1915, Case #1536, Estate Papers of William A. Ferrell, p.201-211; digital images *Family Search* (https://www.familysearch.org/ark:/61903/3:1:33S7-9TW5-Z9J?cc=1978117&personaUrl=%2Fark%3A%2F61903%2F1%3A1%3AVNTV-6DZ : accessed 26 Jan 2021).

The estate records of Salina Wynne Ferrell show that from 1859-1865 Charles and his family were rented out for the benefit of the estate, under the direction of O.A. Wynne.

According to Alabama Black McGruder oral history, Charles and his family were sent from plantation to plantation to provide labor to the region's white families. As a consequence, Mariah, Charles and their family were divided and rented out to different individuals, enduring continual disruption to their lives. A family letter also indicates that the Magruder family may have briefly provided services to the family of O.A. Wynne at the dawn of the Civil War. On January 29, 1860, Laura Wynne wrote to her sister Betty that their father, O.A. Wynne, had "sent all the kinky heads over on yesterday. They were a great many. You can guess how many we own."[121]

Between 1860 and 1863, most, possibly all, of the black Magruder family was rented to A.J. Mayfield, most likely working on the Ferrell plantation itself, the rental of the land also being part of the transaction. In 1864 and 1865, however, Charles and his mother Mariah were rented to a neighbor, J.W. Melton, a future Postmaster of Sawyerville, who also rented a portion of the Ferrell land, while Matilda and her six children were rented to D.V. Patterson. This circumstance separated Matilda and her children from Charles Magruder. The rest of the Mariah Magruder family was divided and rented between various individuals who successfully bid for the enslaved labor of the family.

It is unknown whether Charles continued to be exploited as a breeder during this period. However, if one is to adopt the Alabama Black McGruder oral history that Charles had one hundred children, it is likely that he was.

---

[121] Alice Coleman Griffin. *Laura's Letters* (Privately printed, 2008), 186. Alternatively, the note may also provide a firsthand account of the return of the Alabama Black McGruders from the control of Andrew J. Mayfield to O.A. Wynne pursuant to the 1859 court order.

O.A. Wynne — Adm'r.

Adm't rented Land & Slaves by the Estate

Charles
Martha Ann & Children
John
Matelda
Isaah
Rose
Mary
Isaac
Virginia
Jake
Jasper
Caroline

List of Black Magruders and others rented out

122

122 Greene Co, Alabama, Probate Court, Estate Case Files, 1820-1915, Case #1545, Estate Papers of Salina A. Ferrell, 1868, pp.184-85; digital images, *FamilySearch* (https://www.familysearch.org/ark:/61903/3:1:33S7-9TW5-4PC?i=29&cc=1978117 : accessed 26 Jan 2021; citing FHL#5008479, image 1039-1303).

Mary May Ferrell Magruder, later Inge. Date and location unknown.
Courtesy of Maryln Rawls.

Below is a summary of slave rentals by the estate from 1860 to 1864, including rental of the labor of Mariah Magruder and her family.[123]

---

123 Greene Co, Alabama, Probate Court, Estate Case Files, 1820-1915, Case #1545, Estate Papers of Salina A. Ferrell, 1868, pp.184-85; digital images, *FamilySearch* (https://www.familysearch.org/ark:/61903/3:1:33S7-9TW5-4PC?i=29&cc=1978117 : accessed 26 Jan 2021; citing FHL#5008479, image 1039-1303).

Am't brot over .... $ 716.25
1864 Hired Mary to W H Applegate .... $ 75. "
          Rose " Tho' M Roberts ...... " 25. "
          Sarah " J L Ryan .... " 60. "
          Matilda & child D V Patterson ... " 50. "
          " ―― to J M Melton
     Charles, Creecy Maria Fanny
     Martha Ann & children .... $ 500. 00
     Hired John to M' Christian ..... " 200. "
     Rent & Hires for 1864 .... $ 1626.25

The Adm'r would also return & report
to the Court that she held in this
business belonging to the Estate on the 1st
of March last 1864 about $8000.00
in Confederate Treasury Notes which
he funded in 4 pr ct Certificates under
the Act of The Confed' Congress of the
17th Feby 1864 – as follows to wit
N° 198. March 5 1864 Certificate .... $1200. "
N°216   "   7 "   "   .... $6800. "
for which he asks the Court to allow
him a Credit under the Act of the
Legislature of 1864

                                    A A Wynne

Rachel Hill

It was in this period of being rented from plantation to plantation that Charles, at the dawn of a great war, met Rachel Hill, the last, and most important, of what Gwendolyn Hubbard describes as Charles's "legitimate" wives. It is unclear whether Charles met Rachel in the context of being wielded as a stud, or whether the two met individually and formed a natural affection.

Rachel Hill was born in 1845, most likely in Alabama,[124] the daughter of Edmond and Manerva Hill, both of whom are reported to be from Virginia.[125] Rachel had at least two siblings.[126]

---

[124] Different birth dates are given for Rachel, including 1845, 1848, 1849, and 1850. In the 1880 census, she is listed as being born in Alabama. Her father's place of birth is listed as Virginia and her mother's as North Carolina. In the 1900 census, Rachel is listed as being born March 1850, in Virginia. In the 1910 census, she is listed as a mulatta living in Sawyerville, Alabama, having been born in Virginia along with both of her parents. According to her death certificate, she was born in Hale County, Alabama—although Hale County was not incorporated out of Greene County until 1867. These matters remain unresolved and need further research.

[125] Two researchers have put forth alternative names for Rachel's father—James Hill or Wiley Hill. Both these researchers have agreed that her mother's name was Manerva. Rachel's death certificate names her parents as Edmond and Manerva Hill, both born in Virginia. However, if one is to adopt the oral history of Rachel's Creek ancestry, then at least one of her parents would have had to have deeper Alabama roots. This would also undermine the accuracy of a Virginia birth for Rachel. These matters remain unresolved and need further research.

[126] One of Rachel's siblings was Nathan Hill, whose picture Rachel kept on the wall of her home. It is unclear whether Nathan Hill was her full or half-brother. According to Lucille B. Osborne, Nathan "looked exactly like" a full Indian. Nathan was reportedly a member of the Creek tribe who voluntarily left Alabama to follow his people west after their removal from Alabama. He suffered a lot on his journey to Oklahoma.

According to Geneva Gibbs Wesley, Rachel wanted to go west with her brother, but had sixteen children, was married to Charles McGruder Sr., and was unable or unwilling to go, possibly because she was still enslaved. According to Lucille B. Osborne, "When the Creeks were given a chance to get out of that area and go to Oklahoma, half breeds (half black and half Indian) were given the opportunity to stay where they were or go with the tribe, and Nathan decided to go with the tribe." Lucille thinks that Nathan may have had black ancestry but had been passing for Indian and was accepted by the tribe because he looked Indian. Lucille also notes the possibility that Nathan was a freedman with African ancestry who applied to join the Indian nation after slavery.

This narrative would imply that Rachel or parts of her family had been enslaved by the Creeks. The 1832 census-takers commissioned by the U.S. government in Creek country struggled to categorize the diverse people who resided there, unsure how to count African-American wives of Creek men, nor where to place people of mixed African-Native descent.

Rachel is reported to have had light skin, a mulatto complexion, and to have been petite and thin with long hair. Catherine Gibbs Robertson, writing in the 1960's, reported that Rachel was one-sixteenth Creek Indian. However, Lucille B. Osborne reported that that Rachel may have had a Native American father or grandfather. [127] As Rachel was part Native-American, she *could* have had ancestors enslaved by a Native-American slave-holder, though this was not necessarily the case. Sue Magruder Smith, a relative of O.A. Wynne, writing on the background that enslaved people like Rachel descended from, observed as follows:

> Apparently one of the most pathetic phases in the history of Alabama was the forceful removal of the Indians from their native homes to the Reservations in Indian Territory in 1836. The Indians in Alabama were friendly, intermarrying with negroes on the large plantations and often working with the slaves, that is, when they felt like working. It proved to be a bad combination however, for their descendants were mostly known to be "sassy" negroes who had often to be taught better manners. [128]

There also were Creeks who managed to stay behind in Alabama after the Trail of Tears in 1836. By the 1840's, Creeks are estimated to have enslaved three to four thousand people. Between 1842 and 1859 the Creeks passed oppressive "black codes" to protect their "property," such as banning intermarriage and abolitionist school teachers.

Nathan Hill did eventually return to Alabama, at the end of his life, reportedly to die, and did so at the age of ninety-eight. The author located the death certificate of a Nathan Hill, identified as a black man born in 1835 who died March 16, 1929, at the age of 94, in Akron, Hale County, and was buried in Sawyerville. This could be the Nathan Hill of this family. However, according to a handwritten entry contained in the Archive of Wilmar McGruder, Nathan lived to be 102 years old, which indicates that the death certificate might refer to a different Nathan Hill. Nathan Hill also is reported to have had a granddaughter named Edith Cunningham. While the arc of this oral history account may be true, not all the nuances align with historical events. More research is required to construct a fuller picture.

According to Lucille B. Osborne, Rachel also had an older sister named Fannie, whom Lucille suspects was a half-sister. Fannie didn't look like Rachel but looked plainly African-American. Charles McGruder Sr. also had a sister named Fannie (b. 1822). A handwritten entry in the Archive of Wilmar McGruder provides that Fannie married Henry Green and lived to be 104 years old.

[127] Lucille B. Osborne relates that Rachel looked Indian, though with an African influence. She isn't certain if it was one side or both sides of Rachel's family that were part Indian, but believes that her father was either Indian or part Indian.

[128] Sue Magruder Smith, "William Reardon Magruder," *Yearbook of the American Clan Gregor Society* XV (1928): 117 [gathering of 1927].

Rachel Hill was apparently one of these "sassy negroes." According to Lucille B. Osborne, abolitionist missionaries taught Rachel to read and write while she was still enslaved.[129] The missionaries reportedly also taught her how to cook and sew.

According to Lucille B. Osborne, when Rachel was about twelve years old, she "was a slight build and wasn't strong enough to work in the fields." Rachel had to work in the house, "and they had her in the kitchen." Rachel's job was to feed the slaves. Rachel "had to take the buttermilk and cornbread out to feed [the slaves] and she had to put this in a big wooden tub and then [the slaves] would have to come and take it out in a bowl." The field slaves apparently did this in a chaotic manner. Rachel couldn't stand to watch them fret because she had lived in the house and had gotten accustomed to eating at a table. Rachel "felt terrible" about the enslaved people outside the house. Rachel hated her job specifically, and enslavement broadly, with a passion, but had no choice but to perform what was required of her. Rachel wasn't very happy as a teenager, but her lot reportedly "improved" when at approximately seventeen she coupled with Charles, who was twenty-five to thirty years her senior.[130]

Amos, Charles's first child with Rachel Hill, was born in 1862. Although separated from his previous wives, Charles did maintain contact with them. Mary Ann Magruder was born to Matilda in 1862. Roena, Charles's second child born to Rachel Hill, was born in 1864.

The dispute between the Wynne and Ferrell families, which raged in the courts for years, ended with neither side retaining any true ownership over Charles, rather, with him gaining his own dominion as the consequence of the Emancipation Proclamation and the victory of the United States over the rebellious Confederate States. Charles's new freedom was enforced by the occupation of Alabama by troops of the United States Army. Years later, it was determined by the courts that Salina Ann Wynne would have been the rightful owner of the Mariah Magruder family should the institution of slavery have endured.

Hope of a New World

In the Spring of 1865, enslaved people in Alabama attained freedom. One can imagine the 36-year-old Charles Magruder proudly and anxiously marching along the road to Wynnewood, returning from a period of rental enslavement on a

---

[129] In one version of the story, this happened shortly after Emancipation.

[130] The 1900 census indicates that the couple married in 1860.

neighboring plantation. On the way, Charles would have observed chaos around him: occupation troops of the Union army, newly indigent white Southerners—some connected to the very people who had once persecuted and enslaved him—and newly freed black men and women also traveling the road with hope in their eyes. Arriving at Wynnewood, Charles would have reunited with family and friends whom he may not have seen, or spent true companionship with, in years. Together, they no doubt celebrated the good news of freedom, and later mourned the assassination of their great emancipator, Abraham Lincoln.

With freedom for Charles, however, came responsibility. Before him lay the arduous task of providing for his numerous families. A letter written on December 3, 1866, by Jack W. Wynne to Julia E. Wynne, one of his sisters, provides details about Mariah Magruder and her family's ongoing economic relationship with the Wynne family. He writes, in part:

> I have neither bought nor rented a place yet don't know what I will do next year, but I am determined not to be idle. I could not be content and stay at home and do nothing. I think Pa calculates on farming more extensively next year. I think all of his old negroes are anxious to return, so he will have no difficulty in getting hands. Those he employed this year I think have done remarkably well considering the times. His crop is better than the average in the neighborhood. App[131] & Mine is about like his. The house servants are doing tolerably well, no changes in their favor since you left, there is such a turn of them that as usual they are in each other's way. I think Ma wants only a few about the house next year just enough to do business necessary & no surplus ones, for instance have one to do what Lila[132] and Rowena[133] does, & one in the place of Wash & Mitchell[134] and so on. Cornelia is already here. Pa has employed her husband also for the next year or rather has agreed to take him [but they] have made no contract as yet.

> The freedman are already having a lively time anticipating Christmas, have quilting parties[135] every Saturday night. Cary, I

---

[131] William Appling "App" Wynne, a.k.a. "Master William," son of O.A. Wynne.

[132] Lilly, Mariah's daughter.

[133] Another Roena—not the one who is the daughter of Charles and Rachel (b. 1862).

[134] This is likely John Mitchell, husband of Martha, Mariah's daughter.

[135] An Alabama Black McGruder pastime, whose tradition and style of weaving are preserved in the quilts produced by Lucille B. Osborne.

understand, will be married next Saturday night to Martha Seay and the Freedman are going to have a huge time of it generally on the occasion. I don't think there will be any amusements in the neighborhood during the Christmas holydays. I doubt if we have our usual eggnog Christmas morning judging from the number of eggs we have on hand at present. Mitchell brought in one the other day for Christmas, the first. I believe Maria[136] is trying parched corn on the old hens perhaps we may succeed better if there is any virtue in it. There seems to be an epidemic chicken cholera in the chicken family at present & they are dying rapidly.[137]

A letter dated December 16, 1866, from O.A. Wynne's wife, Frances Laura, to her other daughter, Laura F. Wynne, strikes a different tone regarding the new realities of labor and production at the dawn of the Reconstruction era. Frances writes:

I feel that I know not what a day may bring fourth [sic]. It seems to me that these are days of darkness and uncertainty both of a spiritual and temporal nature. Your Papa is not enjoying very good helth [sic] at this time. He and the boys are both a good deal perplexed at this time about getting hands for another year. App will still cultivate the same place which he did last year. Jack has bought out Mr. Evans and of course they will need a good many more hands though why none of them expects to hire very extensively. This is no doubt to be a usual business and a source of no little trouble to us all Forever, but I think the negroes up here are more docile and less disposed to be troublesome than they were last year about hiring, though your Papa seems to be as usual all the time uneasy and restless. He has just disappeared up the road taking his usual Sunday evening visit or ride which you know he is compelled to take.[138]

---

[136] Mariah, the matriarch of the Alabama Black McGruders and mother of Charles.

[137] Alice Coleman Griffin. *Laura's Family Letters*, 227-28. There is another reference to Mariah on p.250, in a letter from Frances to Julia, on March 24, 1869, as follows: "I have very few young chickens yet, but Mariah is making quite an effort to raise some. I hope she will succeed."

[138] Alice Coleman Griffin. *Laura's Letters*, 69.

Charles Gathers His Children & Breaks Hearts

It was in the context of the financial and social upheaval after the Civil War that Charles reunited with his family. At Wynnewood, Charles reconnected with his mother, wife Matilda, and many, but not all, of his children. Charles later sought out Mary May, from whom he seems to have been separated by the squabbling between the Wynne and Ferrell families over the estate of Salina Ann Wynne Ferrell. The couple seems to have reconciled, albeit temporarily, and a son, James Daniel "J.D." McGruder, was born in October of 1865.[139]

The first known act of Charles Magruder as a free man was to gather his wives and children into a central location at or near Wynnewood—an act which took inordinate effort. Some of the women with whom he had children no doubt did not want to reconnect, and some of his children found homes among their mothers' families. Others were no doubt lost to Charles due to the violence towards familial connections endemic to enslavement generally, and "slave breeding" specifically. However, by 1866, Charles had found partial success in uniting his family. He is listed in the 1866 Alabama state census as a resident of Greene County, Alabama, having 37 people in his household, including 22 males and 15 females. Among Charles's first directives was that all of his children acquire literacy.

Darkie's Soliloquy.

Don't tell me what a blessin'
  'Tis for niggers to be free;
Freedom don't bring bred and bacon,
  Things ain't like they used to be.

Vittles is the thing—without 'em
  Liberty ain't worth a cuss;
Readin' and writin', and such doings,
  Was'nt meant for folks like us.

A comment on the economic struggle of freedmen, published in a local white-run newspaper.[140]

Taking responsibility for several woman and numerous children created not only financial difficulty but also social challenges in Charles's life. It is likely that

---

[139] According to oral history accounts, James D. "Jim" Magruder spoke with a white accent, had red hair, and some people thought he was white. He was successful and respected locally by whites and blacks.

[140] Selected Poetry: Darkie's Soliloquy, *The (Greensboro) Alabama* Beacon, 16 February 1867, p.1, col. 1; digital image *Newspapers.com* (https://www.newspapers.com/image/355814222/?terms= : accessed 23 Sept 2021).

the unification of the various women with whom Charles had relations was the origin of some of the tension between Charles's wives and their children that would continue in some form among their descendants until the middle of the twentieth century. By the close of 1866, there were at least three women—Matilda, Mary May, and Rachel Hill—all living in the vicinity of one another.

During slavery, there was no legal marriage between enslaved people. However, on September 29, 1865, an ordinance ratifying marriage between freedmen and freedwomen was adopted. By the terms of this ordinance, all marriages before and after Emancipation were legalized. Children who had been born of enslaved parents were legitimized, and their parents called on to assume the full responsibility of parenthood. Freedom therefore presented the question of to whom Charles Magruder would legally and spiritually bind himself—as one man with one woman. Picking one woman meant excluding all the others. Freedom had created the opportunity to marry, which consequently created the freedom to break hearts and inspire resentment.

Mary May was the first to leave the "homestead," or "Magruder Plantation," and set up her own farmstead, no doubt with the assistance of her son, Charles Magruder Jr. By 1868, Mary May and Charles Magruder Sr. had become fully separated, and on April 23, 1869, Mary May married Pleasant Inge before the Justice of the Peace. Unlike Charles McGruder and Mary May, Pleasant was described, according to Maryln Rawls, as having a pure African complexion. Like Charles, Pleasant was one of the brave African-American men who had registered to vote, despite voter intimidation, in 1867.[141]

---

[141] On her marriage certificate Mary May's surname is recorded as Ferrell. The 1870 census provides that Pleasant and Mary Inge were living with one another with ten children, including an Irene Inge. The oldest child, Irene, then age 16, is known to be a child of Charles and is referenced as Irene McGruder on her marriage certificate. This raises the possibility that other children of Charles McGruder Sr. and Mary May may have adopted the surname Inge. The 1870 and 1880 census records therefore provide additional possible names of children of Charles McGruder Sr. This requires further research and DNA testing. See more about this topic in Chapter 9.

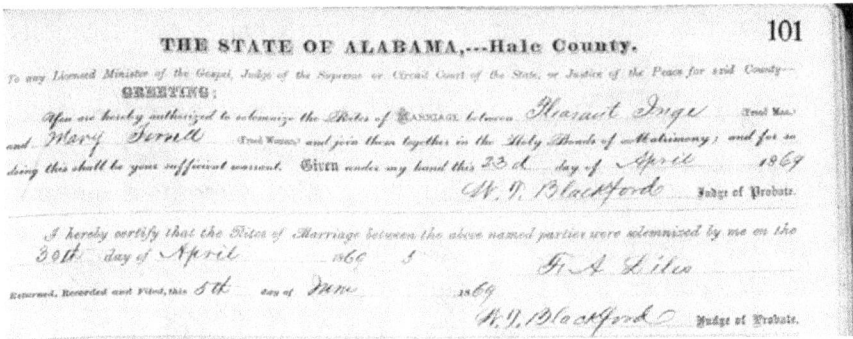

The marriage record of Mary May-Ferrell-McGruder-Inge.[142]

Unlike Mary, Matilda and Rachel Hill continued to live in the vicinity of the Magruder Compound, each giving birth to children in 1869, Rachel to Edmund Magruder and Allen Magruder, and Matilda to Israel Magruder.

According to Lucille B. Osborne, Rachel was the only woman ever legally married to Charles. Of all the women with whom Charles had relationships, he picked Rachel to be his wife. According to Lucille B. Osborne, Charles loved Rachel more than any other woman with whom he had ever coupled. Moreover, Rachel was with Charles at the end of slavery, the youngest of his wives, and best positioned to procure a legal marriage. However, to date, no marriage certificate has been located. Whether the couple ever did legally marry, oral history provided by the Rachel Hill branch of the Alabama Black McGruders makes clear that Charles's affection for Rachel was unparalleled, and he therefore chose her as his wife—before God and before the law. This caused resentment towards Rachel from the other women and some of their children.

From the end of slavery through the end of the Reconstruction era, Charles and Rachel had sixteen children together.[143] They were: Amos (b. 1862), Roena (b.

---

[142] Hale County, Alabama, Probate Courts, marriage records, Pleasant Inge and Mary Ferrell, 30 Apr 1869; digital image *FamilySearch.org* (https://familysearch.org/ark:/61903/1:1:QKZS-2H28 : 19 February 2021).

[143] The census lists a Chapin McGruder (b. 1879) as a child of Rachel and Charles. Lucille B. Osborne says this is a mistake, and/or that it may have been a relative or another son of Charles McGruder, but not a child he had with Rachel Hill. Others have reported that Rachel had eighteen children. His death certificate of May 8, 1939, states that Chafman McGruder was born in 1882 and married a woman named Mary. Chafin and Chapin are believed to be one and the same person.

It's possible that Chapin McGruder is actually a child of Fanny Magruder (b. 1822). Sabrina Franklin has conducted extensive research into the Magruder-Chapin line. In her 2005 McGruder reunion pamphlet, "The Alabama Black McGruders," she wrote: "Fanny was born about 1822. Her husband was named Creed (?-c. 1870) and was a bit older than Fanny. He

1864), Samuel (b. 1866), Julia Ann (b. 1868), Allen (b. 1869, reported to have died as a baby), Jonathan (reported to have died as a baby), Edmond (b. 1869/1870), Wiley (b. 1871), Minerva (b. 1873), William (1876-1921), Jasper (b. 1878), Chase (b. 1882), Rembert (1883-1910), Joshua (b. 1886), Creed (b. 1888), and Paul (1889-1910). Three of these children married siblings born to Thomas and Lizzie Edmonds. [144]

The blossoming of Rachel's relationship with Charles no doubt also negatively impacted his relationship with Matilda. By 1880, the census reports that Matilda also had left the compound and was living in one of her own. She reported to the census-taker that she was a widow.

---

also was owned by the Wynne family. After slavery, Fanny and her children took the surname Chapin or Chafin. Fanny and Creed were the alleged parents of twelve children, all of whom were born during slavery. Fanny's life is documented in a series of slave inventories, and there are numerous doctor bills showing the medical attention she received while enslaved."

Fanny had a daughter named Rose, who had a son named Creed. According to Franklin, "in 1870, five years after emancipation, Fanny's daughter Rose was married to an older man named Winston Childs. The 1870 Census in Greene County, Alabama, lists Winston's occupation as a liquor dealer and Rose as a housewife. By the 1880s, Rose was a widow living in Dallas County, Alabama, with her son, Creed. Her occupation is listed as a dressmaker. . ."

"By the 1880s, Rose's siblings, William, Luke, and Paul, lived with her and her son, Creed. William's occupation is listed as a carpenter. Luke's occupation is listed as a domestic servant, and Paul's occupation is listed as a shoemaker. Rose's son, Creed, at only sixteen years of age, is listed as a teacher. Creed must have been extremely bright, because by 1900 he is listed as a physician living in Washington, DC. There are numerous references to him in *The Washington Post* in the early 1900s and he was also a member of the Board of Education. It is quite an accomplishment to have been born a slave and become a doctor. This should be inspirational to future generations."

[144] Oral history received by Lucille B. Osborne asserts that none of Rachel's children were born during slavery. However, this may have been wishful thinking on the part of her informants, as numerous documents provide that Amos was born in 1862, which is prior to both the Emancipation Proclamation and the actual liberation of the black Magruders from enslavement by troops of the United States Army.

The thought of only being a creature of the present and past was troubling. I longed for a future too, with hope in it. The desire to be free, awakened my determination to act, to think, and to speak.

Frederick Douglass

My Bondage and My Freedom

8 - Reconstruction & Recognition

By J.R. Rothstein, Esq.

Charles Magruder Registers to Vote
& the Alabama Black McGruders Are Born

After the Civil War, Congress—dominated by radical Republicans, mostly abolitionists who represented Northern states—mandated that the treasonous Southern states rewrite their constitutions, ratify the 14th Amendment, and grant black men the right to vote, in order to gain reentry into the United States. During this period of Reconstruction, the black Magruders and other newly freed men and woman asserted their right to vote and to play a role in reshaping their state governments.

In March of 1867, Congress passed the Reconstruction Act, which temporarily divided the South into five military districts and outlined how governments based on universal male suffrage were to be organized. The new laws incensed white supremacists in the South, giving rise to the Ku Klux Klan. In that context, in 1867, Charles Magruder Sr.,[145] Charles Magruder Jr., Pleasant Inge, and John Mitchell, understanding the power of the ballot box, resisted race supremacy and courageously registered to vote. With them that day were other relatives, Jasper Magruder,[146] Henry C. Magruder, John Magruder,[147] and Madison Magruder.[148]

---

[145] There are two records of a Charles Magruder registering to vote. Both were residents of Hale County. (As outlined above, Hale County was created in 1867 from parts of three counties, with most of its territory coming from Greene County). One record was in precinct 6, election district 19, and the other in election district 19, precinct 6. The records are likely of father and son. An index of Hale County voter registrations for 1867-68 is available at the Alabama Department of Archives and History (https://digital.archives.alabama.gov/digital/collection/voter1867/id/3780/rec/1 : accessed 25 Jan 2021).

[146] Likely the brother of Charles Magruder.

[147] John Magruder/McGruder appears in the 1870 census as born in 1835 in Alabama. He is listed with three children: (1) William; (2) George; and (3) Henry. However, in the 1880 census, he is listed as born in Virginia.

[148] How all these men were related needs more investigation. Madison McGruder (b. 1825, North Carolina) appears in the 1870 census living in Greensboro, Hale County. With him is a woman who appears to be his mother, Rose McGruder, born 1790 in North Carolina. It is not unreasonable to assume that this family is related to our McGruders. However, how they fit into the puzzle remains unknown.

Despite asserting his right to vote, Charles's economic freedom remained tenuous. From 1865 onwards, Charles was renting land from the estate of Salina Ann Wynne Ferrell.[149] The records of the estate, of which Osmun A. Wynne remained one of the administrators, provide that the administrator managed:

> a small tract of land near Hollow Square, in Hale County, which he [the administrator] has been renting out for several years during the war and since which he accounted for in his previous settlement and is charged up for in the settlement now to be made. He rented out a part only of the land for the year 1868, as follows . . . and to Chas Magruder, about 23 acres for $40 which has been collected and is charged for. And he rented only a part of the land for this year, 1869 . . . and to Chas Magruder about 30 acres for $50. The land is very much worn, and out of the 250 acres of cleared land there is about 125 acres (in small patches) tillable. All of the rest of it is waste land and the fencing very much dilapidated, and it was offered at public auction and could not be rented at any price. The administrator further reports that he hired out the negroes of the estate during the war and had charged himself with all the hires... and has tried in vain to collect the notes which he holds for the hires of 1864 and 1865.[150]

A business partner and close ally of Charles Magruder in his struggle for civil rights, was his brother-in-law, John Mitchell. John had married Martha, Charles's elder sister.[151] According to research conducted by Sabrina Franklin, Martha was

---

[149] The record is unclear when this arrangement ended, but the evidence provides that Charles was also sharecropping for some other white landowners in the area, such as J.W. Melton. This requires further research.

[150] Greene County, Alabama, Probate Court, Estate Case Files, 1820-1915, Case #1545, Estate Papers of Salina A. Ferrell, pp.30-31; digital images *Family Search* (https://www.familysearch.org/ark:/61903/3:1:33S7-9TW5-4PC?i=29&wc=MXR9-6PV%3A314241801%2C316387401&cc=1978117 : accessed 26 Jan 2021).

[151] The following note contains research gathered by Sabrina Franklin in her 2005 McGruder reunion pamphlet:

> Martha was born in 1825, the second child of Ned and Mariah. Most likely, she was born on the Wynnewood Plantation, in Greene County, Alabama. There are few records left behind about Martha, except for slave inventories, doctor's bills, and contracts that show that she was leased out to work on other plantations. Evidence provides that she had six to seven children, the oldest being a son she named Ned, after her father. . .

sickly throughout her life. During slavery, this was reflected in her lower valuation in estate inventories. By 1870, she had passed, leaving her husband, John Mitchell, and a new wife, to care for their youngest children. Sabrina Franklin has located an 1870 census entry that identifies John Mitchell.[152] Born in South Carolina in 1823, Mitchell was trafficked as an enslaved person to Greene County, Alabama. Evidence suggests that, at some point, he was acquired by O.A. Wynne and that is when he met Martha. He also appears with other extended family members in the 1859 inventory of Salina Wynne Ferrell's estate. After enslavement, Mitchell continued to work for O.A. Wynne.

In 1870, John Mitchell, Charles McGruder Sr., and the other black McGruders were witness to one of the greatest acts of racial violence in United States history, as well as a pivotal moment in the Reconstruction era. The Eutaw Massacre of October 25th was part of an extended period of political and racial violence before the gubernatorial election of 1870, in which white Alabama Democrats used racial terrorism to suppress black Republican voting.

Earlier in the year, on the night of March 31, 1870, James Martin, a black Republican from Union, Alabama, was killed. A physician attempting to remove the bullet from his body was interrupted by a group of armed men, who carried his live body away. His final resting place is unknown. On the same night white Republican County Solicitor Alexander Boyd was shot in his hotel in Eutaw, the county seat, by a 30-member masked and costumed lynching party that rode into town on horseback. Both Martin and Boyd were promoting racial justice. Boyd's

---

Salina Ann Wynne Ferrell's estate was appraised on August 15, 1859. Martha is valued at only $133. It is possible a health issue determined that amount, because in the same inventory her older sister was valued at $1,433, an exceptionally high figure. . .

There is no evidence to show that Martha was alive in 1870. By 1870, her husband John was living with another woman, Lucretia "Creasy," along with Martha's youngest children, Walton and Lucy. Martha's son, Ned, was born in Greene County, Alabama.

Franklin initially proposed that Ned II was brought to Huntsville, Walker County, Texas, in 1852/4 by his slave owner, Erasmus Wynne. However, Franklin has retracted this assertion. Franklin also posits, without evidence, that Ned Wynne's father was Erasmus Wynne. This needs further research and DNA testing.

[152] 1870 U.S. Census, Hale County, Alabama, population schedule, Beat 6, p127A, family #476, John Mitchell; NARA Microform Publication, Roll: M593_18; digital image *Ancestry.com* (https://www.ancestry.com/imageviewer/collections/7163/images/4257571_00259?usePUB=true&_phsrc=BBS1326&_phstart=successSource&usePUBJs=true&pId=13272764 : accessed 25 Sept 2021).

death was eventually "investigated" by local officials, but no one was successfully prosecuted. Martin's murder, on the other hand, was not even considered worth investigating. In July of the same year, in Calhoun County, four blacks and one white were lynched for similar reasons. Closer to home for the black Magruders, in Greene County, Gilford Coleman, a black Republican leader, was lynched; he was fatally shot and his body mutilated after being taken from his home.

On October 25, 1870, a Republican political rally was held at the county courthouse in Eutaw, attracting 2,000 blacks—a crowd which almost certainly included John Mitchell and other members of the Alabama Black McGruders. The rally was attacked by Klansmen (supporting Democrats), who first verbally harassed the attendees and then started shooting at them, killing as many as four and wounding 54. Federal troops in the area did not intervene. As a consequence, fear spread throughout black Hale and Greene Counties and black voters stayed away from the polls on election day in fear of more violence, resulting in Democratic electoral success. In the 1868 presidential election, Greene County had voted for Republican Ulysses S. Grant by a margin of 2,000 votes; in the 1870 gubernatorial election, voters carried Democrat Robert B. Lindsay to the governorship by a margin of 43 votes.

These events, traumatic to all the black people in Hale and Greene Counties, raised fundamental questions about the future for Charles Magruder and his family. The collective experience of enslavement, Emancipation, Reconstruction, the Eutaw massacre, and sharecropping forced Charles to consider his identity and his family's story. Was he part of the larger Magruder tribe? Yes, but he also was different—separated by the color of his skin and the experience of enslavement. Charles desired a fresh start in a new era. Throughout the 1870s, he experimented with the spelling of his surname, perhaps as an act of asserting independence and distinction from the white Magruders, while at the same time still claiming them as his own. At the end of the decade Charles settled on the surname he would employ for this rest of his life and by which he is known to this day: *McGruder*. Most of his family, including the vast majority of his sons, followed his lead and used the *McGruder* spelling, and in that decision the Alabama Black McGruders were born.[153] According to Alabama Black McGruder oral history, some of his

---

[153] Marie McGruder posits that Charles intentionally rejected the American spelling of the surname, Magruder, and instead adopted the Scottish version of the surname. It has also been suggested that the different spellings of the surname are of no significance other than the random ways in which the surname could be phonetically spelled. According to Dora Coleman McGruder, a former census-taker and schoolteacher, census-takers were not allowed to ask people how to spell their names. Due to the high level of illiteracy the question could

children, perhaps acting from feelings of estrangement towards Charles and motivated by the same desire for a new beginning, decided on other variants of the surname, such as *McCruder* or *McCruter*.[154]

Charles's experimentation with the spelling of the McGruder surname is reflected in an entry by O.A. Wynne in the estate records of Salina Wynne Ferrell, dated May 23, 1871, referencing "Chas McGruder freedman" renting what appears to be the same land, but this time more acres, "for the sum of $200 Dollars, and he also … bargained to [renovate]… two small log cabins on the place, which he has done." A note dated April 24, 1872, provides that the administrator rented out "about 125 to 135 acres of … land in Hale County near Hollow Square, for $200.00 Dollars to … Charles McGruder, a freedman, secured by his note, for which the crop is bound. The said land… [has] no improvements of any value on it and cannot be rented out at public auction."[155]

Public support for Reconstruction policies, requiring continued supervision of the South, faded in the North with the rise of the Liberal Republicans in 1872, and after the Democrats, who strongly opposed Reconstruction, regained control of

---

be embarrassing. Therefore, many different spellings of a surname could be recorded and perhaps adopted by descendants.

[154] Some have reported that the changes of the surname resulted from certain family members' "feelings of superiority." According to Juan McGruder, "members of our family have spelled the surname MaGruder, McGruder, Mccruder, Mcgruda, McGouder, Mcruder, and Mcgruter." According to Juan, in the second generation some members of the Alabama Black McGruders would tease the McCruter children for spelling their surname incorrectly.

DNA testing conducted on Robert McCruter, a direct male descendant of Tennessee McGruter (1875-1954), son of Bob McCruter (1849-1904) and Rose Coalman, contradicts this oral history. Tennessee McGruter married Ada Inge (1876-1956), daughter of Mary May Ferrell and Pleasant Inge. DNA testing confirms that Robert McCruter matches autosomally with the descendants of Charles McGruder Jr., but not with any of the descendants of Charles McGruder Sr. and Rachel Hill. Y-Chromosome testing on Robert McCruter places him in haplotype group-O-M175, a different haplotype group than the Alabama Black McGruder males which belong to R-M269. This suggests that Charles McGruder Sr. was not the biological father of Robert "Bob" McCruter (1849-1904). As of the date of this publication, a second DNA test is being conducted on another descendant of Robert McCruter (1849-1904) as a control subject. However, these initial results suggest that the McCruter family is related genetically to the descendants of Charles McGruder Jr., but not paternally via Charles McGruder Sr.

[155] Greene Co, Alabama, Probate Court, Estate Case Files, 1820-1915, Case #1545, Estate Papers of Salina A. Ferrell, p.53; digital image *Family Search* (https://www.familysearch.org/ark:/61903/3:1:33S7-9TW5-4PL?i=52&wc=MXR9-6PV%3A314241801%2C316387401&cc=1978117 : accessed 26 Jan 2021).

the House of Representatives in 1874. Around him, Charles began to see the hopes of newly freed men and women fade with the rise of the Ku Klux Klan and its violent tactics to enforce the white supremacy of the Democratic party. Moreover, Charles understood the economic trap sharecropping represented. What became apparent to him in discussions with his sons, particularly Charles McGruder Jr., and his brother-in-law John Mitchell,[156] was that true freedom was economic freedom, which meant the ownership of land. Land and money, and the power they represented, would guarantee his security and place in society—not the power of the Federal government and its ever-evolving laws and policies about his God-given inalienable rights.

By 1875, Charles, the black McGruders, and African-Americans as a whole, had witnessed the increasing exhaustion of the Republican party and its steady retreat from both the racial egalitarianism and the broad definition of federal power spawned by the Civil War. The presence of federal troops in Alabama had not ended the deadly violence black people faced on a daily basis. Yet Charles remained steadfast. From the perspective of the Alabama Black McGruders, the election of 1876 symbolized a last effort to achieve the egalitarian dream of the Republican Party. Charles McGruder Sr. and the other eligible men of the Alabama Black McGruders registered to vote and designated John Mitchell, Charles's brother-in-law, as an inspector at the polls to resist both voter intimidation and fraud.

---

[156] Ironically, John Mitchell shared the name of a famous racist intellectual of the era.

The gravesite of Bob McCruter. Sawyerville, Alabama.
2020 photo courtesy of Stephen May III.

The 1875 Hale County voter registration list
containing reference to Charles Magruder Sr.

157

---

[157] Charles Magruder Sr. is listed here as Charles Magruda. His occupation is farmer—self-employed. Charles had at least one employee/laborer, a Ned Freeman, listed a few rows below Charles. Also on the same page is John Mitchell, working for O.A. Wynne; his son Blocker is on another page, also working for O.A. Wynne.

Inspectors of Election and Returning Officers.

IN accordance with Section 21 of the New Election Law, the following named persons have been appointed Inspectors and Returning officers:

BEAT No. 1, HAVANA.
Inspectors—J. W. Strudwick, Jno. H. Jack, Dick Harris, colored. Chesley D. Cummings, Returning Officer.

BEAT No. 2, NEW PROSPECT.
Inspectors—Geo. B. Sheldon, T. J. Mc Faddin, Ro. C. Hanna. Jno. May, Jr., Returning Officer.

BEAT No. 3, HARRISON.
Inspectors—Ben. S. Evans, C. C. Gewin, Henry Levert, colored. Jno. H. Gewin, Returning Officer.

BEAT No. 4, GREENSBORO.
Inspectors—R. H. Stickney, W. G. Hafner, A. S. Duval, colored. Sheriff, Returning Officer.

BEAT No. 5, NEWBERN.
Inspectors—Thos. J. Ramey, Wm. N. Knight, Oliver Ward, colored. Chas. W. Turpin, Returning Officer.

BEAT No. 6, HOLLOW SQUARE.
Inspectors—E. V. Melton, W. G. Britton, Jno. Mitchell, colored. Jas. P. Rogers, Returning Officer.

BEAT No. 7, CEDARVILLE.
Inspectors—Ro. C. Oliver, Mat Moore, Henry Smith, colored. P. A. Britton, Returning Officer.

BEAT No. 8, MACON.
Inspectors—Jas. A. Styron, R. L. Maupin, Darby Willis, colored. Ard B. Johnson, Returning Officer.

BEAT No. 9, DRAKE's STORE.
Inspectors—P. J. Knox, R. B. Waller, Jr., Geo. Bryant. Alex. Sledge, Returning Officer.

BEAT No. 10, WARREN's STORE.
Inspectors—A. M. Avery, J. T. Latimer, Chas. L. Madison. Jas. A. Stokes, Returning Officer.

BEAT No. 11, FIVE MILE.
Inspectors—Burrel Johnston, Thos. W. Payne, Geo. W. Morris. E. J. Ivie, Returning Officer.

BEAT No. 12, CARTHAGE.
Inspectors—Virginius F. Lewis, Geo. P. Browne, O. T. Anthon. Thos. P. Grimes, Returning Officer.

JOHN ATKINS,
Probate Judge.
JNO. S. TUCKER,
Sheriff.
V. BOARDMAN,
Clerk.
Supervisors of Elections.

———

The attention of Inspectors of Elections is directed to Sections 22, 24 to 35, inclusive, 37, 40, 41 and 91 of the New Election Law, approved March 3, 1875.

Returning Officers are hereby appointed Special Deputy Sheriffs on the day of Election, and are referred to Sections 23, 40, 43, 91, 95, 96, 98 and 100 of said Law for information respecting their duties.

158

———

158 Inspectors of Election and Returning Officers, *Greensboro) Alabama Beacon*, p. 1, col. 7; digital image *Newspapers.com* (https://www.newspapers.com/image/355765346/?terms=%22Inspectors%20of%20Elections%22&match=1 : accessed 27 Sept 2021). Note that John Mitchell is listed as an inspector.

GENERAL ELECTION

IN pursuance of law, I, John S. Tucker, Sheriff of Hale county, Alabama, hereby announce an election to be held at the various Precincts in said county, on TUESDAY, the 7th day of NOVEMBER, 1876, for the purpose of voting for Electors for President and Vice-President of the United States, and a Member of Congress for the 4th Congressional District of Alabama. Said election will be conducted and returns made in the manner provided and required by an Act of the General Assembly, entitled "An Act to regulate Elections in the State of Alabama," approved March 3d, 1875, and amended on the 27th of January, 29th of February, and 6th of March, 1876.

Inspectors and Returning Officers.

In accordance with Section 21 of the new Election Law, the following named persons have been appointed Inspectors and Returning Officers, to conduct said Election, to-wit:

HAVANA, PRECINCT NO 1
Inspectors—Joe Whatley, G B Sheldon, Dick Harris. J H Jack, Returning Officer.

NEW PROSPECT, PRECINCT NO 2
Inspectors—W P Loyd, T J McFadden, H Sylvers. N H Gewin, Returning Officer.

HARRISON, PRECINCT NO 3
Inspectors—D H Britton, J H Gewin, C C Gewin. F M Moore, Returning Officer.

GREENSBORO, PRECINCT NO 4
Inspectors—W G Hafner, W B Young, Marshal Thornton. Sheriff, Returning Officer.

NEWBERN, PRECINCT NO 5
Inspectors—J W Ramey, W N Knight, Dock Lane, Sr. J N Williamson, Returning Officer.

HOLLOW SQUARE, PRECINCT NO 6
Inspectors—H C Kelley, P M Britton, John Mitchell. J P Rogers, Returning Officer.

CEDARVILLE, PRECINCT No 7

Inspectors—Mat Moore, P A Britton, Ed Smith. Harvey Sutton, Returning Officer.

MACON, PRECINCT No 8

Inspectors—R L Maupin, A T Henley, Gus Wright. A B Johnson, Returning Officer.

LANEVILLE, PRECINCT No 9

Inspectors—Thos Hylton, P J Knox, Geo Bryant. R B Waller, Returning Officer.

WARREN'S, PRECINCT No 10

Inspectors—J T Latimer, A M Avery, C L Madison. J H Warren, Returning Officer.

FIVE MILE, PRECINCT No 11

Inspectors—F M Johnston, T W Payne, G W Morris. Isaac Ryan, Returning Officer.

CARTHAGE, PRECINCT No 12

Inspectors—Geo Brown, T J Powers, O T Anthon. John S Powers, Returning Officer.

PHIPPS', PRECINCT No 13

Inspectors—Wm Phipps, Isaac Phares, Sr, Wm H Johnson. John I Clary, Returning Officer.

JOHN ATKINS,
Probate Judge,
JOHN S. TUCKER,
Sheriff,
V. BOARDMAN,
Clerk,
Supervisors of Elections.

The attention of Inspectors is directed to Sections 22, 24, 25, 26, 27, 28, 29, 32, 33, 35, 36, 37 and 40 of the Election Law, approved March 3, 1875, and Sections 23, 30, 31, 34, 41 and 91, as amended in the Acts of 1875-76.

Returning Officers are hereby appointed Special Deputy Sheriffs on the day of Election, and are referred to Sections 95, 96, 98, 99 and 100 of the Election Law of 1874-75, and Section 43, as amended in Acts of 1875-76.

JOHN S. TUCKER,
Sheriff Hale county.
October 7, 1876   41-13in-5w

---

159 General Election, *Greensboro) Alabama Beacon*, 14 October 1876, p.1, col. 8; digital image *Newspapers.com* (https://www.newspapers.com/image/355768978/?terms=John%20S.%20Tucker&match=1 : accessed 27 Sept 2021).

At the Sunset of Reconstruction, Charles McGruder Sr. Acquires Land

It was in this political climate that Charles McGruder Sr. acquired land. Accounts within the family of how Charles McGruder Sr. acquired the hundreds of acres he would own by the 1880's are inconsistent and at times contradictory. Oral history provides that both Charles McGruder Sr. and Charles McGruder Jr. were zealously driven to acquire land. There are numerous stories as to how Charles's *initial* land was acquired. In addition, among the descendants of Charles McGruder Jr., the stories about the land purchases of Charles Sr. and Charles Jr. have become so conflated that they are difficult to separate.[160]

I will outline the numerous variations of the oral history, and how I believe they relate to Charles McGruder Sr., before integrating these accounts with the archival record.[161] I believe that each of these stories may hold an element of truth, reflecting different land purchases, different aspects of the same story, or different motivating factors of the parties involved.

The following are various oral history accounts of the land acquisition:

1.   Charles McGruder Sr. was given the land by his father;[162]

2.   Charles McGruder Sr. was given the land by his former slave owner(s);

3.   Charles McGruder Sr. was given the land by his former slave owner(s), who were biologically "related to him in some way;"

---

[160] Accordingly, when constructing the narrative in the next subsection, I give deference to the oral history narratives of the descendants of Rachel Hill over those of Mary May.

[161] The story of Charles McGruder Sr. and his acquisition of land most popularly circulated at family reunions is summarized in an entry found in the Archives of Wilmar McGruder. The entry, likely provided to Wilmar by a descendant of Minerva McGruder, states:

> Charles McGruder/McCruder (slave breeder) . . . mother was Marie [and] his father was Ned. He had three sets of children—100 children. He [later] married Rachel Hill. He conceived (100) children. He was light skin[ed] with straight black hair. He was a carpenter and his master gave him 365 acres . . . [and] many years later his sons lost the property because of their laziness. They weren't work[ing] and [did not] pay the taxes. (Lost 240 acres because brothers wouldn't pay mortgages).

[162] According to one source, "Charles's former master gave him 360 acres of land, of which his sons lost 240 acres due to not paying taxes."

4. Charles McGruder Sr. was assisted with the purchase of land by his father;

5. Charles McGruder Sr. was assisted with the purchase of land by his former slave owner(s);

6. Charles McGruder Sr. was assisted with the purchase of land by his former slave owner(s), who were biologically "related to him in some way";

7. Charles McGruder Sr. was given land (or assisted with the purchase of land) "because he was a breeder and had so many children;"

8. Charles McGruder Sr. was given land (or assisted with the purchase of land) "because he was family;"

9. Charles McGruder Sr.'s "white brother" helped him purchase land (from the local Indians);

10. Charles McGruder Sr.'s father helped him purchase land from the local Indians;[163]

11. The court (or some other legal entity, like an administrator) *directed* Charles McGruder Sr.'s former enslaver/brother/father/white relatives to give him land;

12. The court (or some other legal entity, like an administrator) played a role in giving Charles McGruder Sr. land;

13. The court (or some other legal entity, like an administrator) played a role in assisting Charles McGruder Sr. to acquire land;

14. Charles McGruder Sr. "saved up money"[164] and purchased the land "entirely by himself;"[165]

15. Charles McGruder Sr. "saved up money" and purchased the land "entirely by himself" and without the help of any white person or family member;[166]

---

[163] A narrative likely more accurately associated with Charles McGruder Jr.

[164] Susan Tichy reports that some enslaved people, especially those favored by their owners, were allowed to earn and save money, the funds usually held by the slave-owners themselves, as slaves could not use banks. Charles could have gone to O.A. Wynne not to ask for money, but to collect his savings. However, as the event in question occurred nearly a decade after the end of enslavement, this scenario is unlikely.

[165] A narrative likely more accurately associated with Charles McGruder Jr.

[166] A narrative likely more accurately associated with Charles McGruder Jr.

16. Charles McGruder Sr. "saved up money" and purchased the land "entirely by himself" and with minimal help of any white person or family member;[167]

17. Charles McGruder Sr. received reparations/compensation from his former enslavers; and

18. When other African-Americans received 40 acres and a mule, Charles McGruder Sr.'s white family members helped him instead to get 100 acres.[168]

Additionally, according to Lucille B. Osborne, when he acquired the land Charles McGruder Sr. was advised by an "old white man"—likely connected to the Wynne family—where there were water wells on the property and, thus, where to build.

Considering the DNA results, the year of the land acquisition, and the timing of Osmun A. Wynne's death relative to the purchase of the land, the author believes that after enslavement Charles was assisted in some manner in the acquisition of his *initial* land by O.A. Wynne, Charles McGruder Sr.'s white first cousin. O.A. Wynne's roles as leader of the Wynne family and administrator of the estate of Salina Ann Wynne Ferrell, along with the fact that his brothers had migrated to Texas more than a decade earlier, makes him the obvious and only candidate to match the Alabama Black McGruder oral history.

Osmun Appling Wynne

Eleanor Magruder Wynne's first son, Osmun Appling Wynne (1804-1877) was born November 9, 1804, in Oglethorpe County, Georgia. As a young man, O.A. Wynne migrated with his family and their enslaved people from Georgia to Hollow Square (later Sawyerville), Alabama. On January 26, 1829, at age twenty-four, he married Frances Laura Anderson, in Greene County, Alabama—just months before the death of this father, Williamson Wynne, and the birth of Charles Magruder Sr. to Ned and Mariah Magruder.

At twenty-five, massive responsibility was thrust upon Osmun, all within the period of a single year. As the eldest son, he became the new master of Wynnewood, while also serving as the administrator of his father's estate.

---

[167] A narrative likely more accurately associated with Charles McGruder Jr.

[168] Official reparations for enslavement were never made to African-Americans or their descendants. Although it is an inaccurate statement by the informant, it is relevant in that it reflects an understanding of the intent and circumstances surrounding around these historic events.

Wynnewood had been established only a few years before, and it would be his task not only to stabilize the plantation's finances but to ensure that it thrived. Exploiting the labor of enslaved people towards that end, including the black Magruders, Osmun directed the clearing of frontier land and building of his family's home. After his father's estate was settled, he assisted his mother, Eleanor Magruder Wynne, in repurchasing the family of Ned Magruder in 1830, including baby Charles.

By 1850, O.A. Wynne's efforts had succeeded. Osmun and his family were, collectively, the owners of approximately 192 enslaved human beings, including the family of Ned and Mariah Magruder. Directing such a large plantation would not have been easy for the Wynne family and it is likely that they employed numerous overseers to repress and control the enslaved people of Wynnewood— overseers which O.A. Wynne likely supervised.

At the same time, O.A. Wynne's share of the inheritance had remained in probate since his mother Eleanor's death in 1848. Something in her will was controversial—perhaps her leaving nearly her entire estate to her daughter—and it created a long and drawn-out legal process. Nevertheless, according to the 1850 Slave Schedule, 62 of the 192 enslaved people had been designated to Osmun.

By 1852, it became apparent to the younger Wynne siblings that, whatever the outcome of the probate process, Wynnewood would remain under the leadership of Osmun. At this time, a breakaway group of Wynnes, led by Erasmus Wynne, migrated from Alabama to Texas.[169]

O.A. Wynne's support of the Confederate States of America and the institution of slavery on which it was founded set in course a series of tragic events for his family during the 1860's and 1870's. When Alabama seceded from the United States, O.A. Wynne whole-heartedly joined the Confederate cause, sending members of his family to the Confederate Army and leading other local planters to join the war effort.

During the war, Osmun blessed the decision of his two sons, along with his nephew William O. Ferrell, to fight for the Confederate cause. His son John Williamson "Jack" Wynne enlisted for the Confederacy on April 13, 1861. In

---

[169] In Texas, Erasmus and his siblings founded the town of Wynnewood and built plantations on the San Jacinto River in western Walker County, modeled on the world they had left behind and that O.A. Wynne now presided over. Descendants of those Texas Wynnes, with the enslaved friends and possibly relatives of Charles Magruder Sr., continued to grow tobacco and cotton in Wynnewood, until the early 1940s. The ancestors of Sabrina Franklin, a historian of the Alabama Black McGruders, were among those trafficked to Texas from Alabama with the Wynne family.

1862, his nephew Gustavus Wynne died at the Battle of Antietam, in Maryland. Throughout these years, O.A. Wynne continued to grow cotton for the Confederacy. He was pardoned for his actions by President Abraham Lincoln, shortly before the latter's assassination in 1865.

After the war, in a span of two years, O.A. Wynne buried two sons and a daughter: John W. "Jack" Wynne died in May 1867, only a few weeks after his wedding; Elizabeth "Betty" Webster, a daughter of O.A. Wynne, died at about the same time; and William "App" Wynne, Osmun's favorite son, died in May 1869. Osmun became the administrator for all these estates. During this same period, the husbands of his two remaining daughters, Martha Ann Sturdivant and Laura Wynne Coleman,[170] also died, as did William O. Ferrell, in 1868—Salina's son and Osmun's nephew, whom Osmun and his wife, Frances Laura, had raised. Salina's estate was finally settled in 1872, when Salina's daughter, Emerette, turned 21.

After the Civil War, in 1870, Osmun was a delegate to the Alabama state convention of the Democratic party, whose platform included resistance to reconstruction efforts, and overtly racist and hostile treatment of newly freed blacks. In 1874, when Osmun's daughter Martha Lavinia Sturdivaunt died, she too named her father executor of her estate. Osmun's wife, Frances Laura, most likely had also died before this time, as only her father and two sisters, Julia Wynne and Laura Frances Wynne, are mentioned in her will.[171] In 1875, Julia Wynne's husband, Dr. John Scott, was killed in the explosion of a steam mill, just twelve or fifteen months

DISTRESSING ACCIDENT.—The Steam Mill of Messrs. Boyd, Scott & Co., situated 5 miles West of Marion, was blown up last Saturday evening, killing Dr. John Scott, one of the proprietors, Alex. Fagan, colored, engineer, and mortally wounding Mr. —— Parker, of Marion,—since reported as having died; and slightly wounding several others. The whole machinery, building, etc., were destroyed. Capt. Boyd and Mr. D. B. Scott, the other partners, had just left the mill before the explosion. The mill was but recently put in operation, the building not having reached completion. Mr. Parker, aided by Mr. Mitchell, (who was blown a considerable distance) was roofing the building at the time, with tin.

Dr. Scott was a gentleman of high standing, and was highly respected by all who knew him. He married some twelve or fifteen months ago, Miss Julia Wynne, daughter of Mr. O. A. Wynne, of this county.

No cause can be ascertained for the sad calamity, as the greatest caution was used by the engineer.

[170] Martha Ann Wynne (1834-1875) married Dr. Lewis L. Sturdivant on October 9, 1860.

[171] Greene Co, AL Probate Ct. Estate Case Files 1820-1915, Case#1546, Estate of Martha Lavina Ferrell; digital images Family Search (https://www.familysearch.org/ark:/61903/3:1:33SQ-GTW5-W4D?wc=MXR9-XPL%3A314241801%2C316387101&cc=1978117 FHL#5008479 : accessed 26 Jan 2021); image1731.

after their wedding.[172] This list does not include deceased grandchildren of O.A. Wynne.

In the view of the author, it was O.A. Wynne's close acquaintance with death that played a transformative role in his character. In addition, O.A. Wynne knew firsthand the hardships that Charles and his family had experienced as a result of the actions of his former brother-in-law, William A. Ferrell. Osmun had observed the legal chaos resulting from his sister's divorce, compounded by the untimely death of both his sister and her husband, and how that wreaked havoc on the family of Ned and Mariah Magruder.

O.A. Wynne had not been a detached observer to these events. It was O.A. Wynne who, as administrator for Salina Ann Wynne Ferrell's estate, managed the war between the Wynnes and Ferrells for possession of the Mariah Magruder family. It was O.A. Wynne who, after the deaths of the Ferrells, continued to rent Charles out from plantation to plantation. It was O.A. Wynne who sold cotton to the Confederate States of America during the Civil War. It was O.A. Wynne who—after slavery and on behalf of his sister's estate—contracted with Charles and his family to work on Salina Ann Wynne's land as sharecroppers. O.A. Wynne, more than any other white man, knew Charles's story.

It was in this context, in late 1876 or early 1877, at the sunset of Reconstruction and the eve of a contentious national election, that Charles McGruder Sr. and Osmun A. Wynne met. What precisely was spoken between the two men, and what exactly was requested or offered, we will never know. Perhaps Charles had saved enough money to purchase land on his own, but was a few hundred dollars short. Perhaps, as some assert, Charles had all the money he needed, but needed O.A. Wynne's political support or legal advice to conduct the transaction. Perhaps it was a heated conversation. Perhaps Charles reminded Osmun that they were of one blood, that he and the other Alabama Black McGruders had toiled on behalf of the white Magruders and Wynnes, without compensation, for generations. Perhaps Charles reminded Osmun of the dehumanization which he had experienced as a breeder of enslaved people, in which Osmun had been complicit. Perhaps Charles pointed out that now, as a result of past events, he was father to dozens of people and needed the means to support them. Perhaps Charles argued that it was O.A. Wynne's moral responsibility to provide him and his family with financial recompense.

---

[172] Distressing Accident, *(Greensboro) Alabama Beacon*, p. 4, col. 2; digital image *Newspapers.com* (https://www.newspapers.com/image/355765548/?terms=%22John%20Scott%22&match=1 : accessed 27 Sept 2021).

What motivated O.A. Wynne to heed Charles's words, we likewise will never know. Perhaps Osmun was merely fulfilling a promise made to Charles in the days of enslavement. Perhaps Osmun was fundamentally a good man who had been corrupted by an evil institution and now wished to atone for his sins. Perhaps he felt that helping Charles and his family was one way to do that. Perhaps the experiences of a Civil War, Southern dispossession, and the approaching end of his own life gave O.A. Wynne some feelings of Christian repentance and perspective on the evils of slavery from which he had profited all his life. Perhaps, as Juan McGruder posits, having been born again, now having accepted the teachings of Jesus and Christianity into his heart, Osmun sought to make amends for his past sins. Perhaps O.A. Wynne, reflecting upon the curses and tragedies which God Almighty had brought upon his house for being an enslaver of his fellow humans— including members of his own family—saw before him an opportunity to banish the angel of death which had visited his shattered dynasty. Perhaps O.A. Wynne could see before him the social devastation which enslavement and the breeding of enslaved people had wrought, not just for him and the South but in the family structures and economics of the black men and women whose bodies he had dominated, suppressed, and exploited.

Or perhaps O.A. Wynne felt none of these things. Perhaps he cared nothing for Charles McGruder Sr., and the proposed transaction simply provided him with some unknown political or economic benefit. Perhaps whatever money was given, if any, was given grudgingly.

We don't know.

Whatever his motivation, the Alabama Black McGruder oral history provides that O.A. Wynne would hear Charles's words and, in some manner, lend Charles the assistance he needed to accomplish his goal of acquiring land.

On February 17, 1877, Osmun Appling Wynne, son of Williamson Wynne and Eleanor Magruder, and first cousin to Charles Magruder Sr., died.[173] An obituary

---

[173] No will was filed with the courts and his three surviving children agreed to distribute his estate amongst them without aid of court appointed administration. Hale County Alabama, Probate Court General Index, 1867-1918, Deeds 1867-1902, Deed Book I, p 485-487, Estate of Osmun A. Wynne; digital images *Family Search* (https://www.familysearch.org/ark:/61903/3:1:3Q9M-C375-X383-J?i=47&cat=487823 : accessed 25 Jan 2021); citing FHL#8586683, image# 48-49.

Osmun died with about $6,000 in cash and/or gold on hand. One of his daughters, Julia Scott, died a few months later. Laura Frances Wynne Coleman lived until 1891, and probably looked after her brother Thomas. Her son, Bestor Coleman, became guardian of Thomas after her death, Thomas having been declared incompetent. Thomas died in 1911, never married

in *The Montgomery Advertiser* described him as a "most excellent citizen," "of great personal wealth."[174]

The Land

Eight months after the death of Osmun A. Wynne, Charles Magruder acquired land. On November 6, 1877, Charles and Rachel Magruder purchased 240 acres of land from Frances and Sarah Liles for $1,500, the exact amount at which Charles was assessed in value in 1859.[175] That Rachel Hill appeared on the deed as Charles's wife, and that only Charles's children with Rachel were listed on the deed as well, was no doubt hurtful to some.[176] This deed, being a significant document in the history of the Alabama Black McGruders, is presented here in its entirety as follows: [177]

Francis A. Liles and Wife Deed

To Chas. Magruder Et.al

State of Alabama Perry County

Nov. Sixth One thousand eight hundred and Seventy-seven

---

and childless. Alice Coleman Griffin, a contributor to this work, is a descendant of O.A. Wynne via Laura Frances Wynne Coleman.

Susan Tichy questions whether the eight-month lapse between Charles's death and the purchase of land might suggest that it was one of Osmun's children who assisted Charles. Tichy suggests that O.A. Wynne may have been an obstacle removed. This theory, however, is rejected by the author.

[174] Death of Mr. O. A. Wynne, *The Montgomery (Alabama) Advertiser*, 9 March 1877, p. 1; digital image Newspapers,.com (https://www.newspapers.com/image/355639965/?terms=Wynne&match=1 : accessed 30 Dec 2021).

[175] On November 12, 1877, a few days after Charles purchased his first land, Liberty African CME Church was established. The church had grown out of the quasi-integrated CME church, forced to segregate with the sunset of Reconstruction. The Alabama Black McGruders were instrumental in the church's formation and growth. The church's official history is included in the documents relevant to Chapter 11 annexed to this book.

[176] It raises the possibility that Rachel had a unique influence or role in the acquisition of this land.

[177] Hale County, Alabama, Probate Court General Index, 1867-1918, Deeds 1867-1902, Deed Book I, p 420; digital image *Family Search* (https://www.familysearch.org/ark:/61903/3:1:3Q9M-C375-X3ZF3?i=15&cat=487823 : accessed 25 Jan 2021); citing FHL# 8586683, image#16.

This indenture made and entered into on the day and date above written, witnesseth that Francis A. Liles and his wife Sarah A. Liles of Perry County, Alabama, for and in consideration of the sum of fifteen hundred dollars in hand, paid as and before sealing and delivering these presents the receipt of which is hereby acknowledged have bargained and sold, and by these presents do bargain and sell unto Charles Magruder and Rachel Magruder, his wife, and heirs, viz: Amos Magruder, Revena[178] Magruder, Sam Magruder, Julia Magruder, Edmund Magruder, Wiley Magruder, Nerva[179] Magruder, William Magruder, and Jasper Magruder, and assigns administrators and executors forever of Hale County, Alabama, a certain tract or parcel of land lying in Hale County, Alabama, known and described as follows: the west-half of the Southeast quarter Sec (13) thirteen, East half of the South west quarter Sec (13) thirteen N.W. ¼ of the N.E. ¼, Sec. 24, and the N.E. ¼ of the N.W. qr. Sec 24, all in Township 21, Range 3 three east, containing 240 two hundred and forty more or less, together with the building rights, privileges, advantages, and appurtenances belonging thereunto or in any wise appertaining to the same.

To have and to hold himself, his wife, and heirs whose names are herein given and assigns forever, free from all and every claim of my heirs, executors, and administrators forever, together with all and singular the appurtenances thereunto belonging.

In witness whereof we have hereunto subscribed our names on this 6th day of Nov. Eighteen Hundred and Seventy-Seven.

Francis A. Liles   *L.S.*

Sarah A. Liles   *L.S.*

Witness

E.E. Tramill

E.R. Liles

The State of Alabama, Hale County

---

[178] Roena

[179] Manerva

I, S.C. Tramill, Notary Public and Ex. Office Justice of the Peace in [and] for said County, hereby certify that on the 6th day of November A.D. 1877, personally came before me Francis A. Liles who acknowledge before me, that being informed of the contents of the foregoing conveyance, he executed the same voluntarily on the day the same bears date.

And also, on the same day personally came before me, Sarah A. Liles, known to me to be the wife of the within Frances A. Liles, who being by me examined separate and apart from her husband did sign the foregoing conveyance after being informed of the contents of the same of her own free will and accord and without fear, constraint, or persuasion of her husband.

In witness whereof, I have hereunto set my hand this the 6th day of November A.D. 1877.

S.C. Tramill

Notary Public & Ex. Off. J.P.

The foregoing conveyance was filed for Record November 7, 1877, and duly recorded the same day.

420

Francis A Files & wife
&c &c Deed
Chas McGruder Etal

State of Alabama } For sixth One
Perry County } thousand eight
hundred and Seventy Seven

This Indenture made and entered into on the day and date above written, Witnesseth, that Francis A Files and his wife Sarah A Files of Perry County Alabama, for and in consideration of the Sum of Fifteen Hundred dollars in hand paid as and before sealing and delivering these presents the receipt of which is hereby acknowledged have bargained and sold and by these presents do bargain and sell unto Charles Magruder and Rachel Magruder his wife and heirs viz Amos Magruder, Stevena Magruder, Sam Magruder, Julia Magruder, Edmund Magruder, Riley Magruder, Serena Magruder, William Magruder and Jasper Magruder, and assigns administrators & Executors forever of Hale County Alabama, a certain tract or parcel of land lying in Hale County Alabama known and described as follows; the west half of the south east quarter sec No thirteen, East half of the south west quarter sec No thirteen N W½ of the N E¼ Sec 24, and the N E¼ of the N W¼ Sec 24 all in Township 21 Range 0 three east containing 240, two hundred and forty more or less together with the buildings rights privileges advantages and appurtenances belonging thereunto or in any wise appertaining to the same To have and to hold himself, his wife, and heirs above named are herein given and assigns forever, free from all and every claim of my heirs executors and Administrators forever, together with all and singular the appurtenances thereunto belonging In witness whereof we have hereunto subscribed our names on this 6th day of Nov Eighteen hundred and Seventy Seven

Witness
E. E. Tramell
E. R. Files

Francis A Files [S.S.]
Sarah A Files [S.S.]

The State of Alabama } I E Tramell Notary Public and
Hale County } Ex Officio Justice of the Peace in for said county, hereby certify that on the 6th day of November A D 1877, personally came before me Francis A Files who Acknowledged before me, that being informed of the contents of the foregoing conveyance, he executed the same voluntarily on the day the Same bears date

And also on the same day personally came before me Sarah A Files known to me to be the wife of the within Francis A Files who being by me examined separate and apart from her husband did sign the foregoing Conveyance after being

Land Deed of Charles Magruder Sr and Rachel Hill,
Sawyerville, Alabama, 1877.

Photo of O. A. Wynne (1804 - 1877), circa 1870's, Hale County Alabama.
Courtesy Alice Coleman Griffin.

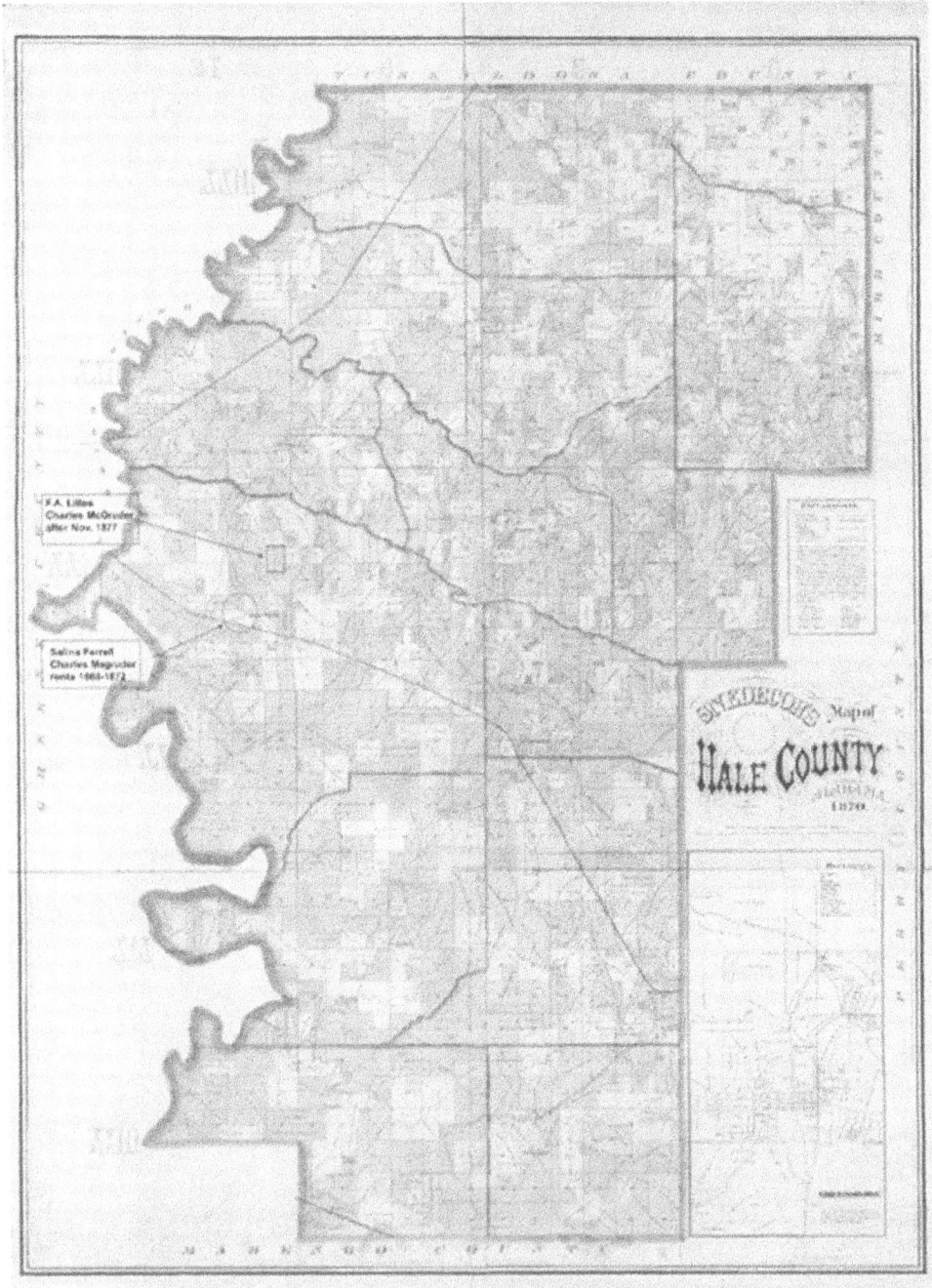

Snedecor's 1870 Map of Hale County, annotated to show location of land rented and purchased by Charles McGruder, Sr.

180

180 V. Gayle Snedecor, *Snedecor's Map of Hale County, Alabama* (Boston: Walling & Gray, 1870); digital image, Library of Congress, county land ownership maps

The 1880 Selected U.S. Federal Census Non-Population Schedule for Hale County provides further details regarding the nature of this purchase. The record provides that Charles McGruder Sr. owned 80 acres of tilled soil, had 10 acres of orchards or vineyards, and 140 acres in woodland in the greater Sawyerville area, all valued at about $800. With this economic foundation, Charles would go on to acquire more land and establish several businesses, including a store. Charles also helped members of his extended family and network to acquire land. For example, in 1886, Charles, with a number of other closely related African-Americans families, syndicated a real estate deal which involved the acquisition of a storefront.[181]

Among the first things Charles did with this prosperity was procure advanced education for his children and grandchildren, directing his children Charles McGruder Jr., Jim D. McGruder,[182] Amos McGruder, and others to reject the mediocre level of education then provided to freedmen. Instead, Charles directed his children to acquire the highest forms of literacy possible and achieve academic excellence.[183] Only after the educational and economic foundations of his children were established did Charles Sr. purchase for himself a grand prized horse which he rode proudly around Sawyerville and its environs.

The Resilience of the McGruders During Jim Crow

After the Reconstruction period ended in 1877, white supremacy raged unopposed across the South and the segregationist policies known as Jim Crow soon became the law of the land. Southern blacks were forced to make their living working the land as sharecroppers, which offered little in the way of economic opportunity. The Ku Klux Klan (KKK) had been officially dissolved in 1869, but continued underground. Intimidation and violence, including lynching, were not uncommon in Jim Crow Greene and Hale Counties, Alabama.

(https://www.loc.gov/resource/g3973h.la000003/?r=-0.479,-0.013,1.787,1.537,0 : accessed 20 Feb 2021).

[181] A copy of the deed of syndication is annexed as one of the important documents of this chapter.

[182] Jim was a businessman, and local leader. He was also a schoolteacher and promoted the education of the Alabama Black McGruders.

[183] Following his father's example, Charles McGruder Jr. prioritized the advanced education of his exceptionally talented son, Ethew A. McGruder, saving enough money to send him to university at Tuskegee to study with Booker T. Washington, with the hope that he would return and educate the other Alabama Black McGruders. Ethew would subsequently return to Sawyerville, and, in 1917, along with other members of the Alabama Black McGruders, establish Wynne Academy, a school for black children.

In this context, Charles worked with his brother-in-law, John Mitchell, in supporting local Republican leaders and black political efforts in the county. The following account of John Mitchell's efforts appeared in a local white racist newspaper, the *Greensboro Watchman*.[184]

— According to previous notice, the Republican party of Hale county met in Greensboro Saturday, for the purpose of electing delegates to the District Congressional Convention, and for the "transaction of other important business."— At about 12:30 o'clock, the writer in company with a number of other gentlemen. repaired to Tullibody Academy, the place of meeting, where we found a house fairly packed with negroes, delegates and visitors. Hon. Geo. M. Duskin, one of the aspirants for Congressional honors, appeared on the scene, and was escorted into the meeting by a number of his Democratic friends.

We met there with Jas. K. Greene, of Montgomery, and asked him to secure us a seat in the body as a representative of the Press. Jim Greene made a motion to that effect which prevailed, and we were furnished a chair.

The Chairman of the Republican Ex-

---

[184] Hale County Republicans elect Delegates to the District Congressional Convention. *Greensboro (Alabama) Watchman*, 3 August 1882, p. 3, col. 3; digital image *Newspapers.com* (https://www.newspapers.com/image/308391976/?terms=%22previous%20notice%22&match=1 : accessed 27 Sept 2021).

ecutive Committee—Geo. B. Griffin—had the floor, and made several harrangues in trying to perfect an organization. He boasted of his true Republican principles, his honesty and faithfulness to the party,—and let off in a most spiteful and venemous manner a great quantity of nonsensical and disgusting gas. He was frequently interrupted by cries of "Mr. Cheerman;" "I rise to a pint of order," etc., but was so much enthused that he continued in his mad career until he was almost out of wind.

Rev. A. W. Atwaters moved that the visitors, black and white, be invited to take seats in the Convention. Finding that the motion would probably be defeated, he arose and said: "Mr. Chairman, feeling that the Republican party of Hale has so little courtesy as to deny this privilege to my fellow-citizens, I beg to withdraw my motion.

From subsequent proceedings it would seem that two parties had been suggested for temporary Chairman—Rev. Mr. Atwaters, a delegate, and T. A. Motley, a visitor, in fact the Chair so stated, and placed before the meeting the name of the latter, announcing "all in favor of his election make it known by the usual voting sign, I."

There were some ayes in the house as well as outside. Right here for some minutes the wildest confusion prevailed, and everybody except a few who got out the windows, made a rush for the speaker's stand. Knives and razors were drawn, and but for the presence of Sheriff Locke, who took the stand, and in a few remarks, commanded the peace, the scene would have been one of bloodshed. Motley took the Chair and endeavored to call the meeting to order, but failed. Griffin stood on his right, and read out what was said to be a list of the delegates to the Congressional Convention, but the confusion was so great that no one heard the names. At this juncture the Chairman of the Convention, which had never been organized, announced its adjournment, and with his McDuffie followers, quit the scene.

Prof. Williams, of Tullibody Academy, said that he had never attended a political meeting of his race before, and if all were conducted in the shameful and disgraceful manner that this one was, he would certainly never attend another.

Preacher Atwaters then took the Chair, and called the meeting to order and organized a Mass Meeting. He made a sensible and conservative speech, highly conservative for a Republican.

Mr. W. W. Jones, the only white delegate, was made Secretary.

A committee of five was appointed to select nine delegates to the Congressional Convention, to be held in Selma, the 24th inst. The following names were reported and elected :

A. W. Atwaters,	W. W. Jones,
B. W. Reese,	Mantly Wynne,
Jack Morris,	John Mitchel,
George Jackson,	Dock Lane.
	Isanc Silvers.

An Executive Committee was then appointed, consisting of one member from each Beat, with B. W. Reese as the Chairman.

Speeches were made by Mr. Geo. M. Duskin, Jas. K. Green, and others, after which the Mass Meeting adjourned.

With two sets of Delegates from Hale county the Republicans will have trouble in the Selma Convention.

The 1880's was also a decade of loss for Charles. He witnessed not only the death of the dream of Reconstruction, but the deaths of his mother Mariah, brother Jasper,[185] and brother-in-law John Mitchell, allies in the struggle for economic and spiritual self-development for the Alabama Black McGruders. Racist scorn is evident in the following death notice, printed in an anti-black newspaper, *The Alabama Watchman*. Its venom suggests that John Mitchell's civil rights activities had been extensive.

> John Mitchell, colored, a shining light of the Radical party, in Hollow Square Beat, passed in his chips last week. Those who knew him best say nothing good of him.[186]

Yet despite death of the civil rights agenda of the Reconstruction era, Charles remained relatively successful. His economic success during this period, rooted in land ownership, can be put into perspective by a June 1887 article in the *Alabama Beacon* which noted that "blacks have not been able, as a general thing, to buy farms, although there is plenty of land for sale cheap in the South."[187]

---

[185] Jasper was born in 1832/1837 in Greene County. According to Franklin, he married a woman named Rhoda Fells. The couple had at least nine children, and he was a farmer by profession. According to a letter preserved by Alice Coleman Griffin, Jasper died in 1881. "The country is in commotion (I mean negroes)," wrote Laura Frances Coleman to Wynne Coleman on May 24, 1881, "about going to a funeral Sunday, Jasper Magruda's." Alice Coleman Griffin, *Laura And Her Children's Letters* (Privately printed, 2009), 165.

According to the 1880 Census, Jasper had the following children: (1) James McGruder; (2) Amos McGruder; (3) Numa McGruder; (4) Fannie McGruder; (5) Henry C. McGruder; (6) Clara L.P. McGruder; (7) Julius C. McGruder. Numah is not a common name. In Hausa it means beautiful, or pleasant. The name may be a loan word from Arabic. It may also have its origin as Pneuma (πνεῦμα) an ancient Greek word for "breath" and, in a religious context, for "spirit" or "soul".

[186] Death of John Mitchell, *Greensboro (Alabama) Watchman*, 26 July 1883, p. 3, col. 1; digital image *Newspapers.com*

(https://www.newspapers.com/image/308393719/?terms=Mitchell&match=1 : accessed 27 Sept 2021).

[187] A Rapid Sub-division of Land, *(Greensboro) Alabama Beacon*, 9 August 1887, p. 3, col. 2; digital image *Newspapers.com*

Wedgeworth

In this period of Alabama Black McGruder family success, and at the dawn of Jim Crow, an individual named Wedgeworth and his family emerged as white antagonists of at least some of the black McGruders. The Wedgeworth family were among the largest landowners in Sawyerville, second only to the Alabama Black McGruders. According to oral history accounts, Wedgeworth owned a cotton gin and a store, where local farmers would bring raw cotton in their wagons, sometimes a ton at a time. Wedgeworth would process the raw cotton into bales, which the farmers would sell or keep at their homesteads. According to Robert Brasfield, an Alabama Black McGruder, Wedgeworth's store also served as a kind of bartering station where local blacks would bring food and other produce and exchange it for items they needed "because there was little currency in circulation at the time."

Rev. Orlando McGruder Sr. recalls hearing that Mr. Wedgeworth would sit on a white horse to oversee his sharecroppers picking cotton. According to Juan McGruder, when Charles Jr. (and/or Charles Sr.) was interested in purchasing more land, Wedgeworth found out about his plans and "went over to that Indian," who had previously sold Charles his land, and told the Indian "don't you sell that nigger any more land."[188] Rev. Orlando McGruder Sr. relates that Wedgeworth was the archetypical "grabby white person," who sought to own as much land as he could "get his hands on" and would get it by "hook or by crook." According to Robert Brasfield, Wedgeworth would regularly move the property line markers in his favor in order to encroach on McGruder land. In response, Charles[189] built a ditch, thereby creating a permanent border between the two territories. According to Rev. Orlando McGruder Sr., Wedgeworth's greed, and these types of actions, eventually caught up with him and he lost a lot of the land he had acquired.

According to Juan McGruder, some of Wedgeworth's male kin behaved inappropriately and "ill-bred" with some of the McGruder women. Juan explained that "we don't recognize them as family and they don't recognize us." Juan doesn't know which McGruder women were involved, but heard many family members gossip about this.

(https://www.newspapers.com/image/253993500/?terms=%22to%20buy%20farms%22&match=1 : accessed 27 Sept 2021).

[188] Juan McGruder believes this story is about Charles Sr. The author believes, based on speaking with different family members, that the story is about Charles Jr. According to Dorothy McGruder Edwards, the land was purchased from a white person and not an Indian.

[189] Or another McGruder.

> Mr. Will Wedgeworth, of the Akron neighborhood, is among Hale's model farmers. With five mules he made this year fifty-five bales of cotton, over a thousand bushels of corn, and any quantity of fodder, potatoes, etc. [190]

Juan indicated that this race mixing would have occurred around the 1890s to 1900s.

Elmer Brox, on the other hand, reported that relations with the Wedgeworth family were more complex. When Elmer's grandfather, James D. McGruder[191], was sick, the Wedgeworths came to visit him, and Elmer was not aware of any issues between the two families at that time.[192]

The Last Years of Charles Sr.

Lucille B. Osborne relates that each of Charles Sr.'s wives staked out her own section on the McGruder land. Each built her own sub-compound at the "McGruder Place," "McGruder Farm," or "McGruder Plantation," as it was called. In addition, there seem to have been at least two, possibly three, non-adjacent properties owned by Charles Sr. and/or some of his sons, including one in old Wedgeworth and another in old Sawyerville—likely representing lands acquired by Charles McGruder Sr. in 1877, and lands acquired by Charles McGruder Jr. in the following years.

The oral histories present a tension between the different wives and their respective compounds, yet also a sense of solidarity vis-a-vis the outside world. According to Lucille B. Osborne, there was tension or jealousy among the different branches of the Alabama Black McGruders, because each wanted to be favored by Charles McGruder Sr. Additionally, some of Charles McGruder Sr.'s wives were jealous of Rachel Hill because she was legally married to him, had

---

[190] Mr. Will Wedgeworth Among Hale's Model Farmers, *The Marion (Alabama) Times-Standard*, 2 Dec 1891, p. 1, col. 3; digital image *Newspapers,com* (*https://www.newspapers.com/image/319367645/?terms=Wedgeworth&match=1* : accessed 30 Dec 2021).

[191] James D. McGruder was said to look mostly white.

[192] It is possible that some of the stories about Wedgeworth may date to the first decades of the 20th century, rather than to this period. It is also likely that there were several Wedgeworth individuals, over a period of generations, who are the subjects of these various oral history narratives. The narrative of Elmer Brox cautions painting the Wedgeworths in a single light.

benefited most by his acquisition of land in 1877, and received most of his affection.[193]

Charles attempted to visit and mentor his children as often as he could. Lucille Burden Osborne relates that as Charles would ride his grand horse around town, he would frequently gallop to his daughter Minerva's home.[194] After quickly devouring the food she gave him, he would gallop away to some important business matter, or to visit another family member. Until the end of his life, Charles McGruder Sr. was a "man in a hurry."

Charles died sometime between 1900 and 1910, in or around Sawyerville.[195] He left behind a complicated web of relationships—not only with the many women in his life, but also with some of his children. A large and diverse crowd, including many of his children, gathered for his funeral. Lucille B. Osborne reported that an old neighbor of Charles recounted that he was very tall and that the casket purchased for him by his children was too small. Instead of buying a new one, the McGruder sons cut a hole through the end of the casket to let his feet stick out. The sons then wrapped Charles's feet in black cloth. Together, they buried him. Despite Charles's best efforts to establish relationships with his children, one truth remained: he was a father of many, yet a father to few. This is revealed by the gossip of a white woman who attended the funeral: "Old man Charles had so many sons, yet nobody offered to purchase a new casket for him."

Like his large body that could not be contained by a casket, Charles's larger-

---

[193] Nevertheless, according to Anita McGruder McGrew, a descendant of Charles Sr. and Mary May, there are reports of Charles McGruder Sr. having had meetings and/or conjugal visits at his store, where he maintained a cot, with at least some of the other women with whom he had established relationships during enslavement, right to the end of his life, and this too could have been a significant source of tension between the women. Gwen Hubbard, a descendant of Rachel Hill, thinks the story presented by Anita McGruder-McGrew could be about Charles Jr., but not Charles Sr. The rest of the Rachel Hill branch of the family also vehemently reject this story as unconfirmed gossip from the Mary May branch, slanderous against Rachel Hill, and an attack on the integrity of Charles McGruder Sr.

[194] An entry contained in the Archive of Wilmar McGruder provides the following description of Minerva:

> She was a tall, beautiful woman with brown skin and long straight black hair with features of an Indian. She was part Indian and white. She desired to be a schoolteacher but married at an early age. After her husband divorced her, she lost her mind and was unable to raise her youngest daughter, Queen Mary, who was six weeks old. She was a proud black woman!

[195] His name appears on the 1900 census, but not the 1910 census. No death certificate has been located.

than-life personality, ambition, foresight, and determination set him apart from his peers. Charles's vision laid the foundation for his descendants to make rapid economic and educational gains that few of his African-American neighbors were able to match. Whatever conflicted feelings his children had towards Charles, a great number of his children, grandchildren, and great-grandchildren, led by his example, not only entered the middle class but became part of the local black elite. Among them were doctors, lawyers, ministers, scientists, academics, entrepreneurs, and teachers.

The Alabama Black McGruders were inculcated by Charles McGruder Sr. with a deep sense of determination and a drive "to strive for something better." That meant practicing self-development, which for Charles's children meant not only to start and be at the center of businesses and community institutions, but to acquire high levels of education and wealth—not only for themselves, but also in order to be of service to the rest of the Alabama Black McGruders, their communities and the world at large.

Part III

"See that you do not neglect one
of the little ones."

Matthew 18:10

9 – Charles McGruder Sr.'s Known and Potential Children

By J.R. Rothstein, Esq.

Alabama Black McGruder oral history provides that Charles McGruder Sr. was the father of one hundred children. Both Lucille B. Osborne and Anita McGruder report that the common belief within the family was that if one were to meet a black McGruder from anywhere in Alabama, and particularly from Hale and Greene Counties, it was certain they were members of the Alabama Black McGruders.[196] According to Juan McGruder, at least fifty-two of Charles's one hundred children were sons.

An obvious question arises as to whether these oral reports are accurate or exaggerated. It is possible that Charles McGruder Sr. himself never knew exactly how many children he had sired. It is equally possible that Charles developed a system to keep track of his many children and that the number of one hundred, rooted in oral history, is accurate. It is likely that this question will never be satisfactorily answered.

The author is aware of four women with whom Charles had children: Matilda/Matida (surname unknown), Mary May, Mary (surname unknown), and Rachel Hill. Very weak oral history indicates a fifth wife, but her name is unknown. Even assuming the highest known fertility rates for each of these women, we arrive at nowhere near one hundred children, or the one specific oral history account of fifty-two sons. If Charles had one hundred children, then clearly many more women were involved. Both the oral history and the written record are inconclusive as to whether Charles McGruder Sr. was exploited at industrial-level breeding farms, or just sent by his enslavers on a sporadic basis from plantation to plantation as his 'breeding services" were requested.[197]

---

[196] According to Lucille B. Osborne, a newspaper article—which she thinks was in the *Birmingham World News,* though it has not been located—reported that Charles sired some one hundred children. Lucille is not certain that the article mentioned Charles by name. She believes it was published around the end of slavery. Future researchers should survey black newspapers of the era to locate the story.

[197] Sabrina Franklin rejects the entire Alabama Black McGruder oral history that Charles McGruder was a breeder. Franklin argues that if Charles had been a stockman breeder there would have been *explicit* references to these sexual services in the estate documents. Rather,

It is possible that these four or five women represent only the women with whom Charles was able to maintain a connection, and represent his "legitimate" families, as some have called them. Implicit in such a characterization is that there were other women and children who were not recognized as "legitimate," with whom Charles lost contact. It is also possible that Charles's breeding activities were more or less limited to the five wives mentioned, and that the Alabama Black McGruder oral history account that Charles had "one hundred children and fifty-two sons" is an exaggeration and euphemism, employed to convey that Charles had many children with several different women.

We don't know.

As of this writing, Alabama Black McGruder historians have been able to identify approximately 40 children of Charles McGruder Sr., with four or five different women. More may be identified over the coming years. It will be the mandate of the next generation of historians of the Alabama Black McGruders to identify and to document the lives of each of Charles's children.

In addition to relying on evolving DNA technology, future historians of the family could (1) reach out further to the descendants of the *McGruter* family, and to other families with phonetically similar surnames who resided in Sawyerville at the dawn of the 20th century; (2) conduct further DNA testing on the descendants of Pleasant Inge and Mary May Ferrell[198] to determine which of the children may

---

Franklin argues that Charles (and most members of his family) were sent from plantation to plantation due to the estate battles between the Ferrell and Wynne families, and that in each location Charles may have developed casual relationships with women. Franklin argues that the narrative of Charles as a breeder must have developed later to explain or justify his numerous relationships. This position, however, in light of the archival and oral record, is rejected by the author.

[198] According to the 1900 census, Mary Inge (who is thought to be the same as Mary May) had 14 children, 8 of whom were living at the time. According to the 1870, 1880, and 1900 census records combined, Mary had the following "Inge" children: (1) Irene (b. 1854); (2) Cook (b. 1854); (3) Louisa (b. 1856); (4) Susan (b. 1858); (5) Charles (b. 1860); (6) Rufus (b.1862/3); (7) McGruder (b. 1862); (8) Edward (b. 1862); (9) Reese (b. 1864); (10) Jennie (b. 1864); (11) Ried (b. 1865); (12) William (b. 1867/8); (13) Mary (b. 1870); (14) Emma (b. 1871); (15) Alice (b. 1874); (16) Ada (b. 1877); (17) Robert (b. 1895); (18) Willie (Dec 1897); (19) Frank (b. 1899). This list does not include other known children of Mary, which include: (20) Charles McGruder Jr. (b. 1854); (21) James D. McGruder (b. 1866); (22) Emerratte McGruder, all of which are known from other records to have been fathered by Charles McGruder Sr.

The number of these births would make Mary an outlier in terms of modern science regarding fertility. According to the census records, Mary had numerous children during her 50's and early 60's, which is unlikely. In addition, while it is possible she bore two children in a single

have been fathered by Charles; and (3) review the Magruder-Wynne family archive and estate records, located at the University of Alabama, which contains thousands of pieces, including family letters from the 19th century. There is no doubt that much information about the Alabama Black McGruders lies undiscovered in these records; and (4) more thoroughly review the estate records of Salina Ann Wynne Ferrell.

The following is a list of the children of Charles McGruder Sr. known to the Alabama Black McGruders as of this writing:

First Name	Last Name	Mother	DOB
Jeremiah	McGruder	Matilda	1848
Charles Jr.	McGruder	Mary May	1854
Irene	McGruder	Mary May	1857[199]
Dennis	McGruder	Matilda	1857
Duff	McGruder	Matilda	1861
Amos	McGruder	Rachel Hill	1862
Mary Ann	McGruder	Matilda	1862
Samuel	McGruder	Rachel Hill	1864
Rowena	McGruder	Rachel Hill	1864
James	McGruder	Mary May	1865

year, it is unlikely that she twice bore three children in a single year (as shown here for 1854 and possibly 1862). Such a list raises questions as to the accuracy of the oral history narrative that Mary May, Mary Ferrell, and Mary Inge are one and the same person. However, another way of reconciling the oral history with the census, and what is more probable, is that children born in the 1890's are grandchildren, and that some born earlier may be children that Pleasant Inge had with a previous wife. Census records after enslavement often depict blended families, including children without a biological relationship to either parent. DNA testing would need to be conducted on descendants of each of these Inge children to determine which, if any, are descendants of Charles McGruder Sr.

[199] Other dates of birth are given in the records for an Irine: 1854 and 1858.

Julia	McGruder	Rachel Hill	1867
Edmund	McGruder	Rachel Hill	1869
Allen	McGruder	Rachel Hill	1869
Israel	McGruder	Matilda	1869
Wiley	McGruder	Rachel Hill	1871
Mary Ann	McGruder	Rachel Hill	1871
Fed	McGruder	Matilda	1873
Minerva	McGruder	Rachel Hill	1875
William	McGruder	Rachel Hill	1876
Jasper	McGruder	Rachel Hill	1877
Chapin	McGruder	Rachel Hill	1879
Rembert	McGruder	Rachel Hill	1883
Joshua	McGruder	Rachel Hill	1886
Creed	McGruder	Rachel Hill	1888
Paul	McGruder	Rachel Hill	1889
Jonathan	McGruder	Rachel Hill	1890
Emerratte	McGruder	Mary May	
Eva	McGruder	Unknown	
Green	McGruder	Unknown	1857
Elizabeth	McGruder	Unknown	
Wiley	McGruder	Matilda	
Rose	McGruder	Mary	
Martha Anne	McGruder	Mary	
Mary	McGruder	Mary	

Charles McGruder Sr.'s Known and Potential Children

Virginia	McGruder	Mary	

10 – Some Notes on Charles McGruder Jr.

By J.R. Rothstein, Esq.

Deed Index including some purchases by Charles McGruder Sr. and Jr.

According to Anita McGruder McGrew, Charles Jr., like his father, was very concerned with acquiring land and ensuring the development of multi-generational wealth. According to Juan McGruder, after Charles Jr. was emancipated from slavery, he worked on a steamboat as a cook. Later, he was a shoemaker and owned a shop where he performed repairs.[200] In the 1870 census, Charles Magruder Jr. was working as a laborer, yet he reportedly went on to engage in numerous land purchases in the 1870s and 1880s.[201] On January 29, 1885, he married Emmaline Riddle, in Hale County.

According to Kevin McGruder, Charles Jr. saved up the money and purchased a homestead, unlike his father, entirely by himself—without the help of any white relative. However, according to Rev. Orlando McGruder, some white individual

---

[200] Juan McGruder believes it is possible that part of this narrative has been conflated with the experiences of Charles McGruder Sr.

[201] Hale County, Alabama, Probate Court Reverse [Deed] Index, 1896-1918, FHL# 8586678, image#147; digital image FamilySearch.org (https://www.familysearch.org/ark:/61903/3:1:3Q9M-C375-CSML-9?i=146&cat=487823 : accessed 24 Jan 2021)

in Charles McGruder Jr.'s past, possibly a relative, helped him to acquire at least some of his initial land. However, it is likely that Orlando or his source conflated the narratives of father and son. The relatively late acquisition date of Charles McGruder Jr.'s land suggests that Kevin McGruder's narrative is the accurate one. In any event, Charles McGruder Jr. is reported to have acquired at least 300 acres over a period of time, and to have subsequently sold some of the land to his brother, James "Jim" McGruder. Jim McGruder also acquired some land independently, through the Homestead Act of 1902.

According to Juan McGruder, at the end of his life Charles McGruder Jr. lived in a big and beautiful white house with marble pillars, "like the [houses of the] White folks." Anita McGruder McGrew described the house as a mansion with many rooms. Each of Charles's children built their own homes, but the "big house" remained the family's "mansion." Numerous children of Charles lived in the house for a time before staking out their own areas of the compound. Many have reported that the land belonging to Charles McGruder Jr. had a special legal status called "heir property," whereby the land could only be divided among relatives and not sold to third parties.[202]

The home of Charles McGruder Jr. was later destroyed by fire. Dorothy McGruder Edwards relates that it was a fire set by an angry group of white supremacists (most likely the KKK), a story corroborated by Betty McGruder Shaw. Juan McGruder, however, has asserted that it was a naturally occurring fire. Meanwhile, Anita McGruder McGrew remembers the house burning down in or around 1930, but has no knowledge as to its cause.[203]

---

[202] Some of the land belonging to Charles Jr. was subsequently taken by the state through eminent domain. McGruder Crossing is not far from the former town of Wedgeworth, near Robuck Landing, and is marked by a plaque thanking the McGruder family for its contribution of the land to the state.

[203] This story needs further research.

Part IV

It occurred to me

that no matter where I lived,

geography could not save me.

Isabel Wilkerson

The Warmth of Other Suns: The Epic Story of America's Great Migration

11 - From the Darkness of Jim Crow to the Dawn of the Great Migration

By J.R. Rothstein, Esq

During the last years of the life of Charles McGruder Sr., some members of the Alabama Black McGruders began to migrate to other locations within Alabama. By 1900, records show Alabama Black McGruders living in the vicinity of greater Birmingham, contributing to the growth of the city. At the same time, other members of the family, seeking escape from the terror and violence of the Jim Crow South, set their eyes on states such as Kansas, Michigan, Indiana, and Ohio, which offered the dream of economic and racial equality, away from the provincialism of Sawyerville and Hale County.

This chapter will provide a few examples of divergent McGruder experiences during this era.

Lucille McGruder & Her Great Migration

William McGruder (1876-1921), son of Charles McGruder Sr. and Rachel Hill, married the sixteen-year-old Bessie Beatrice Edmonds (Aug 1883-1910)[204] in or

---

[204] Most of what we know about the Edmonds family comes from Catherine Gibbs Robertson's interview with Susie B. Edmonds in the 1960's. Bessie Edmonds, Lucille's mother, was one of 23 children born in Alabama to Thomas Edmonds II (Mar 1839-Dec 1902) and Elizabeth "Lizzie" Hawks (Dec 1845-Nov 13, 1912). According to the 1900 census, Elizabeth Hawks was born in Virginia, as were her parents. According to Catherine Gibbs Robertson, Elizabeth's mother, named Rachel, "was taken away and sold in slave times."

Bessie Edmonds McGruder died at a young age and her sole child, Lucille McGruder, was raised by her sister, Susie B. Edmonds. According to the 1900 census, Bessie's parents, Thomas II and Lizzie, married in 1859 and had six living children. Thomas Edmonds II was said to have been born in Alabama in March 1839, and his parents are said to have born in Virginia. In the 1880 census Thomas was living in Court House district, Tuscaloosa. Lizzie was working as a washer and he as a day laborer. By 1900, Thomas Edmonds and his family had migrated away from Court House and were living in Jefferson County, Alabama.

According to Susie B. Edmonds, Thomas II was said to be the son of Tony and Martha Edmonds. Tony Edmonds was the child of Thomas Edmonds I and a woman named Lucy. Tony was said never to have known his father. Herman English cites a Samuel Edmonds, without any basis, as the father of Thomas II, but in light of Susie B. Edmonds' testimony this is likely inaccurate. The surname is sometimes spelled Edmond.

around 1898. William McGruder and Bessie Beatrice Edmonds were one of three sets of McGruder and Edmonds siblings that married.[205]

According to Lucille Burden Osborne, William was called "Willie" and "old man Will McGruder." Will was also called "Red," because of his ruddy complexion and hair. Will looked like his brothers, Amos and Creed, who were tall, strong-looking, with a tanned complexion, sandy red hair, and greyish or green eyes. Creed was described, in Catherine Gibbs Robertson's McGruder-Edmonds History, as "tall, light, [and] a lady killer."

The couple had a daughter who was born in greater Sawyerville in July 1899. She was named Lucille[206] and affectionately called Lucy or Lilly. According to Catherine Gibbs Robertson, Will's wife, Bessie Beatrice Edmonds, died when Lucille was nine or ten years old. At some point after Bessie's death, due to the precarious financial situation in Sawyerville, Will, along with some of his brothers, left the McGruder Homestead and went to Kansas as migrant workers. The brothers left Sawyerville to earn enough income to sustain the women and children of the McGruder Homestead.[207] As a consequence, Lucille McGruder was left to be raised in Sawyerville by extended members of the Alabama Black McGruders, but also by her Aunt Susan B. Edmonds (1877-1971), also known as Big Mama.

A close childhood cousin and friend of Lucille McGruder was Queen Mary Burge, daughter of Minerva McGruder, granddaughter of Rachel Hill and Charles McGruder Sr. The two became inseparable playmates and companions. The girls

---

[205] Elizabeth Edmonds married Amos McGruder, and, according to Tasha Peace, Julia McGruder married Prince M. Edmonds. By the early 1890s Prince and Julia had migrated to Kansas, where their only child, Earnest Walter Edmonds (called Walter) was born in December of 1894. At some point, Minerva relocated to Kansas and lived with Julia. Walter married Dovie Glenn, and the couple had Prince M. Edmonds, born on August 19, 1921 or 1924, and six more children.

[206] In the 1900 census, Lucille is listed as Lucille Edmonds and her mother, eighteen years-old, as Bessie Edmond. A Green McGruder is listed in the household as a brother-in-law of Bessie.

[207] Lucille Burden Osborne relates that there was some discussion about her Uncle Will leaving. Lucille asked her father where he thought Will had gone and he speculated that Will had gone with his brothers, Amos and Creed, who had migrated to Oklahoma in search of employment. The brothers would then send money back to the family in Sawyerville. After all, the economy in Sawyerville was terrible and there was no work for Will or his brothers locally. It is unclear how long Will worked out of state, but he eventually returned to the McGruder compound. Lucille's father also told her that Will had a paternal relative, Obedia Speed, and they enjoyed talking about their school days together.

were the same age and both had grown up without the presence of a father, though for very different reasons. Queen Mary found Lucille to be a smart, sassy, spunky, funny, confident, and determined woman who said what was on her mind. Both had very light skin and straight or wavy hair. In keeping with the colorism endemic in the beauty standards of the era, both were considered exceptionally beautiful and were sought after by men.

According to Lucille B. Osborne, on one occasion the two girls were chased by a group of boys who were trying to assault them, but the two managed to run home to safety at the McGruder Place. The McGruder men, serious about the obligations of manhood, and the duties, rights, and privileges of family, zealously protected the girls from harm.

It was from this quiet, safe, small-town environment that Lucille McGruder migrated to Birmingham, where she met Nathaniel Robertson. Nathaniel "Manthro" Robertson was born October 7, 1891, in Alabama. He was one of twelve children born to Moses Nathaniel "Mose" Robertson and Bernice W. Johnston, sister of activist Dr. David Johnston of Tuskagee University. Nathaniel is reported to have been charismatic, fun, exceptionally handsome, a ladies' man, and flamboyant in his dress. Nathaniel had a great desire and ambition to be successful and to project success. Perhaps Lucille saw in his ambition a shadow of Charles McGruder Sr.

The two married in April 1917, and their eldest child, Dovie B. Robertson, was born in Birmingham, Alabama, in 1918. She was followed by Nathaniel Moses Robertson Jr. in 1919, and Curtis Bernard Robertson in December 1920.[208] The 1920 census indicates that Nathaniel and Lucille, or "Lucy" as she was recorded, were both literate, owned their own home, and lived together in Birmingham.

Lucille's fortunes, however, would soon take a turn for the worse. In 1921, her father Will, who had years earlier returned from Kansas, died in Sawyerville. A little more than a year later, Nathaniel, whose ambitions in the Jim Crow South did not yield fruit, abandoned the pregnant Lucille and their children, for unknown reasons. According to Catherine Gibbs Robertson, Nathaniel left Lucille on February 7, 1922.[209] This abandonment added to existing intergenerational

---

[208] According to both his birth certificate and oral history, Curtis was born in Gary, Indiana, on December 23, 1920. However, the 1920 census and other sources belie this assertion and indicate that he was born in December 23, 1919/1920 in Birmingham, Alabama. This requires further research. Meanwhile, Susie B. Edmonds is listed as the attending physician on Curtis' birth certificate, which also states that Curtis was named by his mother.

[209] This date was related by Nathaniel to Catherine Robertson. In later years, Nathaniel had regrets about deserting his wife and children and was in correspondence with Catherine.

trauma, the enormous consequences of which can be felt among Nathaniel and Lucille's descendants till this day.

Lucille McGruder was not alone in considering whether to leave home. By February 1922, some one million blacks had left the South, including many Alabama Black McGruders, driven from their homes by the racial violence of hate groups like the KKK, dire poverty, and harsh segregationist laws. In the North they took advantage of the need for industrial workers sparked by the First World War. Many traveled by train, boat or bus, while a smaller number had automobiles or even horse-drawn carts.

The Great Migration, as this phenomenon would come to be called, resulted in the relocation of more than six million African Americans from the rural South to the cities of the North, Midwest, and West from 1916 to 1970. It had a huge impact on urban life in the United States. In the decade between 1910 and 1920 the black population of major northern cities grew by large percentages, including New York (66 percent), Chicago (148 percent), Philadelphia (500 percent), and Detroit (611 percent). Many new arrivals found jobs in factories, slaughterhouses and foundries, where working conditions were arduous and sometimes dangerous. As Northern cities saw their black populations expand exponentially, migrants were forced to deal with poor working conditions and competition for living space, as well as widespread racism and prejudice. Nearly every black family in the South needed to consider whether to remain or go north. Lucille McGruder and her cousins were no exception. They lived this migration and epitomized its experiences.

Deciding to take her future into her own hands, the strong-willed Lucille McGruder ultimately decided to leave Alabama and migrate North, in hopes of creating a better life for herself and her children. However, before leaving, Lucille placed three of her children—Dovie, Nathaniel Jr., and infant Curtis—with her sister-in-law, Dovie Rena Bell Robertson, the younger sister of Nathaniel Robertson Sr.

Lucille left Birmingham and traveled alone to Gary, Indiana, hoping that a new world would also mean a new beginning. In Gary, Lucille initially resided with her aunt, Susie B. Edmonds, who had previously migrated. Thereafter, on September 19, 1922,[210] Richard, her fourth child with Nathaniel Robertson Sr., was born, in Gary. At some point, Lucille returned to Birmingham to recover her infant son, Curtis, and took him to Gary. Lucille left her two eldest children,

---

[210] Some records provide 1923.

Dovie and Nathaniel Jr., behind in Birmingham, with the hope to recover them once she was established up North.

As a single mother, Lucille experienced great hardships raising her children. Sometime around 1923 she partnered with John Anderson, with whom she would later have a daughter, Johnnie Mae. Lucille's union with John Anderson did not last, however, and she eventually returned to Susie B. Edmonds, in Gary, where she settled permanently.

In 1926, in Alabama, Lucille's cousin and childhood friend, Queen Mary Burge Burden, out of love for her cousin, named her new daughter Lucille, in hopes that she would be as sweet, smart, spunky, determined, and sassy as Lucille McGruder, her cousin and childhood friend. Little Lucille would grow up to be the family historian Lucille Burden Osborne.

Back in Gary, Lucille's fortunes did not improve. Working in exceptionally hard, menial, and degrading jobs, she became ill, but remained determined to provide food, shelter, and clothing for her children. Curtis, Lucille's devoted son, recognizing his mother's struggle, did everything he could to assist her, including cooking, cleaning, and household chores. He also helped Lucille take care of his younger siblings, Richard and Johnnie Mae.

One day in the winter of 1927, when Curtis was seven, Richard five, and Johnnie Mae three, Lucille left for work (or acquire food), despite being ill. As she left, she told Curtis to take care of his younger siblings. That evening, however, Lucille did not come home. Lucille McGruder died of lobar pneumonia on October 30, 1927, in Gary, Indiana. She was 27 years old.[211]

An orphan, overlooked for fostering and adoption due to his dark skin and prominent African features, Curtis Bernard Robertson found himself living on the streets of Gary, alone and starving. Far from the world of the McGruder Place in Sawyerville, Curtis vowed to one day become a different kind of man than his father. Carrying around an abandoned and worn-out business briefcase, sleeping in bushes with stray dogs, taking scraps of food from strangers, boy Curtis grasped onto the memory of his mother and her stories of the Alabama Black McGruders. Curtis aspired to one day become a McGruder type of man—one who started and operated businesses, served his community, and most importantly, took care of and provided for his children.

---

[211] According to Michael McGee, both Lucille and her mother Bessie died at the age of 27. When Michael's grandmother, Dovie "Little Dovie" Robertson, was 27 she was very sick, and people thought she was going to die like her mother and grandmother, but she pulled through and lived to an old age.

GRAND FATHER   NATHANIEL ROBERTSON

Nathaniel Robertson Sr. (1891-19??)

Undated photo of Susie B. Edmonds Martin, "Big Mother" or "Big Mama."

Other McGruders in Sawyerville

Back in Sawyerville, life continued for the remaining Alabama Black McGruders. Anita McGruder McGrew doesn't believe the different branches of the family had much communication with one another during the first generation, because they were living in different homesteads. However, subsequent generations, particularly those that remained in Sawyerville, did mingle at school with their cousins who came, as Lucille Burden Osborne characterizes it, "from the other side of the fence," and developed strong bonds with one another.

According to Rev. Orlando McGruder Sr., after Charles Sr. passed away, Jim Crow laws began to take their toll on the economic vitality of the family. According to Betty McGruder Shaw, during the Great Depression multiple branches of the Alabama Black McGruders mortgaged their interest in their land in order to survive. Because these branches jointly owned their land, when the debt of one McGruder came due the entire tribe of McGruders had to bail out the group (or individual) who was unable to pay their debt in order to prevent all the land from being foreclosed upon. Together they rose, and together they would fall.

To keep the land in the family, some of the McGruders coordinated with one another to pay off the mortgages.[212] According to Genie Adele Cooper-Ahanotu, a great-granddaughter of Charles McGruder Sr. via his wife Rachel, Elsee L. Cooper was exceptionally generous in helping the McGruders keep their land by paying others' property taxes for an extended period. He did this to preserve the legacy of Charles McGruder Sr., keep the land in the family, and promote the black ownership of land more generally.[213]

---

[212] Included among the primary documents annexed to this chapter are a selection of legal notices placed on McGruder family land by creditors.

[213] Roena McGruder, daughter of Charles McGruder Sr., married Alfred Cooper. Alfred owned about 160 acres of land, possibly acquired through the Homestead Act. According to Ron Cooper Bey, the land assigned to him was swamp wetlands, considered inferior. Yet Alfred Cooper would figure out how to extract the good from the land and, through his entrepreneurial spirit, raise some of the best ribbon cane in the area. Alfred Cooper was also a veterinarian, able to treat and heal farm animals employing natural and herbal remedies. His healing powers were known county-wide and people from both the white and black communities would call on him to take care of their livestock. Roena was a very religious woman. When she brought Alfred his lunch, she would sing Christian hymns and spirituals. Sometimes she would "catch the spirit" and just start shouting or "speaking in tongues" wherever she was. Roena was very direct and had no problem telling people exactly what was on her mind, though in a respectful manner. Roena and Alfred's son Elsee Cooper Sr. was always family-focused. He worked in the wood industry, and helped his McGruder cousins

Robert Brasfield has provided an explanation for this phenomenon. According to Brasfield, because of a shortage of currency in the region, most were not paid in cash for their labor. Instead, a barter economy developed between blacks and whites. When it came time to pay taxes or make mortgage payments most blacks did not have cash in reserve. Whites from the plantation class benefited from this system because it limited the increase in black land ownership. Poor whites, however, were able to access currency from the plantation class.

Juan McGruder relates that Alabama Black McGruder group solidarity during the Jim Crow era helped shape the future course for many households within the tribe. While other black Sawyerville families became bound to local whites through debt, because the McGruders owned land, took care of each other, exercised group solidarity, and were not sharecroppers, they were free from a whole series of economic challenges faced by others. Most family members did not live in luxury—they often ate rabbits and hunted to survive—but they owned land. This simple fact provided compounding levels of positive impact in the history of the Alabama Black McGruders that can still be felt until today.

Educational Leaders

After the death of Charles McGruder Sr., Rachel relied heavily on her elder son, Amos McGruder, who became the *de facto* head of the Rachel Hill branch of the family and was tasked with helping to educate the next generations of his branch of the Alabama Black McGruders.

Literate, and armed with some of the leadership skills of his father, Amos was the glue that kept the family of Rachel and Charles Sr. together. Amos was respected by his community and known for his humor. Taking Charles McGruder Sr.'s educational mandate seriously, he took it upon himself to instruct the next generation of Alabama Black McGruder children. Sometimes, as part of their lessons in a makeshift school, Amos would entertain the children by going over to the wall of the house, placing his cowboy hat on the ground, and proceeding to stand on his head, allowing the blood to rush to his brain. Amos did this to explain to the children the importance of acquiring an education, and that no matter what one did in life, all of one's blood and energy should go to developing one's mind.

Two other educational leaders of the family during this era also helped

---

keep the family land despite the fact that some were irresponsible in handling their finances. According to Robert Brasfield, some of the Coopers rented land from the McGruders. He would often hear Coopers mention that they needed to go work on their farms at the "McGruder Place." Meanwhile, Etta, Elsee's wife, was a midwife who served both the black and white communities of Sawyerville, sometimes for free.

facilitate the educational and social development of the Alabama Black McGruders. They were Ethew Adolphus McGruder and Rosa Nell McGruder, both from the Mary May branch of the family.

Born on January 27, 1886, to Charles McGruder Jr. and Emmaline Riddle, Ethew Adolphus McGruder was trained in his youth as a brick mason, but through tenacity, hard work, and ambition—plus the support of the entirety of the Alabama Black McGruders—he was able to attend Tuskegee University, where he studied under Dr. Booker T. Washington. Ethew attempted to build upon the educational efforts of Amos, James, Charles McGruder Jr., and others by trying to educate the other Alabama Black McGruders and improve the lot of black people in Sawyerville generally. Despite fierce opposition and interference from racist local whites, Ethew established Wynne Academy in Greensboro, the subject of articles annexed as primary documents to this chapter.

Rosa Nell McGruder was also a teacher at the local "colored school." Unlike those who migrated to Northern cities, Rosa Nell McGruder remained behind in Alabama and attended Miles College in Birmingham. Upon graduation, she returned to Sawyerville to help educate a new generation of Alabama Black McGruder children. She is remembered as someone who loved children, learning, reading, singing and being of service to others.[214]

The Story of Rembert McGruder

The challenges of the era were not entirely economic. After her husband's death, Rachel Hill had a difficult time disciplining some of her younger teenage boys, particularly Rembert. The oral history suggests that Rembert, despite the efforts of his older brother Amos and others, led his younger brother Paul into trouble. On February 28, 1907, *The Greensboro Watchman* published a detailed account of a shootout between local police and these two sons of Charles Sr. and Rachel.[215] The account is as follows:

---

[214] Rosa was most favored by her brothers. She valued her light skin and was afraid to get dark in the sun.

[215] Fight with Desperadoes, *Greensboro (Alabama) Watchman*, 28 February 1907, p. 3, col. 2; digital image *Newspapers,com* (https://www.newspapers.com/image/308321864/?terms=Rembert&match=1 : accessed 2 Oct 2021).

FIGHT WITH DESPERADOES.

On last Friday evening, Feb. 22d, Sheriff Gewin and Mr. Wm. Martin, went to Sawyerville to arrest Rembert McGruder, colored, on the charge of shooting at another negro a few days previous. About dark they located McGruder in the house of his mother two miles north of Sawyerville. Mr. Martin went to the door and after knocking told the parties in the house to open it, as he had a warrant for Rembert McGruder. The only reply to the summons of the officer was the firing of a gun into the door by some one within. Sheriff Gewin then came up and told McGruder not to resist the officers, that the offense with which he was charged was a slight one, and that he could easily make bond; but without replying, fired at the Sheriff. Mr. Gewin told Mr. Martin to remain near the house until he went over to Sawyerville to summon a posse to help him take the man. As he walked off down the road, one of the McGruders stepped into the hallway between the two rooms and fired at him. The Sheriff says he heard the bullet whiz by his head. When the Sheriff returned with several of the citizens of Sawyerville, they were fired upon by those in the house. In the meantime, the Sheriff had sent to Greensboro for Capt. C. C. Gewin, and asked him to bring him a rifle or two and some ammunition. Capt. Gewin secured the weapons and was driven out to the place by Charlie Key, colored, who is in the employ of the sheriff's office. The Captain thought to go to the house and make the arrest, but was stopped by being fired at by those in the house. The posse guarded the house all night, and along towards day the Sheriff and several of the men crept up close to the house and told those within if they did not surrender they would set fire to it and burn them out, but no attention was paid to the proposition but continued to shoot, and the fire was returned. Charlie Key, the colored deputy, was standing at the corner of one of the rooms with his right arm exposed to the view of those in the other room, and some one within shipped a shot gun through a crack in the logs and fired at Key, the whole load entering the arm just below the elbow. He hastily retreated. This drove the posse to desperation, and they gathered up kindling, secured a bottle of kerosene and notified the people within that they proposed to burn the house down over their heads. They lighted the fire, and when the besieged saw that the officers meant what they said, an old woman in the house begged them to put the fire out, and assured them that she would make the boys come out and give up. After parleying a good while, two boys Rembert McGruder, aged 23, and Paul McGruder, aged 18, came out and surrendered. A search of the house revealed the fact that the two negroes were armed with a 38-calibre Colt's pistol, a repeating rifle and a breach-loading shot gun, and that they had exhaused their supply of ammunition, except one cartridge in the pistol and it had been snapped. Besides the two negroes mentioned, there were in the house an old woman, the mother of the prisoners, and a boy about 10 years old, The two McGruders were brought to Greensboro and lodged in jail, where they await the action of the grand jury.

Over a hundred shots were exchanged between the Sheriff's posse and the negroes in the house. It is a marvel that no one was killed.

Charlie Key, the man shot by the McGruders, is in a critical condition, his arm having been amputated.

This was the most daring and defiant action on the part of these men towards the officers of the law that ever occurred in Hale county.

On April 24, 1907, *The Alabama Beacon* reported that in the most recent term of the Hale County Circuit Court, "Paul McGruder, assault with attempt to murder, [was sentenced to] 20 years in the penitentiary. Rembert McGruder same offense, same sentence."[216] *The Greensboro Watchman* of June 2, 1910, provided the following details regarding Paul's fate.[217]

According to Alabama prison records, Rembert was 5'10", had red hair, and yellow eyes. Although the record isn't clear, it appears he died in prison on May 16, 1910, in a fight. The remarks section describes him as "a bad negro." According to Lucille B. Osborne, Rachel was consistently scolding Rembert to behave better. Additionally, Lucille relates that she was told that Paul died after being "struck by a train, or possibly in a mine," and that "the company he was working for at the time offered to compensate the family."[218]

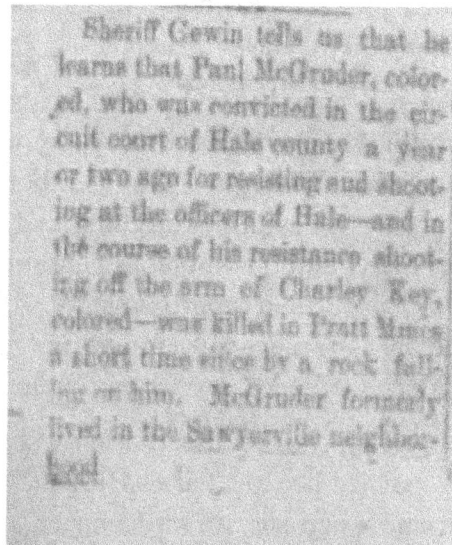

Sheriff Gewin tells us that he learns that Paul McGruder, colored, who was convicted in the circuit court of Hale county a year or two ago for resisting and shooting at the officers of Hale—and in the course of his resistance shooting off the arm of Charley Key, colored—was killed in Pratt Mines a short time since by a rock falling on him. McGruder formerly lived in the Sawyerville neighborhood.

---

[216] Convictions at the Circuit Court, *(Greensboro) Alabama Beacon*, 24 April 1907, p. 2, col, 5; digital image *Newspapers.com* (https://www.newspapers.com/image/253642080/?terms=McGruder&match=1 : accessed 2 Oct 2021).

[217] Death of Paul McGruder, *Greensboro (Alabama) Watchman*, 2 June 1910, p. 3, col. 1; digital image *Newspapers.com* (https://www.newspapers.com/image/308328218/?terms=McGruder&match=1 : accessed 2 Oct 2021).

[218] According to genealogist Robyn N. Smith, "Alabama was one of the worst perpetrators of convict leasing in the decades after the Civil War." (*The Best of Reclaiming Kin: Helpful Tips on Researching Your Roots*, 2015. p39). Paul and Rembert McGruder were convicted of serious crimes, but thousands more served long terms of forced labor for petty crimes, or simply for being unable to pay a fine. Alabama counties signed contracts with plantations, lumber camps, and coal mines to provide a steady source of labor, and sheriffs were paid for delivering prisoners. This practice—which has not entirely disappeared—is often described as the beginning of industrial slavery. See Douglas A. Blackmon's *Slavery by Another Name: The Re-Enslavement of Black Americans from the Civil War to World War II* (New York: Doubleday, 2008). In 2012, this Pulitzer Prize-winning book was adapted into a PBS documentary of the same name.

The Last Days of Rachel Hill

According to Lucille B. Osborne, Rachel lived most of her life in the vicinity of Sawyerville, in the house that her son Amos had built for her. Rachel was a very structured person with a strict daily routine. After Charles McGruder Sr. died, Minerva, his daughter, lived in an adjacent plot of land, and looked after Rachel, although Rachel remained independent, taking care of her garden and chickens till the day she died.

Later, Minerva McGruder's husband, Noah Burge, abandoned Minerva and "her mind snapped." According to Gwendolyn Hubbard, Noah then sought to take Queen Mary (Minerva's daughter, born 1900) with him, but Rachel begged him to leave the child with her, arguing that if he took the child from Minerva, it would make her condition worse. Rachel promised to care for the child, and it was thus that Rachel, then approximately fifty-five, undertook care of her daughter, Minerva McGruder Burge, and her granddaughter, Queen Mary Burge, cousin-friend to Lucille McGruder and future mother to Lucille Burden.[219]

According to Lucille Burden Osborne, Rachel helped raise Queen Mary and later married her to Charles Burden. Mr. Burden asked for Queen Mary's hand in marriage when she was a teenager, and Rachel told him he would have to wait until Queen Mary finished her high school education and turned nineteen. They married in 1919, a month after Queen Mary's nineteenth birthday, and the couple moved away from the vicinity where Rachel lived. Their union produced four children, the fourth of which was Lucille Burden.[220] Lucille and her half-sister Geneva Gibbs Wesley,[221] recall that during the summer Queen Mary would return to Sawyerville and live with her mother Minerva and grandmother Rachel.

During those summers, four generations of strong women lived in the same house and many stories were transmitted to Lucille and Geneva. Lucille recalls that despite having no father, she felt loved because everyone around her was a relative and took care of her. Many of the McGruder men eagerly assumed responsibility for Lucille and Geneva and strived to be a father figure to them—and any other McGruder child in need of affection. Lucille recalls picking

---

[219] The picture below is believed to be of Queen Mary Burge, with either her grandmother, Rachel Hill McGruder, or her mother, Minerva McGruder Burge. Minerva would have been around 28 or 29 when Queen Mary was born and the woman in this picture is much older, so it's more likely a photo of Rachel Hill and Queen Mary. This photo was given to the family by a Mrs. Cunningham of Long Beach, California, who was a granddaughter of Rachel's brother, Nathan Hill.

[220] Some family members chose to spell the name *Burton*.

[221] Queen Mary's second married name was Gibbs.

vegetables with her family, bringing them over to the river to wash, and then cooking what they had harvested on an old-fashioned stove. At all times, Lucille felt safe and protected by those McGruder men around her. Yet, at the same time, Rachel, Minerva, and Queen Mary struggled to make ends meet and pay the taxes on their land. They craved the presence of a primary male financial provider in their lives, absent since the death of Charles McGruder Sr.

Lucille and Geneva describe Rachel as a pious and devout Christian woman who sat in her rocking chair reading the Bible and singing hymns.[222] She rarely, if ever, left her home, and was very protective of her private space. Lucille recalls playing around Rachel, sometimes blocking the view of her Bible. Rachel would then say, "Get out of my rout, grandbaby."[223] Every Sunday, Rachel, her daughter Minerva, granddaughter Queen Mary, and great-granddaughter Lucille would walk together to Liberty African CME Church. At Liberty, a church founded by freed slaves, including the Alabama Black McGruders, the various branches of the McGruder family would socialize with one another. Despite the many challenges of the day, faith and God remained the center of a vibrant McGruder family and community life, as well as a key to their survival—just as it had been for Charles McGruder Sr. and Rachel Hill during enslavement.

Geneva Gibbs Wesley reported that "Grandma Rachel was tall, slim, with black hair that she could sit on.[224] She was very religious and born a slave. She raised Queen Mary until she was eighteen years old. Grandma Rachel was a distant person who allowed few people to get to know her. She was aloof and didn't like a lot of people coming around the house." Lucille Burden Osborne recalls that whenever she asked Rachel about the era of slavery, she would "clam up" and refuse to talk about those times. Lucille was told that she "didn't need to know about slavery," and to stop asking questions about Rachel's experiences during enslavement.[225]

---

[222] Lucille B. Osborne recalls that "every family had a Bible where weddings, births, and deaths were recorded. I saw Rachel's Bible." The Bible was reportedly destroyed and lost to history.

[223] Local dialect for "view" or "way."

[224] However, the surviving photograph shows a woman with short hair.

[225] Though her parents and grandparents generally refused to talk about their experiences during slavery, Lucille, who was particularly curious and inquisitive, made an effort to gather these stories as a child.

*A photo believed to be Rachel Hill McGruder
and her granddaughter, Queen Mary Burge, circa 1902.
Courtesy of Geneva Gibbs Wesley.*

Queen Mary Burton-Gibbs. Courtesy Lucille B. Osborne.
Date and location unknown.

During the last decades of Rachel's life, the economic situation in Sawyerville worsened due to the increased use of machinery and the racism of Jim Crow. In the first two decades of the twentieth century, the men of the McGruder family scattered across the South and Midwest in search of work and new financial opportunities. The women—like Rachel and her daughters—most often remained behind, alone for extended periods with young children. This put stress on the integrity of the family unit. By the 1930s, however, the Great Migration was in full swing and many of the remaining McGruders, this time both men women, abandoned Sawyerville and its environs for opportunities in the North or the big cities of Alabama. Thus, in this context, did many members of the family bid Rachel farewell.

Betty McGruder Shaw, speaking of her personal experiences decades later, spoke of a fantasy held by many Alabama Black McGruders residing in Sawyerville that a promised land existed in the North, free of racism and ripe with opportunity.[226] According to Lucille B. Osborne, having been born enslaved, Rachel wanted her children to maximize their potential even if that meant that they leave Sawyerville. Despite all the hardships she had suffered in her life, she remained persistent and determined to build a respectable life for herself and children.

Like Charles, Rachel above all valued literacy. She pushed her children and grandchildren to succeed in school. Rachel also instructed them to aspire to become people of meticulous excellence in every endeavor they undertook. Unlike Charles, who had gone from place to place and plantation to plantation, Rachel stayed near Sawyerville for the duration of her life never experiencing other parts of the world. While Rachel desired to travel and see more of the world, she never had the opportunity. As a result, she always encouraged her children to leave Alabama and travel the world, to expand their horizons and see new wonders, to seize life and all the financial and educational opportunities formerly enslaved people never had—in short, to take advantage of all the good and godly experiences life has to offer.

Rachel Hill died on January 17, 1935, knowing that most of her children and grandchildren were building a future in the promised lands of the North or Midwest—under the warmth of other suns.

---

[226] Betty Shaw, like many of the Alabama Black McGruders, left the south with great hope, but met the harsh reality that racism was fully operative north of the Mason-Dixon line.

The Last McGruders in Sawyerville

Despite the failings of Rembert, the McGruders overall had a good local reputation throughout the Reconstruction and Jim Crow eras, which has endured into modern times.

> CHAS. McGRUDER, Sr., Heirs—
> W ½ of SE ¼ Sec. 13 Tp. 21 R. 3;
> E ½ of SW ¼ Sec. 13 Tp. 21 R. 3·
> NW ¼ of NE ¼ Sec. 24 Tp. 21 R. 3:
> NE ¼ of NW ¼ Sec. 24 Tp. 21 R. 3.
> MRS M C SCOTT

Location of lands belonging to the heirs of Charles McGruder Sr..[227]

This is what may have led Jonathan May, a white resident of Sawyerville and a local historian, to recount that, "When I was young, some 70 years ago, I had the sense that, at the time, the McGruders were thought to be 'too full of themselves' by *both* whites and local Blacks; and those whites, including my own parents, considered the McGruders to be 'superior' to most of the other blacks in the area. But my own sense was also that the attitude of the [McGruder] family might well have been justified."[228] Today, Sawyerville is economically depressed, there are few jobs, and few members of the family have remained. As of 2022, the overwhelming majority of the Alabama Black McGruders have made their homes elsewhere. The few family members who remain have the distinction of being the oldest landowners in the area, maintaining the tradition started by Charles McGruder Sr. One historical McGruder property, originally purchased by Charles McGruder Jr., remains in the family, at 340 McGruder Road, Sawyerville, Alabama, 36776.[229] Currently home to Juan McGruder, the land is owned in a trust by members of Charles McGruder Jr.'s branch of the family.

---

[227] Delinquent Tax Sale, including land owned by heirs of Charles McGruder Sr., *Greensboro (Alabama) Watchman*, 22 November 1934, p. 4, col. 3; digital image *Newspapers,com* (https://www.newspapers.com/image/538107789/?terms=McGruder&match=1 : accessed 2 Oct 2021).

[228] According to Jonathan May, "The McGruder lands [when I was a child] were on the outer reaches of what would be considered Sawyerville, a good five miles away, serious distance during the 1940s, and my main contact with them was when they came into my father's post office."

[229] It is reported that the road itself was named for Jim McGruder.

In recent years, Marie McGruder has returned to the McGruder Homestead owned by Charles McGruder Jr., and has established McGruder Farms LLC, located next to the home of Juan McGruder, at 338 McGruder Road, with the aspiration of creating a new chapter of Alabama Black McGruder history in Sawyerville.

The Alabama Black McGruder Legacy

According to Lucille B. Osborne, the story of Charles McGruder Sr. and the Alabama Black McGruders is a painful history which his children and descendants have worked hard to turn into a positive legacy.

Lucille urges the next generation of the Alabama Black McGruders to do better than the generation before them, saying, "Look at the legacy you have. If we made it through here, then you [the next generation] can do even better." Juan McGruder recounts that the family ethic was to love and support one another, and to respect everyone.

Despite internal differences between the wives and their children in the first generation, subsequent generations came together in unity, particularly at school. Members of the Alabama Black McGruders established, and continue to establish, broad networks to assist one another. As Juan McGruder says, they believed, and continue to believe, that if they stuck together, "nobody could break them" and "nobody could get to you." Their common blood was, and is, thicker than water.

Part V

Timeline of the Lives of Ned, Mariah, & Charles Magruder Sr.

By J.R. Rothstein, Esq.

August 1619	"20 and odd Negroes" are brought ashore from the White Lion, a Dutch man-o-war, in the Colony of Virginia. This is one of the first records of enslaved Africans in the colonies of the British Empire in North America.
17th or 18th century	The ancestors of the mother of Ned Magruder are kidnapped and trafficked from Africa, likely via the West Indies, to one of the colonies of British North America.
1744	Ninian Offutt Magruder, a white man, son of John Magruder and Jane Offutt, is born in Prince George's County in the Colony of Maryland.
April 19, 1775	A rebellion begins with the exchange of gunfire between British troops and colonists at Lexington and Concord in the Colony of Massachusetts.
July 4, 1776	The Declaration of Independence is adopted by 13 British North American colonies, claiming independence from the British Empire, condemning monarchial rule, and asserting "that all men are created equal, that they are endowed by their Creator with certain unalienable Rights."
Summer 1776	The military forces of Great Britain mobilize to crush the colonial rebellion and commence invasion of the newly formed nation calling itself the United States of America.

Circa 1778	Ninian Offutt Magruder takes the Patriot's Oath in Montgomery County, Maryland, to fight for freedom from British rule.
September 3, 1783	The Treaty of Paris ends what comes to be known as the American Revolution. Great Britain recognizes the United States, the first republic formed in over two thousand years.
1782-1783	Ninian Offutt Magruder, along with his cousin, Ninian Beall Magruder, migrates to Georgia to settle land granted to him by the new country. It is probable that during this period he enslaves an unknown woman who would one day give birth to Ned Magruder, the patriarch of the Alabama Black McGruders
Circa 1785	Eleanor Magruder, daughter of Ninian O. Magruder, is born in Columbia County, Georgia.
May 1787	The Constitutional Convention meets in Philadelphia with delegates from thirteen states, the former colonies of the British Empire, to draft a constitution to govern the new nation. The delegates are divided between Northern and Southern states over slavery. The division threatens to derail the convention and ultimately the experiment of self-government embodied by the new republic.
June 1787	Charles Pinckney of South Carolina proposes the Three-Fifths Compromise, providing that three-fifths of each state's enslaved population will count towards that state's total population for the purpose of apportioning the House of Representatives. The compromise is adopted by the majority of the delegates.
1795	Birth of Ned Magruder in Columbia County, Georgia, to Ninian O. Magruder and an unknown enslaved woman.

Timeline of the Lives of Ned, Mariah, and Charles Magruder Sr.

1800	Birth of Mariah, future wife of Ned Magruder, in Georgia.
March 3, 1803	Ninian O. Magruder dies in Georgia. He wills Ned to his youngest daughter, Eleanor Magruder. He wills Mariah to his son Archibald Magruder.
December 17, 1803	Eleanor marries Williamson Wynne in Columbia County, Georgia. Williamson in effect becomes the new enslaver of Ned Magruder.
Circa 1819	Ned Magruder (re)unites with Mariah and the two marry.
Circa 1819	The white Wynne and black Magruder families move from Columbia County, Georgia, to Greene County, Alabama. They establish Wynnewood, a plantation near Hollow Square, now Sawyerville, Alabama.
1823	Salina Ann Wynne, daughter of Eleanor Magruder Wynne and Williamson Wynne, is born at Wynnewood.
January 26, 1829	Osmun Appling Wynne, son of Eleanor Magruder Wynne, marries Frances Laura Anderson.
April 1829	Williamson Wynne dies intestate at Wynnewood, Greene County, Alabama.
May 11, 1829	The court orders an appraisal of Williamson Wynne's property. Ned is appraised at $500, and Mariah at $350.
Late May 1829	Charles Magruder is born to Ned and Mariah Magruder at Wynnewood, Greene County, Alabama.
January 8, 1830	Ned, Mariah, and their three children—Fanny, Martha, and Charles—are sold at a public auction of Williamson Wynne's Estate. They are redeemed by Eleanor Magruder Wynne.

August 1831	Nat Turner leads a rebellion against enslavement.
December 7, 1832	William Appling Wynne is born to Osmun A. Wynne and Frances Laura Anderson Wynne at Wynnewood, Greene County, Alabama.
1832	Jasper Magruder, sibling to Charles, is born to Ned and Mariah Magruder at Wynnewood, Greene County, Alabama.
April 1835	Mary May, future wife of Charles Magruder, is born in South Carolina.
October 14, 1839	Salina Ann Wynne marries William A. Ferrell at Wynnewood
Circa 1839	Archibald Magruder, brother of Eleanor Magruder and former owner of Mariah, dies.
March 1845	Rachel Hill, future wife of Charles Magruder, is born in Virginia or Alabama.
June 1849	Jeremiah Magruder is born to Charles Magruder and Matilda (surname unknown). This is the first record we have of a child of Charles.
July 1849	Eleanor Magruder Wynne dies at Wynnewood.
July 1849	Eleanor Magruder Wynne wills Ned, Mariah, Charles, and the rest of the black Magruder family to her daughter, Salina Ann Wynne Ferrell, effectively placing them under the control of Salina's husband, William A. Ferrell. However, the will remains in probate for almost four years.
Winter 1853	Ned Magruder dies.

Timeline of the Lives of Ned, Mariah, and Charles Magruder Sr.

April 11,1853	Mariah Magruder is appraised for the purposes of settling the estate of Eleanor Magruder Wynne.
Circa 1853	This year marks the likely beginning of Charles Magruder's activities as a breeder of enslaved people.
Circa 1853	Mary May couples with Charles Magruder Sr.
1854	Mary May gives birth to Charles Magruder Jr.
1852-1854	Some of Eleanor Magruder Wynne's children, led by Erasmus Wynne, migrate West with their enslaved people, and establish the town of Wynnewood, Texas.
Circa 1855	Salina Ann Wynne Ferrell initiates a divorce from William A. Ferrell, sparking a legal battle that will rage for years.
March 6, 1857	At the peak of Charles's breeding activities, the United States Supreme Court, in *Dred Scott v. Sanford*, rules that, as a slave, Dred Scott, was a piece of property having none of the legal rights or recognitions afforded to a "person." The decision is condemned in Northern states, but praised in the South.
Spring & Summer 1859	Both Salina Ann Wynne and William A. Ferrell die, complicating ongoing legal proceedings arising from their divorce.
1859	Charles Magruder Sr. is appraised at a value of $1,500.
October 1859	John Brown, a white Christian abolitionist, raids Harpers Ferry, in what is then Virginia, hoping to spark a holy war to free enslaved people.

November 6, 1860	Abraham Lincoln is elected President with a mandate to complete the unfinished work of the American Revolution and end the institution of slavery.
December 1860	South Carolina secedes from the United States.
January 11, 1861	Alabama secedes from the United States.
Circa 1861	Charles McGruder Sr. and Rachel Hill couple.
February 8, 1861	The Confederate States of America declare independence. Alexander H. Stephen is appointed Vice President and declares that the cornerstone value of the new nation "rests upon the great truth that the negro is not equal to the white man; that slavery, subordination to the superior race, is his natural and normal condition."
1860-1865	O.A. Wynne rents the labor of Charles Magruder Sr. and his family to a number of local planters, particularly A.J. Mayfield, administrator of William A. Ferrell's estate.
January 1, 1863	President Abraham Lincoln signs the Emancipation Proclamation, declaring "that all persons held as slaves within said designated States, and parts of States, are, and henceforward shall be free." The proclamation does not apply to slave states that are not in rebellion.
January 16, 1865	General William Tecumseh Sherman issues Special Field Order No. 15, confiscating Confederate land, and orders that "40 acres and a mule" be given to thousands of Black families as reparations for enslavement.

Timeline of the Lives of Ned, Mariah, and Charles Magruder Sr.

April 15, 1865	Abraham Lincoln is assassinated. Sherman's Special Field Order No. 15 is retracted.
June 19, 1865	The last enslaved people are freed in Texas.
1865	The Reconstruction era begins in Alabama.
Circa 1865	Charles Magruder Sr. claims some of his many children and "wives" and establishes a homestead.
1866	Mariah Magruder, matriarch of the Alabama Black McGruders, is enumerated in the Alabama state census of the colored population. She is living with her son, Charles Magruder Sr., in Greene County, Alabama.
June 13, 1866	Congress passes the 14th Amendment to the Constitution, extending the rights and liberties granted by the Bill of Rights to formerly enslaved people.
1867	Congress passes the Reconstruction Act of 1867, codifying the policies of Radical Reconstruction. Alabama, along with other Southern states, refuses to ratify the 14th Amendment and is placed under military occupation.
Spring 1867	Charles Magruder Sr. commences his civil rights work, leading a group of black men to register to vote.
Spring 1867	The Alabama Black McGruders and other African-Americans elect James K. Greene, a formerly enslaved man, to the state legislature.
1868	The Ku Klux Klan is established in response to black economic and political advancement.
April 23, 1869	Mary May, former wife of Charles Magruder Sr., marries Pleasant Inge.

March 31, 1870	James Martin, a prominent Aalabama black Republican activist, and Alexander Boyd, a white civil rights activist and ally of Martin, are murdered by the Ku Klux Klan. Martin's murder is never investigated. Boyd's murder, which took place in Eutaw, is investigated but leads to no convictions.
July 8, 1870	Mariah Magruder is 70 years old. She lives independently in Hale County, next to her son, Jasper and her daughter, Lilly.
October 25, 1870	In the courthouse square of Eutaw, Ku Klux Klan members attack a civil rights rally of 2,000 black citizens, which likely include members of the Alabama Black McGruders, killing at least four and wounding 54 in an act of voter intimidation.
1870	Charles Magruder Sr. is sharecropping, renting about 150 acres of land and two log cabins from the estate of Salina Ann Wynne Ferrell for $200.
February 1871	The Ku Klux Klan marches through Hollow Square, home of the Alabama Black McGruders, on their way to raid Greensboro.
1875	Despite voter intimidation, Charles Magruder and other Alabama Black McGruders register to vote.
1865-1876	1,982 African-Americans are lynched throughout the South.
November 7, 1876	Republican President Rutherford B. Hayes is narrowly elected President, after campaigning for equal rights for black people.

Timeline of the Lives of Ned, Mariah,and Charles Magruder Sr.

December 1876	Democrats and Southerners contest the presidential election results, raising fears across the nation of a second civil war.
January 29, 1877	President Ulysses S. Grant signs the Electoral Commission Act, setting up a commission of eight Republicans and seven Democrats to settle the disputed 1876 election.
Circa 1877	Charles Magruder Sr. meets with Osmun Appling Wynne about purchasing land. O.A. Wynne assists Charles in some manner in the endeavor.
Early February 1877	The Reconstruction era ends with the Compromise of 1877, mandating the end of military occupation of the South by federal troops. The act is viewed by the Alabama Black McGruders and other southern blacks as a grand act of betrayal by the federal government and an abandonment of the promises of Reconstruction.
February 17, 1877	Osmun Appling Wynne, son of Williamson Wynne and Eleanor Magruder Wynne, dies.
November 6, 1877	Charles and Rachel Magruder, and some of their children, purchase 240 acres of land for the sum of $1,500.
November 12, 1877	The Liberty African CME Church is established in Sawyerville, Alabama, as an outgrowth of an earlier quasi-integrated CME Church.
Mid to Late 1877	The United States federal government begins to withdraw the last troops from the South, thereby initiating the Jim Crow era.
Late 1870's	In an act of independence, Charles Magruder Sr. adopts the spelling of his surname as *McGruder*, thereby establishing the Alabama Black McGruders.

1880	Mariah McGruder is 80 years old, living with her daughter, Lilly Ellis, in Hale County, Alabama. This is the last record we have of her life.
July 2, 1881	Republican President James Garfield, a strong advocate for black civil rights, is assassinated.
1881 – 1896	Jim Crow laws predominate throughout the South, while KKK membership expands exponentially and lynchings continue.
April 13, 1896	U.S. Supreme Court rules in *Plessy v. Ferguson* that as long as segregated facilities are equal in quality, black Americans can be served separately from white Americans.
Circa 1900-1910	Charles McGruder Sr. dies.
Circa 1917	Ethew A. McGruder, son of Charles McGruder Jr., grandson of Charles McGruder Sr., and student of Booker T. Washington, establishes the Wynne Academy, a school for "colored" children.
Date Unknown	Matilda dies.
Date Unknown	Mary May dies.
January 17, 1935	Rachel Hill dies.

Timeline of the Lives of Ned, Mariah,and Charles Magruder Sr.

Part VI

Do we not all have one Father?

Did not one God create us?

Why do we profane...our ancestors by

being unfaithful to one another?

Malachi 2:10

Letters Between Black & White McGruders & Magruders

a.   <u>Letter from Lucille Burden Osborne</u>

Dear McGruder Family,

I am so privileged to be a member of this unique clan. I agree whole heartedly with what Marie has so eloquently written and Juan has expressed so spiritually.[230]

There is much for which I am grateful. Never in my ninety-five years did I think I'd have the opportunity to address the white Magruders in a letter of this kind.

I hold no animosity in my heart toward any member of their family. I am grateful to them for keeping Ned and Mariah in a cohesive family group that would eventually become my forbears. I'm grateful to Charles and Rachel for becoming my great-grandparents and keeping their sixteen children together.

Let us not forget that God was watching over us through it all and He's still in our corner. This means we can now concede what the DNA has proven—that we're connected forever.

Much love,

Aunt Lucille

---

[230] *See infra.*

b.   **Letter from a White Magruder to the Alabama Black McGruders**

Dear Alabama Black McGruders,

I am Jill Magruder, descended from the Scottish immigrant. Alexander. and his sons and grandsons, who farmed tobacco in Maryland, and their descendants, who fought in the Revolutionary War and later in the Civil War (on the wrong side). My line of Magruders moved west to Texas; my dad was born in El Paso and I live in Albuquerque, New Mexico.

For many years, I have corresponded with a number of African-American genealogists, some of whom had oral histories passed down from their family elders mentioning a white Magruder slave owner in the mix, possibly even as their ancestor. I contacted many other folks I found during my research, who I thought might be able to help us trace these stories. Some—Black AND White— outright denied any possibility of such a history and, understandably, many didn't want to talk about it.

I was excited and astonished to learn about you all and your amazing family history. While I descend from a different branch of Magruders, one that diverged from Ninian Offutt Magruder's line long ago, I know—through the magic of DNA—that I am your blood kin. The Y-DNA of Alabama Black McGruder men perfectly matches the Y-DNA of my white Magruder brother.

We know that at least one enslaved woman produced children by a white Magruder slaveowner. (We know his name, but we will probably never know hers.) We cannot deny or sweep this painful history under the rug, and it should not be romanticized. It is important that the truth be told, and I really appreciate the research, documentation, and meticulous oral history that went into bringing this history to life in this book. Thank God these stories survived.

Our intertwined history is a complicated one. Together, we are proof of an appalling period in American history. Your ancestors endured the unspeakable cruelties of enslavement and families torn apart. As a white Magruder, I grew up hearing an air-brushed version of my family history that included "Confederate heroes." It is difficult to reconcile these alternate historical perspectives in what is now one big family. I just know that this has been an eye-opening journey for me and I am honored to meet the Alabama McGruders.

Reading this account makes me admire even more your strength, resilience, and love of family. I am humbled and touched to be accepted by some of you as part of your family. The way I see it is that we can't change the past; rather, we must learn from it. We still have a lot of healing to do today and I hope we can do that together to make the future better for all our descendants.

Love,

Cousin Jill

c. **Letter from an Alabama Black McGruder to All Magruders/McGruders, White and Black**

Dear family:

Thank you to this team of storytellers, writers, editors, and supporters who, through hours of research & dedication, present our family story, which is the true American story, a woven tapestry of documented fact, legacy, legends, and personal accounts from our elders.

To my white & black Magruder/McGruder family (through genetic heritage and/or Magruder family affiliation), what we cannot do is change the very complex, painful, and stained past of our forefathers. What we can do is decide what we will do with our shared story, how we heal from wounds of the past that still plague our society today, and walk together into our future with love, empathy, and a commitment to connect and celebrate the beauty in the racially, ethnically, and culturally diverse family that is today's Magruder/McGruder Tribe. We each have a larger-than-life responsibility to bring our ancestors into our today with dignity and honor, and we each take the delicate handoff of the torch from our ancestors, forward into the hands of generations to come. So, let us be the model of humanity and "…be the change you want to see happen."

I look forward to the day when we have the opportunity to come together as one big family on the Alabama Black McGruder Homestead.

I love you all,

Marie A. McGruder

d.   **Letter from a White Magruder to the Alabama Black McGruders**

Dear Black McGruders,

I am so grateful to be part of this project, discovering the extraordinary resilience of generations of Alabama Black McGruders, and the dedication, curiosity, and moral courage of those who have gathered and preserved the family story. I will always be thankful to J.R. Rothstein for inviting me into the fold.

I was raised in a white Maryland family with such a strong Magruder and Scottish-American identity that I sometimes call myself, only half-jokingly, an eleventh-generation immigrant. Whatever its faults, that upbringing taught me to see connection rather than isolation, and family as a microcosm of history. As a poet and professor, I have always used the personal as an instrument for gaining entry into historical and political subjects, revealing their complexity and endless variety.

In the 1990s, I began work on a hybrid book of history and poetry called *Trafficke*, tracing my mother's Magruder family through Scotland and Maryland over several hundred years. It was during the research for *Trafficke* that I first discovered—or, more accurately, allowed myself to see—how deeply my family had been involved in slavery, and how complicit I had been in the silence surrounding that fact. Acknowledging the truth of our past meant learning to see myself not only as an inheritor of a violent and exploitive history, but also as a beneficiary of a violent and exploitive present.

I have come to believe that there is no right way for a descendant of enslavers to write about slavery, and there is no right way to be silent. All there is is to do whatever work falls to me, to contribute what my background and professional skills can provide.

And so, in 2011, I launched *Magruder's Landing*, a website *where all are welcome to come ashore*, as the subtitle says. One function of the site is to publish information from archival sources about families and individuals enslaved by Magruders, hoping that African-Americans seeking their ancestors might find some helpful detail, some missing name, anything to push their search onward.

That's where J.R. found me, and how I came to the great honor of editing this manuscript and learning your stories. Working on this project helps me set aside the anger and bitterness I feel toward my ancestors and to dwell instead in our shared present, with hope for a future of respect and forgiveness, grounded in historical truth.

What a huge, complicated tribe we are, an image of the messy, painful, yet hopeful business of being American. Thank you for preserving memory and doing the work that pushes us all just a little bit closer to justice.

With love to all,

Susan Tichy

e.   **<u>Letter from a Black McGruder to All McGruders and Magruders</u>**

To my Magruder/McGruder Family,

The only person who thinks it is important to be a McGruder/Magruder is another McGruder/Magruder—just as a Smith or a Jones is as important to his family members as we are to ours. The only true difference between us is the way we treat each other. God wants us all to lovingly treat each other as human beings. Showing general respect towards each other is how we know that we love one another.

A lot of the times when bad things happen in our lives, God is allowing us to be tested so that we can find out who He (God) is. In the past, and today, God is testing white and black McGruder/Magruders about how we will treat one another. Just as with our ancestors, God is interested in our soul and not our body. Our soul is neither black nor white, male nor female.

We are truly thankful for the gift of love that we are capable of showing, one for another. May God help us to be a living instrument to show man who God is. As Christians, if we know God, and we know what God wants, and we do not tell others about our knowledge of God, then we are not doing the will of God. And our salvation is for naught. We are directed to love our fellow human, black and white, and we are to help lead others to God and his love.

I love you in the Name of Jesus Christ,

Juan McGruder

f.   Letter from a White Magruder to the Black McGruders

Dear McGruders,

Thank you for maintaining this collective family history, sharing it with the rest of us, and with the world. This family story is a story of one arc of our country's history. People who are not Magruders will also see elements of their family experiences in our family's experience. There is often not enough information for black people to know so much detail about their family histories, and what you have accomplished here is tremendous for so many reasons.

I have been learning more of my family history in recent years. I have always known I am Scottish, due to more recent grandparents, but have found also that I am descended from a different descendant of Alexander, the Immigrant, than your branch, one who sought their fortune in the wilds of Kentucky. I did not know very much about the Magruder part of my family, and am excited for our shared common ancestry, humbled by how our family story is such a deeply American story. I want to continue to learn about the experiences and stories of black Magruders and McGruders. Families like ours, and the new generations that we are, get to decide what comes next. Every day we are alive is a day in which we have the power to decide. Armed with knowledge and so much inspiration (thanks to you all and the team that put together this publication), we are inevitably moving into a new direction together. While the publication of this book is the culmination of much work and the collection of oral history by many people over years, I hope it is also a beginning of a new era of our family.

Kind regards,

Katea Ravega

g.   **Letter from a Black McGruder to All McGruders and Magruders**

Dear McGruders and Magruders,

One might argue successfully that the effort undertaken to put into written form centuries of information has been a great faith journey. The journey began ignobly, and perhaps unbeknownst to its earliest progenitors. It meandered through states, places, and people in unplanned ways that required faith and hope in even modest amounts in order to persevere. And persevere it did. Family members dared to cling to faith and hope of a better tomorrow—even when all they could see was utter darkness. Year by year they were rewarded with short-lived glimpses of the light reinforcing hope of that better tomorrow. Without those glimmers of light, neither this book nor the lives portrayed within would have existed.

Just as the holy scriptures are replete with accounts of struggle by people who maintained a measure of faith and hope, despite many twists, turns, and downright hardships experienced, those whom God called His have always survived and moved forward. No, not all of them, but at least a remnant. Our family history is replete with similar incidences and yet we, the family, exist today and continue moving forward. And now, in this time and space, a loving reach across racial, economic, and cultural lines has become our new reality as we move forward and reconcile the past and present in hopes of an ever-brighter future. After all, it has been said by one much more erudite than I, "You can't really know where you are going until you know where you have been." (Maya Angelou) Knowing our roots is important to shaping our future.

                                            Reverend Orlando McGruder

h.   Letter from a White Magruder to All McGruders and Magruders

When I was growing up in Santa Cruz, California, I didn't realize there were many black Magruders/McGruders. I knew vaguely that I had Scottish ancestry, but beyond my immediate family and my Magruder uncles living with their families in Seattle and Japan, I didn't know many other Magruders at all. But as I got older, and more curious about my ancestry, I began to learn more about how the Magruder story is woven into the broader American story, a journey of learning and connection I'm still in the early stages of today.

In America, we're often reluctant to discuss or acknowledge the complexities of the painful and unjust moments from our history and, in the process, we lose the ability to learn, to heal, and to connect in ways that are long overdue. In the spring of 2018, my wife—whose family hails from Georgia—and I attended the opening of the National Memorial for Peace and Justice in Montgomery, Alabama, honoring the lives lost to lynching in America. I was struck by the number of Magruder names I saw etched in the weathered steel columns that display the names of those who were lynched. It was a heart-wrenching, soulful, and eye-opening experience. I am grateful there is a sacred space in Alabama that acknowledges these Magruders/McGruders existed, that they were somebody's someone, and that they were unjustly taken from this earth. Generations later, we might find a way to mourn them, and, by remembering them, honor their life's divine preciousness in a way that both slavery and the Jim Crow South so brutally denied.

I continue to want to learn more and better understand the experience of black Magruders and McGruders in America. Since 2018, I've had the pleasure of meeting several black Magruders and McGruders and learning about the project that J.R. and so many others have put together in this book. While I'm not a descendant of the Magruder/McGruder line in Alabama, I share common ancestry with J.R., Marie, and all other Magruders who are descendants of Alexander Magruder, The Immigrant, and am looking forward to getting to know my cousins better. Your warmth and generosity have inspired me.

I hope that through this incredible project, and the connections that have come from it, the story of Magruders can help shed light on the complexities of the American story. I still keep faith in the promise of America, despite its difficult past, hoping that we might be more ambitious in our interpretation of the creed "all men are created equal." And I believe that transformation lies on the other side of acknowledging what Juan Magruder so beautifully wrote, that each generation is tested by how we treat each other.

Warmly,

Ian Magruder

i.   **Letter from a Black McGruder to the White Magruders**

By Tanya Robertson-Rothstein, a great-great-granddaughter of
Charles McGruder Sr.

On the occasion of the publication of *The Alabama Black McGruders*, by my
son J.R. Rothstein, I would like to extend my heartfelt respect and gratitude to
those "White" Magruders for your writing us letters and your participation in this
work. Reaching across the racial lines is an important contribution to the divinely
ordained destiny of an evolving United States of America. Your gesture honors
the soul of our common ancestor, Ninian Offutt Magruder, notwithstanding the
horrors and tragedies in the early life of our country in which he participated.
"America the Beautiful," an American anthem, eloquently indicates the nature of
our collective redemption:

And crown thy good with brotherhood

From sea to shining sea.

I am a product of an interracial marriage in the late 1940's, when interracial
marriage was not legal at the federal level. However, interracial marriage was
legal in Chicago, where my parents, of blessed memory, were married at
Rockefeller Chapel. I am a product of a union that took place legally and with
honor, unlike those disgraceful unions that took place between a master and an
enslaved person during slavery.

Our great country is presently in the painful labor pangs of brotherhood and
sisterhood, to deliver divinely ordained healing for our country. The word of the
Lord rules and transcends the perceived reality of our historic processes with
penetrating power. It shines through in the historic response of the
"White" Magruders to this history. This contributes the binding of our souls to the
healing that must take place within the United States.

This dialogue promotes the healing of historic pain, not only for past
generations of the Magruder and McGruder family; it promotes healing of the
wounds of our present Magruder and McGruder generation as well. I have found
much strengthening of my identity as a McGruder by the detailed historical
account of the two families, and I appreciate the courage of your involvement in
this project.

Warmly,

Tanya Robertson-Rothstein

j.   Letter from a Black McGruder to All McGruders and Magruders

Dear Magruder/McGruder Family,

I do not have all the words to put into context just how much this coming together, the retelling and aligning of our historical origin and the tragedy of slavery that this bloodline was founded on, means to me. The stories my father and grandfather told me are not only true but are being shared with the world—how amazing!

McGruders, *you are special.* It is not just happenstance. God foresaw this day and allowed us to discover our individual paths back to Charles McGruder Sr. through many obstacles and circumstances. My prayer is that we will embrace our story, however tragic, this family and its history, with open arms, and show the world what can be when we set aside our differences. I cannot wait to meet each of you. Thank you, J.R. Because of you, I found the pieces of me that have been missing. It is an honor to be a part of this remarkable family.

Genuinely,

Nikki (McGruder) Smith

k. Letter from an Alabama Black McGruder to All McGruders / Magruders

Dear White McGruder,

Wait. That doesn't work. Most everyone has at least a little melanin.

Dear Purple McGruders,

Well. That doesn't work, that's the color of the crayon you use.

Dear Kinfolk,

Yeah. I'll go with this one.

I am thankful for the work of J.R. Rothstein and those he acknowledged at the beginning of the book. I was able to discover [Susan Tichy's] *Magruder's Landing* and friend Jill Gatwood. I am also thankful for Anita McGruder-Johnson, my sister and our family genealogist, who shared with me the work of J.R.

> **HOPEFUL**, *adjective* Having qualities which excite hope; promising or giving ground to expect good or success; as a *hopeful* youth; a *hopeful* prospect.

Full of hope or desire, with expectation.

This is how I feel based on what I have read so far. Though the racial divide is in the spotlight in our country, as I read the letters of others I know there is hope. It's not that we can show others how it's done; we are doing it now.

That is, in Christ, God was reconciling the world to himself, not counting their trespasses against them, and He has committed the message of reconciliation to us. (2 Corinthians 5:19 CSB).

Sincerely,

Diana McGruder

l. **<u>Letter from an Alabama Black McGruder to All McGruders/ Magruders</u>**

Dear cousins,

I have a love for genealogy, so I was elated to learn about our rich, shared history. Often when African-Americans attempt to trace our roots, we are limited by the impact of slavery. There were minimal records kept during that time for most African-ancestored families, and few that included names. I appreciate the gift you have shared with us through historical records and DNA.

In my personal experiences learning American history, I have been dismayed. In this case, although our shared story is complicated, I am encouraged that our families can acknowledge the past and share a positive future together!

Sincerely,

Dr. Anita McGruder-Johnson

Part VII

The ABC's of (McGruder) Attainment

By Dora Lee McGruder[231]

A	Aspire for a worthwhile goal.
B	Be sincere about it.
C	Count on achievement.
D.	Don't give up.
E	Envision the outcome.
F.	Focus upon success.
G.	Grasp every cord attached to it.
H.	Hold fast to progressive ideas.
I.	Invest your time and talent.
J.	Justify every move toward its accomplishment.
K.	Kindle a flame of it. Excite the world.
L.	Lavish the success of it.
M.	Make a joyful noise about it.
N.	Never forget it.
O.	Ought is accomplished by quitting.
P.	Persevere, diligently to the end.
Q.	Quitters never win.
R.	Rest is reserved for constant toilers.
S.	Satisfaction comes when the task is complete.
T.	Take time and plan for success.
U.	Undertake only worthwhile tasks.
V.	Venture into the unknown
W.	Work hard.
X.	Exclude Weakness.
Y.	You set your standards.
Z.	Zeal in action pays off.

---

[231] Written for a family reunion, this ABC takes a few creative liberties in summarizing Alabama Black McGruder family values. A profile of Dora Lee McGruder may be found in the Gallery.

The Alabama Black McGruders

You got it from your father,

it was all he had to give.

So it's yours to use and cherish

for as long as you may live.

If you lose the watch he gave you

it can always be replaced,

but a mark on your name, dears,

can never be erased.

It was clean the day you took it,

and a worthy name to bear,

when he got it from his father

there was no dishonor there.

So make sure you guard it wisely,

after all is said and done,

you'll be glad the name is spotless

when you give it onto someone.

Submitted by Obra McGruder.

Some Alabama Black McGruders—A Gallery

1 - Patrice Aggs

Patrice Osborne Aggs was born in Detroit, Michigan, in 1952. In 1972 she paused her education at St. John's College, Maryland, to travel in Europe, and has lived in England ever since.

She studied fine arts at the City and Guilds of London Art School from 1976 to 1979. While a student, she worked part time in the BBC radio newsroom, and sketches made there resulted in a painting bought by their schools education program.

Patrice won a travelling scholarship to Italy in her penultimate year at art college, and illustrated her first children's book, for Methuen, in 1979. Since then, she has illustrated over forty picture books for various publishers, both in Britain and the US. In the early 1980s, she was co-opted into the team producing the animated film *The Snowman* by TVC Animation. At the same time, Patrice began producing limited edition, hand-colored etchings on nursery themes.

Married to the landscape painter Chris Aggs in 1983, Patrice began exhibiting etchings and watercolors at two-man shows with her husband. Original paintings and prints are now in collections in Europe, the United States, and Japan.

Acceptance at the Royal Academy Summer Exhibition has been a regular feature, with seven etchings making it into the show, all of which have sold out. One image, "Dogs", was chosen by the Academy as one of the postcard designs to promote the 1995 exhibition.

Away from her drawing board, Patrice has run children's workshops for a number of primary and secondary schools in Sussex, Hampshire, and London. She spent three years as a volunteer for the Ford Prison Board of Visitors and has completed commissions for Worthing Hospital's Children's Ward and Art in Hospitals.

Patrice is currently illustrator of *The Boss*, a new children's weekly illustrated magazine featuring stories by Philip Pullman. She continues work as a printmaker, writer of children's fiction, and illustrator for magazines and educational publishing. She lives on a farm in West Sussex with her husband and two teenagers. Her first author/illustrator picture book, *The Visitor*, was published by Orchard Books in 1999. *The Visitor*, retitled *The Giraffe Who Came to Dinner*, is currently published by O'Brien Press.

2 - E. Napoleon Burton (1924-2018)

Edward Burton, age 94, died peacefully on August 5, 2018, in the company of his beloved wife and daughter. He was born April 3, 1924, in Sawyerville, Alabama, to Queen Mary and Charlie Burton. He attended Dunbar High School in Bessemer, Alabama, where he graduated as senior class president in 1943. He was drafted into the United States Army during WWII, and afterwards pursued a BA in chemistry at the University of Iowa. While completing his degree at Michigan State Normal College (Eastern Michigan University), he met his future wife, Helen Virginia Dudley. They married in 1955 and settled in Detroit. Mr. Burton worked for the City of Detroit Waste Water Department and advanced to the position of Senior Water Systems Chemist. On retirement in 1984 he received a citation from Mayor Coleman Young for his dedication and years of service to the city.

Edward Burton enjoyed being of service, especially to the Catholic church. He was a member of IHM and, later, St. Scholastica parish in Detroit. In earlier years, he became one of the first lay lecturers at S.S. Andrew and Benedict parish where he lead the local society of The Legion of Mary, and co-sponsored a vacation Bible school. Ed became an instructor for the Gabriel Richard leadership course and was once invited by the Archbishop to teach Catholics in British Honduras (Belize). He volunteered as retreat captain for many years and served on the Board of Governors at St. Paul of the Cross Retreat Center. Edward was president of his neighborhood 7-8 Schaeffer Lodge Association, lending his talents to designing the signs that once stood proudly at entrances to the community.

Besides work and volunteerism, E. Napoleon indulged in several hobbies. He was an enthusiastic photographer, enjoyed gardening around the house, and occasionally dabbled in fishing. An avid reader, he embraced a lifetime of self-education and continued attending classes at WC3 well into his seventies. Ed's love of classical music led him to usher at a variety of music venues in Detroit. His most famous pastime, however, was traveling around the world. By age 65, E. Napoleon had managed to visit all seven continents. In his late eighties he laid claim to having reached both ends of the Pan American Highway, which extends from Fairbanks, Alaska, to Ushuaia, Argentina.

E. Napoleon Burton was the proud patriarch of the Charles McGruder-Burton-Gibbs families. He is survived by Helen Burton, his wife of 63 years; his daughter, Ann Y. Burton MD; five sisters: Lucille Osborne, Ernestine Graham, Geneva Wesley, Shirley Garrison, and Marie Diggs; and one brother, Jack Bernard Gibbs, as well as a host of relatives and friends.

Submitted by Dr. Ann Burton

3 - Sabrina Franklin

Although not technically a member of the Alabama Black McGruder family, Sabrina has been fully adopted by them due to her extensive research on their behalf. Sabrina Franklin is a proud native Texan and graduate of Texas Christian University. After a 23-year career as a federal law enforcement officer, she retired to focus on her family. As a young child, she became fascinated with genealogy after watching the television mini-series, *Roots*. She vowed to herself that she would spend her spare time unlocking the mysteries of her family tree. Next to spending time with her six children and extended family, genealogy is her fondest passion. She writes:

My oldest daughter was my first foster baby. It was love at first sight! Then, my oldest son came into the picture, when he was two months old. His adoption became final on his 2nd birthday. His birth mom gave birth twice after I adopted him, and I couldn't say "no" when those babies needed a home. I was fostering two more girls and fell in love with them, too.

4 - Diana Yvonne McGruder Harper

Diana Yvonne McGruder Harper is the oldest child of Deorsey Earl McGruder Jr., D.V.M., and Vera Etta Evans McGruder.

Diana's formal education began in Dallas ISD schools: Robert L. Thornton Elementary, D.A. Hulcy Middle, and Skyline Career Development Center. Undergraduate studies were completed at The University of Texas at Austin (B.A. with major in biology and minor in chemistry), and graduate studies at Texas Women's University in Denton (M.S.S.E. in Biology).

After completing her student teaching at David W. Carter High School and Zumwalt Middle School, Diana was assigned to John B. Hood Middle School to teach Life Science. After two years there, she became a member of the staff of Edison Middle Learning Center. The move was precipitated by marriage to a co-worker, math instructor (and pastor) Anthony Ray Harper Sr. At the time, married couples could not work at the same school. In addition to teaching Life Science, she sponsored the student council and the science club, and served as chairperson for the Science Department.

Six years later, Diana began teaching biology pre-AP at the Science and Engineering Magnet at Townview Center. While there, through contacts from summer grants, Diana was able to bring a scanning electron microscope to the school and develop a scientific research and design course. She was also a member of the Site-Based Decision-Making team and the school team for the Southern Association Accreditation Evaluation team.

Her next step was serving as the Secondary Science Instructional Specialist. In this role, Diana was responsible for providing professional development and curricular support for grade 8-12 science teachers.

Two years later, Diana resigned from the district to homeschool her then three children. Two more children have since been added to the number. For Diana, homeschooling is about more than academics. It is about discipleship and developing a love for lifelong learning.

Diana has demonstrated a love of learning. During the pandemic of 2020, she became a certified holistic health coach, and is studying to become a certified aromatherapist.

Besides being an educator, Diana is a pastor's wife, minister of the gospel, a dancer, a scrapbooker, and Gia to her first grandchild.

5 - Gwendolyn Elaine Hubbard

My name is Gwendolyn Elaine Hubbard and for years my family called me *Gwenlaine*. I am the tenth child and fifth daughter of the union of Mattie Lorene Burton (aka Burden-Hubbard) and George Lorenzo Hubbard. I am not the youngest of the family, and family stories state that I was not happy when my sister Evylon, "The Baby," was born.

I came from a family of eleven children (five boys and six girls). As a child, I had a thirst for knowledge, loved clothing, was very competitive, and talked my way out of many uncomfortable situations. At a young age, I understood the value of interpersonal and intrapersonal skills. I loved school. My brother taught me to read at the age of four. My inquisitive nature led me to become the genealogist in the Burton-Hubbard Family. I asked questions, loved storytelling, and wanted to know the truth, so that I would know my history and not "his story." These characteristics remain with me today.

My grandfather, Charley Burden, made his own guitar and would entertain people after church on Sundays. I inherited his love of music and was a member of my junior high school jazz band—one of very few females. My favorite solo was "Mercy, Mercy, Mercy" (1966) by the Cannonball Adderley Quintet. When I entered high school, I had to choose between cheerleading and band. I chose cheerleading and made the varsity squad as a freshman. As a senior, I was the team captain.

My mother stressed the value of a college education to me, as well as to my siblings. I entered high school in the college prep program and attended Michigan State University (MSU), where I received a Bachelor of Arts in Clothing and Textile Design. I was quite active in that, wrote an article for the school newspaper, *The State News*, was the Director of the Office of Black Affairs, and runner-up in the Black MSU pageant. I earned the Master of Science Degree at Central Michigan University. While I originally aspired to be a professional buyer of women's clothing, I've spent the last twenty years of my career working at Pfizer, the largest pharmaceutical company in the world. I was awarded a CMR and Advanced Sales Management Certification. I value education, so my goal is to earn a doctorate degree.

My family was blessed with many storytellers, who provided the foundation for my love of history. As a child, I listened to many stories from my mother, aunt, and uncle about the McGruder family. I asked questions, recorded answers, and obtained documentation when possible. Of all my careers and professional decisions, I derive the most pleasure from being the McGruder-Hubbard Family Genealogist. It is an honor and a privilege that my Aunt Lucille has passed the torch to me. I look forward to retiring and having the opportunity to pursue entrepreneur interests, as well as hobbies such as reading and listening to jazz.

6 - Aaron McGruder

Aaron McGruder was born on May 29, 1974, in Chicago, Illinois. He is a cartoonist best known for writing and drawing The Boondocks, a Universal Press Syndicate comic strip about two young African-American brothers from inner-city Chicago now living with their grandfather in a sedate suburb.

Aaron McGruder graduated from the University of Maryland with a degree in African-American Studies. The Boondocks debuted in the campus newspaper, *The Diamondback*, in late 1997. He recently worked as a screenwriter in the final treatment of the upcoming film *Red Tails*. With George Lucas as executive producer, the story is based on the Tuskegee Airmen, a group of African-American combat pilots during World War II. McGruder currently lives in Los Angeles.

7 - Anita McGruder Johnson

A native of Dallas, Dr. Anita McGruder-Johnson graduated from Skyline High School of the Dallas Independent School District. She earned Baccalaureate, Masters, and PhD degrees from Texas A&M University, concentrating in Clinical Psychology. During training, she volunteered for the Brazos Valley AIDS Foundation as a hotline counselor. She also counseled domestic violence survivors, children residing in an emergency shelter, and assaultive offenders on probation. These experiences influenced her research interests, culminating in a thesis and dissertation examining the prevalence of exposure to interpersonal violence and emotional aftermath including PTSD, dissociation, and fear of interpersonal victimization. In 2000, she published a co-authored a now-classic article in the field, "Interpersonal violence and posttraumatic symptomatology: the effects of ethnicity, gender, and exposure to violent events," in *Journal of Interpersonal Violence.*

Dr. McGruder-Johnson completed an internship and post-doctoral fellowship at Michael Reese Hospital in Chicago, where she specialized in pediatric clinical psychology, medical psychology, and addiction. Since 2004, she has devoted her clinical expertise to training the next generation of psychologists who assess and treat medical patients with stress-related conditions, emotional disturbance, and addiction.

Dr. McGruder-Johnson has combined over 20 years of mental health experience with spiritual foundations to create children's books, sleep-assistance audios, and the guidebook journal, *7 Days To A Stress-Free Life!*, teaching how to experience more satisfaction and less stress by integrating God's stress defense tasks into a daily routine. Seek peace, break off smaller bits, expect positive outcomes, encourage yourself often, seek supportive companionship, reflect on the positive, and immerse in appreciation. She followed this journal with *The Genesis 1:2-3 30-Day Stress Defense Challenge*. Each day, for one month, she presents a scripture, a related stress defense task, and a prayer. The goal is to develop a repertoire to imitate God by employing Stress Defense strategies daily to reduce chaos and enhance emotional and spiritual health. Living the life God intended is possible with peace, optimism, control, harmony, appreciation, and rest.

Finally, a favorite activity is researching Black Native American genealogy and publishing it in her blog: https://african-cherokee-genealogy.com.

8 - Dr. Deorsey Earl McGruder Jr. (1937-2019)

When former slave Charles McGruder Sr. purchased land in Alabama to create a permanent home for his numerous children, he paved the way for his great-great grandson, Dr. Deorsey Earl McGruder Jr. (1937-2019), to become the first African-Cherokee-American to graduate from Oklahoma State University School of Veterinary Medicine, in 1964.

Of his birth, Dr. McGruder wrote: "I was told [that] upon my arrival, they [my parents] were very happy and filled with joy, because not only was I the fourth child, but the first boy. I was born May 1, 1937, to Deorsey Earl McGruder Sr. and Sadie Mae Olivia Toneta Seals McGruder, by midwife, in Muskogee, Oklahoma."

Dr. Deorsey Earl McGruder Jr. is a direct descendant of Cherokee citizen Chas. Forman and Patsey Bushyhead, a slave. The couple had four daughters in the Cherokee Nation Indian Territory during the 1800's: Dorcas Forman, Narcissa Forman, Lucy Forman, and Polly Forman. Dorcas Forman was owned by Jesse Bushyhead, 2nd Chief and minister. According to her enrollment interview, Dorcas bought her freedom "six years before the Civil War."

Dr. McGruder's mother, Sadie Mae Olivia Toneta Seals McGruder, is the great-great-granddaughter of Dorcas Forman. Sadie Mae Olivia Toneta Seals married Deorsey Earl McGruder Sr., son of Robert McGruder (who was the son of Amos McGruder, the first-born son of Rachel Hill and Charles McGruder Sr.). Deorsey Sr. spent his early years in Alabama with his parents, Viola and Robert, and several siblings. At age four, he was adopted by his aunt and uncle, Elizabeth Moseley and Convis Burton. He lived with them in Muskogee, Oklahoma, and visited his Alabama McGruder family once per year.

McGruder Family

Deorsey Earl Sr. and Sadie Mae Seals McGruder

Sadie and Deorsey Sr. resided on a small farm in Muskogee. Deorsey Sr. worked as a hospital aid at the Veterans' Hospital. Sadie Mae worked in the home rearing their nine offspring: Viola, Sadie, Gladiola, Deorsey Jr., Geneva, Sterlin, Monroe, Barbara, and Wilma. Dr. Deorsey McGruder Jr. grew up in rural Muskogee with his parents and eight siblings. He was very industrious, picking crops at age four and printing newspapers for his paper route at age eleven. He also sold chickens as he delivered newspapers.

Attending Manual Training High School, Dr. McGruder was active in agricultural studies, helping the school raise money by cultivating crops and cattle for New Farmers of America (comparable to FFA). His father, Deorsey McGruder Sr., created Career Day, encouraging young Deorsey to seek the field of Veterinary Medicine and introducing him to Dr. John Montgomery, an African-American Veterinarian in Poteau, Oklahoma. His future wife, Vera Etta Evans, was working with Dr. Montgomery in her hometown.

Dr. McGruder attended Langston University for two years, then transferred to Oklahoma State University, achieving a BS in Agriculture. In 1960, he was accepted into the Oklahoma State University School of Veterinary Medicine, becoming the first African-Cherokee-American to be admitted.

He married his sweetheart, Vera Etta Evans McGruder, in 1963, and graduated in 1964. To this union were born three offspring: Diana McGruder Harper, Edward Deorsey McGruder, and Anita Kay McGruder-Johnson.

Dr. McGruder made numerous contributions to the fields of agriculture and veterinary medicine. After graduating, Dr. McGruder was recruited to teach large animal medicine at Tuskegee Institute, becoming the first Veterinary Professor to use sterile surgical techniques outdoors. He was next employed by the Food and Drug Administration, inspecting chickens on farms throughout the South.

Eventually, he achieved his dream of owning a veterinary practice in Dallas, Texas. Dr. McGruder was the first African-Cherokee-American Veterinarian in Dallas and the third in Texas. He volunteered with the ASPCA, providing free medical exams to newly adopted pets. Dr. McGruder was appointed by Governor Ann Richards to the Texas Racing Commission, where he served from 1993-1999. He was instrumental in getting legislation passed requiring that only veterinarians could administer rabies vaccinations. Dr. McGruder served the Dallas community for 50 years.

9 - Dora Lee Coleman McGruder

Dora Lee Coleman McGruder (1902-1999) was the wife of Alphonso Alonzo McGruder (1894-1982), who was a son of Charles McGruder, Jr. and Emmaline Riddle. She was a public-school teacher from the early 1920s, when she taught at one-room schoolhouses in the Sawyerville area, and later in Fairfield Public Schools near Birmingham. She was one of the organizers of an early McGruder reunion in Sawyerville in the 1960s, and attended them regularly when they began to be scheduled in alternating years. By the 1980s and 1990s, as one of the few of her generation remaining, she was often asked to give remarks. She and Alphonso were the parents of Charles, Elmer, Anita, Dorothy, Alphonso, Jr., Orlando, and Betty.

10 - Captain Geneva Kay McGruder Moore (1939-2009)

Captain Geneva Kay McGruder Moore was born on May 10, 1939, the fifth child and fourth daughter of Deorsey Earl McGruder Sr. and Sadie Mae Olivia Toneta Seals. She was active in church and studied home economics in high school. She enjoyed sewing and made identical dresses for her sisters.

Captain McGruder Moore was commissioned as a dietitian in the Air Force, serving at Clark Air Force Base in the Philippines, at Dover, Colorado, at Delaware in Dayton, Ohio, and Lackland in San Antonio.

She was highly skilled in business, real estate, and stocks, acquiring an extensive portfolio and advising friends and family members throughout the years. Geneva McGruder Moore retired as a Captain and served as a Chaplain for the Disabled American Veterans in San Antonio, Texas.

She enjoyed gardening, played some mean chess, and kept Christmas in her heart throughout the year.

11 - Gregory McGruder

Gregory McGruder serves as Vice President for live events at the National Geographic Society, overseeing its lectures, film screenings, panel discussions, and other public events. Gregory began his career at National Geographic in 1987, and has served on various grant-making committees. He is currently a member of the committee that selects and mentors Fulbright-National Geographic Fellows.

Additionally, he frequently takes part in the Society's Science-telling Bootcamps, in which he trains and coaches grantees on public speaking. For four years, he has served on the jury of the D.C. International Film Festival Circle Award. He also serves on the jury for the Barbados Independent Film Festival and is a member of the board of the D.C. Environmental Film Festival. Additionally, he serves as vice president of the board of the D.C. Arts and Humanities Education Collaborative.

12 - Jeff McGruder

Jeff McGruder's strengths are in personal and commercial credit analysis, financial structuring, and community outreach. Jeff's business and real estate philosophies were built on conservative practices. He has a passion for teaching financial literacy to clients and the rest of the community.

He was a student assistant coach/walk-on at David Lipscomb University under head coach Don Meyers. He was a recruiting assistant/walk-on at the University of Tennessee under head coaches Jerry Green and Buzz Peterson. Jeff is an East Nashville native, an Eagle Scout, and "Basketball Aficionado." He has a Master's of Business Administration, with a minor in Healthcare Administration, from Trevecca Nazarene University.

Jeff's financial services background began with Wells Fargo Financial in Knoxville, Tennessee. He transitioned his client base to Regions Bank in Franklin, where, after two years, he was promoted to business banking sales manager for the southern region of Middle Tennessee. From January 2012 to August 2013 he trained as an underwriter for Regions Large Corporate and Middle Market group. He was employed with Regions Bank for over ten years.

Jeff moved on to senior vice president roles with BB&T and Pinnacle Financial Partners. He is now serving on the executive team of Citizens Savings and Trust Bank as Chief Relationship Officer. Jeff is also a founding partner of the business/real estate consulting firm Urban Campus and Core.

Jeff's wife is Jessica McGruder, they have two daughters and a son— Marlee, Ansley, and William. His family lives in Brentwood, Tennessee. He currently serves on the board of directors for KIPP Academy, Nashville, and WPLN Nashville Public Radio. He has been active as a volunteer and community partner with several other organizations, such as CE McGruder Family Resource Center, Williamson County Chamber of Commerce, Leadership Franklin, Boy Scouts of America, New Hope Academy Board of Trustees, Nashville Celtics AAU basketball program, and HustleStrong Foundation.

13 - Juan McGruder

I was born on November 28, 1938, in the Historic Wedgeworth Community, born on the land at Highway 60 and Alabama State Road 14 at the time of the Great Depression, when black people had a hard time just surviving. We were among the fortunate people, because we had our own farm. When the War was over and soldiers were settling in houses down in Texas, my mother and brothers and I left Hale County on the train headed for Dallas. My mother had cooked a lot of food, so we wouldn't have to buy any food on the train. Momma had made some cakes as well, so we had a birthday party for me on the train. Since we were going to eat anyway, she called it a party for me.

In Texas, my momma saw electric lights for the first time. I vividly remember my brother and her playing with them. My momma would cut the light switch on and my brother, standing on the other side of the room, would cut it off with a different switch. There were limits and boundaries when playing with Momma. When Momma played with us, she always remained Momma. She was really strict. Well, as a little boy I liked to fight, and I stayed in Texas until I was eleven years old, when my Ainnie came for a visit and my daddy told her how bad I was. "Ainnie" is a term of endearment for my Aunt Rosie Nelle Winston. She convinced Daddy to let me come home with her. I was crazy about Alabama and always wanted to come back home. So I came back home to Alabama with my Ainnie, and went to school.

I remember one night my uncle and I were traveling, and as we were traveling down the road, all of a sudden we saw all of these lanterns being waved out there in the distance. My uncle slowed down, and we saw all of these hooded guys standing around with these sheets on, as my uncle slowly rolled up. All of a sudden, a man—one of the Klu Klux Klan—said "HARVEY!! We're taking up a donation for the …. Would you like to give a donation?" My uncle, stammering over his words, said, "Oh yeaah, yeaah, OK cappin, yeaah yeaah—I'll give a donation…" I was so mad at my uncle that I was about to burst. I was so mad at my uncle for yesssa-bossing them. When we got down the road, my uncle said he knew who the hooded man was, that he was the sheriff. My uncle knew who he was because he knew his voice, and the sheriff knew who my uncle was because they knew each other. That encounter made me so mad I couldn't hardly sleep that night, thinking about how my uncle disrespected himself with them Ku Klux Klansmen. The KKK did whatever they wanted, because no one was ever going to say anything.

My Ainnie required me to attend Revival, and one night in particular a young man caught me as I got out of the car to go into the church. He grabbed me by my hand, looked me right in my eye, and said, "I'm so glad that I got Jesus. I got him all over, way down in my soul." He said, "I'm so glad I got him (Jesus) all over, I got him way down in my soul." Now I'mma tell you something. I was eleven years old. That young man convinced me that he knew what he was talking about. Not that he convinced me about Jesus, but that he was convinced that what he was saying was true to him. I did not join the church that night. The next week, at my Ainnie's church revival, I sat on the moaning bench that Monday night, Tuesday night, Wednesday night, and Thursday. I would just sit there listening to everything they were talking about—how good Jesus was and about what Jesus had done for us and everything. How He died on Calvary's cross for my sins. I remember when I would come home each night that I would be walking around in the house praying, asking God to change me and come into my life. Well, that Friday night when they opened the doors of the church, I remember them saying, "If you have someone in church that you believe you have confidence in, then I want you to go to them and ask them to pray for you." I went to my cousin, Joe Johnson, because I really believed that he knew God, and he prayed with me. When the minister opened the doors of the church I went up and gave my hand to him and I gave my life to Christ Jesus. Afterwards, I started singing in the churches with my Ainnie.

A year and half later, my daddy came up from Dallas and got me, because my momma did not want me to be around the bad influences in Alabama. Every Sunday morning we went to our church service, and every Sunday evening my daddy would take me around to other local churches to sing solo, absent of any instruments. The congregation would pat their feet on the wooden floors, and you would have to sing by the rhythm they were patting.

In 1957, my brother, who was in the Navy and lived in Kansas, bought a 1957 Chevrolet convertible. I lived in Texas and I was always working, and I kept money. He sold me half of the car, and I would send him half of the payment. When my brother went overseas, he asked me to drive his wife and young child from Kansas to Oakland, California. Instead of returning to Texas, I drove the car from California over to Alabama, where I stayed and worked for a while. My Texas family wanted me back, so my sister got me a job working for American Airlines at Love Field Airport. So, once again, I left Alabama. While in Texas, I met my first wife, who was working for Love Field Airport at the time. A year later, I was drafted into the U.S. Army, where I worked as a cook for two years. We had two sons. I worked two jobs so I could buy a home and my wife could quit her job and stay at home with our children.

In 1984, my wife and I split. I left to my wife and children our home and all our possessions, and (consistently) paid support for my children. The first thing that I did when I got my paycheck was to pay my boys. I always said, "I didn't need no white judge to sit up and tell me what these two little black boys need. I am their daddy and I know more about what they need than he did." I sent both of my boys to college.

While in Dallas, I ran several very large and successful black-owned night clubs. My job was to walk around and watch the money. Later on, I moved to Kansas where my brother Sherby (who had retired from the Navy) lived. I bought and ran a restaurant in Wichita. After seven years, I sold my restaurant and moved back to Dallas, where I stayed with Momma. Two years later, I gave up the city life, sold my sports car, bought me a GMC truck and trailer, put everything I owned in that trailer, and came back to Alabama. Out of respect and good standing I communicated my intentions to set up on the McGruder family land. When I arrived that first night, I parked up the road at Elmer Brox's house. The next day I pulled the truck and trailer onto the McGruder family land and began building me a house. With the permission of my family, I dug a pond and went and bought me some cows. I put fences all around my place out of my own money. I later purchased and now hold title to sixteen acres of the McGruder family land where I live to this day, at the age of 82. I will pass my land on to my two sons, Juan Jr. and Michael.

14 - Kevin McGruder

Kevin McGruder is Associate Professor of History at Antioch College, Yellow Springs, Ohio. He received a B.A. in Economics from Harvard University, an M.B.A. in Real Estate Finance from Columbia University, and a Ph.D. in History from the Graduate Center of the City University of New York.

Before pursuing doctoral studies, he worked for many years in nonprofit community development, and also owned two retail businesses with products celebrating Harlem. His most recent book is *Philip Payton: The Father of Black Harlem*, published by Columbia University Press in 2021. He is also co-author of *The Emancipation Proclamation: Forever Free,* and *Witness: Two Hundred Years of African-American Faith and Practice at the Abyssinian Baptist Church of Harlem, New York*, and sole author of *Race and Real Estate: Conflict and Cooperation in Harlem, 1890-1920.*

15 - Marie McGruder

I am Marie Antoinette McGruder, the granddaughter of Marvin McGruder and the great-granddaughter of Charles McGruder Jr., the original owner of McGruder Landing on the Black Warrior River. Starting business ventures and materializing a vision is in my DNA. With a Bachelor of Science Degree (Mathematics & Statistics) from the University of South Florida and a Master of International Business Studies from the University of South Carolina, I have always pursued my dreams and my passions as they have evolved over my lifetime. From the age of eight, one of my biggest dreams has been to farm on the land that has been in my family for nearly 160 years.

Today, I am the owner of McGruder Farms, LLC. I own ten acres of McGruder land and control more than 50 acres of farmable McGruder land. My vision is to develop an infrastructure to grow and market highly desirable, nutritious, non-chemically grown, non-GMO produce and other edibles right here on our McGruder family land. We also have the Tribe of Jacobs Ladder, Inc., a non-profit organization in Sawyerville, embarking on the adventure of a lifetime and playing a role in elevating the economic development and sustainability of my community.

16 - Rev. Orlando McGruder Sr.

Orlando McGruder Sr., the 6th child of Alphonso McGruder and Dora McGruder (née Coleman) and grandson of Charles McGruder Jr. and Emmaline McGruder, and the great grandson of Charles and Mary McGruder, was born in Hale County, Alabama, in 1936.

At a young age, Orlando joined Jones Chapel A.M.E. Church, Fairfield, Alabama, where he began a lifetime of religious and community service, starting as a Sunday School teacher to younger children. After his marriage to Alberlena Robinson in 1958, he was baptized in the Baptist Church and affiliated with several Baptist churches over the years until he moved to Baltimore and affiliated with Calvary Baptist Church in 1968. During his affiliation with Calvary, he continued as a Sunday School teacher and has served as a gospel choir soloist, trustee, deacon, and leader of the senior ministry.

Orlando Sr. graduated Westfield High School, Westfield, Alabama, in 1953, number one in a class of 100, and attended the University of Toledo from September 1953 to June 1954. Orlando Sr. entered the U.S. Air Force in August 1954. With rank frozen and having been in the same grade for five years, he left the Air Force in 1963, after nearly ten years of honorable service, seeking to pursue greater advancement opportunity. Orlando Sr. obtained employment with the State of Kentucky as a Social Worker, a job he held while obtaining a college degree. Due to his leadership as a civil rights/labor advocate, social workers of all races in the State of Kentucky received substantial pay increases.

In 1965, Orlando Sr. received the Bachelor of Science degree in Sociology from the University of Louisville. While matriculating at University of Louisville, he became involved in minority recruitment initiatives. Once again not seeing advancement opportunity in a low-paying job, he left state employment for federal employment. Early in his federal employment, he completed one year at Wayne State University Law School.

Over the years, Orlando Sr. pursued studies in the areas of public administration, management information systems, and leadership development. His theological studies were at Chesapeake Theological Seminary in Maryland.

Orlando Sr. retired from the Social Security Administration as a senior level executive. Throughout his years of service, he received numerous commendations for management excellence, including the Extraordinary Public Service Award, and the Social Security Administration's highest award, the Commissioner's Citation. Decades after his retirement, his former colleagues remembered him fondly as a trailblazer in federal service and mentor to many whose careers had stalled before his intervention.

Orlando Sr. was licensed to preach the good news of Jesus Christ by St. John Baptist Church in October 1997. In recognition of his faithfulness and commitment to his calling, Rev. McGruder was ordained on September 29, 2013.

Since 2005, he has led the Ministry Without Walls, which he organized. He and his team members provide weekly worship services to five nursing homes/assisted living facilities throughout the Baltimore area. He makes visits to the sick and shut-in, regardless of church affiliation. Additionally, Rev. McGruder performs funerals and other religious services upon request by the various institutions and families. He has passed along to his two children, Orlando Jr. and Shawn, his passion for lifelong learning and the arts.

17 - Rev. Orlando McGruder Jr. (1963-1993)

Orlando McGruder Jr., the first-born child and only son of Orlando McGruder Sr. and Alberlena McGruder (née Robinson), the grandson of Alphonso McGruder and Dora McGruder (née Coleman), the great-grandson of Charles Jr. and Emmaline McGruder, and the great-great-grandson of Charles and Mary McGruder, was born in Louisville, Kentucky in 1963.

As a child, Orlando Jr. moved with his parents from Louisville to Detroit, before settling in the emerging Baltimore suburb of Columbia, Maryland, where he and his family were charter members of the Columbia Chapter of Jack and Jill of America, Inc. At a young age, he joined Calvary Baptist Church in Baltimore, Maryland, where he was a member of various youth ministries, became the church's first percussionist (drummer), and delivered his first religious message during a youth service.

He enjoyed a normal childhood and, in 1981, graduated from Wilde Lake High School, Columbia, Maryland, in the top 5% of his class. *Affable, studious, athletic*, and *helpful* were descriptors very appropriate to him. During his teen years, his parents installed a separate phone line in his room so he could counsel the many classmates who sought guidance from the young sage; he counseled friends at all hours on personal matters, including those fighting suicidal ideation. He also began proselytizing to his younger sister, stating that he wanted to ensure she would be with him in Heaven one day.

Orlando Jr. attended Fisk University for one year then transferred to Morehouse College. While at Morehouse, he entered the dual degree program in math and engineering with Georgia Institute of Technology. He received a degree in Mathematics in June 1986. In December 1986, upon receiving a degree in electrical engineering from Georgia Tech, he became gainfully employed with Wisconsin Power and Light.

Active in the community of Madison, Wisconsin, he became an accomplished speaker and trainer with the Dale Carnegie Institute and affiliated with the Mt. Zion Baptist Church youth programs. Also during this time, Orlando Jr. answered the call to ministry and became a licensed minister—serving as the youth pastor of his congregation and as a founding member of the African-American Ministers Clergy Association, exploring the issues and concerns of African Americans and other minorities. In July 1992, he married Felitia Nesbary of Chicago. He was married for approximately eleven months prior to his untimely death in June 1993. Orlando Jr., an avid reader and dancer in life, lies at rest beside his beloved mother in Anderson County, South Carolina.

18 - Sadie Mae McGruder

Sadie Mae McGruder, born February 8, 1933, in Omaha, Nebraska, is the second child born to Deorsey Earl McGruder Sr. and Sadie Mae Olivia Toneta Seals. Viola Leanna McGruder, Deorsey and Sadie's first child, was born February 16, 1931, in Omaha. The family moved to Muskogee, Oklahoma, in 1934, where, due to complications from pneumonia, Viola passed away on March 18, 1947, at age sixteen. Sadie Mae became Deorsey and Sadie's eldest child by default.

Sadie Made was very active in church and at seventeen represented the Sunday School department at the National Baptist Convention. In 1952, after a year of education at Langston University, Sadie Mae traveled with her maternal grandmother, Elizabeth Mosley Burton, to Los Angeles. In California, she attended East Los Angeles College, studying nursing. Her experiential learning at Los Angeles County General Hospital led to her calling to work in pediatrics. For 40 years, she worked for the county of Los Angeles, in both the nursing department and payroll, setting up the system before electronic scheduling and payroll were introduced countywide. She was married, raised three children, learned to drive in her early 40s, served as secretary of the Langston University Alumni Association (Los Angeles chapter) and as treasurer of the Oklahoma Charity and Social Club (Los Angeles). She enjoys traveling and gardening. Sadie Mae resides in Los Angeles, is a grandmother of three, great-grandmother of two, and is enjoying her 28th year of retirement.

19 - Reverend Sterlin Henry McGruder Sr.

Reverend Sterlin Henry McGruder Sr. was born October 3, 1942, in Muskogee, Oklahoma, the 6th child and 2nd son of Deorsey Earl McGruder Sr. and Sadie Mae Olivia Toneta Seals. He worked cutting yards with a push mower at young age. He also worked as a dishwasher at a restaurant and sold newspapers.

Rev. McGruder learned leather craft and shoe repair at Manual Training High School, making billfolds, handbags, and belts. After graduating high school, he moved to Los Angeles, California. He worked at the International House of Pancakes and at a fish and poultry store. In 1962 he followed his brother, Deorsey Jr. to Oklahoma State University, completing a degree in Biological Sciences. In 1965 he was commissioned as a Second Lieutenant in the U. S. Army, serving in Korea from 1965 to 1967. Upon returning to the United States, he was stationed at Ft. Sill, Oklahoma.

Rev. McGruder completed a second bachelor's degree in Accounting, in May 1970. On August 2, 1976, he became one of the first Certified Public Accountants in the Dallas area of African-Cherokee descent. He worked for the government as a federal auditor and completed his MBA on August 14, 1981.

On July 14, 1984, Sterlin Henry McGruder Sr. accepted his calling to the ministry, becoming a licensed minister by attending the Southern Bible Institute. He has alternated as Assistant Pastor and Interim Pastor at New Hope Church in Grand Prairie, Texas, for 33 years. During those years, he has inspired numerous teachers, ministers, and congregants.

Rev. McGruder retired as a Lieutenant Colonel in the United States Army Reserve, and now enjoys spending time with his wife, Kerry. Joy abounds with his children, Geneva and Sterlin Jr., and many grandchildren.

20 - Shawn Shyrlena McGruder

Shawn S. McGruder, the second child and only daughter of Orlando McGruder Sr. and Alberlena McGruder (née Robinson), the granddaughter of Alphonso McGruder and Dora McGruder (née Coleman), the great-granddaughter of Charles McGruder Jr. and Emmaline McGruder, and the great-great-granddaughter of Charles and Mary McGruder, was born in Baltimore, Maryland, in 1968.

Shawn was raised in the Baltimore suburb of Columbia, Maryland, where her family became charter members of the Columbia Chapter of Jack and Jill of America, Inc. At a young age, she joined Calvary Baptist Church in Baltimore, Maryland, where she was a member of various youth ministries, including the usher board, and played piano for the Sunday School throughout her teen years, while attending the Peabody Conservatory of Music.

In 1986, Shawn graduated in the Top 5% of her class at Centennial High School in Ellicott City, Maryland, and then attended Howard University in Washington, D.C. In 1990, she graduated cum laude from Howard University's School of Business and Public Administration with a degree in Finance. During her undergraduate years she performed with the Howard University Showtime Marching Band, where she played alto saxophone. In 1993, she graduated from the Howard University School of Law, where she served on the editorial board of the Howard Law Journal. She also holds a Certificate of Public Policy from the

Harvard University Kennedy School, and has been admitted to practice law in Maryland, Pennsylvania, the District of Columbia, and before the U.S. Supreme Court.

After serving legal internships with the Pension Benefit Guaranty Corporation, the Commodity Futures Trading Commission, and the Social Security Administration (SSA), and passing the bar in December 1993, Shawn began her career as an attorney for SSA, where she built a career as a civil rights, labor, and employment law attorney and senior litigator. Proceeding through progressively responsible positions, she accepted jobs as a Supervisory Attorney in SSA's Philadelphia Regional Office and then at SSA Headquarters in Baltimore, where she managed complex litigation, including nationwide class-action litigation, and provided national oversight for civil rights matters. She also received appointments as a Special Assistant U.S. Attorney for the District of Maryland and the Western District of Virginia. She was lead counsel in landmark litigation governing the federal workforce, notably Tunik v. SSA, overturning 20 years of precedent.

After completing SSA's Senior Executive Service (SES) Candidate Development Program, Shawn accepted an SES appointment as the Assistant General Counsel for General Law at the U.S. Department of Agriculture (USDA), where she managed a full range of general law and litigation matters for all 20+ USDA sub-agencies and staff offices. Ultimately, the Secretary of Agriculture appointed her to serve as USDA's Executive Director for Civil Rights Enforcement, where she provided executive leadership to approximately 75 federal and contract staff in the intake, investigation, and adjudication of discrimination complaints filed by USDA staff and members of the public seeking to participate in some 400 federally conducted or assisted programs administered by USDA.

In May 2019, Shawn accepted a position as the Senior Associate General Counsel for the Equal Employment Opportunity Office at the Johns Hopkins University Applied Physics Laboratory in Laurel, Maryland.

In her spare time, since 2005 Shawn has been a Tae Bo® certified cardio kickboxing instructor who also enjoys all forms of dance and music. She performs community service at local nursing homes as part of the Ministry Without Walls founded by her father, Orlando McGruder Sr.

21 - Sharon McGrew Sommerville

I am Sharon McGrew Sommerville. I am one of six children born to O'Neal McGrew and Anita McGruder McGrew. My linkage to the McGruder family is through my mother, Anita McGruder McGrew; my grandfather, Alphonso McGruder; my great-grandfather, Charles McGruder Jr.; and great-great-grandfather, Charles McGruder Sr. I was born and raised in Fairfield, Alabama. My mother often shared stories about life in Wedgeworth, Alabama, and offered many details regarding the McGruder family tree. My grandparents, Alphonso McGruder and Dora McGruder, lived close by and I also heard many family stories while spending time with them. As a child, I knew that in our community the McGruder name was associated with education, a strong work ethic, and strong family values.

After graduating from the University of Alabama, Birmingham, with a degree in Occupational Therapy, I relocated with my husband to Durham, North Carolina. After relocating to Indianapolis, I obtained a Master's degree in Public Health from Indiana University. My career choice was influenced by my uncle, Dr. Charles McGruder. He told me I was "smart and could be anything I wanted," and suggested that I consider the health field. I did some research and immediately knew Occupational Therapy was the perfect choice for me. His encouragement gave me the confidence to pursue a competitive occupation that many people were not familiar with. For over 40 years, I have worked in a variety of settings including administration, early intervention, and geriatric specialties. I am currently employed in the school system.

For 40 years, I have been married to Ron Sommerville. His career as an educator and historian has afforded us the opportunity to visit several countries, including Ghana, South Africa, and Kenya. One of my most memorable experiences was visiting the Cape Coast Castle and seeing the Door of No Return. We are the parents of two children—Raymond Sommerville (Tosha) and Maya Mimms (Adrian). We are also the proud grandparents of seven grandchildren under the age of 12—Nautica, Ray, Gabriel, Micah, Jonas, Nahum, and Nia. Their parents have instilled in them a love for reading and several of them also have a keen interest in history.

22 - Alvin McGrew Sr.

Faye McGrew, Alvin McGrew, A.J. McGrew, and Michael McGrew.
Birmingham, Alabama, 2019.

My name is Alvin McGrew Sr. I am one of six children born to O'Neal McGrew and Anita McGruder McGrew. My linkage to the McGruder family is through my mother, Anita McGruder McGrew; grandfather, Alphonso McGruder; great-grandfather, Charles McGruder Jr.; and great-great-grandfather, Charles McGruder Sr. Following graduation from high school in 1969, I played professional baseball for eight years with the Cleveland Indians, New York Yankees, and the Baltimore Oriole organizations. Concurrent with my baseball career, I attended the University of Alabama, where I received a B.S. degree in 1977 and enlisted in the United States Army in 1971.

I retired from Southern Company in October 2019, as a Supervisor at the nuclear operations subsidiary, Southern Nuclear Operating Company. Prior to that, I retired from the United States Army Reserve with over 34 years of service, having attained the rank of Colonel.

I am married to Faye Bryant McGrew, whom I met at the University of Alabama, and we have two sons, Alvin (A.J.) Jr. and Michael.

A.J. graduated in 2000 with a B.S degree from Vanderbilt University, where he was a member of the Vanderbilt football team. He is married to Juana Elizabeth Rodriguez-McGrew and they have one son Ayden (eight years old). A.J. works in Corporate Development-Acquisitions for Pinnacle Treatment Centers.

Michael graduated from the University of Virginia (UVA) in 2005, where he also played football. Following his graduation, he played two years with the New England Patriots. He is married to Prima Patterson McGrew and they have two daughters Kayla (nine years old) and Alayna (six years old). Michael and Prima own and operate Cavalier Healthcare Services, located in Alexandria, Virginia.

23 - Marva McGrew

I am Marva McGrew. I am the oldest of six children born to O'Neal McGrew and Anita McGruder McGrew. My linkage to the McGruder family is through my mother, Anita McGruder McGrew; my grandfather, Alphonso McGruder; my great-grandfather, Charles McGruder Jr.; and my great-great -grandfather, Charles McGruder Sr.

After graduating from Tuskegee University, I relocated to Baltimore, Maryland, where I enjoyed a 30-year career with the Social Security Administration. I was also an active member of the Baltimore Tuskegee Alumni Club. I treasure friendships, and to this day I maintain many that were formed during those years. I call them my "Baltimore friends." One friend is a genealogist and she often said, "Tell your story. No one knows it like you do." Inspired by her, I launched a McGruder newsletter and edited several issues. My mother also inspired my interest in family history, and I remember how she loved attending family reunions and telling stories about our family.

Both my grandparents and parents were determined to educate their children. My grandmother graduated from college after her children were grown. My mother was a 1948 graduate of Miles College. This education value-system was inherited by my siblings, all of whom shared the goal of a college education for their children. Our father said each generation should do better than the previous one. We should be grateful for the opportunity to document our history, as we recall the following Sumer legend:

"What became of the Black People of Sumer?" the traveler asked the old man, "for ancient records show that the people of Sumer were Black. What happened to them?" "Ah," the old man sighed. "They lost their history, so they died."

24 - Vernal Ulelah Reese

Mrs. Vernal Ulelah "Mamma," "Auntie Vana," "Aunt Vernal," "Coach" Reese entered this life on Tuesday, May 6, 1930, to Mr. Ethew Adolphus McGruder and Mrs. Maggie Sawyer McGruder in Hale County, Alabama. Vernal was the youngest of nine children. She received her education in the schools of Alabama and attended Dunbar High School. Upon graduation she went on to Alabama State (now known as Bishop State) on an academic scholarship for best all-around student. Upon graduating from Alabama State in 1949, with a degree in General Education, she moved to Chicago and became employed by the largest post office in the world.

While working full-time at the post office she also attended George Williams College full-time, where she received her Bachelor of Science degree in Physical Education in 1956. After receiving her undergraduate degree, she attended Concordia College in Montreal, Quebec, and toured several European countries, including Denmark, Germany, Sweden and Austria. After touring Europe, she attended Saint Xavier College in Chicago (now known as Saint Xavier University). In 1972 she received her Master's Degree in Physical Education from George Williams College. She devoted over 30 years to the youth at Eisenhower High School in Blue Island, Illinois, as a physical education teacher, until she retired in 1987. It was at the age of five, while working in the fields carrying water, that Vernal decided "this won't be my life." She has educated herself and everyone around her for her entire life. "A mind is a terrible thing to waste," she would say. In addition to raising her son Edwin, with the help of her two sisters Manuella McGruder Walston and Vlasta Fleming, she raised five grand-nieces: Wynona, Pocquilla, Elizabeth, Dominyque, and Deana. She was a devoted member of St. Mark AME Zion Church in Chicago, where she served in many capacities including the Usher Board, Trustee Board, Class Leader, and a short time in the Choir. In 1967, she met her husband, Henry Van Reese. Four years later they united as one, and she remained a devoted and loving wife until he departed this life on December 28, 2015. After retirement, she and her husband moved to Union Pier, Michigan. As "Snow Birds" they traveled all over the United States, and in 2015 moved back to Mobile, Alabama, where they were faithful attendees of Hope Chapel AME Zion Church. Her favorite pastimes included traveling, flowers, listening to gospel music, watching TV, reading, and participating in athletics.

Vernal was preceeded in death by her mother, father, all eight of her siblings, and her husband Henry Van Reese. She leaves to cherish his memory a loving son, Edwin Echols; a devoted adopted daughter, Pocquilla J. McGruder McNeely (Samuel); two granddaughters, Zoya D. Baker and Mya L. McNeely; a dedicated grand-niece, Wynona (Curtis) Nicholson; eight nephews: Ronald (Constance) Fleming, Earthel (Harolyn) Fleming, Manuel (Margaret) Fleming, Zandy (Charlotte) McGruder, Victor (Veronica) McGruder, Calvin McGruder, Ethew McGruder, and Johnny McGruder; and two nieces, Patricia McKinley and Ivy McGruder.

25 - Curtis Robertson Sr. (1919 – 1994)

Curtis C. Robertson, Sr., age 73, a Southside insurance Broker and Agent of over forty-one years, succumbed to cancer on June 14, 1994. A World War II Veteran and an engineer by profession, he fulfilled his dream of having his own business when he established the Cooperative Insurance Agency, initially in South Shore, and by 1960 in the Hyde Park Bank building.

A prominent member of the community, he had been active in the Cooperative movement, Ingleside Evergreen Cooperatives, the Masons, the Hyde Park Business Men's Association, the Hyde Park Co-op, the Methodist Church, the American West Indian Association, the Universal Negro Improvement Association, Second Ward, and numerous other groups. He and his family were citizenship sponsors for many from Africa and the Islands. Various are those who will always remember his marvelous smile, sunny disposition, and captivating personality. Many were the beneficiaries of his outstanding generosity, sharing, counseling, and unwavering assistance. Through his interest in genealogy, he was able to trace the McGruder/Robertson family tree to 1822.

A connoisseur of the arts, he was a loving, caring patron to local and international artists, sculptors and importers, who benefitted from his guiding sponsorship and support. During his numerous trips to Africa, he was always able to renew contacts with former exchange students and heads of state, and make new friends.

26 - Tanya Maria Robertson-Rothstein

Tanya M. Robertson-Rothstein is Director of the Transformational Breath Center in Rockland County, New York. She is a certified Transformational Breath Facilitator with advanced certifications and holds three advanced certifications each in Yoga and Reiki. Tanya's specializations include working with children and with trauma victims.

Tanya Rothstein came of age at the height of the Civil Rights movement in Hyde Park, a vibrant, progressive, and diverse community centered around the University of Chicago. She attended undergraduate at Coe College and graduate school at the University of Chicago. Tanya taught African-American history in the Chicago Public Schools and worked for a number of years in Human Resource Management, with an emphasis on Affirmative Action, for two major corporations. She married Jay Rothstein and had three children, whom they raised to be committed to racial and social justice. More recently, Tanya has served as a licensed real estate agent with a leading brokerage firm.

Tanya, an observant Jew, comes from a multi-racial family committed to strong ethnic identity and social justice. Her father, Curtis Robertson, of the Alabama Black McGruder family, was raised by Marcus Garveyites and went on to be a successful businessman and community leader. Her mother, Catherine Dove Gibbs, a member of the Daughters of the American Revolution, was a prominent, award-winning social worker. Both parents were active in a number of organizations that promoted racial and social justice. Tanya's maternal grandfather, Bernard Gibbs, a white minister who invited people of color into his church against the established convention of his day, is the subject of *The Preacher of Morgantown*, by J.R. Rothstein.

27 - Joshua Rothstein

Joshua Rothstein is a specialist in Early Childhood Education with a bachelor's degree from Touro College and a Master's Degree in Education from Hunter College. He has taught in various preparatory schools throughout New York City and the tristate area, with a background in Reggio Emilia, Waldorf Education, and Diversity, Equity and Inclusion in early childhood curriculums. Josh is known for his sensitivity to others and ability to work with people from all walks and backgrounds of life.

In the field of Real Estate and Real Estate Management, Josh has previously served as the manager of three multi-family buildings in New York City and as a licensed real estate agent. He has a keen eye for properties of value in unconventional locations. Josh is universally liked and respected, with connections worldwide. Josh is a nature enthusiast who loves to hike with friends, including a recent trip to Machu Picchu, in Peru. He has traveled to over thirty-six countries on nearly all the continents.

Josh is a successful organic farmer and creative vegetable fermenter. He is highly conscious of the challenges in our society and the necessity of achieving true racial conciliation and justice.

28 - J.R. Rothstein

J.R. is a transactional attorney who practices on an extensive range of matters, with both law firm and in-house counsel experience. His real estate law practice includes development, acquisitions and dispositions, and leasing transactions of real property. During his career, J.R. has worked with numerous corporate and individual clients, including property managers, investors, developers, and cooperatives. He provides legal support and advice on all real estate matters. His legal advice goes beyond the law and responds creatively and strategically to meet business needs. J.R., who studies real estate development part-time at New York University, often assists his clients in syndicating real estate deals.

J.R. received his Juris Doctor from Cornell Law School, where he was Editor of the *Journal of Law and Public Policy* and an Albert Heit Scholarship recipient. He simultaneously obtained an L.L.M, Master of Laws in International and Comparative Law from Cornell Law School, and spent time studying Islamic Law at the American University of Cairo. After obtaining his J.D. and L.L.M., he began his legal career serving as a federal law clerk in the Eastern District of New York for the Honorable I. Leo Glasser.

J.R. completed his undergraduate degree at the University of Michigan, Ann Arbor, in Middle-Eastern & North African Studies and African-American Studies. After university, he was a Legacy Heritage Fellow doing human rights work at the United Nations. Later, he was an Ariana De Rothschild Fellow at the University of Cambridge Judge Business School in Cambridge, United Kingdom, focusing on Social Entrepreneurship and impact investing with faith-based communities. J.R. was also a Fulbright visiting scholar at the University of Toronto Faculty of Law, where he focused on comparative real estate transactions.

Today, J.R. is a member of DOROT, Sons of the American Revolution, and the NAACP. He also serves as a member of the Steering and Board of AJC ACCESS. He has lived, worked, studied, and traveled in over two dozen countries. He is the author of five books, including the children's book, *The Adventures of Rumi & Bixby Bear.*

29 - Rabbi Isaiah Rothstein

Rabbi Isaiah Joseph Rothstein recently joined The Jewish Federations of North America professional team as a Rabbinic Scholar and Public Affairs Advisor. Previously, he served as Rabbi-in-Residence at Hazon: The Jewish Lab for Sustainability. Before that, he was the Spiritual and Experiential Educator at Carmel Academy of Greenwich in Greenwich, Connecticut, and worked on the faculty of Camp Yavneh in New Hampshire. Rabbi Isaiah received his rabbinic ordination and Master of Social Work at Yeshiva University. Growing up in a multi-racial Chabad family in Monsey, New York, Rabbi Rothstein sees himself as a human bridge, connecting disparate parts of the Jewish and non-Jewish communities. Rothstein is a member of the Schusterman Foundation's ROI Fellowship and was listed as one of *Jewish Week*'s *36 Under 36*. During his spare time, Rabbi Isaiah is writing a musical about Queen Esther and performs music with his band. Isaiah currently lives in Harlem, New York.

30 - Nikki McGruder Smith

Nikki McGruder Smith is the eldest grandchild of Horace and Leola McGruder, who had three sons between them: Donald, Ralph (Nikki's father), and Horace Jr. ("Junior"). Her great-grandparents are Adam and Pearla ("Pearl") McGruder, two McGruder first cousins who married, one of whom is suspected to be a descendant of Charles McGruder Sr., though no evidence has yet been located. Nikki has one daughter, Victorya, and is an international recording artist who goes by the artist name, The Nu Chic©. She was born and has spent most of her life in Miami, Florida. Currently residing in Atlanta, Nikki owns and operates LionFish Music & Entertainment Group LLC, an independent record label and production company. Nikki is a published writer, singer, songwriter, music, and film producer. Currently pursuing her degree in Music Production at Full Sail University, she plans to continue her education after graduation and acquire her Master's in Entertainment Business at Berkeley College.

The Ancestors Call Us Back Home to Alabama

By Marie McGruder

Who am I that God chose me to be the next steward of the Alabama Black McGruder land that has been passed down through the generations for more than 150 years? I am but the least of many in a family that is as numerous as the sands of the sea. It is on this 25th day of December, 2021, that Elder Juan McGruder, Sr. (aged 84) and I (aged 59) sit together on the Charles McGruder Jr. homestead and give thanks.

Thanks to our Father in Heaven for the life, health, strength, and prosperity of each member of the McGruder/McCruter/Magruder tribe.

We laugh, we praise, and we sing Halleluiah because as we look back over the past year and a half, and as we think about all the family members that have come together from near and far, we are overwhelmed, and we are amazed. We are as giddy little children grinning like cheesier cats at the great fortune we have to wake up on the land daily, walk through the woods, grow amazing food and drink from the well that was handed down from our forefathers.

I am Marie Antoinette McGruder, the second child of Marvin L. & Thelma J. Miller-McGruder (family line: Marvin L. & Leola Tabb-McGruder Sr., Charles & Emmaline Riddle-McGruder Jr., Charles Sr. & Mary May McGruder, Ned & Mariah Magruder, Ninian O. Magruder & Empress sent by God—name unknown).

My earliest memory of the land is when at eight years old, on our drive home from summer vacation in Kansas City, Daddy stopped in to visit his aunt who lived on the McGruder family land. We city kids had little appreciation for rural living or farm life. Like the other matriarchs in my life, Aunt Doll was a larger-than-life figure—regal, independent, and stern, with a commanding presence. My dad was so happy to be there and it was as if he became a little boy again. Aunt Doll was welcoming, gracious, and took us all on a tour of the "McGruder estate." As if just yesterday, I remember coming to the artesian well dug by great-grandaddy Charles, putting my hands together under the hand pump as the clear and very cold water came up from the well and ran over my fingers. The water tasted magical, and that was when I told myself that I wanted to live here forever.

Well, that was a short-lived moment, because within hours we saw a mouse, and us city kids cried and screamed until my daddy relented, loaded us four kids back into the station wagon, said his goodbyes, and headed down the highway back to Tampa. He was so disappointed that he couldn't enjoy more time with his Auntie and time on the land.

We were always told by my grandmother Leola about our McGruder family values and about the Alabama family land off the banks of the Black Warrior River. On occasion, at family gatherings, the topic discussed among the elders would be my grandfather Marvin's defection, seeking a better life in the North, and how he "put the family land in hoc" to finance his journey, leaving his siblings behind on the land to pay off his debt and save the McGruder family land. It always hurt my heart. It was a painful stain on my grandfather's name and passed down from father to sons and on to us the grandchildren.

Two years ago, as fate would have it, I was empowered, enabled, and appointed by the Great Creator to purchase a small part of the family land, Great Uncle Calvin's parcel. I have also restored the honor of the Marvin McGruder line. I am healed, and I now call this land home.

I tell you this story because through it all I have always had great faith, felt loved, nurtured, empowered, and even emboldened to dream big, live free, show up and be present. In God's time and in God's perfect timing the universe has manifested my very heart's desires. As a family member, I know our ancestors smile down on us. So YES, family, this Alabama Black McGruder homestead is here and will be here for all to enjoy.

It was passed forward for us as a remnant, and as a piece of heaven right here on earth, to nurture our body, our soul, and our spirit.

We are present, we are proud, we are chosen!

Part VIII

Documents Pertaining to Chapter Four

Links for some entries appear after the table.

Summary of Early Georgia Records for Ninian Beall & Ninian Offutt Magruder		
Date	**Who**	**Description & Source**
July 1782	Ninian O.	Receipt of Bounty Warrant, below, means he was resident of Georgia before July 1782, when the British fled Georgia
February 1784	Ninian O.	Ninian O. as "Citizen of Georgia," petitions for 250 acres in Washington County on certificate of Col. Green Berry Lee; granted 287+ acres in Washington County, surveyed lands recorded March 1784 *GA Headright & Bounty Land Records, 1783-1909, FHL#5203602, image#211-216, FamilySearch – link below*
March 1784	Ninian O.	Ninian O.'s son, Zadok, petitions for warrant as a resident of Georgia during British occupation before July 1782 (not heard/paid?) *GA Headright & Bounty Land Records, 1783-1909, FHL#5203602, image#199-200, FamilySearch – link below*

---

[232] This is not an exhaustive list of Georgia records related to Ninian Offutt or Ninian Beall Magruder. The family surname is recorded as Magruder, McGruder, MacGruder, Gruder, Grooder, Magrooder, Magrunder, and McGrunder. *Ninian* may be Ninion or Ningin, and *Offutt* may be Offet or Offum. Ninian's O.'s son Zadock fares better, but is recorded at least once as Tadock.

February 1785	Ninian O.	Ninian O. purchases warrant from P. Few & patents 200 acres *Columbia Co GA, Plats and Land Grants, 1783-1794, Bk A p 82, FHL#8657180, image#78, FamilySearch – link below*
February 1785	Ninian O.	Ninian O. purchases warrant from Wm Glascock & patents 100 acres *Columbia Co GA, Plats and Land Grants, 1783-1794, Bk A v, p 82, FHL#8657180, image#78, FamilySearch – link below*
January 1786	Ninan B.	Ninian B. purchases land from Richard Castleberry, DB A 1 Folio 109, Richard Castleberry to Ninian B. Magruder of St. Pauls Parish *Records of Richmond Co GA, formerly St Paul's Parish, v 2 p 287, Historical Collection of Georgia Chapters of the DAR, 1929, FamilySearch – link below*
February 1786	Ninian B.	Houlton J. to Ninian Magruder of Richmond, DB A 1 - Folio 112 *Records of Richmond Co GA, formerly St Paul's Parish, v 2, p 290, Historical Collection of Georgia Chapters of the DAR, 1929, FamilySearch – link below*
September 1786	Ninian O.	Ninian O. purchases warrant from Chas Crawford & patents 100 acres *Columbia Co GA Plats and Land Grants, 1783-1794, Bk A p 162, FHL#8657180, image#124, FamilySearch – link below*
September 1786	Ninian B.	Ninian B. is security for marriage bond of Mann Simms to marry Margaret Magruder, his daughter *Records of Richmond Co GA, formerly St Paul's Parish, v 2, p 185, Historical Collection of Georgia Chapters of the DAR, 1929, FamilySearch – link below*

March 1787	Ninian O.	Ninian O. purchases warrant from Chas Crawford & patents 200 acres *Columbia Co GA Plats and Land Grants, 1783-1794, Bk A p 244 FHL#8657180, image#170, FamilySearch – link below*
August 1787	Ninian B.	Ninian B. purchases warrant for 150 acres from James McNeil, surveyed August 1787 *Columbia Co GA Plats and Land Grants, 1783-1794, Bk A p 245, FHL#8657180, image#170, FamilySearch – link below*
December 1787	Ninian O.	Ninian O. is appraiser for John Matthew's estate *Records of Richmond Co GA, formerly St Paul's Parish, v 2, p 103, Historical Collection of Georgia Chapters of the DAR, 1929, FamilySearch – link below*
December 1788	Ninian O.	Ninian O. testator for Daniel Praytor, deceased *Records of Richmond Co GA, formerly St Paul's Parish, v 2, p 114, Historical Collection of Georgia Chapters of the DAR, 1929, FamilySearch – link below*
January 1789	Ninian O.	Ninian O. purchases warrant from James McNeil & patents 850 acres *Columbia Co GA Plats and Land Grants, 1783-1794, p 280, FHL#8657180, image#190, FamilySearch – link below*
March 1789	Ninian O.	Ninian O. 200 acres to Mark Roberson, recorded 1807 *Columbia Co GA, Superior Ct Deeds and Mortgages, 1791-1911, v O, p 16, FHL#847821, image#275, FamilySearch* https://www.familysearch.org/ark:/61903/3:1:3Q9M-C3Q2-P3LG-W?i=274&cat=112848

March 1793	Ninian B.	Ninian B. purchases 250 acres from Lewis Gardner *Columbia Co GA, Superior Ct Deeds and Mortgages, 1791-1911, v B p272, FHL#8135388, image#247, FamilySearch -* https://www.familysearch.org/ark:/61903/3:1:3Q9M-CSVB-JC81?i=246&cat=112848
December 1793	Ninian O.	Son, Zadock Magruder late in paying taxes *Augusta Chronicle & gazette of the state, December 7, 1793, image 6 – persistent link:* https://gahistoricnewspapers.galileo.usg.edu/lccn/sn82015 220/1793-12-07/ed-1/seq-6/print/image_431x817_from_0,0_to_2857,5405/
November 1794	Ninian O.	Son, George Magruder, late paying taxes *Augusta Chronicle & gazette of the State, November 8 1794, image 4, - persistent link:* ttps://gahistoricnewspapers.galileo.usg.edu/lccn/sn820152 20/1794-11-01/ed-1/seq-4/print/image_464x817_from_0,0_to_4102,7209/
October 1798	Ninian B.	Ninian B. to son Samuel Magruder, for 1,150 acres *Columbia Co GA, Superior Ct Deeds and Mortgages, 1791-1911, DB I, p 60, FHL#847820, image#45, FamilySearch* https://www.familysearch.org/ark:/61903/3:1:3Q9M-CS4X-K3YY-S?i=44&cat=112848
November 1799	Ninian O.	Son, Basil, marries Elizabeth Graves (Magruder?), marriage bond November 26, 1799, *Georgia County Marriages, 1785-1950, link below*:
April 1800	Ninian O.	Ninian O. sells to John Magruder 420 acres - *Columbia Co GA, Superior Ct Deeds and Mortgages, 1791-1911, v I p 425, FHL#847820, image# 234, FamilySearch* https://www.familysearch.org/ark:/61903/3:1:3Q9M-CS4X-K3YL-1?i=233&cat=112848

October 1801	Ninian O.	Ninian O. places ad for runaway slave Ambrose, 18 yrs. old with yellow complexion *Augusta Chronicle & gazette of the state, Oct 17, 1801, image 4* https://gahistoricnewspapers.galileo.usg.edu/lccn/sn8201 5220/1801-10-17/ed-1/seq-4/print/image_477x817_from_1115,5709_to_2170,7514/
February 1802	Ninian O.	Son, Basil, personal estate including negroes to be sold, February 1802 *Augusta Chronicle & gazette of the state, January 16, 1802, image3* https://gahistoricnewspapers.galileo.usg.edu/lccn/sn82015 220/1802-01-16/ed-1/seq-3/print/image_484x817_from_0,0_to_4081,6885/

Columbia Co GA, Plats and Land Grants, 1783-1794
https://www.familysearch.org/search/catalog/113351

Columbia Co GA, Superior Ct Deeds and Mortgages, 1791-1911
https://www.familysearch.org/search/catalog/112848

Georgia Headright & Bounty Land Records, 1783-1909; Collection Search link: https://www.familysearch.org/search/collection/1914217

Georgia County Marriages, 1785-1950; Collection Search link: https://www.familysearch.org/search/collection/1927197

Historical Collection of Georgia Chapters of the DAR, v. 2, Records of Richmond Co GA, formerly St Paul's Parish, p 114, Historical Collection of Georgia Chapters of the DAR, 1929
http://www.familysearch.org/library/books/idurl/1/283919

Augusta Chronicle & gazette of the state is part of the Georgia Historical Newspapers collection, University of Georgia

Last Will & Testament of Ninian Offutt Magruder

Recorded 24 June 1803[233]

Georgia Columbia County

Personally appeared in open court James Olive, Bury Olive, and Reuben Reynolds being duly sworn on the Gospels of Almighty God saith that they were present and saw Ninian O. Magruder deceased, sign the within will and that they subscribed the same as witness in the presence and at the request of the deceased and at the time of signing the same the deceased was of sound mind and disposing memory.

James Olive

Bury Olive

Reuben Reynolds

Sworn to in open court

Subscribed this 20 June 1803

R. Reynolds excepted that he saw the testator sign

A.Crawford
Clk

---

[233] Columbia County, Georgia, Court of the Ordinary, Wills Arranged Alphabetically, Will of Ninian Offutt Magruder; digital images *FamilySearch* (https://www.familysearch.org/ark:/61903/3:1:3QSQ-G9QM-FVHJ?i=338&cc=1999178&cat=285564 : accessed 24 Jan 21); citing FHL 5782677, image 337-342.

Georgia Columbia County

By their Honors the Judges of the Court of Ordinary for said county

To whom these presents shall come –

Greetings!

Know Ye that on the twentieth day of June one thousand and eight hundred and three, the last will and testament of Ninian Offutt Magruder, late of this county and state aforesaid deceased was proved approved and allowed of the said deceased having whilst he lived and at the time of his death divers goods, rights chattels and credits within the county aforesaid by means whereof the approbation and allowing testament and the power of granting the administration of all and singular the goods and chattels rights and credits of the said deceased to us is manifestly known to belong and that the goods chattels rights and credits of the said deceased and his testament of anyone concerning was granted and committed to Zadok, George, and Archibald Magruder named executors in the last will and testament. They being just[ly] sworn according to law to make a true and perfect [*document incomplete*].

In the Name of God, Amen

I, Ninian Offutt Magruder, of the State of Georgia and County of Columbia, being low and weak but of sound mind and disposing memory and calling to mind the mortality of my body and that it is ordained of God for all men once to die do make and confirm this instrument of writing to comprise my last will and testament.

> 1.   I recommend my soul to god who gave it and my body to be decently interred in the earth from whence it came at the discretion of my executors herein after named and that all my just debts be payed out of my Estate.

> 2.   I give and bequeath to my son, Zadok Magruder, a certain parcel of land including the Plantation whereon the said Zadok lives beginning at Water's ford on the East fork of Kioka Creek running with the stream to the Mouth of said Zadok's using Spring branch from thence to Wyley Olive's Post Oak Corner across the Mill Creek thence on Wyley Olive's line to my corner thence along my line to the beginning [illegible] the same more or less to be freely enjoyed by him and his heirs forever.

> 3.   My desire is that three hundred and fifty acres of land in Washington County and three hundred acres in Glyn County be sold under the direction of my sons Zadok & George Magruder and the money

equally divided between the said Zadok and George to be freely enjoyed by them and their heirs forever.

4. I give and bequeath to my son Zadok one negro girl named **Charlotte** to be by him received out of my Estate after the death or marriage of my dearly beloved wife, Mary.

5. I give and bequeath to my son George one negro boy named **Daniel** to be by him received out of my Estate after the death or marriage of my widow.

6. I give and bequeath to my son John Magruder, one negro woman named **Pat** and her increase to be delivered over immediately after my death, that is as soon as conveniency will admit; and also at the death or marriage of my widow, my desire is that my executors deliver to my said son, John, one other negro named **Prince**.

7. I give and bequeath to my son Archibald **Tom**, **Nancey**, **Mariah**, and **Charity**, my four negroes to be delivered over as soon as convenient after my death; also after the death or marriage of my widow one other Negro named **Middleton** to be freely enjoyed by him and his heirs forever—and further, I wish the plantation whereon I now live containing seven hundred acres [illegible] more or less to be possessed and freely be enjoyed by my son Archibald after the death or marriage of my widow.

8. I give and bequeath to my daughter Sarah Olive the following negroes **Fan Nan & Dave** to be delivered over to my son-in-law John Olive as soon as convenient after my death and also after the death or marriage of my widow, my two negroes **Bob** and **Will** to be by her and her heirs freely enjoyed forever.

9. I give and bequeath to my daughter Eleanor Magruder my two negroes **Ned** and **Ben** as soon as convenient after my death and also after the death or marriage of my widow, my two other negroes, **Harry** and **Cate**, to be by her and her heirs freely enjoyed forever.

10. I give and bequeath to my granddaughter Polly Magruder and daughter of John Magruder one negro girl named **Henny** and also my granddaughter Eliza Magruder and daughter of John Magruder one negro girl named **Matilda** to be by them enjoyed forever.

11. My further desire is that all the remaining part of Estate not before disposed (say) Stock of every kind plantation tools be and remain on the Plantation and to be freely enjoyed by my beloved wife Mary Magruder during her natural life or widowhood and at her death or marriage the said

property then remaining of my Estate to be equally divided between my children, share and share alike to wit, Zadok, George, John, Archibald, Sarah, and Eleanor or their heirs. Know, this clause is not to be understood to interfere or include any property that my children are now in possession of or is understood in the family they have a just claim to.

12. My further desire is having gone through the disposition of my property that if any of my children herein before named do die before having any heir of their body that then their bequest revert to my estate again be equally divided among the surviving legates.

Lastly, I hereby appoint my sons Zadok, George, and Archibald as my executors to this my last will and testament revoking all other therefore made or implied requiring that the said Executors do carry this will and Instrument of Writing into full effect according to the intent and meaning therein expressed and my further wish and desire is that in case any dispute may arise in the distribution of my estate between my executors and the legates that they mutually agree to submit the same to honest men of discernment to evade Litigation Suits at Law. In witness whereof, I have hereunto set my hand and seal this seventeenth day of March Anno Domino 1803.

Ninian O. Magruder

Signed, sealed, and acknowledged.

In presence of the said George

The last clause before signed

James Olive

Bury Olive

Reuben Reynolds

Inventory of the Estate of Ninian Offutt Magruder

Recorded October 26, 1803[234]

An inventory of all the goods and chattels of Ninian Offutt Magruder, deceased:

One Bay gelding 13 years old $60 One mare 6 do $110	$170
One gelding 8 do $90, 1 yellow bay mare 4 do $130	$220
1 yellow bay gelding 8 do $100 One sorrel calf 1 do $45	$145
40 head of cattle $252 36 head of geese $18	$270
13 head of sheep $19.50 5 Shovel plows Singletree plows $18	$27.50
4 coulters and stocks $3.50 2 bars hare plows doubletrees & harness $10	$13.50
Waggon and one p. [illegible] $75 16 weeding hoes $8	$83
5 Pair of chains harness, collars, and bridles	$10
11 Beehives $22 One Grind Stone $2	$24

[234] Columbia Co, GA, Court of the Ordinary, Estate Records, 1788-1940, Inventories, appraisements, sales, v. E-G 1790-1822, Book F, p 213-215; digital images, FamilySearch (https://www.familysearch.org/ark:/61903/3:1:3Q9M-C9YP-2DJH?i=113&cat=298373: accessed 24 Jan 21); citing FHL7701375, image#114-115.

Set of blacksmiths tools & bellow $30 2 Scythes & Cradles $2	$32
4 rum hogs heads $5 Five Stands $3.75 8 Sides seal leather $16	$24.75
Quantity of rough rice $4 4000lbs of fodder $20	$24
5 axels and one hatchet $6 2 Mattocks & grubbing hoe $3	$9
3 Spinning wheels $3. Jackscrew $6 3 Iron wedges $1.25	$10.25
7 barrels $3 Crop cut saw $1 Two old saddles $2	$6
20lbs wool $5 1000lbs bacon $125 6 bushels salt $6	$136
5 old casks $2 One lot pewter $13 Quantity of lard $18	$33
Set of wooden ware $6 4 pots 2 ovens skillet 2 frying pans $15	$21
1 Loom $6 A web in the loom $12 Six sickles $1	$19
150 bushels of corn $75 Lot of jugs and jars $4.50	$79.50

1 mans saddle and bridle $8 1 Coopers jointer $1	$9
Coopers and foot adz [adze] $2 Lot of carpenters tools $4	$6
15lbs bees wax $3.75 2 barrels 37 cents 1 Small keg 50 cents	$4.62
Coffee Mill 75 cents 4 Slays $4 1 Riddle 50 cents	$5.25
Lot of crockery ware $20 15 teaspoon Teaspoon 50 cents	$20.50
One lot books $8 1 linnen wheel and hackle $3	$11
8 yds cotton cloth $3 Quantity of spun cotton $15	$18
3 hides and a piece of upper leather $6.50	$6.50
3 beds bedstead & furniture $80 4 woolen bed covers $24	$104
1 bed quilt 1 pr sheets, 3 pillowcases $9.50 5 Counterpanes $10	$19.50
3 roses blankets $6 Six dutch blankets $15	$21
1 lot of Harness $1 22 Split bottomed chairs $11	$12
4 beds bedstead & furniture $120 3 pine chests $9	$129

3 pine Tables $4.50 One desk $20 1 looking glass $18 ¾	$24.68 ¾
1 Morocco pocketbook $2 Shaving box case razors & hone $2.50	$4.50
1 lot Phials $1 Quantity brown sugar $7 Quantity coffee $3	$11
One pair flat iron tea kettle Two candle sticks	$2.50
Three [illegible] pr cotton cards one pr. wool cards	$2.50
[page damaged] cloth & 7 towels $5.75 1 pr. fire dogs $2 One [illegible] $4	$14.75
Quantity of brandy $6 1 pr plated [spurs] $1 1 felling ax $1.50	$8.50
9 large hogs $36 8 Second size $20 10 third size $15	$71
4 Sows 21 pigs $24 1 piece of blistered steel 87 ½ as 1 piece of steel	$25.87 ½
1 p Sheep shears 25 cents Lot of knives and forks $2	$2.25
1 Cutting knife & box $2.50 SixHh^s Tob° [hogsheads of tobacco] supposed at 1100 lbs each	$132

Fan Han Bob Will & Dave $1300. **Nancey Tom Mariah Charity Cofy**[235] and **Mider** $1400	$2700
Charlotte $350 **Harry Kate Jim**[236] **& Ned** $900	$1,250
Prince, Pat, Henny, Matilda $800 **Daniel** $375	$1,175
Quantity of tallow and candles	$3.50

We do certify that the foregoing is a just and true inventory of all the goods and chattels of Ninian O. Magruder deceased. Shown to us by the Executors thereof Certified by us and given under our hands and seals this 24th day of October 1803.

Wim. Hoge

Joshua Wynne

William Drane

We do hereby certify that we rec'd the foregoing Inventory from the appraisers who have thereunto subscribed their names certified by us this 24th day of October 1803.

Zadok Magruder

Geo Magruder

Archibald Magruder

---

[235] Difficult to read; may be Cofy, derived from the West African name Kofi.

[236] May be read as Ben.

Application of Lucille B. Osborne to the Daughters of the American Revolution, based on descent from Ninian O. Magruder

** ONLINE APPLICATION PROOFING DOCUMENT ***

Generation: 3   was the biological child of:

Noah Burge   born: - Mar - 1872   at: AL

died: Demopolis Morengo Co AL   on: 21 - Oct - 1950   and his (**1**) wife

Minerva McGruder   born: - Feb - 1875   at: AL

died at: Sawyerville Hale Co AL   on: p - - 1930   Married - Date   4 - Jan - 1891

                                                                  at: Hale Co AL

Source Citation: DC; MC;1900 Census; 1910 Census; 1930 Census

The next generation added will be the parents of: This Female

---

Generation: 4   was the biological child of:

Charles McGruder   born: c - - 1829   at: AL

died: Hollow Square Hale Co AL   on: p - - 1900   and his ( ) wife

Racheal Hill   born: - Mar - 1818   at: Hale Co AL

died at: Sawyerville Hale Co AL   on: 17 - Jan - 1935   Married - Date   c - - 1860

                                                                  at:

Source Citation: **Probate   record**

The next generation added will be the parents of: This Male

Generation: 5   was the biological child of:

Ned Magruder   born: c - - 1795   at: GA

died: prob Greene Co AL   on: a 11 - Apr - 1853   and his ( ) wife

Mariah X   born: c - - 1800   at:

died at: Hollow Square Hale Co AL   on: p - - 1880   Married - Date   - -

                                                                  at:

Source Citation: Y-Chromosome Report; analysis; AL Wills & Probate, ancesty

The next generation added will be the parents of: This Male

The Alabama Black McGruders

** ONLINE APPLICATION PROOFING DOCUMENT ***

Generation: 6   was the biological child of:

Ninian Offutt Magruder   born: - - 1744   at:

died: Columbia Co GA   on: a 24 - Jun - 1803   and his (**1**) wife

X X   born: - -   at:

died at: on: - -   Married - Date   - -

                                                                   at:

Source Citation: 878789 Add Vol 1231 A073127, Ninian Offutt Magruder

The next generation added will be the parents of: **Patriot**

The following analysis was written by Rhea Mihalisin and Ellen Fancy as part of Lucille Osborne's historic application to the Daughters of the American Revolution (DAR National Number 1017233) based upon descent from Ninian O. Magruder (A073127). The citations referenced are within file 1017233 as below

The purpose of this analysis is to prove that Ned Magruder is the son of Ninian Ouffit Magruder.

Summary of Research Strategy

Ned Magruder was born about 1795 (DOC B), the son of a slave woman and his presumed father, Ninian Ouffit Magruder. No birth records would have been recorded, except by the owner or overseer—none were located. Ned died before 1853 (DOC C), still enslaved; again, no record of his biological parents was located, only that he was part of the estate of Eleanor Wynne. However, a collection of existing records and yDNA reports were located that together indicate that Ninian Offutt Magruder was the father of Ned Magruder.

Supporting Documentation

- DOC A - GA Wills & Probate Records, 1742-1992, Columbia Co, v A, p 175-177, Ancestry

- DOC B – Greene Co, AL, Probate Ct, WB C, p 203-205, FHL#5175959, image#645-646, FamilySearch

- DOC C - Greene County, AL, Probate Ct. Court Records, v N, p 756, FHL#5176175, image#50, FamilySearch

- DOC D – Greene Co, AL, Orphan's Ct., Court Records v C-1830, p 68-70, FHL#7736049, images 443-444

- DOC E – Greene Co, AL, Orphan's Ct., Court Records v C-1830, p 258-263, FHL#7736049, images 539-541

- DOC F - AL State Census, 1866, Greene Co, p 44, Colored Population, Ancestry

- DOC G – 1870C, Hale Co, AL, Beat No. 6, p 17 hh#175, 176, p 18, hh#177

- DOC H –Baltimore Sun, Oct 25, p 14

- DOC I -1850C Slave Schedule, Greene Co, AL, Hollow Square, p 33

- DOC J – Greene Co, AL, Probate Ct., Probate Minutes, v. H, p 777, FHL#7738730, image#167

Interpretation

In 1803, Ninian Ouffit Magruder wrote his last testament and will, leaving four slaves to his unwed daughter, Eleanor: Ned, Ben, Kate, and Harvey[237] (DOC A). A few months later Eleanor married Williamson Wynne. (NN#) In her will dated 1848, Eleanor Magruder Wynne gave Ned and his family to her daughter Salina A Ferrell (DOC B). Eleanor's will makes it clear that she is giving Ned and his family to Salina by naming them specifically: Ned, his wife Mariah, and their children, one of which was Ned's son Charles.

Property and estate law in force during Eleanor's lifetime prove that the Ned mentioned in Eleanor's will is the same Ned that is listed in her father's will. When Eleanor wrote her will in 1848, estate law in force at the time limited her to bequeathing property she owned prior to her marriage. She did not have any legal right to bequeath property received as a dower via a will. Property she received as part of her dower when her husband died would be for her use only during her natural life. After her death that dower property reverted back to the estate of her husband. Thus, by law, the only slave named Ned that Eleanor could bequeath to Salina was the slave named Ned that Ninian O Magruder bequeathed to his daughter in 1803.

Although legally belonging to Eleanor, upon her marriage to Williamson Wynne, Ned and his family became 'property' under the control of Eleanor's husband in accordance with coveture law. An inventory of Williamson Wynne's property appraised in Feb 1829 includes Ned and his family (DOC D). Eleanor, now widowed, a femme sole, (a single woman), could retake control of her property, which by 1829 included Ned, his wife Mariah, and their children, Fanny, Martha & Charles (DOC E).

Ned did not live long enough to be emancipated and recorded with a surname. However we know that his surname was Magruder; his wife, Mariah, sons Charles and Jasper, and unmarried daughter Lilly all adopted the name MGruder. (DOC F

---

[237] Could be read Harry.

G). The only "Magruder" for this family, was Ned, whom Ninian Offutt Magruder bequeathed to Eleanor in 1803. There are no other Magruders in the area where Ned and his family had resided since before 1829. That the family adopted MGruder indicates they knew that Ned's father was Ninian Offutt Magruder.

Several other records support this. Descendants of Ninian Offutt Magruder believed he had a son named Ned, and that Ned was the youngest born of his children (DOC H). Descendants of Ned Magruder believed Ned had been fathered by a white man because his children had fair skin (oral history shared with Lucille Osborne). And indeed, Ned can be found on the 1850 Slave schedule identified as mulatto (DOC I). The 1850 Slave schedule was enumerated in Hale County in Oct., about the same time Eleanor Wynne's estate was settled. (DOC J). Salina Ferrell's slaves are listed in the household of husband, William Ferrell since he was the head of the household. Although there are no names on the slave schedule, the sex and age of the slaves are in nearly the same order as listed in Eleanor Wynne's will (DOC C). Ned, age 54, was still living in 1850, and is listed first and described as a mulatto; his wife Mariah is listed next, age 51, followed by Fanny, Martha, and Charles. Thus it was well known to the family and enumerator that Ned was the son of a white man and female slave.

To confirm that Ned Magruder was the son of Ninian Offutt Magruder, Black descendants of Ned Magruder and white descendants of Ninian Offutt Magruder submitted yDNA test results. The DNA test results show that descendants of Ned Magruder share a common ancestor with descendants of Ninian Offutt Magruder within 10 generations. Traditional written records indicate that the common ancestor is a male who lived in Georgia about 1795. Given that Ned Magruder was born in 1795 in Georgia, that Ned Magruder, at age 8, was the property of Ninian Magruder, and that Ninian Magruder bequeathed Ned to his daughter, Eleanor, not to one of his sons, allows for only one interpretation of the yDNA results: Ned Magruder was fathered by his owner, Ninian Offutt Magruder.

Documents Pertaining to Chapter Five

Newspaper Clippings, 19th Century, Hale and Greene Counties

COUNTY MEETING.

Pursuant to previous notice, a Public Meeting of the citizens of Greene county, without respect to party, was held in the Court House at Eutaw, on Monday, the 9th inst.,—when on motion of Col. John Erwin, the Hon. Harry I. Thornton was appointed President of the meeting. The President on taking the chair explained the objects of the meeting in a few very appropriate and happy remarks. On motion of Wm. M. Murphy, Esq., Dr. D. J. Means was appointed Vice President; and on motion, Wiley Coleman was appointed Secretary,—and John G. Harvey and G. G. Snedecor, Assistant Secretaries. Dr. P. W. Kittrell then moved that a committee of 21 be appointed by the President, to be selected from the two parties,—which was amended by Col. James B. Clarke, so that the committee should be composed of *ten whigs, ten democrats* and one *Taylor democrat,*—whereupon the chair appointed the following gentlemen as members of said committee:

Zach'y Meriwether,	John Erwin,
Solomon McAlpin,	Alexander Graham,
Stephen F. Hale,	Z. Horn,
James Wills	Sydenham Moore,
John G. Friend,	John H. Copp,
Wm. M. Murphy,	John G. Harvey,
F. W. Kittrell,	J. J. Harry,
Elias C. Field,	Samuel Pickens,
A. Benners,	John W. Womack,
Alfred Hatch,	Erasmus Wynne.

On motion, the meeting then adjourned till 2 o'clock, to afford the committee time to prepare their report.

At 2 o'clock the meeting convened again, when the committee submitted through Col. H. M. Judge, their report, which he prefaced with a few very appropriate remarks.

Col. John Erwin addressed the meeting in an able and highly interesting speech, urging the great importance of firm and united action on the part of the South.— The President then proceeded to take the sense of the meeting on the adoption of the preamble and resolutions, when Col. James B. Clarke moved that they be adopted *unanimously,*—and no objection having been raised, the preamble and resolutions as reported by the committee, were submitted to the meeting and adopted *unanimously:*

REPORT OF THE COMMITTEE.

In as much as we have been admonished in the most solemn manner by the recent Convention of Southern Members of Congress, and by the facts contained in the Addresses submitted on that occasion, that daring *encroachments* have been, and are still being made upon the institutions of the South, in palpable violation of the Constitution,—that the peace and safety of the South—the political equality of the States, and the integrity of the Union, are in *imminent peril,* requiring prompt, energetic, and concerted action on the part of the slave-holding States, be it therefore

238

Greene County Meeting, *(Greeensboro) Alabama Beacon*, 11 April 1849, p. 3, col. 1; digital image *Newspapers.com* (https://www.newspapers.com/image/253602700/?terms=Eutaw&match=1 : accessed 17 Sept 2021).

Resolved, 1st. That the political union established by the constitution, is one of perfect *equality* among the States—that any legislation on the part of Congress, had with the view of impairing this equality, is not only degrading and oppressive in its character, but is also a manifest breach of the constitution; and that whilst we love and cherish the Union, as conducing to our prosperity at home and importance abroad, yet we will never consent that it shall be perverted from its true object, and used as an instrument of oppression, dishonor and degradation to any portion of the sovereign States of this confederacy.

Resolved, 2d. That we regard the territories of the Union, however acquired, as the common property of the several States composing the Union—that the passage by Congress of any law which shall directly or indirectly prevent the citizens of any State from emigrating to California or New Mexico with their property of *any* and *every* description, will be a gross and palpable violation of the constitution—a direct assault upon the institutions of the South—endangering the stability and permanence of the Republic, and which ought to be resisted by every freeman, who cherishes his liberty and equality, at any and all hazards, and to the last extremity.

Resolved, 3d. That the slaveholding States, actuated alone by patriotic considerations and a high appreciation of the Union, have long submitted, without retaliation or attempt at revolution, to a wanton and systematic assault by the non-slaveholding States upon their interest, feelings and clear constitutional rights.—They have seen the influences of early education, of religion, of the press and of organized associations, directed against an institution, which is recognised by the Constitution and sanctioned by the Christian religion—they have seen the constitutional provision for the surrender of fugitive slaves *annulled* by enactments of the Legislatures of the Northern States, defeating their just rights in property, and exposing the border slaveholding States to the predatory incursions of organized bands of fanatical and felonious abolitionists—they have witnessed the attempts made in Congress to violate the constitution by excluding the South from a participancy in the common territories of the Union—to abolish slavery in the District of Columbia, and to interdict the slave commerce between the States. We now say, in a spirit of frankness, to our Northern brethren, *that aggression upon our rights has reached that point, beyond which* it shall not go—that a further submission to insult and injury, would be incompatible with a just regard for our honor and future safety, and degrading to our character as freemen and co-equals in the confederacy.

Resolved, 4th. That we cordially approve the resolutions adopted by the Virginia Legislature, and we recommend their adoption to the Legislature of this State at its next session.

Resolved, 5th. That we disclaim any intention and deprecate any attempt to agitate the slave question for party purposes or party effect—that we discard all partizan bias or prejudice, and look upon this great question as *Southern freemen* and *American patriots*, who are determined to maintain the political equality of the States —to uphold the constitution, and preserve the integrity of the Union,—and recommend to our Southern brethren moderation, but at the same time, firm and concerted action.

Resolved, 6th. That we do not intend by these resolutions to refuse our assent to have the Missouri Compromise bill applied to any territory of the United States, by way of *conciliation and to preserve the Union,*—should a returning sense of justice on the part of our Northern brethren lead them to adopt the same.

Resolved, 7th. That we cordially approve of the address adopted by the convention of the Southern Members of Congress in January, 1849, at Washington City.

Jno. Erwin,	Zach'y Meriwether,
Wm. M. Murphy,	Alex. Graham,
P. W. Kittrell,	Solomon McAlpin,
John W. Womack,	Hilliard M. Judge,
Samuel Pickens,	S. F. Hale,
Erasmus Wynne,	A. Bonners,
Sydenham Moore,	Alfred Hatch,
James Wills,	John H. Copp,
John G Harvey,	John G. Friend,
Z. Horn,	Elias C. Field,

J. J. Harry.

On motion of Wm. M. Murphy, Esq., it was resolved that the proceedings of the meeting be signed by the officers, and that they be published in the Eutaw Whig and Alabama Beacon, and that the papers throughout the State be requested to copy.

The meeting then, on motion, adjourned,

HARRY I. THORNTON,
President.

D. J. MEANS, Vice-Pres't.

W. COLEMAN, Secretary.

JOHN G. HARVEY, ⎰ Ass't Secretaries.
G. G. SNEDECOR, ⎱

GIVE ME A TRIAL.

HAVING purchased the entire interest of S. M. Cole at Hollow-Square, I shall continue to carry on the Mercantile Business as formerly, under the care of B. P. Ferrell, my authorized agent.

In addition to my present stock I have just received, and will continue to receive, a fresh supply of Goods suitable for my customers.

From the many advantages I possess relative to contingent expenses, I am confident I shall be able to compete with any house of a similar order in point of prices. With these inducements and close attention to business, I earnestly solicit a liberal share of patronage from my friends.

JOHN Q. A. CLEVELAND.

Dec. 25, 1849.   35 tf

239

---

239 Give Me a Trial, notice placed by John Q.A. Cleveland, *(Greeensboro) Alabama Beacon*, 12 January 1850, p.3, col. 5; digital image *Newspapers.com* (https://www.newspapers.com/image/253603640/?terms=give%20me%20a%20trial&match= 1 : accessed 17 Sept 2021).

RANAWAY,

FROM the neighborhood of Greensboro', about the 1st of April, a negro man by the name of ULYSSES—a Plasterer by trade—about 5 feet 8 to 10 inches high—about 50 years of age,—his complexion is between that of a black and a mulatto—no distinctive marks recollected. He can read and write—is a negro of a great deal of shrewdness and cunning, and can play the hypocrite very successfully whenever he has any particular object to effect. He was brought some twelve years ago from Newbern, N. C., and having made three previous attempts to get back to that place, the probability is that he is again making his way there.

A liberal reward will be paid for his delivery to Captain C. Jones, Greenesboro', or to the subscriber, at Camden, Wilcox county.

JESSE GIBSON.

April 19, 1851.   51 tf

☞The Montgomery Advertiser & Gazette will copy till forbid.   J. G.

240

---

[240] Runaway advertisement placed by Jesse Gibson, *(Greeensboro) Alabama Beacon*, 19 April 1851, p.3, col. 1; digital image *Newspapers.com* (https://www.newspapers.com/image/253282879/?terms=%22Jesse%20Gibson%22&match=1 : accessed 17 Sept 2021).

NOTICE.

ADMINISTRATOR'S SALE OF SLAVES.

BY virtue of an order of the Probote Court of Sumter county, I will, on Wednesday, the first day of June next, at Hollow Square, in Greene county, as administrator, with the will annexed, of Richard Jenkins, deceased, sell to the highest bidder, for cash, the undivided one half interest of the said Richard Jenkins, deceased, in the slaves hereinafter named, for and during the natural life time of James Ferrell, to wit:— Nancy, about 52 years old; Eliza, about 25; Harriet, about 24; John, 20; Allen, 16; Fanny, 7; Louisa, 9; Sarah, 3, and London, 3 years old.   P. G. NASH, Adm'r.

  April 29, 1859.   15 2s 5w

241

---

[241] Administrator's Sale of Slaves, estate of Richard Jenkins, *(Greeensboro) Alabama Beacon*, 29 April 1859, p.2, col. 6; digital image *Newspapers.com* (https://www.newspapers.com/image/253255025/?terms=Jenkins&match=1 : accessed 17 Sept 2021).

RANAWAY, MAY 12, '59,

FROM the subscriber. on the night of the 11th of May, 1859. one negro man, as follows : WASHINGTON, supposed to be about 23 or 24 years old, near six feet high, spare made, weighing about 150 or 160 pounds; had on when he left a roundabout coat, drab color, a drab hat, a pair of ditcher's boots. and took with him a pair of gaiter shoes ; is quick spoken, and a very intelligent negro, of a coper color. He can read and write well, and is rather thick-lipped.

Any one taking him up and confining him, or bringing him to me, will be liberally rewarded ; and any information concerning him will be thankfully received.

W. F. MONETTE.

Hollow Square, Ala.. may 20. '59. 18 3s 4w

242

---

242 Runaway advertisement placed by W.F. Monette, *(Greeensboro) Alabama Beacon*, 10 Jun 1859, p.3, col. 1; digital image *Newspapers.com* (https://www.newspapers.com/image/253255132/?terms=Monette&match=1 : accessed 17 Sept 2021). On the same day (p.2, col. 7) Monette adverstised both Washington and a man named Henry, as runaways.

HORRIBLE MURDER.—The editor of the Pensacola Gazette has seen a private letter from Hollow Square P. O., (Green County Ala.,) from which he makes the following extract :

A terrible thing has occurred since I wrote you last—the murder of our postmaster at Hollow Square. He took his meals about a mile from the postoffice, and was returning from his supper, when, it is supposed, he was met and followed into the office, and there knocked in the head with an axe ; then robbed of all his money. The letters were then all broken open, and a great deal of money taken from them. He was then dragged about three-quarters of a mile, with the intention of putting him in an old well, but the murderer fled before he accomplished this. Before he left, to make sure of his victim, he shot him through the head. The postmaster was a very inoffensive man, and was very much liked, but was murdered in cold blood merely for his money. The murderer has not been taken up, although it is well known who he is, but not having sufficient evidence to hang him, they think it best to let him alone.—Negro evidence is pretty much all there is, and you know that is of no avail in court.

Later news states that suspicion rests on a man by the name of Jones, an overseer by occupation, as the murderer of Hercefield. He is now in Green county jail.

243

---

243 Horrible Murder, *The Weekly Advertiser (Montgomery, Alabama)*, 25 April 1860, p. 1, col. 2; digital image *Newspapers.com* (https://www.newspapers.com/image/355842745/?terms=murder%20%22hollow%20square%22&match=1 : accessed 17 Sept 2021).

NOTICE.

THE Court of County Commissioners in and for Greene County, will please attend a call session of said Court at the Court-house of said county, on MONDAY, the 27th October, instant. And the Precinct Commissioners below named, appointed at the August term of said Court to look after the necessities of the destitute families of our brave volunteer soldiers, to wit:

1. IN HAVANA PRECINCT.—D. D. Harris, Geo. H. Sheldon, T. J. Sorsby, and W. K. Brown.

2. NEW PROSPECT.—D. B. Sample, Solomon George, and E. C. Harris.

3. FIVE MILE CREEK.—A. S. Jeffries, R. C. Davis, and A. F. Flinn.

4. GREENSBORO.—T. K. Carson, C. Avery, and Wm. Morris.

5. NEWBERN.—J. Huggins, John Atkins, R. W. Moore.

6. HOLLOW SQUARE.—O. A. Wynne, W. G. Sadler, and C. L. Stickney.

7. DRAKE'S LANDING.—J. R. Webster, and A. S. Nelson.

8. FORKLAND.—M. R. Brassfield, W. M. High, and J. C. Taylor.

9. GARRETT'S SHOP.—R. F. Shelton, R. Taylor, and B. Gulley.

10. EUTAW.—W. R. Hardaway, Jno. Sears, and J. M. Durham.

11. SPRINGFIELD.—Samuel Crawford, John Hall, and T. M. Colvin.

12. KNOXVILLE.—D. S. White, J. M. Knox, and T. J. Patton.

13. UNION.—Aquilla Hardy, A. R. Davis, and J. M. Chambers.

14. PLEASANT RIDGE.—J. M. McGowan, John D. Horton, and J. D. Duncan.

15. MT. HEBRON.—Arnold Jolly, J. Stephens and C. L. Wilson.

16. CLINTON.—D. Harris, B. Turnipseed, and J. M. Chambers.

17. BOLIGEE.—N. F. Smith and D. C. Mayes.

Are particularly invited to attend, and they are furthermore particularly requested to prepare themselves to report as fully as can be done the destitute in their respective precincts, and all other good citizens who feel an interest in the welfare of the destitute families of soldiers are also invited to attend and confer with the Commissioners' Court as to what would be best to be done. It is earnestly hoped that one Precinct Commissioner at least from each Precinct Committee will attend.

Families destitute will please make their situation known to their Precinct Commissioners.

W. C OLIVER,
Judge P. C. G. C
Eutaw, October 14, 1862.   40 6s 2w

244

---

244 Call to Greene County Commissioners re: destitute families of soldiers, *(Greensboro) Alabama Beacon*, 24 October 1862, p. 3, col. 4; digital image *Newspapers.com* (https://www.newspapers.com/image/355657581/?terms=Sheldon&match=1 : accessed 17 Sept 2021).

No advertisement received for a longer period than three months.

SELMA:
TUESDAY, APRIL 19, 1864.

NEW ADVERTISEMENTS.—A list of enrolling officers appointed in this district will be found in another column.

A meeting of the stockholders of the Alabama Coal Mining Company will be held in Montgomery on the 4th day of May next.

The members of Phœnix Fire Company No. 1 will meet at their engine room tonight.

Miss Deegan has opened a dressmaking establishment at the corner of Broad and Dallas streets.

A well improved house and lot will be sold at Dayton on the 25th inst.

Geo. Marlow has Cuba tobacco seed for sale.

A good blacksmith is wanted at Forte's postoffice.

Fifty dollars reward is offered for the negro boy Charles, runaway from near Newbern, Ala.

E. T. Watts wants has a good cook for hire

Aram & Purviance have for sale a set of jewelry garnets set in pearl.

Sink & Thompson will sell on Wednesday next beds and bedding, guns, jugs, pitchers, &c.

The perishable property belonging to the estate of Wellington Dallas, deceased, will be sold on the 23d day of May next.

245

245 Notice of Stockholders' Meeting, Alabama Coal Mining Company, *The Daily Selma (Alabama) Reporter*, 19 April 1864, p. 4, col. 1; digital image *Newspapers.com* (https://www.newspapers.com/image/573970824/?terms=%22Alabama%20Coal%20Mining%22&match=1 : accessed 17 Sept 2021).

NOTICE.
Administrator's Sale.

BY virtue of the will of Jonathan May, deceased, I will sell at Public Auction, on the premises of said deceased, near Hollow Square, Greene county, Alabama, on the 12th day of December next, (1862) the following property, to wit:

Eleven Negroes,
ONE GIN, 1 GIN BAND,
—ALSO,—
200 ACRES OF LAND,

160 of which is enclosed, a portion of which is

Good Bottom Land.

Call and examine.

The terms of sale will be on a credit of 12 months. The purchaser will be required to give note and two approved securities before the property is delivered.   JOHN W. MAY,
                              Administrator.

November 7, 1862.   43 3s 6w

School Books,

(NEW SUPPLY,)

Such as used by Schools in this vicinity, just received at
          RUSSELL'S BOOK STORE.
Greensboro, Nov. 7, 1862.

246

---

246 Administrator's Sale, estate of Jonathan May, *(Greensboro) Alabama Beacon*, 21 November 1862, p. 3, col. 6; digital image *Newspapers.com* (https://www.newspapers.com/image/355657632/?terms=Jonathan%20May&match=1 : accessed 17 Sept 2021).

WANTED,
300,000 Bushels of Corn.

THE subscriber has been appointed Agent for the purchase of Corn for indigent soldiers families. He is authorized to pay $1 50 per bushel for it, delivered at any landing on the Warrior or Bigbee rivers, or at any point on the Newbern, or Alabama and Mississippi Railroads. He can be addressed at Hollow Square, Ala.

SAMUEL COWIN.

December 25. 1863.   50 2s 4w

☞ Whig & Observer requested to copy.

247

---

247 Wanted: 300,000 Bushels of Corn, *(Greensboro) Alabama Beacon*, 15 January 1864, p. 4, col. 2; digital image *Newspapers.com* (https://www.newspapers.com/image/355658130/?terms=300%2C000%20bushels&match=1 : accessed 17 Sept 2021).

ELECTION NOTICE.

IN pursuance of the act of the Legislature of the State of Alabama for the formation of the new county of Hale, approved January 30th, 1867, the undersigned appointed Commissioners by said act, and in accordance with the requirements thereof hereby give notice that the polls will be opened at each of the old election precincts within the limits of said new county, on the

First Monday in March Next,

for the election, by the qualified voters residing within the limits of said new county, for such public officers for said county as are required by law to be elected in the other counties of this State, viz: For Judge of Probate, Sheriff. Clerk of the Circuit Court, Tax Assessor, Tax Collector. Four County Commissioners, County Superintendent of Education. also for two Justices of the Peace and one Constable in each election precinct, and at the same time and place there will also be held an election for a county site for said new county, and the following named persons are hereby appointed to conduct said elections at the respective precincts:

Carthage Precinct.

Thos. C. Hardwick.   Tharion Brown.
W A Bishop.
Frank Whatley, Returning Officer.

Havana Precinct.

R B Allen,   T J Sorsby,
J M Jack,
Thos M Lavender, Returning Officer.

New Prospect Precinct.

Jno B Watkins.   Doct. —— Anderson,
Jno Wedgeworth.
Archie Jones, Returning Officer.

Harrison Precinct.

J W Williams,   F M Harris,
J H Gewin,
Belton Singley, Returning Officer.

Hollow Square Precinct.

O F Wynne,   James Melton.
Seaborn Travis,
Robt Redding. Returning Officer.

Greensboro Precinct.

Gustavus Stollenwerck.   A S Jeffries,
Gaston Drake,
Geo Briggs, Returning Officer.

Drake's Landing Precinct.

Jno R Webster,   T B Lipscomb.

248

---

248 Precinct Returns and limits of new (Greene) county, *(Greensboro) Alabama Beacon*, 23 February 1867, p. 3, col. 6; digital image *Newspapers.com* (https://www.newspapers.com/image/355814368/?terms=Hollow%20Square&match=1 : accessed 17 Sept 2021).

A J Dunlap.
L L Singleton, Returning Officer.

Newbern Precinct.

J L Burton,　　　　　　A Parker Hatch.
James W McCarn.
Joseph Allison, Returning Officer.

Macon Precinct.

James D Browder,　　　　Henry A Tayloe,
A P Blount.
Jno D Wilburn, Returning Officer.

Picken's Mill Precinct.

R N Harris,　　　　　　Robt Drake.
Robt Henley.
W C Christian, Returning Officer.

Five Mile Prec'nct —Perry.

Marion Johnston,　　　　Jno D Ryan.
Green B Wilson.
Wm H Wilson, Returning Officer.

The limits of said new county are as follows, viz: All that portion of the county of Greene East of the Warrior river; Township 18, Range 5, Township 18, Range 4, all of the North half of Township 18, Range 3, East of the Warrior river, and all of Township 19, Range 3, in the county of Marengo. Townships 22 and 23, and the West ½ of Township 21, Range 6, in the county of Perry, Township 23 in Range 5, and of that portion of Township 23 in Range 4, and Township 25 in Range 5, lying East of the Warrior river in the county of Tuscaloosa.

The managers and returning officers of said elections shall be governed by the same rules as govern managers of elections in this State, and the returns of all such elections shall be made as required by the said act to the undersigned Commissioners at the town of Greensboro within three days after said elections.

A. M. DORMAN, ⎫
A. C. JONES, ｜
WM. T. HENDON, ⎬ Commissioners.
I. H. OSBORN. ｜
G. H. SHELDON, ⎭

Greensboro, Feb 16.　　　　6-12in-tds.

THE COTTON CROP OF HALE.—We have made special inquiry this week of our planting friends in town attending court, as to the cotton crop of their respective neighborhoods. The reports from the Carthage neighborhood are extremely unfavorable,—crop not likely to turn out more than *one-third* of last year's crop.— From the Havana neighborhood the reports are bad,—crop estimated at scarcly half of that of last year. The estimate for the Hollow Square neighborhood, about half of last year's crop. From the New Prospect neighborhood the reports are better than from any other part of the county —estimated yield, about *two-thirds* of last year's crop.

South of this, though we have heard of a few crops that will probably reach two-thirds to three-fourths of last year's yield, we have heard of others that will not exceed one-third of a good crop. The aggregate yield for the portion of Hale, South of this, is estimated at about half of that of last year.

249

---

249 The Cotton Crop of Hale, *(Greensboro) Alabama Beacon*, 7 October 1871, p. 3, col. 2; digital image *Newspapers.com* (https://www.newspapers.com/image/355689996/?terms=%22cotton%20crop%22&match=1 : accessed 17 Sept 2021).

J. T. Walshe, who killed a negro at Hollow Square, some two weeks ago, had a hearing in this place, last Tuesday, before Justices Melton and Roulhac. The evidence showed that the killing was done in self-defence, and the accused was discharged.

250

---

250 J. T. Walshe Killed a Negro, *(Greensboro) Alabama Beacon*, 27 April 1872, p.3, col. 1; digital image *Newspapers.com* (https://www.newspapers.com/image/355690096/?terms=Hollow%20Square&match=1 : accessed 17 Sept 2021).

.... Jim. K. Green, negro member of Parsons' Museum, from Hale county, made a chatter the other day, in which he dwelt upon the approaching dawn of a brighter day for negrodom, when little niggers would go to the same schools with white children, play with them, kiss them, and, when they get large enough, intermarry with them. This fellow Green, a few years ago, was a well-behaved negro member of Harrington's Menagerie, but since the change of keepers, he grows insolent apace. This talk of Jim. Green's beats anything yet. Alabama surely is drifting into the same dark channel with Louisiana, and we doubt not that Green expects to be the next Governor of the State. Would'nt be surprised.—[Tuscaloosa Blade..

251

251 Jim K. Green: Negro Member of Parson's Museum, *(Greensboro) Alabama Beacon*, 15 February 1873 p. 2, col. 3; digital image *Newspapers.com* (https://www.newspapers.com/image/355690203/?terms=%22Jim%20Green%22&match=1 : accessed 28 Sept 2021)..

The Beacon.

PUBLISHED EVERY SATURDAY MORNING.

JOHN G. HARVEY, Editor.

GREENSBORO, ALA.

SATURDAY, MARCH 1, 1873.

Subscription, Advertising and Job-work due in advance.

THE "CIVIL RIGHTS BILL."

The most important measure now before the Alabama Legislature, is what is called the "Civil Rights Bill," which was introduced in the House some three weeks ago, and finally referred to the Judiciary Committee.

The Committee made their report last Monday. Some of the provisions of the bill are so objectionable that Parsons, White, and other of the more intelligent Radicals, are opposed to it,—but the colored members, with Jim Green at their head, say that nothing short of that bill will satisfy them.

The Committee reported adversely to the bill, but presented a substitute. The minority reported the original bill. The report of the majority was discussed at considerable length. Jim Green made quite a long speech against the report,—in which he said, referring to his condition as a slave: "I was compelled to work from the time the sun first kissed the morning breezes until it sunk behind the western horizon. I could not look up but my back was lashed. * * These Black Republicans said there would be an inter marriage of the races. We don't want it The prettiest thing I ever saw was a black woman. * * The Constitution gives us equal rights. I read from the Constitution Niggers, where are you? *I tell you, the leading colored men are done with party.— I don't know whether I will be a Democra or a Republican. We intend to go with those who give us our rights."*

I don't know whether I will be a Democrat or a Republican. We intend to go with those who give us our rights."

Now, in reference to the matter in hand, we have this to say. And we think the great body of the Conservative party of Alabama occupy on this subject the same ground:

Let the colored men have all the rights civil and political, to which the Federal or State Constitutions, and laws passed in accordance with the same, entitle them.

Railroads, and other common carriers where they charge colored people full fare, should furnish them with as good accommodations as they do to whites. But those accommodations should be separate and distinct from those furnished the whites.

As to hotels, restaurants, etc., they should not—nor can they, in our opinion, constitutionally—be required to give accommodations to any particular race or class of individuals. There should, and doubtless will, in course of time, be hotels and res taurants in the towns of the country for the special accommodation of colored people. To those places the colored people should go, and not attempt to force them selves where their company is not wanted It seems to us that a colored man of sense and self-respect would feel ashamed to try to force himself where he knows his company would be unacceptable.

Castes have existed in all ages of the world, and will continue to exist for all time to come. And the white men of this country, however kindly disposed toward the colored race, *will never consent to a obliteration of the distinctions of race* The colored people may as well, once for all, be distinctly informed on this point An attempt on their part to carry into practical effect the doctrine of *social equa ity, will certainly lead to bloodshed ; and in the end, the extermination of the black race in this country, where the whites o number the blacks about nine to one.*

252 The Civil Rights Bill, *(Greensboro) Alabama Beacon*, 1 March 1873, p. 2, col, 1; digital image *Newspapers.com* (https://www.newspapers.com/image/355690211/?terms=%22Civil%20Rights%22&match=1 : accessed 28 Sept 2021).

EMIGRATION OF COLORED LABORERS.

The Eutaw *Whig and Observer* of last week publishes a communication, signed "An Old Citizen," from which we make the following extract:

Mr. W. O Monroe:

Dear Sir—A few days since a neighbor called and startled me with the news that "the country is utterly ruined; the negroes—the laborers of the country"—as he called them, "are all gone or going to Louisiana." I thought the matter over, and came to the conclusion that to the few money kings, who are purchasing large tracts of our best lands to rent to them, it is, doubtless, a serious matter; but for the rest of us a great deliverance. Why, Sir, let them go—the more the better—for we will be the sooner freed from Radical rule."

Our readers will recollect an editorial published a few weeks ago in the BEACON, on this subject. We took the ground, that, while a material diminution in the number of farm-laborers in this section, would be attended with inconvenience, and, to some planters, loss,—it would, in the end, prove a general good.

Though the subject does not appear to be engaging much of public attention, the more we reflect upon it, the stronger are our convictions that Hale county would, in the end, be benefitted, by having at least half of the colored laborers now in it to seek homes elsewhere.

As we contended, in the editorial referred to,—one of the effects of a large diminution in the number of our colored laborers, would be, *the inauguration of a better system of farming.*

Another would be,—*the whites would do more work themselves.*

Another—and one for the consummation of which every good citizen of Hale should earnestly labor—would be, *a change in the politics of the county.*

Let the number of colored voters be reduced, say one-half, and those remaining behind would not be so much inflated with their political strength. Nor would they be able to intimidate, as they now are those inclined to vote the Conservative ticket.

That the intelligent county of Hale should be represented in the lower branch of the Legislature by negroes, who are as unfit to make laws as an elephant to teach music, is certainly a most humiliating reflection.

But this state of things is likely not only to continue, but to grow worse,—so long as the negroes of the county can out vote the whites three or four to one.

We earnestly commend this matter to the attention of those who are so deeply interested in it, and who have it in their power, by concert of action, to remedy the evil.

---

253 Emigration of Colored Laborers, *(Greensboro) Alabama Beacon*, 1 March 1873, p. 2, col 2; digital image *Newspapers.com* (https://www.newspapers.com/image/355690211/?terms=%22Civil%20Rights%22&match=1 : 28 Sept 2021).

[For the Beacon,
HOLLOW SQUARE, ALA. }
October 2d, 1873. }

The citizens of Hollow Square and Saw-yerville neighborhoods, met at the latter place to-day, for the purpose of listening to an address by Capt. W. C. Zimmerman, upon the subject of organizing a "Grange of Patrons of Husbandry."

The meeting was well attended, and after Capt. Zimmerman's interesting and appropriate discourse, a Grange was organized, with the following named officers:

Master.—Samuel Pickens.
Overseer.—Gilliam James.
Lecturer.—Dr. B. Grigg.
Steward.—A. P. Evans.
Chaplain.—J. W. May.
Secretary.—E. V. Melton.
Treasurer.—J. A. Grigg.
Ass't Steward.—W. C. Pickens.
Gate Keeper.—E. L. Connolly.
Ceres.—Mrs. T. F. Stickney.
Flora.—Mattie Sawyer.
Pomona.—Mrs. Elina Melton.
Lady Ass't Steward.—Mrs. J. W. May.

After transacting the necessary business, the Grange adjourned to meet again at Sawyerville, on Thursday, the 9th inst., at 10 o'clock, A. M. We hope to see all good citizens out.

SAM'L PICKENS,
E. V. MELTON,   Master.
Secretary.

254

---

254 Organizing a "Grange of Patrons of Husbandry," *(Greensboro) Alabama Beacon*, 11 October 1873, p. 2, col. 4; digital image *Newspapers.com* (https://www.newspapers.com/image/355690303/?terms=Zimmerman&match=1 : accessed 17 Sept 2021).

The democrats of Hollow Square, Hale county, organized a Houston club the 5th; John W. May president, Dr. B. Grigg and A. J. Mayfield vice-presidents, E. V. Melton secretary, and W. G. Britton treasurer.

255

---

255 Campaign Notes: Democrats of Hollow Square Organize a Houston Club, *The Times-Argus (Selma, Alabama)*, 25 September 1874, p.3, col. 3; digital image (https://www.newspapers.com/image/355758308/?terms=Hollow%20Square&match=1 : accessed 17 Sept 21).

The communication signed "Now and Then," giving an account of a political meeting, held at Hollow Square, on the 11th inst., came to hand too late for our last week's issue. We quote as follows from the letter:

"Thos. J. Seay, Esqr., delivered a chaste and elegant address, having, if we may judge from the attention of his audience and the frequent applause, a decided effect. Several colored men signified their intention to vote the Democratic ticket. In fact, Mr. Seay's remarks to them were so appropriate and so clearly stated, that it is strange every one present was not immediately converted. Tom knows no such word as fail. With such men as Seay, Hobson, and Jack, we should certainly reclaim our county, and instead of a representation which is a disgrace to the intelligent portion of our people, have such as they shall be proud of."

256

---

256 Political Meeting at Hollow Square, *Alabama Beacon*, 22 July 1876, p.4, col. 1; digital image *Newspapers.com* (https://www.newspapers.com/image/355768326/?terms=Hollow%20square&match=1 : accessed 17 Sept 2021).

PUB- LIC

SPEAK- ING!

The voters of Hale county will be addressed politically, by the gentlemen below named, as follows:

Havana, Wednesday, July 11th; Carthage, Thursday, July 12th; and Phipps', Friday, July 13th. by Hons. J. M. JACK, J. M. HOBSON, and THOS. SEAY.

Flinn's Mill, Saturday, July 14th, by Hon. A. A. COLEMAN, and C. E. WALLER, Esqr.

Hollow Square, Tuesday, July 24th, by Hon. THOS. SEAY, and JAS. J. GARRETT, Esqr.

New Prospect, Wednesday, July 25th, by Hon. JAS. M. HOBSON, and THOS. R. ROULHAC, Esqr.

Mt. Hermon Church, Thursday, July 26th, by Hons. A. A. COLEMAN, THOS. SEAY, J. M. HOBSON, and JAS. E. WEBB, Esqr.

It is hoped that all—and especially the colored people—will attend these meetings.

257

---

257 Voters of Hale County to Be Addressed, *(Greensboro) Alabama Beacon*, 7 July 1877, p. 1, col. 6; digital image *Newspapers.com* (https://www.newspapers.com/image/355772047/?terms=voter%20hale%20county&match=1 : accessed 17 Sept 2021).

☞ Political meetings have been held this week at Hollow Square, New Prospect, and Mt. Herman Church. To-day (Saturday) there will be a meeting at Cedarville, at which Messrs. Thos. Seay, Thos. R. Roulhac, and W. B. Young are expected to speak.

We are gratified to learn that the meetings are generally well attended. Where the people take a proper degree of interest in an approaching election they are likely to attend the political meetings. That, by the way, is a pretty fair test.

Though there are no important political issues involved in the election,—there are *interests* involved, which should prompt the Democrats of the county generally to attend the meetings, and to turn out on the day of the election and cast their votes for the ticket nominated by the County Convention of the party.— The election of that ticket would promote the good of the county,— as well as strengthen the party.—

Personal considerations, or individual preferences, should be subordinated in exercising the elective franchise to the public good. By observing that rule, people would generally vote right.

Next week, there will be meetings and barbecues at the following places:

Newbern, Tuesday, the 31st.

Knight & Booker's Mill, Wednesday, August 1st.

Laneville, Thursday, August 2d.

Macon, Friday, August 3d.

Harrison, Saturday, August 4th.

Speakers have been appointed for each place,—some of whom will no doubt be in attendance.

The Democrats and Conservatives of those Precincts should not only attend the meetings themselves, but they should induce as many of the colored voters as possible to attend also. We need the help of colored Republicans, and should use all fair and honorable means to secure it.

258

---

258 Political Meeting at Hollow Square, *Greensboro (Alabama) Watchman*, 25 July 1877, p. 3, col. 3; digital image *Newspapers.com* (https://www.newspapers.com/image/356077499/?terms=%22Hollow%20Square%22&match =1 : accessed 17 Sept 2021).

Political meeting at Hollow Square on Tuesday.—Quite a large crowd of both whites and blacks attended this meeting, notwithstanding the unpropitious weather. The people are fully alive to the issues of this campaign, are enthusiastic and determined to do their duty to a man from this to sundown election day, and we predict a rousing majority from that precinct for our ticket.

Messrs. Seay and Garrett were to have addressed the meeting, it being impossible for Mr. Seay to attend, only Mr. G. was on hand.

259

---

259 Political Meetings at Hollow Square, *(Greensboro) Alabama Beacon*, 27 July 1877, p. 1, col. 2; digital image *Newspapers.com* (https://www.newspapers.com/image/355772567/?terms=%22Hollow%20Square%22&match =1 : accessed 17 Sept 2021).

THE LEE MONUMENT.—The managers of the Lee Monument Association have made another appeal to the people of the South, and "especially to her daughters," for funds for the proposed monument. They recommend that ladies be appointed in all the towns, to solicit subscriptions, rejecting no offering, however small; and that on the night of January 19, the anniversary of Lee's birth, "tableaux, balls, musical soirees, dramatic representations, feasts, or some like entertainment" be given.

260

---

[260] The Lee Monument, *(Greensboro) Alabama Beacon*, p. 1, col. 5; digital image *Newspapers.com* (https://www.newspapers.com/image/355774267/?terms=%22Lee%20monument%22&match=1 : accessed 17 Sept 2021).

A very large crowd assembled at Sawyerville, on the 4th, to witness the Tournament, Base Ball match game, and to enjoy the hospitality of the good people of that neighborhood. Visitors were there from all portions of the county, and the day was spent most pleasantly.

The Tournament came off in the morning. Some thirteen Knights competed for the prizes, and the riding was very exciting and spirited. Mr. W. M. KING took the first prize; Mr. J. BROOKS MAY, the second; and Mr. WILLIE TORBERT, the third.

Capt. J. B. WILEY was chosen Herald, and Mr. WM. G. BRITTON Trumpeter.

After the riding, a pic-nic dinner was spread, and the party, as one whole family, enjoyed the bountiful repast in the highest degree,—and there was enough left for another such party.

Dinner over, the coronation took place. Mr. KING crowned Miss MARY SAWYER Queen of Love and Beauty; Mr. MAY crowned Miss SALLIE TORBERT, first Maid of Honor; Mr. TORBERT crowned Miss SALLIE KING, second Maid.

MISS SALLIE KING, second maid.

The match game between the "Elm Club," of Hollow Square, and the "Useless Club," of Greensboro, began about 3 o'clock. The game was about half finished, when the former Club—owing to the illness of some of its members—gave up the game. The score stood—"Useless Nine," 22; "Elm Nine," 4.

After nightfall, Mr. ENOCH SAWYER threw open the doors of his residence to the assemblage,—and to the excellent music furnished by Prof. E. BAYOL, the young people responded most willingly. "Partners for a cotillion" was sung out, and eight couple took the floor, and the maizy dance continued till a late hour.

The enjoyments of the day, and the hospitality of the people of that section are very flatteringly spoken of by those whom we have heard express an opinion.

261

---

261 Sawyerville Base Ball Tournament, (Greensboro) Alabama Beacon, p. 4. col. 2; digital image Newspapers.com (https://www.newspapers.com/image/355782647/?terms=Sawyerville%20base%20ball&match=2 : 17 Sept 2021).

According to Robert Brasfield, there was a "Negro" team in Sawyerville. Many members of the family felt that it was wrong of some of the others to play baseball, because they should instead be focused on God and on acquiring an education. Moreover, baseball games were a location where one would encounter gambling, which was considered sinful and contrary to the Alabama Black McGruder family ethic. Nonetheless, some of the McCruters were known

copy 45 cents; Trial subscription for three months, $1.

HOLLOW SQUARE, Aug. 25th, 1880,

Mr. Editor:

Once annually for several years past, you have kindly given place in the WATCHMAN to a line or two from this quarter of our "moral vineyard." Then, presuming, as we do upon your past generosity, and with commingled thanks therefor, we would again ask for our wonted space in the columns of your valuable journal.

As in politics, so in enterprise, and every good cause, Beat No. 6 is in the foremost rank. We have clever, chivalrous, sociable and thrifty men and boys; our girls are beautiful and accomplished; we have good, faithful and Democratic colored people, and lovely homes. Our schools are good, and we have three well supplied churches. A ride through our farms will show that we are thrifty and prosperous. Enquire into the management of our political interests, and our elections, and you will find perfect harmony. Go to our social gatherings, and you will find perfection in every line. In fine, we have the higher types of sociability, chivalry, industry and enterprise. Our barbecues and pic-nics are unexcelled; our tournaments are grand, and the gallantry of our boys unrivalled.

In response to a cordial invitation from our sister county of Greene, for they know we gloried in such things, a good number of old and young people, not only from our section, but from other parts of Hale, attended a Tournament at Eutaw, on the 20th, and participating as they always do on such occasions, our boys bore the laurels off the field. Messrs. W. E. Torbert and J. B. May, of Hollow Square, winning the 1st and 2nd prizes. Mr. T. J. McFaddin, of Acron the 3rd. The crowns were very handsome and costly; the 1st and 2nd were awarded to Misses Laura Martin, of Mobile, and Tommie Kinnard, of Hale. Mr. McFaddin reserving his for whom, we have not been informed.

We are wide awake out here, and in due time we will have our Hancock and English club and banner.

X.

to be very good at baseball. According to Robert Brasfield, had some of these individual McCruters been given the opportunity, they could have been professional baseball players.

262 Letter to the Editor, from Hollow Square, *Greensboro (Alabama) Watchman*, 2 September 1880, p. 3, col. 4; digital image *Newspapers.com* (https://www.newspapers.com/image/356080622/?terms=%22moral%20vineyard%22&match=1 : accessed 17 Sept 2021).

— A Marion gentleman, who had dismounted from his horse, at Sawyerville, on Saturday morning, for the purpose of fastening his saddle, was approached by a negro, who asked the traveler to let him hold his horse; no sooner had Sambo gotten possession of the lines, till he snatched the gentleman's watch, mounted the horse, and was soon out of sight. The horse was found hitched to a fence in Greensboro the next morning. A bold robbery for this country.

263

263 Robbery by a Negro in Sawyerville, *Greensboro (Alabama) Watchman,* 9 December 1880, p. 3, col. 3; digital image *Newspapers.com* (https://www.newspapers.com/image/356080911/?terms=Sawyerville%20Marion&match=1 : accessed 17 Sept 2021).

☞ We are requested to announce that the Knights of Sawyerville will have, on Thursday, the 18th inst., a Tournament and Basket Picnic, to which the Knights of Hale and adjoining counties, as also the public generally, are cordially invited. Marion and Eutaw papers are respectfully requested to copy the announcement.

264

264 Knights of Sawyerville Tournament, *(Greensboro) Alabama Beacon*, 12 August 1881, p. 4, col. 1; digital image *Newspapers.com* (https://www.newspapers.com/image/253603866/?terms=%22knights%20of%20sawyerville %22&match=1 : accessed 17 Sept 2021).

HALE COUNTY.

Greensboro Beacon;—A telegraph office will shortly be established in Greensboro.

Up to the first of this month, there was an increase in the receipts of cotton at the Greensboro depot, of 700 bales.

There has been, as we learn Maj. Fowlkes stated when here last Wednesday, a considerable increase in the amount of freight coming to Greensboro over this road.

The latest indications are, that the old Sawyerville route will be selected for the extension of the Greensboro railroad. In that event, there will be no change in the location of the Greensboro depot, which the citizens of the town generally will regret.

The demand for dwelling houses here is greater than the supply. There are two or three families troubled to get residences. If some of our capitalists would erect half a dozen, or more, small residences, that could be rented at about $100 a year, they would readily find tenants for them.

265

265 Telegraph Office to Be Established in Greensboro, *The Montgomery Advertiser*, 17 Jan 1882, p. 1, col. 7; digital image *Newspapers.com* (https://www.newspapers.com/image/272367517/?terms=%22Greensboro%20Beacon%22&match=1 : accessed 18 Sept 2021)..

George Griffin, perhaps the only obnoxious Nigger in town, left last week for Chicago, to attend the National Republican Convention. He may, perhaps, get a job of shining shoes for his Radical brethren, but will return home convinced that they have no use for his race further than to use them as political tools.

266

George Griffin, perhaps the most unprincipled Nigger in this county, made up money among his colored brethren to carry him to the Chicago Show. Hope he will have saved enough to settle his subscription bill at this office.

267

266 Perhaps The Only Obnoxious Nigger in Town, *Greensboro (Alabama) Watchman*, 5 June 1884, p. 3, col.2; digital image *Newspapers.com* (https://www.newspapers.com/image/308395432/?terms=obnoxious&match=1 : accessed 18 Sept 2021).

267 Perhaps The Most Unprincipled Nigger in the County, *Greensboro (Alabama) Watchman*, 12 June 1884, p. 3, col. ; digital image *Newspapers.com* (https://www.newspapers.com/image/308395480/?terms=%22George%20Griffin%22&match =1 : accessed 18 Sept 2021).

The Sawyerville Neighborhood on the Prohibition Question.

Mr. Enoch Sawyer called at the BEACON Office last Saturday to advise us of public sentiment in his neighborhood on the prohibition question. He represented his neighborhood as strongly opposed to the liquor traffic, and that in deference to that sentiment, Mr. Sample, who is doing business at Sawyerville, Mr. Cook, who has a store three miles from there. and Mr. Torbert, who is doing business at Hollow Square, had, on the first of January, all three left off selling alcoholic liquors. That good results had already grown out of the discontinuance of the sale of liquor in that neighborhood. But that those gentlemen, learning that a drinking establishment was to be started soon, two miles this side of Sawyerville, say that they will be compelled, if that is done, to resume the sale of liquor in self-defense.

Mr. Sawyer says that neighborhood, generally, would greatly regret having the sale of liquor resumed in their midst, and that he had been requested to bring the matter to our attention, to see if some plan could not be devised for guarding against the evil, from which they have heretofore suffered.

We replied that nothing could now be done in the premises, the Legislature having adjourned. As we suggested, two weeks ago, the prohibition bill should have been made to apply to the entire county.

Here we take occasion to congratulate Mr. Sawyer on the lively interest he is taking in the temperance cause. Though a slave. for many long years, to the use of alcoholic liquors, he assures us that he has abstained entirely for the last four years. His course is not only highly creditable to him, but an example to all who labor under the same infirmity. It proves that men of firmness *can* refrain from strong drink, when they try half as hard to do so, as some men do to get liquor when their appetites crave it

268

---

268 The Sawyerville Neighborhood on the Prohibition Question, *(Greensboro) Alabama Beacon*, 24 February 1885, p. 4, col. 4; digital image *Newspapers.com* (https://www.newspapers.com/image/253992542/?terms=Sawyerville%20prohibition&match =1 : accessed 17 Sept 2021).

Capt. S. J. Monette, of Sawyer-ville, brought five bales of cotton to Greensboro this week, each of which averaged 717 pounds. The largest bale weighed 780 pounds.

The merchants inform us that the farmers of Hale are in a better condition than for five or six years past. They judge from the fact that most of them have paid up their accounts, and will begin the new year with a clean balance sheet.

269

---

269 Capt. S. J Monette Bought Five Bales of Cotton, *Greensboro (Alabama) Watchman*, 22 December 1887, p. 3, col. 1; digital image *Newspapers.com* (https://www.newspapers.com/search/#query=Monette&t=5658&ymd=1887-12-22 : accessed 18 Sept 2021).

The Colored People and Lynchings

Under a call made by the Bishops and other members of the colored churches, for a day of prayer for deliverance of those of their race guilty of crimes from the hands of mobs, meetings were held last Tuesday throughout Alabama by the colored people. The proceedings of the one held in Greensboro will be found in to-day's paper. The assembly is conservative in its appeal for protection against mob violence.

We wish to say to our colored citizens that the white people as a class are opposed to lynchings,—except for one crime. They know what that crime is. It is a crime for which nine out of every ten men —whether white or black—are summarily dealt with. It is a crime for which hemp will continue to be grown and used as long as that crime is committed. The combined powers of the world could hardly protect a man,—no matter to what race he belongs—from the vengeance of an outraged public when guilty of that crime.

This is said in all kindness. There is nothing wrong or objectionable in your demand that the laws should be impartially executed. It is right that you should pray over the matter. But do not forget to preach and talk and argue with your race upon the importance of never committing the unmentionable crime for which speedy death is the inevitable penalty. The white man guilty of it forfeits his life just as surely as does the colored man.

270

---

270 The Colored People and Lynchings, *Greensboro (Alabama) Watchman*, p. 2, col. 2; *Newspapers.com*

Death of Mr. Enoch Sawyer

Mr. Enoch Sawyer died at the home of his daughter, Mrs. Mary Pickens, in Greensboro on the 6th inst., aged about 74 years. He had been ill for several months prior to his death. Mr. Sawyer was one of Hale's oldest citizens. He resided at Sawyerville, ten miles west of Greensboro, for a number of years, which place was his home at the time of his death. He leaves a wife, four daughters and other relatives and friends to mourn his loss.

Funeral services, conducted by Dr. Cobbs, were held in the Episcopal church Wednesday, and the remains interred in the Greensboro cemetery.

271

(https://www.newspapers.com/image/308139679/?terms=Lynchings&match=1 : accessed 18 Sept 2021).

[271] Death of Mr. Enoch Sawyer, *Greensboro (Alabama) Watchman*, p. 3, col. 2; digital image (https://www.newspapers.com/image/308140228/?terms=%22Enoch%20Sawyer%22&match =1 : accessed 18 Sept 2021).

The corner stone laying of Springfield Baptist church, colored, near Sawyerville on last Sunday was an occasion of great interest to those interested. It is estimated that there were at least two thousand people present. The land on which the church will be built was a gift to the congregation from Hon. Wm. Smaw. The corner stone sermon was preached by Rev. D. M. Coleman, the district missionary. Rev. W. H. Reddick is the pastor of the church. A collection amounting to seventy-five dollars was taken up.

272

272 Corner Stone Laying of Springfield Baptist Church, *Greensboro (Alabama) Watchman*, 3 June 1897, p. 3, col, 1; digital image *Newspapers.com* (https://www.newspapers.com/image/308154211/?terms=corner%20stone&match=1 : accessed 18 Sept 2021).

There were political rallies at Havana and Sawyerville last week which were largely attended by Democrats and Populites. Speeches were made by Messrs. Waller and Knight, Chadwick and Tunstall for the Democracy, and for the Pops by Judge Hobson and Geo Nabors. Both rallies proved to be field days for Democracy. Hale is coming up all right for Oates and the balance of the ticket next Monday.

273

---

273 Political Rallies at Havavana and Sawyerville, *Greensboro (Alabama) Watchman*, 2 August 1894, p. 3, col. 1; digital image *Newspapers.com* (https://www.newspapers.com/image/308146337/?terms=Sawyerville&match=1 : accessed 18 Sept 2021).

Documents Pertaining to Chapter Six

Inventory of the Estate of Williamson Wynne[274]

Ordered by the Court to be Recorded

The State of Alabama Green County

Orphan Court May Term

11th May 1829

Present the Honorable Thomas F. Moody[275] Judge of Said Court

April 23, 1829

An Inventory & Appraisement of the Estate of Williamson Wynne dec'd.

Ordered by the Court that the appraisement bill presented by Osmund A. Wynne, the administrator of the Estate of Williamson Wynne deceased be received and recorded according to laws.

One Lot of Hogs 7 Sows & 21 Pigs	$ 30.00
One Spotted Boar	2.00
One Cow & Calf $8.00 One do do $9.00	17.00
One do do $8 1 do do $10.00 1 do do $9.00	27.00
One do $10 1 do do $7	26.00

---

274 Greene Co, AL, Orphan's Ct., Court Records v C-1830, p 68-70, FHL#7736049, images 443-444, https://www.familysearch.org/ark:/61903/3:1:3Q9M-C91Q-NQ5L-V?i=442&cat=518808

275 May be read as Mordy

1 do do $9	
One do $8 One do $9.00 One do $8.00	23.00
One do $6 1 small Steer & Heifer $9.00	15.00
7 Yearling Calves $15.00 1 Yoke of Oxen $16	31.00
One Sorrel Horse	65.00
One Grey Horse	30.00
One Mare Mule	80.00
One Grey Mule	60.00
One Horse Mule Iron Grey	75.00
One Road Wagon	30.00
One Ox Cart & Yoke $14 One 60 Saw Gin [illegible] $75	89.00
One Cotton Thrasher	20.00
One Cutting Knife & Box	5.00
Five small Ploughs $5 Carry ploughs $3	8.00
3 Carry Plough $12 5 sweeps $5.00	17.00
1 Lot of Shovel Irons $2.00 1 Hogshead Cask $1.50	3.50
5 Pr. of gear, Singletrees [illegible] & [illegible] & Pea	10.00

At May Term 1839 (p.2)

1 Pr. of steelyards	$ 4.00
1 Log Chain	4.00
5 Grubbing Hoes	3.00
4 Axes	6.00
13 Weeding hoes	3.00
1 Lot of Old Tools	2.00
1 Pr. of Sad Irons	1.30
1 Lot of wooden Vessels Tabs & Trays	8.00
1 Lot of Pales, Churns, & Kelers [illegible]	4.00
1 Lot of Tin Ware	5.00
3 Jugs 1 Jar	3.00
1 Lot of Kitchen Pot Ware	15.00
1 Spinning Wheels & 1 Reel	10.00
1 Loom & Llay [illegible]	3.00
4 Pin Tables	8.00
2 Dining Tables	15.00
1 Large Chest	5.00
1 Lot of Chairs 15	7.50
1 do of Glassware Crockery & Knives & Forks	25.00
1 Shot Gun	6.00
5 Beds & 6 Bed Steads & Furniture	130.00
3 Trunks $4; 1 Lot of Books $20	24.00
1 Looking Glass	24.50
1 Pr. of Fire Dogs & Tongs	3.50
1 Slave Man named **Frederick**	400.00
1 Slave Man named **Ned**	500.00
1 Slave Man named **George**	500.00

1 Slave Man named **Charles**[276]	300.00
1 Slave Man named **Jim**[277] [illegible]	250.00
1 Slave Boy named **Ceaser**	300.00
1 Slave Man named **Ben**[278] [illegible]	275.00
1 Slave Man named **Allen**	150.00
1 Slave Man named **Anderson**	200.00
1 Slave Man named **William**	115.00
Amt carried over	

Ordered by the Court to be Amt Brot forward (p.3)

1 Negro Boy Slave named **Anthony**	175.00
1 Negro Boy Slave named **Naci**	150.00
1 Negro Boy Slave named **Israel**	125.00
1 Negro Boy Slave named **Tom**	100.00
1 Negro Woman **Suckey**[279] & Child	300.00
1 Negro Girl **Sidney**	225.00
1 Negro Girl **Dilly**	150.00
1 Negro Woman **Frances**	100.00
1 Negro Woman **Ann**	300.00
1 Negro Woman **Lucy** & Child	400.00
1 Negro Girl **Peggy**	125.00
1 Negro Woman **Kate**[280]	175.00
1 Negro Girl **Orncy**[281]	175.00

[276] This is not the Charles of our work.
[277] Likely the same person with that name referenced in Ninian O. Magruder's 1803 will.
[278] Likely the same person with that name referenced in Ninian O. Magruder's 1803 will.
[279] May be read as Lucky
[280] Likely the same person with that name referenced in Ninian O. Magruder's 1803 will.

1 Negro Girl **Jam**	150.00
1 Negro Woman **Silva**	250.00
1 Negro Girl **Amanda**	250.00
1 Negro Woman **Sophy**	225.00
1 Negro Woman **Maria**	350.00
1 Negro Woman **Marian**	300.00
1 Negro Girl **Louisa**	230.00
1 Negro Girl **Fanny**	175.00
1 Negro Girl **Martha**	125.00
1 Negro Girl **Kenot** [illegible]	120.00

We whose names are hereto subscribed being appointed by the Judge of the Orphans Court of Green County appraisers of the Estate of Williamson Wynne Dec[d] after being duly qualified preceded on the 23rd Day of April 1829. To value & appraise the within mentioned Slaves & Personal Property. To the sums of Money Respectively [illegible] to the foregoing slaves & articles of property.

Given under our hands & Seal this 23rd day of April 1829

Th[s] Williams

A. McAlpine

[illegible]

Limin Ashford

W[m] B.M. [illegible]

---

281 May be read as Viney

Guardian Bond for Salina A. Wynne

Erasmus Wynne, guardian bond

To Salina, Minor of W. Wynne dec.

The State of Alabama, Greene County

Know all men by these presents that we Erasmus Wynne, Osmund A. Wynne, & Willis Sanders are held and firmly bound unto Thomas F. Moody, Esquire, Judge of the Orphans Court for the County in the sum of five thousand dollars to be paid to the said Thomas F. Moody, Esq. or his successors in office to which payment well and truly to be made we bind ourselves our heirs executors and administrators jointly severally and firmly by these presents sealed with our seals and dated this ninth day of November 1829.

The condition of the above obligation is such that whereas the above bound Erasmus Wynne has been duly appointed guardian to Salina Ann Wynne, a minor of the age about six years, heir of Williamson Wynne, deceased. Now, if the above Erasmus Wynne shall well and truly perform all the duties which are or may be by law required of him as such guardian, then the above obligation to be void otherwise to remain in full force.

Signed, sealed, and acknowledged in open court,

I.C. [illegible]

Clerk

Erasmus Wynne

O.A. Wynne

Willis Sanders

HOLLOW SQUARE, Oct. 18, 1838.

Mr. J. G. Harvey Esq.:

Dear sir---I give you a statement of cotton picked out by 5 of my hands in one day, and in day light---good clean cotton, clear of trash. The boys' names, and the number of pounds picked out by each are as follows:

Green,		517
Amos,		500
Edmond,		410
Phill,		400
Philander, a boy 12 years old,		326

Respectfully,

E. WYNNE.

282

---

282 This note to the publisher was submitted by either Eleanor Magruder Wynne or her son, Erasmus Wynne. The author believes it to be the former. Statement of Cotton Picked Out, *(Greensboro) Alabama Beacon*, 21 Oct 1838, p. 3, col. 2; digital image *Newspapers.com* (https://www.newspapers.com/image/253602424/?terms=Wynne&match=1 : accessed 18 Sept 2021).

Planters' Meeting.

A large number of the Planters of Greene county, assembled at the Lyceum Hall, in Greensboro', on the 16th inst, and the meeting was organised by the appointment of the Rev. Wm. W. HILL chairman, and Dr. JAS. L. TUNSTALL, Secretary.

The chairman having explained the objects of the meeting, the following gentlemen were, on motion, appointed a committee to report resolutions expressive of the views and feelings of the meeting in relation to those objects and to aid in accomplishing the same—viz:

Col. Wm. Armistead, Wiley J. Croom,
T. B. Randolph, Matthew Hobson,
Dr. R. C. Randolph, Rev. L. D. Hatch,
John Nelson, Gen. P. May,
Alfred Hatch, Isaac Croom,
Dr. P. W. Kittrell, Col. Sam'l Pickens,
Dr. J. M. Witherspoon, R. B. Waller,
O. Wynne, A. Norwood,
and John May.

The committee having retired for a short time, reported through their chairman, Col. Armistead, the following preamble and resolutions:

WHEREAS, we have for several years past, believed the rates of wharfage and the tariff of charges by the Cotton Presses, imposed upon our cotton and supplies in the city of Mobile, were onerous and exorbitant, and from whatever causes proceeding, without justification or example; and whereas, the appreciation of our currency, the reduction in the prices of labor, provisions, city property, and more especially the great decline in value of our chief staple, all admonish us, that these exactions are no longer to be endured;—therefore

Resolved 1st. That in the opinion of this meeting, the rates of wharfage and tariffs of Cotton Press charges, as they have existed for several years past, in the city of Mobile, both as they affect our cotton and supplies of merchandise, will bear a material reduction, probably of one half, and still afford to their proprietors liberal and reasonable profits.

2dly. That we will patronise those persons worthy of our confidence, who will aid us in accomplishing such reduction.

283

---

283 Planters' Meeting of Greene County, *(Greensboro) Alabama Beacon*, 23 Nov 1844, p. 3, col. 1; digital image *Newspapers.com*

FATAL ACCIDENT.—We regret to learn that a son of Mr. Erasmus Wynne of this county, a young man about 14 years of age, was killed on the 31st ult. by the accidental discharge of a pistol, which he was handling without being aware that it was loaded.

284

(https://www.newspapers.com/image/253603203/?terms=%22Planters%20meeting%22&match=1 : accessed 18 Sept 2021).

284 Fatal Accident, *(Greensboro) Alabama Beacon*, 3 Jan 1846, p. 2, col. 6; digital image *Newspapers.com*
(https://www.newspapers.com/image/253604541/?terms=%22fatal%20accident%22&match=1 : accessed 18 Sept 2021).

Last Will & Testament of Eleanor Magruder Wynne[285]

In the name of God, Amen, I, Eleanor Wynne, at present of the County of Greene State of Alabama, being in feeble health of body, but of sound and disposing mind and memory and being desirous to settle my worldly affairs whilst I have strength and capacity so to do make ordain and publish this my last will and testament hereby revoking and making void all former wills by me at any time heretofore made, and as to such worldly estate wherewith it has pleased God to entrust to me I dispose of the same in manner following that is to say:

First, I do give and bequeath to each of my four sons hereinafter named, to wit, Osmun A. Wynne, Erasmus Wynne, Williamson Wynne, and Robert Wynne the sum of Eight Hundred Dollars to be allotted to them respectively on a settlement of accounts with my Executors and to be deducted out of any debts or demands which may be due and owing to me from them or either of them at the time of my death.

Secondly, I give and bequeath to my daughter Salina Ann Eleanor Ferrell the sum of eight hundred dollars to be allowed or paid her by my Executors in all respects in like manner with the sum of Eight hundred dollars by me hereinbefore given to each of my said sons. I furthermore give, grant, and bequeath to my said daughter Salina Ann Eleanor Ferrell all my real estate consisting of Three Hundred and sixty acres of Land the disposition of which will more fully appear by reference to a Deed from James Ferrell to me. It being the same I have purchased from him the said James Ferrell.

I furthermore give grant and bequeath to my daughter Salina Ann Eleanor Ferrell the following negro slaves, that is to say **Ned** aged about fifty three years, and **Maria** wife of **Ned** aged about Forty eight years, **Fanny** daughter of **Maria** aged about twenty seven years, **Martha** daughter of **Maria** aged about twenty four years, **Charles** son of **Maria** aged about Eighteen years, **Jasper** son of **Maria** aged about twelve years, **Lilly** daughter of **Maria** aged about eight years, **Rose** daughter of **Fanny** about eight years, **Mary** daughter of **Fanny** aged about six years, **Martha Ann** daughter of **Fanny** aged about four years, **Virginia Lauretta**[286] daughter of **Fanny** aged about two years, **Ned** son of Martha aged

---

[285] Greene County, Alabama, Probate Court, Will Records, Will Book C p 203-204, will of Eleanor Wynne; digital images, *FamilySearch* (https://www.familysearch.org/ark:/61903/3:1:33S7-9B35-WMV?i=644&cc=1925446&cat=132937 : accessed 24 Jan 21); citing FHL 5175959, image#645-655.

[286] Could be read as Lorella.

about seven years, **George** son of Martha aged about five years, **Isaiah** son of **Martha** aged about three years, **Matilda** aged about sixteen years, **Jeremiah** son of **Matilda** aged about four months, **Creed** aged about forty two years, **Reddick** aged about twenty two years, **Thomas** aged about twenty five years, **Jacob** aged about twenty three years, **John** aged about thirty years, **Harry** aged about thirty six years, **Isaac** aged about thirty eight years, **Caroline** aged about sixteen years, together with all the offspring or natural increase of the said female Negro slaves and each and every of them. To Have and to Hold the said slaves and all their increase as aforesaid to her the said Salina Ann Eleanor Ferrell her Heirs and assigns forever. Furthermore, I do give grant and bequeath to my said daughter Salina Ann Eleanor Ferrell all my personal and perishable property, which I may have at the time of my death, and not specially deeded or willed away. And the said property hereinbefore given and bequeathed to my said daughter Sarah Ann Eleanor Ferrell shall in no manner be subjected to the debts, management or control or benefit of William A. Ferrell, husband of Salina Ann Eleanor Ferrell, on the said property real, personal or mixed, increase on proceeds or profits or any investments or purchase made with any funds missing therefrom. But the same and every part and parcel for the sole, entire and exclusive use and benefit of the said Salina Ann Ferrell, to all intents and purposes as if she were a *Feme sole.*

Thirdly, I give and bequeath to my granddaughter Martha Lavinia Ferrell, daughter of William A. Ferrell and Salina Ann Eleanor Ferrell, a negro girl, daughter of **Fanny**, named **Sarah Ann** aged about nine years; also [a] negro girl **Mary,** aged about thirteen years, the last mentioned of the said negro girls I have previously given to the said Martha Lavinia Ferrell by deed of gift, the same having been recorded in the County Court Clerks Office at Eutaw, as will more fully appear by reference and all the offspring or natural increase to her the said Martha Lavinia Ferrell of the said Female negro slaves and each and every of them to have and to hold the said slaves all their increase as aforesaid to her the said Martha Lavinia Ferrell her heirs and assigns forever.

And lastly, I do hereby make and ordain Erasmus Wynne and William A. Ferrell Executors of this my last will and testament in Witness of all which I, Eleanor Wynne, have to this, my will written on three half sheets paper, set my hand and seal this fourteenth day of February in the year of our Lord One Thousand Eight Hundred and Forty-Eight.

Signed and published by the said Eleanor Wynne as her last will and testament in the presence of us who at her request in her presence and in presence of each other have hereunto set our names as witnesses.

Eleanor Wynne

(mark and seal)

B. F. Ferrell

Alfred Perry

John J. Cleveland

Probated Nov 26, 1849

Inventory of the Estate of Eleanor Magruder Wynne[287]

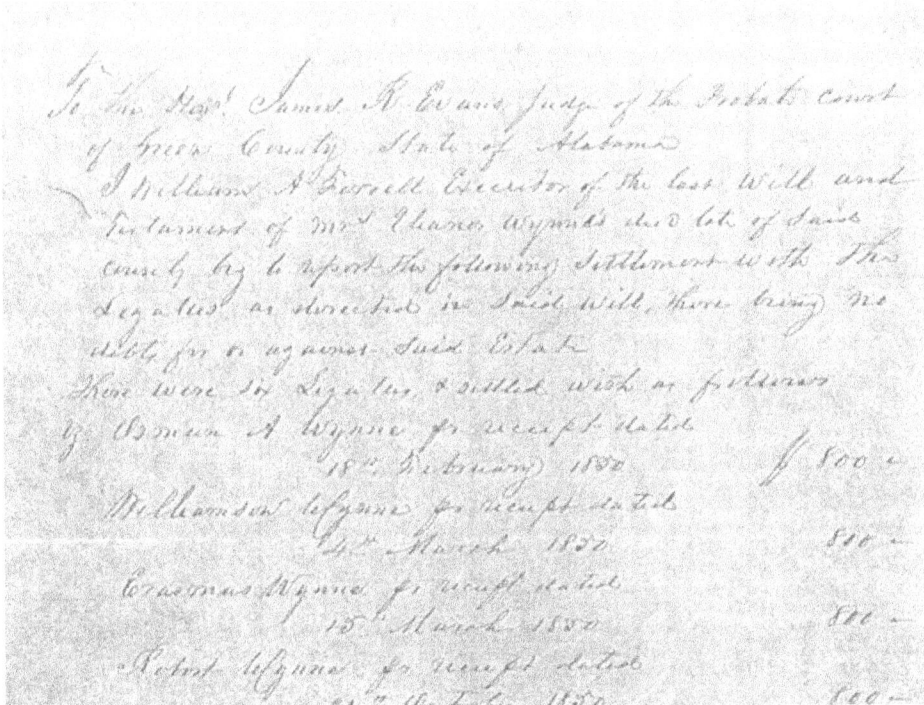

To the Honorable James R. Evans,

Judge of the Probate Court of Greene County State of Alabama

I, William A. Ferrell, Executor of the last will and testament of Mrs. Eleanor Wynne's dec'd late of said county beg to report the following settlement with the legatees as directed in said will, there being no debt for or against said Estate.

There were six legatees and settled with as follows:

Osmun A. Wynne from receipt dated 18 February 1850	$800
Williamson Wynne from receipt dated 4 March 1850	$800

287 Greene Co, Alabama, Probate Court, Estate Case Files 1820-1915, Case# 1144, Eleanor Wynne inventory; digital images, *FamilySearch* (https://www.familysearch.org/ark:/61903/3:1:33SQ-GRTS-KDJ?i=83&cc=1978117&cat=1134600 : accessed 24 Jan 21); citing FHL 5007940, image 84-90; distribution & final settlement Apr 1853, image 2-3.

Erasmus Wynne from receipt dated 15th March 1850	$800
Robert Wynne from receipt dated 24th October 1850	$800
Salina Ann E. Ferrell, wife of William A. Ferrell	$800

To Salina Ann E. Ferrell, wife of William A. Ferrell the following negro slaves:

1. **Ned** aged about ___ years since dead
2. **Maria**, aged about 57 years, wife of Ned
3. **Fanny**, aged about 28 years, daughter of Maria
4. **Martha**, aged about 26 years, daughter of Maria
5. **Charles**, aged about 20 years, son of Maria
6. **Jasper**, aged about 14 years, son of Maria
7. **Lilly**, aged about 10 years, daughter of Maria
8. **Rose**, aged about 9 years, daughter of Fanny
9. **Mary**, aged about 7 years, daughter of Fanny
10. **Martha Ann**, aged about 5 years, daughter of Fanny
11. **Virginia**, aged about 3 years, daughter of Fanny
12. **Roena**, aged about 2 years, daughter of Fanny
13. **Ned**, aged about 8 years, son of Martha
14. **Isaiah**, aged about 4 years, son of Martha
15. **Matilda**, aged about 18 years
16. **Jeremiah**, aged about 2 years, son of Matilda
17. **Creed**, aged about 45 years
18. **John**, aged about 32 years
19. **Reddick**, aged about 25 years
20. **Jacob**, aged about 25 years
21. **Harvey**, aged about 38 years

22. **Caroline**, aged about 18 years

23. **Isaac**, aged about 39 years

The following lands:

    Y(?)   E. H., S.W., _ Sect 26, T. 21, R. 3. E

            M. H., S.W., _, Sect 26, T. 21, R. 3. E.

      N. H., S.W., _ Sect 26, T. 21, R. 3. E

      W. H., A.W., _ Sect 26, T. 21, R. 3. E

      E. H. of the E. H., _ Sect 27, T. 21, R. 3. E 360 acres

1 Pleasure Carriage

Also, all the household and kitchen furniture do [ditto].

Martha Lavinia Ferrell daughter of William A. and Salina Ann E. Ferrell

Negro girl, **Sarah Ann**, daughter of **Fanny**, aged about 11 years.

    Also, **Mary** mentioned in said will but previously conveyed by deed of gift and regularly recorded.

The above account is submitted to the orphan court and by a final settlement of said Estate.

William A. Ferrell, Executor

Subscribed to before me in open court

April 11, 1853

JR Evans, Judge

The State of Alabama,
Greene County

To the Hon. Wiley Coleman

Judge of the Orphans court of said county.

We, the undersigned heirs and Legatees of Mrs. Eleanor Wynne dec'd do hereby assent that the last will and testament of the said decedent be admitted to probate and registration in the Orphans Court of said county, hereby waving the necessity of citations.

W^mSon Wynne

November 10, 1849

Excerpt from Inventory of Eleanor Magruder Wynne, 1849.

From the Estate Papers of William A. Ferrell

Account for Medical Treatment of Enslaved People

1858 & 1859 to G.B. Wilson for:

½ Ounce quinine used for Negroes when sick	$2.00
Small box of blue [illegible]	$0.50
2 Bottles of mustard used when **Rose** was sick with congestion, chill and **Jasper** also	$1.00
2 Boxes pills bought of Atkins	$0.50
2do. bought of Copley	$0.50
1 Bottle of [Abrin?] Liniment bought for my own purpose but authorized by Ferrell to rub **Lucinda** in case of rheumatism large bottle	$0.50
1 Bottle of castor oil brought with me to Mr. Ferrell and in case of sickness sent down to Ferrell to give his negroes when he was out of oil and there was more at Hollow Square	$0.50
1 Dose of Calomel Scent down to Ferrell for some of his negroes	$0.25
	$5.25

Last Will & Testament of William A. Ferrell[288]

In the name of God, Amen. I, William A. Ferrell, of the County of Greene and State of Alabama, being of sound mind and memory and considering the uncertainty of this frail and transitory life do therefore make ordain, publish, and declare this to be my last will and testament:

That is to say, first, after all my lawful debts are paid and discharged the residue of my estate real and personal, I give, bequeath, and dispose of as follows: To wit to my beloved wife, Torzah Mary Ferrell, in addition to her separate estate which she had when I married her a list of which is here unto appended amounting in notes to nine thousand three hundred and sixty two dollars and fifty eight cents, besides negro woman **Delpha** and piano & household furniture mentioned in said list.

In addition to the above mentioned nine thousand three hundred & sixty dollars and fifty-eight cents I give & bequeath to my wife Torzah Mary Ferrell, three thousand and six hundred and thirty-seven dollars & forty-two cents out of my estate amounting to thirteen thousand dollars which she agrees to take in lieu of domain.

It is my wish that in payment of her legacy that all the notes contained in the list hereunto appended be given up to her in part payment of said legacy that is to say such of the notes as are unpaid at my death.

It is my wish furthermore that if my estate does not, in five years, pay the balance between what may be due on said legacy, that **Dick & his family** be sold. That is to say **Dick Martha his wife & their children** for the full satisfaction of the legacy hereunto bequeathed unto my wife. It is my request that my Executor send to any point designated by my wife, the furniture & contents belonging to her at the expense of my estate. It is also my desire that she take charge of the children but in the event the two eldest refuse to go with her, I wish her to take charge of & raise Emerette.

It is also my desire that the Executor keep my estate together till my youngest child becomes of age or marries. It is my desire furthermore that William O.

---

[288] Greene Co, Alabama, Probate Court. Will Records, 1821-1935, Will Book C, p 583-587, will of William A. Ferrell; digital images, *FamilySearch* (https://www.familysearch.org/ark:/61903/3:1:33SQ-GB3T-PW?i=176&cc=1925446&cat=132937 : accessed 24 Jan 21); citing FHL 5175960, image# 177-179.

Ferrell & Emerette Ferrell be maintained & educated out of my estate investment any charge against any portion of my estate that they may be heir to. It is my desire that my Executor, after the ratification of the legacy bequeath to my wife, do annually divide equally between my three children. That is to say Martha L. Ferrell, William O. Ferrell, and Emerette Ferrell, the profits, if any, arising from my estate. In as much as Eleanor Wynne, the grandmother of my children, did during her life give to my daughter Martha L. Ferrell two negroes as a special legacy, it is my desire that in the division of my negroes that two negroes be set apart for W'm. O. Ferrell and Emerette Ferrell each to make them equal in number with their sister Martha L. Ferrell, after that, the negroes to be divided equally between my three children share and share alike. It is my will and desire that after my beloved wife leave my house that all the furniture & other articles unnecessary in keeping up a plantation be sold at public auction.

It is my desire that after my youngest child become of age or marries that all my land be sold, and the proceeds thereof be equally divided between my three children.

It is my will & desire that after my Executor submit to the court an appraisement of my property, that he be not required to make annual statements to the court but only a final statement after the distribution of my property.

Likewise, I make constitute and appoint Osmun A. Wynne to be Executor of this my last will & testament hereby revoking all former wills by me made. In witness whereof I have hereunto subscribed my name and affixed my seal the sixteenth day of March in the year of our Lord One thousand eight hundred & fifty-nine.

Will. A. Ferrell

The above written instrument was subscribed by the said W'm A. Ferrell in our presence and acknowledged by him to each of us and he, at the same time, published & declared into above instrument to subscribe to be his last will and testament, and we, at the testators' request, in his presence have signed our names in witness hereunto and written opposite our names are respective places of residence.

Beverly Gregg, Green Co. Ala.
Jas A. Brown   "   "   "
G.B. Wilson   "   "   "

The State of Alabama,
Greene County

Formally [appeared] before the undersigned an acting Justice of the Peace in & for the said County & State, A.J. Mayfield, who being by me first duly sworn [illegible] that the [illegible] in the foregoing petition of his own knowledge & such as one should in the [private use] & belief he believes to be true.

A.J. Mayfield

Sworn to [illegible] before me

the 2nd Sept. 1859

O.A. Wynne

MASONIC.

The Grand Lodge, Grand Chapter and Grand Council, at their sessions last week made the following election of officers. The attendance was large, and composed of much of the talent and ability of our State. Among the important acts of the Grand Lodge, we understand that the surplus fund on hand was divided out among the subordinate Lodges of the State. Hoping that the worthy Grand Secretary will furnish the newspaper press a synopsis of the *public* actions of the respective bodies of which he is the medium, we append the list of officers of the Grand Chapter and Grand Lodge:

Adv. & Gaz.

OFFICERS OF THE GRAND LODGE OF ALABAMA.

W. M.—Sterling A. M. Wood, of Florence, G. M.

R. W.—J. McCaleb Wiley, of Troy, Dep. G. M.

" " H. S. Shelton, Pickensville, Sen. G. W.

" " J. H. Danforth, Eufaula, Jr. G. W.

" " Thos. Welsh, Montgomery, G. T.

" " Amand P. Pfister, " G. S.

" " Rev. S. E. Norton, " G. C.

" " N. D. Guerry, Enon, Grand Mar.
. " A. C. Taylor, Mulberry, Sen. G. D.
" J. H. Prince, Dayton, Jun. G. D.
J. P. Dickinson, } Mont., G. Stewards.
W. J. Reese, }
Thomas Henry, Mobile, Southern Dist.
Wm. A. Ferrell, Hollow Square, Middle
   District,
Jas. Crumlidge, Athens, Northern Dis-
   trict, Grand Lecturers.
Thos. McDugal, Mont., Grand Tyler.

OFFICERS OF THE GRAND CHAPTER.

M. E.—W. A. Ferrell, Hollow Square,
                              G. H. P.
   " J. R. Clark, Jacksonville, Dep. G.
                                    H. P
   " H. S. Shelton, Pickensville, G. K.
   " M W Davis, Uchee, G S
   " Rev M F Padgett, Midway, G C
   " D Hartwell, Lowndesboro, G L
   " E M Hastings, Montgomery, G T
   " A P Pfister,   "   G S
H P Watson,   "   G C H
A B Darby, Clinton, G P S
J W Drake, Auburn, G R C
D L Ayres, Livingston, G M 2 V
J H Danforth, Eufaula, " " 3 V
A J Terrell, Wetumpka, " " 1 V
T. McDugal, Montgomery, G. Sentinel.

289

---

289 Masonic Lodge Sessions, *Jacksonville (Alabama) Republican*, 19 December 1854, p. 2, col. 5; digital image *Newspapers.com* (https://www.newspapers.com/image/308892931/?terms=Masonic : accessed 25 Sept 2021).

HEAD QUARTERS, 2D BATTALION, 38TH REG'T, ALA. MILITIA.

An Election will be held in Greensboro' on Wednesday the 8th August, to elect Captain, and 1st and 2d Lieutenants for Beat No. 5. By order of

H. C. CHILDRESS, Major.

W. R. HARDAWAY, Adj't.

The undersigned, candidates for Captain, in Beat No. 5, will address their fellow-citizens on Tuesday evening, 7th inst., at Mr. Dugger's Hotel.

R. O. BURTON,
W. A. WYNNE.

Please announce F. A. BROWN and W. B. BRIGGS candidates for 1st Lieutenant, in Beat No. 5. Also, R. S. WADDLE a candidate for 2d Lieutenant.

VOTER.

290

---

290 Notice of Election of Officers, 2nd Battalion, 38th Alabama Militia, *The (Greensboro) Alabama Beacon*, 3 August 1855, p. 2, col. 2; digital image *Newspapers.com* (https://www.newspapers.com/image/253283982/?terms=%22HEAD%20QUARTERS%22& match=1 : accessed 25 Sept 2021).

> ☞We are authorized to announce the fol-
> lowing gentlemen as candidates for the the of-
> fice of Justice of the Peace for the Greensbo-
> ro' Beat—Election in March 1856:
>
> ## *W. A. WYNNE, ESQ.* *
> ## *P. T. WRIGHT.*

291

---

291 Candidates for Justice of the Peace, *The Greensboro) Alabama* Beacon, 7 December 1855, p. 3, col. 4; digital image *Newspapers.com* (https://www.newspapers.com/image/253284025/?terms=WYNNE&match=1 : accessed 25 Sept 2021).

Proceedings of the Town Council.

At a meeting of the Intendant and Council of Greensboro, held at the office of Charles Whelan, pursuant to adjournment, on Monday, 30th inst., present, Chas. Whelan, Intendant, R. D. Huckabee, Wm. A. Lanier, and H. C. Childress. The committee reported in favor of the adoption of the ordinances as they now stand, except the 5th ordinance, and the 2nd section of ordinance 9th, which report was adopted.

On motion of R. D. Huckabee, the Council then proceeded to the election of Marshall, when George Briggs having received a majority of the votes cast was declared duly elected. On motion the Council proceeded to examine the report of W. A. Wynne, the Intendant for 1855.

On motion, it was decided to place the report of the committee, appointed by the Council, to examine the report of R. S. Waddle, Marshall for 1855, in the hands of the Intendant to effect a settlement.

On motion, the Intendant, in conjunction with the Marshall, was authorized to contract for the hauling and placing the dirt out of A. M. Dorman's cellar on the front street. On motion, the Council adjourned.

CHAS. WHELAN, Intendant.
H. C. CHILDRESS, Sec.

292

---

292 Proceedings of the Town Council, *The (Greensboro) Alabama Beacon*, p. 2, col. 4; digital image *Newspapers.com* (https://www.newspapers.com/image/253253090/?terms=Proceedings&match=1 : accessed 25 Sept 2021).

NOTICE.

A. WYNNE, Justice of the Peace,
has removed to the office now occu-
by P. T. Wright, Esq., two doors North
K. Carson's Store, where one or both
always be found.

eensboro, Ala., Feb. 20, 1857,   5 2w

293

---

293 Notice of A. Wynne, Justice of the Peace, moving his office, *The (Greensboro) Alabama Beacon*, 20 February 1857, p.3, col. 1; digital image *Newspapers.com* (https://www.newspapers.com/image/253253035/?terms=WYNNE&match=1 : accessed 25 Sept 2021).

JOS. W. TAYLOR,
Eutaw, Ala.

W. A. WYNNE,
Greensboro, Ala.

. . . .

TAYLOR & WYNNE.
Attorneys At Law,

WILL practice in Greene and the adjoining counties.
November 6, 1857.   42 3m.

294

ANNOUNCEMENTS.

W. A. WYNNE, INDEPENDENT Candidate for Justice of the Peace in Beat No. 5—Election 1st Monday in March, A. D. 1859.
Greensboro, Dec. 31, 1858.   50 2m

295

294 Taylor & Wynne, Attorneys at Law, *The (Greensboro) Alabama Beacon*, 13 November 1857, p. 3, col. 4; digital image *Newspapers.com* (https://www.newspapers.com/image/253253564/?terms=Wynne&match=1 : accessed 25 Sept 2021).

295 W. A. Wynne, Independent Candidate, *The (Greensboro) Alabama Beacon . Alabama Beacon*, 4 March 1859, p. 3, col. 5; digital image *Newspapers.com* (https://www.newspapers.com/image/253254932/?terms=Wynne&match=1

WM. A. WYNNE, ESQ., of this place, is announced in last week's Whig, "a Whig and American candidate for a seat in the Representative branch of the next Legislature."

296

JUSTICE OF THE PEACE.—H. F. Evans, Esqr., was elected, on the 25th ult., Justice of the Peace for the Greensboro Beat, in place of W. A. Wynne, Esqr., who has recently moved out of the Beat.

297

296 W.A. Wynne, A Whig and American Candidate, *The (Greensboro) Alabama Beacon*, 17 June 1859, p. 2, col. 5; digital image *Newspapers.com* (https://www.newspapers.com/image/253254932/?terms=Wynne&match=1 : Accessed 25 Sept 2021).

297 Election of Justice of the Peace, *The (Greensboro) Alabama Beacon*, 9 March 1860, p.2, col. 3; digital image *Newspapers.com* (https://www.newspapers.com/image/355740227/?terms=Wynne&match=1 : accessed 25 Sept 2021).

TRIBUTE OF RESPECT.

At a call communication of Beacon Lodge No. 66, held at the residence of Mr. O. A. Wynne, May 15th, 1859, the following preamble and resolutions were unanimously adopted:

Whereas, It has pleased the Supreme Architect of the universe, to call from his labors our brother, WM. A. FERRELL, for many years the Worshipful Master of this Lodge, whose name has long been identified with the order throughout this State, and who, by his Masonic intelligence and fidelity has done much to spread abroad the true light of Masonry, and

Whereas, This Lodge, over which he has so long presided, are sorely bereaved by this dispensation of an All-Wise Providence, yet in the midst of their affliction recognize the hand of Him "who doeth all things well," and before whom we should all bow with that reverential awe due from the creature to the Creator; therefore,

Resolved, That in the death of brother WM. A. FERRELL this Lodge has sustained an irreparable loss, and the Craft throughout the State have lost a brother, who, by the purity of his life and rectitude of his conduct, afforded a bright example to others.

Resolved, That we tender our heart-felt condolence and sympathy to the bereaved family of our deceased brother.

Resolved, That we wear the usual badge of mourning for thirty days, and that our Lodge-room be draped in mourning for six months.

Resolved, That this preamble and resolutions be spread upon the minutes, and a copy, under the seal of the Lodge, be forwarded to the widow of our deceased brother; and also copies furnished to the newspapers published in this county, and they be requested to publish the same.

Resolved, That we tender our kindest thanks to Mr. O. A. Wynne, for his kindness in furnishing us a room.

J. M. BROWN, Secretary.

298

298 Tribute of Respect to Wm. A. Ferrell, *The (Greensboro) Alabama Beacon*, p. 2, col. 6; digital image *Newspapers.com*

399

We have been favored with a letter from Dr. C. J. Clark, to Mr. R. H Wynne, Esq., from which we obtain an item which speaks volumes in favor of the faithful labors and scientific skill of Dr. C. and the able assistants in the Alabama hospitals. Out of 40J men received in the hospital from the late battles, 29 only have died.

Dr. Clarke also estimates the entire number of killed and wounded at from 12 to 15,000, and of these 3,000 were only slightly wounded. Among the various and conflicting estimates and statements which have been made, we take this to be as correct a statement as can be obtained.

299

(https://www.newspapers.com/image/253255087/?terms=Tribute&match=1 : accessed 25 Sept 2021).

299 Letter re: casualties, *Jacksonville (Alabama) Republican*, 24 July 1862, p. 2, col. 1; digital image *Newspapers.com* (https://www.newspapers.com/image/358346250/?terms=Clarke&match=1 : accessed 25 Sept 2021).

Documents from the Estate Records of
Salina Ann Ferrell & William A. Ferrell

Court Ordered Appraisal of Slaves[300]

We the undersigned appraisers appointed by the Judge of the Probate Court of Greene County Ala. to appraise the personal property of Salina AE Ferrell dec'd proceeded to appraise the Property as shown as by O.A. Wynne Administrator which is as follows to such August the Fifteenth, 1859.

Inventory	Appraisement
1 negro man **Creed** aged 57 years	$1500
Woman **Fanny** aged 39 and child **Viola** aged 1 year	$133
Woman **Rose** aged 18 years	$800
Woman **Mary** aged 17 years	$1266
Girl **Martha** aged 15 years	$1100
Girl **Virginia** aged 13 years	$1100
Girl **Roena** aged 12 years	$1000
Boy **Paul** aged 10 years	$900
Boy **Joshua** aged 7 years	$600
Girl **Sophronia** aged 4 years	$500
Boy **Luke** aged 2 years	$350
Man **John** aged 45 years	$1100
Woman **Martha** aged 37 years	$1133[301]

[300] The inventory can be found in the unbound estate papers: Greene Co, AL, Probate Ct. Estate Case Files, 1820-1915, Case #1545, Estate Papers of Salina A. Ferrell, pp.51-52; digital images, *Family Search* (https://www.familysearch.org/ark:/61903/3:1:33SQ-GTW5-HQF?i=50&wc=MXR9-6PV%3A314241801%2C316387401&cc=1978117 : accessed 26 Jan 2021); and transcribed in Greene County, Alabama, probate minutes, 1854-1929; probate records, 1850-1928, Item 2, p. 627-629; digital images *Family Search* (https://www.familysearch.org/ark:/61903/3:1:33S7-8B31-9Z2?i=316&cc=1925446&cat=518744 : accessed 19 Mar 2022).

[301] It could read $1433

Boy **Isaiah** aged 13 years	$1100
Boy **Blocker** aged 9 years	$950
Girl **Lucy** aged 4 years	$450
Boy **Walton** aged 3 years	$350
Man **Rednick** aged 42 years	$1050
Woman **Matilda** aged 28 years	$1233
Boy **Jeremiah** aged 10 years	$1000
Girl **Malinda** aged 8 years	$900
Boy **Wiley** aged 3 years	$400
Boy **Ellic** aged 2 years	$350
Woman **Maria** aged 70 years	$150
Woman **Lilly** aged 18	$1400
Man **Jacob** aged 40 years	$1100
Man **Isaac** aged 50 years	$850
Man **Jasper** aged 22 years	$1400
Man **Charles** aged 30 years	$1500
Woman **Carolina** aged 27 years	$1100
Man **Harvey** aged 50 years	$1000

Benjamin Travis
J.A. Brown
S. Travis

State of Alabama

Greene County

I, John N. May, an acting Justice of the Peace in and for The County of Greene. Hereby Certify that the Annexed Inventory and Appraisal bill of the Personal property belonging to Salina A. E. Ferrell decreased was sworn to and subscribed before me by B. Travis, S. Travis, & J.A. Brown as appraising of said property on this 15th day of August A.D. 1859.

John N. May, Jr.

State of Alabama

Greene Co.

The above named in the foregoing appraisement Bill is returned by the above as his Inventory of Personal property which has come to his hands. Sworn to & subscribed Sept. 22/59 before me.

M O [illegible]

O.A. Wynne

Opinion of Circuit Court on Wynne-Ferrell Dispute[302]

The State of Alabama,

Greene County

At a Circuit Court begun and held in and for the 7th Judicial Circuit of the State of Alabama, at the Court House of Greene County at Eutaw on the 4th Monday after the 3rd Monday in March, in the year of Our Lord One Thousand Eight Hundred and Sixty-one being the 13th day of April 1861. Present, the Hon. A.A. Coleman, Judge Presiding.

The following proceedings were had.

Osman A. Wynne, Adm[r] of Salina A.E. Ferrell,

Vs.

Andrew J. Mayfield Adm[r] of William A. Ferrell, dec[d]

This cause coming on to be heard on the motion of Osman A. Wynne as Administrator of Salina A.E. Ferrell, deceased, to have the award herein after set out, entered up as the judgment of this Court, and both parties being present by their attorney and it appearing to the Court that Osman A. Wynne, as Administrator of Salina A.E. Ferrell, dec'd, and Andrew J. Mayfield as Administrator of William A. Ferrell, dec'd, having certain matters in controversy between them, no suit pending, agreed in writing to submit the motion to the arbitration of certain persons chosen by them, as follows, to wit,— Whereas the undersigned Osman A. Wynne as the Administrator of Salina A.E. Ferrell claims title to certain slaves now in the possession of the undersigned William Andrew J. Mayfield, Adm[m] with the will annexed of William A. Ferrell deceased, and also the value of the hires of the said slaves, from the death of the said Salina A.E. Ferrell, and whereas the said parties are desirous to save expenses to the Estates, which they respectively represent, but to have such controversy between them adjusted and determined according to law and the rights of the said Estates, they have therefore agreed to submit the same to the arbitrament and award to James

---

[302] Greene County, Alabama, Probate Court Estate Case Files, 1820-1915, Case #1536, Estate Papers of William A. Ferrell, p.201-211; digital images *Family Search* (https://www.familysearch.org/ark:/61903/3:1:33S7-9TW5-Z9J?cc=1978117&personaUrl=%2Fark%3A%2F61903%2F1%3A1%3AVNTV-6DZ accessed 26 Jan 2021).

Dorroh, William, G. Saddler, and Edward L. Kimbrough, upon the following terms, viz.

The said arbitrations shall inquire into and determine as to the title of the slaves, embraced in the inventory of the said Osman A. Wynne filed as the Administrator of the Estate of Salina A.E. Ferrell in the Probate Court of Greene County, and any increase of said slaves born since said inventory was made and if they find and determine that said slaves are the property of the Estate of the said Salina A.E. Ferrell, deceased, they shall then inquire into and determine the value of the hires of said slaves, from the death of the said Salina A. E. Ferrell, to the 25th day of December 1859.

It is further agreed between the parties that the said arbitrators shall be governed in their determination by the provisions of the Code of Alabama in Chapter 9, Title 2 and Part 3 commencing on page 494, and that said award shall be made in compliance therewith. It is further agreed that if the said arbitrators determine that the said slaves are the property of the Estate of the said Salina A.E. Ferrell, they shall not by their award require the same to be delivered up until the 25th day of December 1859, and it is also further agreed that the amount that may be awarded to the said Osman A. Wynne as Administrator as aforesaid for the hire of said slaves, must stand over for payment until the expiration of eighteen months from the grant of letters of Administration to the said Andrew J. Mayfield on the Estate of the said W.A. Ferrell, after which the said award must be entered up as the Judgment of the Circuit Court of Greene County, and if the said Estate of William A. Ferrell, should prove to be insolvent, or be so declared by the proper Court, that the said award and Judgment to stand upon the same footing with other asserted debts against the said Estate.

Given under the hands of the said parties respectively this the eighth day of November A.D. 1859.

A.J. Mayfield, Admin of William A. Ferrell

O.A. Wynne, Admin of S.A.E. Ferrell

Jas Dorroh

M.G. Sadler

E.L. Kimbrough

Attest

Thos H. Hordon [illegible]

J.D. Webb

And it further appearing to the Court, that the said persons so chosen by the parties, did arbitrate said matters and render an award therein in writing, as follows, to wit—.

The State of Alabama,

Greene County

We, James Dorroh, William G. Sadler, and Edward L. Kimbrough having been appointed by Osman A. Wynne, as Administrator of the Estate of Salina A.E. Ferrell Dec'd and Andrew J. Mayfield as Adm^r with the will annexed, of W'm A. Ferrell, Deceased, to determine the matters in controversy in accordance with the terms of submission hereto attached and identified, by our signatures, and having appointed the 13th day of December 1859, as the time, and the late residence of William A. Ferrell deceased as the place for hearing the parties, and making our award, and the said parties having three days notice of such time and place, did at such time and place, the said parties being present, proceed to hear and determine the matters in controversy, and after examining all the witnesses produced before us, and being first sworn impartially to determine the matters submitted to according to the evidence and manifest equity and justice of the case, [to] the best of our judgment, without favor or affection, do make and declare this to be our award.

That the said Osman A. Wynne as the Adm^r of the said Salina A.E. Ferrell is entitled to the following Negroes, viz. —**Creed, Harvey, Charles, John, Rednick, Jacob, Jasper, Mary, Martha Ann, Virginia, Rowena, Paul, Johana [Joshua], Sophronia, Luke, Viola, Fannie, Lily, Caroline, Isaac, Martha, Isaiah, Blocker, Lucy, Walter, Mariah, Rose, Matilda, Jeremiah, Malinda, Wiley, and Ellina [Ellick]**. They being the same embraced in the inventory filed by the said Wynne, and our award is that the said Mayfield do deliver or cause to be delivered the said Negroes to the said Wynne on the 25th day of December 1859.

And we further award that the said Mayfield as the Administrator of the said William A. Ferrell, deceased is liable to the said Osman A. Wynne as Administrator of Salina A.E. Ferrell, deceased for the value of the hires of said

Negroes from the first day of January 1853 in the sum of Eleven Thousand four Hundred and Ninety-Eight Dollars, but in as much as eighteen months have not elapsed since the appointment of said Mayfield as such Administrator, the said sum is to stand over for payment until the 9th day of February 1861, at which time the said Mayfield as such Administrator is by this award to pay the sum with interest from the date of this award to the said Wynne.

It is also our award that if the Estate of the said Ferrell should duly be declared to be insolvent by the Probate Court of Greene County that the amount herein awarded to the said Wynne for the hires of the said slaves is not to be collected, in full, but the same is to be filed in the Probate Court for a Prorated payment out of the assets of the said Estate, as any other debt, against the same.

All of which we hereby certify to be our determination and award in the [illegible] present.[303]

Given under our hands this the 13th day of December 1859.

> *James Dorroh*
> *M.G. Sadler*
> *E.L. Kimbrough*

And it further appearing to the Court by the admission of both parties that a portion of said award has been complied with, by the parties, to wit— The said Mayfield as administrator as aforesaid has delivered in compliance with said award all the slaves therein mentioned to Osman A. Wynne, as administrator as aforesaid.

And it further appearing to the court that said award has not been performed by the said Andrew J. Mayfield as Administrator aforesaid in the following respect, to wit, that the said sum of money awarded in said award to be paid by the said Andrew J. Mayfield, as Administrator of William A. Ferrell, deceased, to the said Osman A. Wynne, as Administrator of Salina A.E. Ferrell, deceased, has not been paid, and that more than ten days have elapsed since the 9th day of February 1861, when said money by said award, was awarded to be paid and the said Parties having also agreed that after the 9th day of February 1861, said award should be entered as the Judgment of this Court and the said parties non-appearing in Court, and consenting and agreeing thereto.

It is therefore ordered and adjudged that the said award, hereinbefore recited, be entered and stand as the judgment of this Court and that the said Osman A. Wynne as Administrator of Salina A.E. Ferrell, deceased have and recover of the

---

[303] Difficult to read; possibly "present."

said Andrew J. Mayfield as aforesaid, with interest from the 10th day of December 1859, to be levied of the goods and chattels lands and tenements of said William A. Ferrell, deceased, in his hands to be Administered for which together with costs Executive may issue.

The State of Alabama,

Greene County

I, David B. Butler, Clerk of the Circuit Court of said County, hereby certify that the foregoing transcript is a true & perfect copy of the proceedings had in said Circuit Court in a matter of Controversy between O.A. Wynne adm'r of Salina A.E. Ferrel, dec[d] & Andrew J. Mayfield, adm'r of the Estate of W[m] A. Ferrell, dec[d.]

Witness my hand this 18th January 1867.

D.B. Butler
Clerk

The State of Alabama,

Greene County

Personally appeared before me, Samuel W. Dunlap, a Justice of the Peace in and for the County of Greene and State of Alabama, O.A. Wynne who being first duly sworn disposeth and saith that the [illegible] judgment in his favour in the Adm[r] of Salina A.E. Ferrell [illegible] on the 15th of April 1861, with [illegible] from 15th day of December 1859, in the Circuit Court of Greene County, against Andrew J. Mayfield Adm[r] of William A. Ferrell for the sum of eleven thousand four hundred and ninety eight dollars, is [illegible] justly due him, and is [illegible] in [illegible] charged again at A.J. Mayfield as the Administrator aforesaid, and that said judgment is unpaid and still due as its payments, executes the following payments have been made to this affiant, one payment four thousand dollars July 31st 1863, 2nd Oct. 1863, amounting to the sum of four thousand five hundred dollars, one payment of $500.00 dollars made 28 Feb 1862.

Sworn to and subscribed before me this 7th day of February 1867

O.A. Wynne

Samuel W. Dunlap
J.C.

Andrew J. Mayfield as administrator of William A. Ferrell, dec'd.

Letter from O.A. Wynne to Judge Regarding Rentals of Land & Slaves, 1860-1864

To the Honorable William C. Oliver,
Judge of the Probate Court of Greene County

Osmun A. Wynne,
Administrator of Estate of S.A.E. Ferrell,
respectfully states unto your Honor:

That as Admin[r] of said Estate, he holds Sundry Notes taken by him for hires of Negroes & rent of lands of said estate, a schedule of which is hereto attached, which were given by the parties during the war and some of which were based upon prices in Confedt money, and if such [illegible] will be attended with costs of litigation.

He therefore prays your Honor to grant unto him an order, authorizing him to settle & compromise the said Notes without [illegible] on the best terms practicable and for such other orders as may be legal & proper.

O A Wynne

By W[m] F Webb

O.A. Wynne, Administrator of the Estate of S.A.E. Ferrell dec'd, makes the following return of the hires of Negroes and Rents of the Lands of the Estate:

1860	Hired the Negroes privately under an order of Court to A.J. Mayfield for 1860	$2130
	and rented the Land to him at public auction	$172
1861	Hired the Negroes to A.J. Mayfield 1861	$1650
	and rented him the Land for 1861	$170
1862	Hired Negroes to A.J. Mayfield for 1862	$300
	And rented him the land " " "	$150
1863	Hired the Negro girl, Rose, to J.M. Dunham and hired all the other Negroes to A.J. Mayfield for the year 1863 for their support clothing & taxes.	$25
	Rented the land to A.J. Mayfield for 1863	"
		$150
1864	Rented the Land to J.W. Melton at public auction for this year 1864	$201.25
	Hired **Isaac** to R.J.M. Lester " " "	$100
	Hired **Virginia** to David May " " "	$50
	Hired **Jake** to G.W. Sims " " "	$140
	Hired **Jasper** to Lewis Windham[304] " " "	$150
	Hired **Caroline** to N.E. Roberts " " "	$75
	Amt cd over	$716.25

Amt carried over $716.25

---

[304] Lewis Wyndham's land adjoined the Ferrell property.

1864	Hired **Mary** to W.H. Applegate	$75
	Hired **Rose** to Thos W. Roberts	$25
	Hired **Isaiah** to J.S. Ryan	$25
	Hired **Matilda** & 6 children to D.V. Patterson	$50
	Hired to J.W. Melton: **Charles**, **Creed**, **Maria** Family **Martha Ann** & children	$500.00
	Hired **John** to William Christian	$200
	Rent & Hires for 1864	$1626.25

The Admr would also return & report to the Court that he held in the records belonging to the Estate on the [illegible] of March [illegible] 1864 about $8000 in Confederate Treasury Notes which he funded in 4 pr ct [percent] Certificates under the Act of The Confedt Congress of the 17th Feb'y 1864 as follows to wit—

No. 198 March 5th 1864 Certificate	$1200
No. 216 March 7th 1864 Certificate	$6800

For which he asks the Court to allow him a Credit under the Act of the Legislature of 1864.

O.A. Wynne

Rental of Enslaved People of Salina A. Wynne for 1865

Osmun A. Wynne, Adm^r of S.A.E. Ferrell Dec'^{d}

In Account on Annual Settlement D^r

1865 Jan'y 1	To^t am^t of JW Melton for Rent of Land in 1864 paid in Confed^t Money	$201.25
	To^t am^t of J.M. Lester for hire of **Isaac** do do	$100
	To^t am^t of Duned May hire of **Vanessa** do do	$50
	To^t am^t of W.H. Applegate hire of **Mary** do do	$75
	To^t am^t of T.W. Roberts hire of **Rose** do do	$25
	To^t am^t of J.L. Ryan hire of **Isaiah** do do	$60
	To^t am^t of J.W. Melton hire of **Chas**, **Creed** and family	$500
	To^t am^t of Ms. Christian for hire of **John** do do	$200
	Amt c^d over	$1211.25

ADMINISTRATOR'S SALE.

BY virtue of an order from the Hon. Probate Court of Hale county, the undersigned will, as administrator of the Estate of John W. Wynne, dec'd., sell to the highest bidder, at public out cry, for Cash, on

Wednesday, the 18th of Dec'r next, (1867,)

all the personal and perishable property of his intestate, consisting in part of

MULES,	HORSES,
CORN,	FODDER,
WAGONS,	FARMING

TOOLS, &c., &c., &c.
HOUSEHOLD & KITCHEN FURNITURE, CROCKERY, GROCERIES & SUNDRIES.

Said sale will take place between the hours prescribed by law, on the premises of the decedent, on the Erie and Greensboro road three miles from Erie, better known as the Kimbrough old place.

O. A. WYNNE,
Administrator.
46-3in-4w

November 23, 1867

305

Administrator's Sale of Estate of John W. Wynne, *The (Greensboro) Alabama Beacon*, 23 November 1867, p. 2, col. 7; digital image *Newspapers.com* (https://www.newspapers.com/image/355816444/?terms=Wynne&match=1 : accessed 25 Sept 2021).

Thoroughly Satisfied.

The Greensboro Beacon says Jim Green, the colored Representative from Hale county, in the Alabama scalawag Legislature, just returned from . Montgomery, expresses himself thoroughly tired of politics. He announces that he has tried politics for three years, and does not see that he has accomplished any good. He is now making an effort to get up an expedition to go to Liberia. He is making speeches and advising all his race who are able to go with him to that country. He truthfully says that this is a white man's government, and that nothing can ever make it anything else. It seems that Green has had a conversation with Gen. Clanton and other leading men of Montgomery, who have convinced him entirely as to what use the Radical party is making of the freedmen.

306

---

306 Thoroughly Satisfied, *The Athens (Alabama) Weekly Post,* 3 September 1868, p. 1, col. 3; digital image *Newspapers.com* (https://www.newspapers.com/image/355775506/?terms=%22Greensboro%20Beacon%22& match=1 : accessed 27 Sept 2021).

Obituary.

WILLIAM APPLING WYNNE, was born on the 7th day of December, 1831, and died on the 2d day of May, 1869, at his residence in this county, in the prime of strong and resolute manhood.

The writer was intimately acquainted with him, and can speak of his character and conduct, both in the private and public relations of life.

In the family circle he was the attentive and respectful son—the kind and considerate brother. He was, indeed, what a refined natural organization, improved by a polite and liberal education, eminently fitted him for—that member of the household whose presence was its light and life.

Socially, his reputation is too well known to need comment. The friends of his boyhood, and of his riper years, scattered as they are, here and there throughout the State, will respond to the statement, that he combined in his life, the virtues of the genial and agreeable companion, and of the steady and trustworthy friend.

His standard of gentlemanly deportment and bearing was pure and elevated. Careful to reserve his opinion of those whom he did not admire, yet when duty demanded, he was ever willing and ready to raise his voice in open and honorable denunciation of the wrong.

Such traits as these rendered him deservedly popular, and make his death a matter of regret to his acquaintances, and of grief to his friends.

With his record as a citizen we are all familiar. He was one whom we could not well afford to lose. Educated for the Bar, he carried into a private station a clear knowledge of his obligation to his fellows, and to the State, with nature's boons, honesty and integrity, to meet and fulfil them. With this knowledge and endowment in a private position of life, he was perhaps better adapted for the repository of public trust and confidence than one in other respects better qualified, but whose opinions were more likely to be warped and biased by the partizanships and prejudices of an active public life.

He was in the opening years of manhood a citizen of our town, and occupied for some time the chief office in the gift of our citizens.

He was taken away in the prime of life.— There is something touching in the sapling nipped by the early frost, and in the oak twisted and felled by the ruthless whirlwind, but there is an awful sadness in the strong oak shivered by the lightning's blast, when its roots have taken a firm hold, and its branches are casting a broad shade.

He died suddenly—not in the promise of the performance, but in the very performance of his duties,—not on the parade grounds of life, but on its battlefields, where his ability to do well had been vindicated by trial and by experience, and long before age had begun to deaden his energies or dampen his ardor.

Though in his earlier years he may have exhibited more indifference on the subject of religion than was meet, yet his manhood years found him abiding by the commandment of his father and in the law of his mother.

He made no loud-mouthed professions, for of such was not his nature, but when asked for the reason for our hope, we point to the record of his life and repeat "I will have mercy and not sacrifice."

T. J....

307

307 Death of William Appling Wynne, *(Greensboro) Alabama Beacon*, 22 May 1869, p. 2, col. 7; digital image *Newspapers.com*

ADMINISTRATOR'S NOTICE.

NOTICE is hereby given that Letters of Administration on the Estate of Wm. A. Wynne, deceased, late of Hale county, Ala., were on the 2d day of June, 1869, granted to the undersigned by the Honorable the Probate Court of Hale county, Ala. All persons having claims against said Estate are required to present them within the time prescribed by law, or the same will be barred, those indebted will make immediate payment.

O. A. WYNNE,
Administrator.

july 3, 1869   26-2in-6w

308

(https://www.newspapers.com/image/355838742/?terms=wynne&match=1 : accessed 27 sept 2021).

308 Administrator's Notice, Estate of Wm. A. Wynne, *(Greensboro) Alabama Beacon*, 31 July 1869, p. 3, col. 4; digital image *Newspapers.com*
(https://www.newspapers.com/image/355841574/?terms=wynne&match=1 : accessed 27 Sept 2021).

Letters from O.A. Wynne to Judge, Regarding Rentals of Land in 1868 & 1869 to Charles Magruder and J.W. Melton, & Slaves Hired Out During the War [309]

To Hon. W^m. Miller,
Judge of Probate of Greene County, State of Alabama

O.A. Wynne, Adm^r of the Est. S.A.E. Ferrell, respectfully states unto your Honor, that the Estate of his Intestate[310] which was in his hands, consisted of a small tract of land near Hollow Square, in Hale County, which he has been renting out for several years during the War and since, for which he has accounted in his former settlements, and is charged up in the settlement now to be made.

He rented a part only of the land for the year 1868, as follows to wit, To J.W. Melton about 15 acres for $30 00/100 and to Chas Magruder, about 23 acres for $40 00/100 which has been collected and is charged up. And he rented only a part of the land for this year 1869, viz:

To J.W. Melton about 60 acres for $100 00/100 and to Chas Magruder about 30 acres for $50 00/100. The land is very much worn, and out of the 250 acres of cleared land, there is about 125 acres (in small patches tillable) all the rest of it, is waste land, and the fencing very much dilapidated, and it was offered at public auction, and could not be rented as any price. The Admin further reports that he hired out the negroes of the Estate during the war, and has charged himself with all the hires he collected, and has tried in vain to collect the notes which he holds for the hires of 1864 and 1865. A schedule of which are hereunto attached to his petition recorded in Book W p. 585.

O.A. Wynne

Sworn and subscribed before me
this 18th day of July 1869.
W^m, Miller, Judge

---

[309] Greene County, Alabama, Probate Court Estate Case Files, 1820-1915, Case #1545, Estate Papers of Salina A. Ferrell, pp.30-31; digital images *Family Search* (https://www.familysearch.org/ark:/61903/3:1:33S7-9TW5-4PC?i=29&wc=MXR9-6PV%3A314241801%2C316387401&cc=1978117 : accessed 26 Jan 2021).

[310] This word, fully legible, seems to have been used by the clerk in place of *testator*.

To the Hon^r A.R. Davis,
Judge of the Probate Court of Greene Co. Ala.

The Report of O.A. Wynne, Adm^r of the Estate of S.A. Ferrell, respectfully shows unto your Honor.

That in pursuance of the order of this Court on or about the 1st of January last, having previously advertised the time & place of the renting, he offered the land of the said Estate for rent at public auction, at Hollow Square, and there being no bid for the same for more than a nominal price, he did not rent it publicly, and afterwards to wit on or about the 5th of January last, he rented the said land (about 150 acres) to Chas McGruder (a freedman) for the sum of Two Hundred Dollars. The said land could not have been rented for more than 10^{cts} per acre probably nor could he get any other security for the payment of the rent, than the sum which the law gives on the crop, for which he now holds the note of said McGruder.

O.A. Wynne

Sworn to subscribed before me this the 13th of May 1870

Judge A.R. Davis

[*For the Beacon*

At a meeting of a portion of the Cotton Planters of Greene county, held at Hollow Square on the 27th of February, 1862, it was unanimously

Resolved, That in the ensuing planting season it will be impolitic and unpatriotic to plant more than one-fourth of our tillable land in cotton, and that every consideration of wisdom and love of country calls upon the planters of the cotton-growing sections to devote *at least* three-fourths of all their lands and industry to the raising of grain and provisions.

For the purpose of carrying our views into practical operation, we, the undersigned, do hereby pledge ourselves to each and the country, that we will faithfully adhere to the above resolution.   (Signed,)

Lemuel Hatch,	R D Redding,
O A Wynne,	J M Wedgworth,
Jas Chapman,	W F Mouette,
B. D. Palmer,	A J Mayfield,
T F Witherspoon,	E Sawyer,

311

---

311 Pledge to plant food crops, *Selma (Alabama) Morning Times*, 16 August 1870, p.2, col. 2; digital image *Newspapers.com* (https://www.newspapers.com/image/571399173/?terms=Wynne&match=1 : accessed 27 Sept 2021).

Benj. Travis,   J W May,
A M Hanna,   M M May,
W L Kennedy,   G W Roberts,
R Hanna,   Benj Evans,
J W Monette,   D D Harris,
B Holbrook,   J H Tarkinton,
E Willingham, Sr.,   Mrs G G Pickens,
C F Burge,   E L Kimbrough,
Chas Stewart,   John Parr,
Andrew Logan,   W T Sawyer,
J A Thompson,   B Grigg.

On motion of Jas. Chapman, it was further

Resolved, That Rev. J. J. Hutchinson be requested to bring this subject to the consideration of the people at such times as may suit his convenience, in public assemblages of our citizens.

On motion of Enoch Sawyer, it was unanimously

Resolved, That the thanks of this meeting are due to the Rev. Mr. Hutchinson for his patriotic exertions among us, and that they are hereby gratefully tendered to him.

Mrs. Bettie Torbert presented, thro' the Rev. Mr. Hutchinson, three large and well-made Bowie knives, of home manufacture, to the Company of volunteers now being raised. Thanks were returned in an appropriate manner by Jas. A. Wemyss, Esqr., in behalf of the Company.

Hale County.

The Democracy of Hale held a Convention on the second, appointed delegates to attend the State Convention, and adopted a series of resolutions, some of which we copy:

Resolved, That as Conservatives and Democrats of Hale county, we declare ourselves in favor of obedience in good faith to the laws of this State and of the United States, so long as the same remain in force; and we pledge ourselves to the support of an honest and faithful administration of them, relying upon the good sense and patriotism of the people for the correction of abuses and bad legislation.

Resolved, That the continued disfranchisement of a large class of the most worthy and intelligent citizens of the South simply because they have been trusted and honored by our people, is at war with the spirit of free institutions and of the age in which we live; and is an infamy peculiar and appropriate to the radical puritanic spirit which has well-nigh destroyed free institutions in our country; and we urge and demand the immediate and unconditional removal of all political disabilities from every class of our citizens.

Resolved, That we denounce the present system of unequal, burdensome and vexatious taxation imposed upon us by the Federal and State Governments, and the extravagance and corruption manifest in the management and expenditure of the public funds; and we demand a reduction of taxes, and an honest and economical appropriation of the people's money for the legitimate purposes of government and no other whatever.

Resolved, That the public school system of the State, as now managed, and the present organization of the State University, are nuisances to the State, and ought to be abated; and we advocate the establishment, instead of the present common school system, of a system upon just and economical principles, which shall afford to all the children of the State alike, in separate schools for white and colored, the means of an elementary English education.

Resolved, That we cordially invite all men, without regard to party affinities in the past, to unite with us in support of the principles we have announced, and in expelling from power the horde of incapable, unscrupulous, and corrupt adventurers and political sepoys, under whose misrule the State now groans, and in placing in their stead, honest, true, and competent men, worthy of the confidence, and regardful of the interests of the people.

The following gentlemen were appointed delegates to the State Convention:

DELEGATES.	ALTERNATES.
Col A C Jones,	Hon A Benners,
Col J G Harvey,	J T Walker,
J J Garrett, Esq.,	J E Love, Esq.,
Hon A A Coleman,	Hon A H Hutchinson
E L Kimbrough,	O A Wynne,
Joseph Chapman,	J H Dorrah,
Dr T J Anderson,	Dr M Wedgworth,
James Jack, Jr.,	J. L. Bozeman,
John H Turpin,	J A Hendon,
Dr J D Browder,	Maj J Wm Tayloe,
Maj I F Lewis,	Thos Armstrong,
John R Webster,	A J Dunlap,
Dan H Britton,	John H Gewin,
Capt A M Avery	A F Flinn,
Harris T Waller,	Matt Jones.

312

312 Hale County Democracy Convention, *Selma (Alabama) Morning Times*, 16 August 1870, p.2, col. 2; digital image *Newspapers.com* (https://www.newspapers.com/image/571399173/?terms=Wynne&match=1 : accessed 27 Sept 2021).

[From the Southern Presbyterian.

DIED—On the 8th of November, 1870, of a protracted and painful illness, in Hale County, Ala., Mrs. FRANCIS L. WYNNE, the wife of Mr. Osmun A. Wynne, and daughter of Mr. Thomas J. and Mrs. Jane Anderson, in the 59th year of her age.

The subject of this memoir was born in the year 1812, in the State of South Carolina, where she spent the first years of childhood and probably received her earliest and most lasting impressions. When about eight years old, her parents removed with her to the State of Alabama, and settled in what was then a portion of Greene County, in the vicinity of Mt. Zion church, where she lived and labored the remainder of her days. When about sixteen years old, she connected herself with the Presbyterian church of her community, then under the pastoral care of Rev. Joseph Cunningham, and was to the end of life an exemplary and useful member of the visible kingdom of Christ. Having been faithfully trained by a pious mother in the doctrines and polity of the Presbyterian church, she was thoroughly indoctrinated and was warmly attached to the faith and usages of her own church, yet charitable and catholic in her feelings toward the people of other denominations. Her house was always the home for all the true ministers of her Master, no matter by what name they may have been called. They always expected and never failed to receive at her hands a cordial welcome to the hospitalities of her house.

She was the mother of a goodly number of children, whom she faithfully trained "in the nurture and admonition of the Lord," and lived long enough to see that she had not labored in vain. She was also once the mistress of many servants, in whose spiritual welfare she ever took a deep interest, and like many other pious Southern ladies, labored long and hard for their salvation and happiness; many of whom highly appreciated her services and fondly clung to her to the end of life, standing by her bedside and kindly ministering to her wants in the hour of death.

Mrs. Wynne was in many respects more than an ordinary woman, and is much missed both by the church and the community with which she was long connected. In the relation of a wife, daughter, mother, and friend, she was all that we could have desired. Possessed with ample means, she gave with a liberal hand to all the calls of benevolence presented to her consideration. Though living some eight or ten miles from her house of worship, she never failed, when circumstances permitted, to be in her place in the sanctuary on the Sabbath.— Though much afflicted of late years in the loss of health and the death of many of her children and friends, yet did she always exhibit the patience and resignation of an humble believer and a true disciple of the Lord Jesus. Having been in feeble health for several years, she was not unmindful of the approach of death; and when it did at last come, she was found ready and willing "to depart and be with Christ, which is far better." As might be expected, her end was peaceful and happy, interspersed at times with more than ordinary joy and exultation. "And devout men," as of old, "followed her to her burial, and made great lamentation over her," exclaiming, "Let me die the death of the righteous, and let my last end be like his." May her mantle fall on some of her surviving kindred and friends, and may the good Master in his mercy favor his church and people on earth with many more such.

313

---

313 Death of Mrs. Francis L. Wynne, *(Greensboro) Alabama Beacon*, 15 April 1871, p. 2, col. 6; (https://www.newspapers.com/image/355689845/?terms=Wynne&match=1 : accessed 28 September 2021).

Election Notice.

BY order of His Excellency, R. B. LIND-SAY, Governor of the State of Alabama, the Polls at the various Precincts in Hale county, will be opened on the FIRST SATURDAY OF MARCH NEXT, (the 4th, 1871,) for the Election of County Superintendent of Education, and two School Directors, for the county of Hale, in accordance with the Acts passed and approved 17th December, 1870, and the Sections of said Acts hereto referred to, to-wit:

"SECTION 5. Be it further enacted, That in each county in this State, a County Superintendent of Education and two School Directors shall be elected by the qualified electors on the first Saturday in March, in the year 1871, and every two years thereafter, who shall hold their office for two years, or until their successors are elected and qualified.

"SEC. 6. Be it further enacted, That at said election all the qualified electors in each county, may vote for County Superintendent of Education, but no one elector shall vote for more than one of the two School Directors provided for in Section 5."

1. HAVANA PRECINCT.—Inspectors—S. A. Wilson, Ben. Travis and Frederick Stickney.—G. H. Sheldon, Registrar and Returning officer.

2. NEW PROSPECT PRECINCT—Inspectors—John Wedgeworth, R. C. Hanna and E. Calloway Harris. Erasmus Ball, Registrar and R. O.

3. HARRISON PRECINCT.—Inspectors—F. M. Moore, B. S. Evans and James Kynard. John Prisock, Registrar and R. O.

4. GREENSBORO PRECINCT.—Inspectors—Jno. H. Y. Webb, A. C. Jones and S. S. Latimer.—Sam'l. G. Briggs, Jr., Registrar and R. O.

5. NEWBERN PRECINCT.—Inspectors—S. G. Spann, J. A. Hendon and Thomas Brown. M. L. D. Moore, Register and R. O.

6. HOLLOW SQUARE PRECINCT.—Inspectors—Jas. W. Melton, Jno. W. May and O. A. Wynne. R. D. Redding, Registrar and R. O.

7. CEDARVILLE PRECINCT.—Inspectors—Jno. R. Webster, A. J. Dunlap and Isaiah S. High. J. V. Childress, Registrar and R. O. ·

8. MACON PRECINCT.—Inspectors—James D. Browder, Edward Sammons and Charles W. Collins. L. W. Dugger, Registrar and R. O.

9. PICKENS' MILL PRECINCT.—Inspectors—W. C. Tunstall, Robert Tinker and Alex. Sledge. M. Jones, Registrar and R. O.

10. WARNER's STORE PRECINCT.—Inspectors—Jno. Warren, A. F. Flinn and James M. Mitchell. Jno. W. Clements, Registrar and R. O.

11. FIVE MILE—Inspectors—Jno. H. Ryan, Geo. W. Morris and D. R. Vaughan, A. J. Russell, Registrar and R. O.

12. CARTHAGE PRECINCT.—Inspectors—T. Brown, Junius T. Wheeler and R. Y. Wood.—A. S. Hamilton, Registrar and R. O.

Inspectors attention is called to the notice of Sections 5 and 6. Polls to open and close according to law, and returns properly made to me. Each Registrar is hereby appointed Special Deputy Sheriff to preserve order.

H. C. CHILDRESS, Sheriff, Hale county, Ala.

January 28, 1871   4-0in-5w

COUNTY ELECTION——1871.

IN accordance with the laws of the State of Alabama, there will be an election held at the different Precincts in Hale county, on the first Tuesday after the first Monday in November next, 1871, the 7th, for the election of the following county officers, to serve for two years, to-wit: One Sheriff, one Coroner, five County Commissioners, one County Treasurer, one Tax Assessor, one Tax Collector, two Justices of the Peace for each Precinct, and one Constable for each Precinct.

HAVANA—Precinct No. 1.—Inspectors, F. G. Stickney, L. L. Sexton. Philip Greene, c. Registrar and Returning officer, G. G. Westcott.

NEW PROSPECT—Precinct No. 2.—Inspectors Robert C. Hanna, Wm. G. Lawless, Sam Speed, c. Registrar and R. O. Erasmus D. Ball.

HARRISON—Precinct No. 3.—Inspectors, Jas. H. Chapman, Jno. Singley, F. M. Moore. Registrar and R. O. H. B. Singley.

GREENSBORO—Precinct No. 4.—Inspectors W. D. Lee, A. C. Waddell, George Williams, c. Registrar and R. O. Jas. E. Griggs.

NEWBERN—Precinct No. 5.—Inspectors, B. L. Bennett, B. Stern, Ellis McCann, c. Registrar and R. O. M. D. L. Moore.

HOLLOW SQUARE—Precinct No. 6.—Inspectors, T. O. Wynne, Jno. W. May, Fred. Evans, c. Registrar and R. O. Seaborn Travis.

CEDARVILLE—Precinct No. 7.—Inspectors, A. J. Dunlap, L. M. Osborn, Levi Holson, c. Registrar and R. O. J. V. Childres.

MACON—Precinct No. 8.—Inspectors, Chas. W. Collins, Wm. A. Roberson, John Collins, c. Registrar and R. O. L. W. Dugger.

PICKENS' MILL—Precinct No. 9.—Inspectors, P. J. Knox, Alex. Sledge, George W. Bryant, c. Registrar and R. O. Mathew Jones.

WARNER's STORE—Precinct No. 10.—Inspectors, Jas. A. Madison, Jno. H. Warren, W. L. Burroughs, c. Registrar and R. O. Jno W. Clements.

FIVE MILE—Precinct No. 11.—Inspectors, George W. Ryan, A. J. Russell, George Thomas. Registrar and R. O. Jos. T. Allen.

CARTHAGE—Precinct No. 12.—Inspectors, Wm. Phipps, John Brown, O. T. Anthon. Registrar and R. O. C. G. Sheldon.

The polls will open at 7 o'clock, a. m., and continue open until 6 o'clock, p. m.

The boxes containing votes, with poll list and registration list, must be returned to the Probate Office within three days after the election, and the attention of Returning Officers and Inspectors is called to the above notice.

JAS. M. HOBSON, Judge of Probate.
V. BOARDMAN, Clerk Circuit Court.
H. C. CHILDRESS, Sheriff.
Supervisors.

The Returning Officers are hereby appointed Deputy Sheriffs, to preserve order on the day of the election.

H. C. CHILDRESS, Sheriff of Hale county, Ala.

September 30, 1871   39-0½in-6x

314   315

---

314 Notice of Election, Superintendent of Education, *(Greensboro) Alabama Beacon*, 4 February 1871, p. 3, col. 3; digital image *Newspapers.com* (https://www.newspapers.com/image/355689775/?terms=Superintendent&match=1 : accessed 28 Sept 2021).

315 County Election—1871, *(Greensboro) Alabama Beacon*, 30 September 1871, p. 2, col. 7; digital image *Newspapeers.com* (https://www.newspapers.com/image/355689991 : accessed 28 Sept 2021).

Rental of Land to Charles McGruder Sr., 1871 & 1872[316]

To the Hon^l A.R. Davis,
Judge of the Probate Court of Greene Co Ala.

O.A. Wynne, Adm^r of S.A.E. Ferrell reports to your Honor.

That on or about the 1st of Jany last (1871), he offered to rent the lands of the Estate (about 100 or 125 acres) at public auction, and not being able to rent it for more than a nominal sum, he withdrew it from public letting, and soon afterwards rented it privately to Chas McGruder Freedman for the sum of $200 Dollars, and he also agreed to put up two small log cabins on the place, which he has done.

Respectfully submitted and filed this 23rd of May 1871.

O.A. Wynne,
Administrator

---

[316] Greene County, Alabama, Probate Court Estate Case Files, 1820-1915, Case #1545, Estate Papers of Salina A. Ferrell, pp.53, 61; digital images Family Search (https://www.familysearch.org/ark:/61903/3:1:33S7-9TW5-4PL?i=52&wc=MXR9-6PV%3A314241801%2C316387401&cc=1978117 : accessed 11 Feb 2021)

Jim Green, legislator from this county, was in attendance, and as will be seen from the following resolution, which was introduced by him, is rather anxious that the negro should emigrate. He addressed the meeting, and endeavored to show to his race the advantages of Kansas:

317

---

317 The Colored Labor Union in Perry (excerpt), *(Greensboro) Alabama Beacon,* 22 July 1871, p. 2, col. 3; digital image *Newspapers.*com (https://www.newspapers.com/image/355689938/?terms=%22Jim%20Green%22&match=1 : accessed 28 Sept 2021).

To the Hon[l] A.R. Davis,
Judge of the Probate Court of Greene Co. Al.

The report of O.A. Wynne, Adm[r] of the Estate S.A.E. Ferrell dec'd, respectfully states unto your Honor.

That in pursuance of an order of Court, about the 5th Jan[y] last, he rented out the lands of his Intestates Estate, privately, about 125 to 150 acres, of open land in Hale County near Hollow Square, for $200 Dollars to one Charles McGruder, a Freedman secured by his note, for which the crop is bound. The said land is poor and no improvement of any value on it and cannot be rented out at public auction on good terms.

O.A. Wynne

April 24th 1872
Sworn to subscribed
A.R. Davis,
Judge

Dissolution of Copartnership.

THE copartnership heretofore existing between the undersigned in the firm name of T. T. May & Co., is this day dissolved by mutual consent. The notes and accounts due said firm are in the hands of T. T. May, for collection, who will pay all liabilities of the late firm.

T. T. MAY,
O. A. WYNNE.

Hollow Square, Ala., Jan'y 1, 1874.

I will continue business at the same old stand, and sell cheap to those who come with the Cash in hand.

T. T. MAY.

January 3, 1874

1-2in-4w*

318

318 Dissolution of Copartnership, *(Greensboro)Alabama Beacon*, 24 January 1874, p. 2, col. 7; digital image *Newspapers.com* (https://www.newspapers.com/image/355690335/?terms=copartnership&match=1 : accessed 28 Sept 2021). Among other things, T.T. May & Co was in the business of retail liquor sales. *See* List of Licenses Under the New Revenue Law, *(Greensboro) Alabama Beacon*, p. 2, col 7; digital image *Newspapers.com* (https://www.newspapers.com/image/355690083/?terms=retail&match=1 : accessed 28 Sept 2021).

Hon. A Benners, of Greenboro, and O. A. Wynne, of Hollow Square, Hale county, returned to their homes from Blount Springs, to vote.

319

RETURNED FROM THE BLOUNT.—Mr. O. A. Wynne, who has been spending the summer at the Blount Springs, returned home a few days ago. We had the pleasure of meeting him in town last Thursday, looking, we were glad to see, in good health.

320

[319] Alabama News (excerpt), *The (Selma Alabama) Times-Argus*, 18 August 1876, p. 3, col. 2; digital image *Newspapers.com* (accessed 28 Sept 2021.

[320] Returned from the Blount, (Greensboro) *Alabama Beacon*, 16 September 1876, p. 4, col. 2; digital image *Newspapers.com* (https://www.newspapers.com/image/355768819/?terms=Returned%20Blount&match=1 : accessed 28 Sept 2021).

1886 Land Syndication Deed of Charles McGruder Sr.[321]

Benj S. Evans & wife

To Stewart Johnson et.al

The State of Alabama County of Hale

Know all men by these presents that we, Benj S. Evans and Bettie S. Evans, his wife of said County and State, for and in consideration of the sum of twenty five dollars to us in hand paid, the receipt whereof we do hereby acknowledge, have this day given, granted, bargained, and sold, and do by these presents convey unto Stewart Johnson, Pink Ellis, Ben Ellis, Geo Washington, Joe Willingham, Marshall Allen, Tobe Collins, Bill Riggins, Bob Hill, Dick Wilson, Marshall Watson, Riley Banks, Luke Charles, John Ethridge, Tom Watson, Allen Wesley, Gabriel Erwin, Bob Logan, Archey Hobson, Oliver Hobson, Dock Hobson, Andrew Hobson, Quintin Johnson, Ben Hobson Sr., Wm Hobson, Higer Hobson, Charles McGruder Sr., Sam McGruder, Alfred Hobson, Treasvau Hobson, Allen Hobson, Ben Hobson Jr., A.C. Ellis, Elisabeth Ellis, Jerry Kennedy, Rachel McGruder, Julia McGruder, Sallie Ellis, Woodard Travis, Sallie Travis, Elisabeth Johnson, Tresvau Johnson, Pleasant Ellis, Gid Ellis, all of said County and State the following two pieces or lots of land lying and being in the village of New Prospect, (or Pin Nook) and in the South West quarter of the North East quarter of Section 36, in T22, of R3 East, to wit 1st commencing at a stake on the East side of the Tuscaloosa and Eric road, thence along said road south westerly 60 feet to within 3 feet of the store house known as the "Callahan Store House," thence due East 85 yards to a ditch, thence 60 feet in a N.W. direction to the beginning: —2nd the store house and lot situated in said Village and formerly owned by T.J. Anderson, purchased by the grantor herein from T. W. Coleman and wife the dimensions of which lot are not exactly known, but which is supposed to contain one third of an acre.

[321] Hale County Alabama, Probate Court General Index, 1867-1918, Deeds 1867-1902, Deed Book L, p 376-377; digital images, *Family Search* (https://www.familysearch.org/ark:/61903/3:1:3Q9M-C375-8S3H-?i=197&cat=487823 : accessed 30 Jan 2021); citing FHL#8586684, image# 198.

To have and to hold unto them, the aforesaid grantees herein, and unto their heirs and assigns forever, together with all and singular the tenements hereditaments, and appurtenances, thereunto belonging or in any wise appertaining. In testimony whereof, we, the Grantors, hereto set our hands and seals this the 29th day of November A.D. 1886

B.S. Evans

Bettie S. Evans

Witness

J.A. Seanbrough,

ER Harris

376

same bears date, that she attested the same in the presence
of the grantor and of the other witness, and that such other
witness subscribed her name as a witness in her presence.
Given under my hand this the 6th day of December
1886.   Charles C. Waller
Filed for Record Dec 10th 1886.   Notary Public

Benj S Evans + w   The State of Alabama
To   County of Hale
Stewart Johnson et al

Know all men by these presents that we Benj S
Evans and Bettie S Evans his wife of said County and
State for and in consideration of the sum of Twenty five
Dollars to us in hand paid the receipt whereof we do
hereby acknowledge, have this day given granted bar-
gained and sold and do by these presents convey un-
to Stewart Johnson, Pink Ellis, Ben Ellis, Geo Washington
Joe Willingham, Marshall Allen, Tobe Collins, Bill Aggins, Bob
Hill, Dick Nelson, Marshall Watson, Riley Banks, Luke Charles
John Ethridge, Tom Watson, Allen Wesley, Gabriel Erwin, Bob
Logan, Archey Hobson, Oliver Hobson, Dock Hobson, Andrew
Hobson, Quinter Johnson, Ben Hobson, & Mc Hobson,
Roger Hobson, Charles McGruder Sr, Sam McGruder, Alfred
Hobson, Freeman Hobson, Allen Hobson, Ben Hobson Jr,
G. A. Ellis, Elizabeth Ellis, Jerry Kennedy, Rachel McGruder,
Julia McGruder, Sallie Ellis, Woodard Travis, Sallie Travis,
Elizabeth Johnson, Freeman Johnson, Plens and Ellis and
Ellis, all of said County and State the following two pie-
ces or lots of land lying and being in the village of New
Prospect (or Pin Hook) and in the South West quarter of the
North East quarter of Section 36 in T 22, of R 8 East, to wit
1st Commencing at a stake on the East side of the Tus-
kaloosa and Erie road, thence along said road
South westerly 60 feet to within 8 feet of the Store house
known as the Callahan Store house, thence due East
85 yards to a ditch, thence 60 feet in a N.W. direction to
the beginning. — 2nd The Store house and lot situated
in said Village and formerly owned by T J Anderson
purchased by the grantor herein from F. W. Coleman + wife
the dimensions of which lot are not exactly known but
which is supposed to contain One third of an acre.
To have and to hold unto them the aforesaid grantees
herein, and unto their heirs and assigns forever together
with all and singular the tenements hereditaments and
appurtenances thereunto belonging or in anywise appertaining. In testimony whereof we the Grantor
herein set our hands and seals this the 29th day of November A.D 1886   B. S. Evans   (seal)
Witness J.H. Scarbrough, E.R. Harris   Bettie S Evans (seal)

*Real Estate Syndication Deal of Charles McGruder Sr.,
Sawyerville, Alabama, 1886.*

Obituaries of Osmun A. Wynne

The following are copied from Stella True's information, in a scrapbook kept by Fannie Coleman Ward and preserved by Alice Coleman Griffin. A source for the first clipping has not been identified.

Obituary of Osmun Appling Wynne

Died at his residence in Hale County, Ala. on the 17th February 1877, Mr. Osmun A. Wynne, in the 73rd year of his age.

Mr. Wynne was born in Georgia but came with his parents to this state in early life. As soon as he arrived at the age of maturity, he married and engaged in planting, a vocation at which he has been eminently successful. In his habits, he was frugal and temperate. In business, prompt and energetic, watching over its minutest details with a vigilance that never slumbered or slept. Endowed with a judgment of rare perspicuity, combined with industry and economy, his success in life was a foregone conclusion.

He adhered to his friends with scrupulous fidelity. He was kind, considerate, and courteous with his neighbors. As a husband and father, he was gentle and affectionate. As a master, indulgent and upright, dealing justice to all, which characteristic integrity, which no pressure could swerve, no casuistry could obscure for a moment.

Modest and retiring, he had an invincible repugnance to notoriety, or any act that would bring him prominently before the public. In dispensing charity, which he did with no niggard hand, his great solicit was not to leave undone, but to keep unknown. In all the duties of his life, he has performed his duties truly and faithful, and "after life's fitful fever," it can be said that "upon his brow shame was ashamed to sit."

Second Obituary: Death of Mr. Osmun A. Wynne

DEATH OF MR. OSMAN A. WYNNE.—We are pained to announce the death of this gentleman, at his residence, near Hollow Square, on Saturday last, at about the age of seventy-one years. Of the precise nature of his disease, we have not been informed; but his health had been infirm for several months.

Mr. Wynne was a native of Georgia, and has been a citizen of our county, uninterruptedly, since 1819, a period of nearly sixty years. He leaves surviving him, but few older citizens in our county, and it is no disparagement to the living to say, that we have left few or none better. We suppose that no one ever heard an unkind or harsh word from him; nor have we ever heard ever: the hint of a question of his strict integrity and honor; nor the slightest reflection upon him as a man, or as a citizen.

His genial disposition made friends of all who knew him. His hospitality was generous and unstinted. His home was the abode of contentment, and happiness.

Few persons have suffered more heavily from affliction, than has Mr. Wynne, during the last fifteen years of his life, in the loss of members of his family. None could

322

---

322 Death of Mr. Osmun A. Wynne, *Eutaw (Alabama) Whig & Observer*, 1 March 1877, p. 3, col. 2; digital image *Newspapers.com* (https://www.newspapers.com/image/356162479/?terms=Wynne&match=1 : accessed 28 Sept 2021).

have felt his numerous bereavements more accurately, and few, we are satisfied could have borne them with more fortitude.

Mr. Wynne, though not a member of any church, profoundly reverenced religion, and so illustrated its virtues and graces, that many who profess and call themselves christains would improve by imitation of his life. We trust that his last moments were cheered by a living faith in Him who is the end of the law for righteousness to all them that believe, and whose messengers had so often found shelter and welcome beneath his hospitable roof.

We would like to say more of our old friend, who has gone from our midst; but our space is limited, and we could hardly do justice to his worth. He filled out the measure of a long and useful life, and has left the fragrant odors of a good name behind him.

May he rest in peace; and may the memory of his well-spent life soften and temper his loss to his much bereaved family.— [Greensboro' Watchman.

Documents & Photographs Pertaining to Chapter Nine

1885 Land Purchase of James McGruder[323]

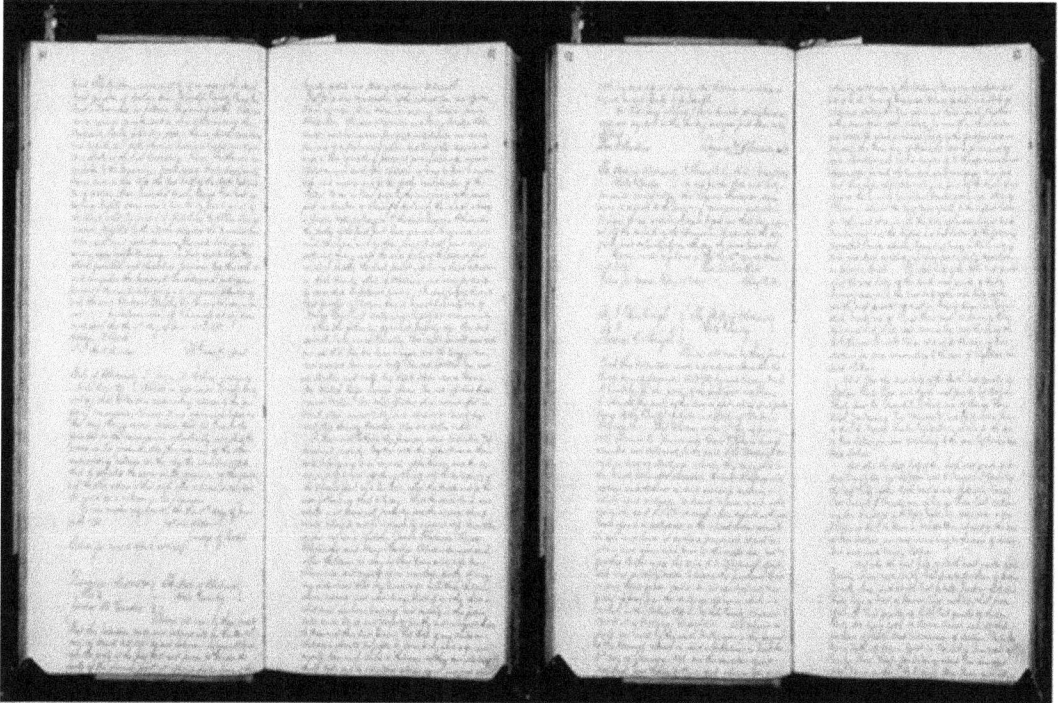

Lazarus Alexander

To James McGruder

The State of Alabama, Hale County

Know all men by these presents that this Indenture, made and entered into, on this 26th day of March A.D. 1885, by and between Lazarus Alexander the party of

---

[323] Land purchase of James McGruder, brother of Charles McGruder Jr., Hale County AL, Probate Ct. General Index, 1867-1918, Deeds 1867-1902, Deed Book M, p 60-62; digital images, *Family Search* (https://www.familysearch.org/ark:/61903/3:1:3Q9M-C375-891M-D?i=367&cat=487823 : accessed 30 Jan 2021); citing FHL#8586684, image# 368-369.

the first part, and James McGruder, the party of the second part, all af'said parties being of the County of Hale and State of Alabama, Witnesseth:

That for and in consideration of the natural love and affection,[324] I bear my wife, Irene Alexander, and my children Jennie Alexander, Clarissa Alexander, and Mary Roselyn Alexander, and being now free of all indebtedness and encumbrances of a pecuniary nature, and being also desirous at such a time of making provision for my said wife, my said children, and such other children as may be born to my said wife and myself, and for the further consideration of One Dollar, to me in hand paid by the said party of the second part as trustee as hereinafter declared, the receipt whereof is hereby acknowledged. I, the said Lazarus Alexander, the party of the first part, have granted, bargained, sold, and conveyed, and by these presents doth grant, bargain, sell, and convey unto the said party of the second part, as such trustee, the track, parcel, or piece of land, situated in Hale County, State of Alabama and more particularly described as follows to wit:— The West half of the South West quarter of section nine in Township Twenty-one of Range Three East, containing Eighty (80) acres more or less.

Also the following personal property viz:— One dark sorrel horse named Charlie, one dark sorrel mare mule named Kit, one two-horse horse wagon, one [illegible] Buggy, one cow named Ann and calf, one red spotted cow named Mollie and calf, one dark steer named Bennie, one Whitish heifer named Snow, one red-spotted heifer named Mollie, one white-spotted steer named Spot, one black steer named Billy, and about (10) ten head of hogs, and one sewing machine, also one silver watch.

To Have and to Hold the premises above described and personal property, together with the appurtenances thereunto belonging or in anywise appertaining and the increase profits and offspring thereof unto the said party of the second part and his heirs, upon the trusts and for the uses following that is to say:— that the said land, real estate, and personal property and the increase thereof shall belong to and be enjoyed by my said wife, Irene Alexander, and Mary Roselyn Alexander, and such other children as may be born to my said wife, Irene Alexander and myself, of our marriage, jointly; it being my intention that my said wife and three children above-named and now living shall, if no other child or children are born to my wife and myself in the future, take said land and property

___

[324] Susan Tichy points out that this deed provides insight into the family dynamic. Lazarus Alexander, married to James' sister, Irene, is conveying his land and property to James so that James will take care of Irene and the children.

jointly and in equal shares to them and their heirs forever; but that if any child or children should hereafter be born to my said wife and myself, then such child or children, as they come into being, shall take and be admitted into an equal and joint interest with my said wife and all my other children in and to said lands and property in fee simple.

In testimony whereof I have hereunto set my hand and affixed my seal on this the day and year first above written.

Lazarus (his mark) Alexander

Attest, Theo R. Roulhac

The State of Alabama,

Hale County

I, Thomas R. Roulhac, a Notary Public in and for the State and County aforesaid, hereby certify that Lazarus Alexander, whose name is signed to the foregoing conveyance and who is known to me, acknowledged before me, that being informed of the contents of the conveyance, he executed the same freely and voluntarily on the day the same bears date.

Given under my hand on this the 26th day of March A.D. 1885.

Filed for Record Febr'y 25th 1889

Tho's R. Roulhac

Notary Public

1891 Land Purchase of Charles McGruder Jr.[325]

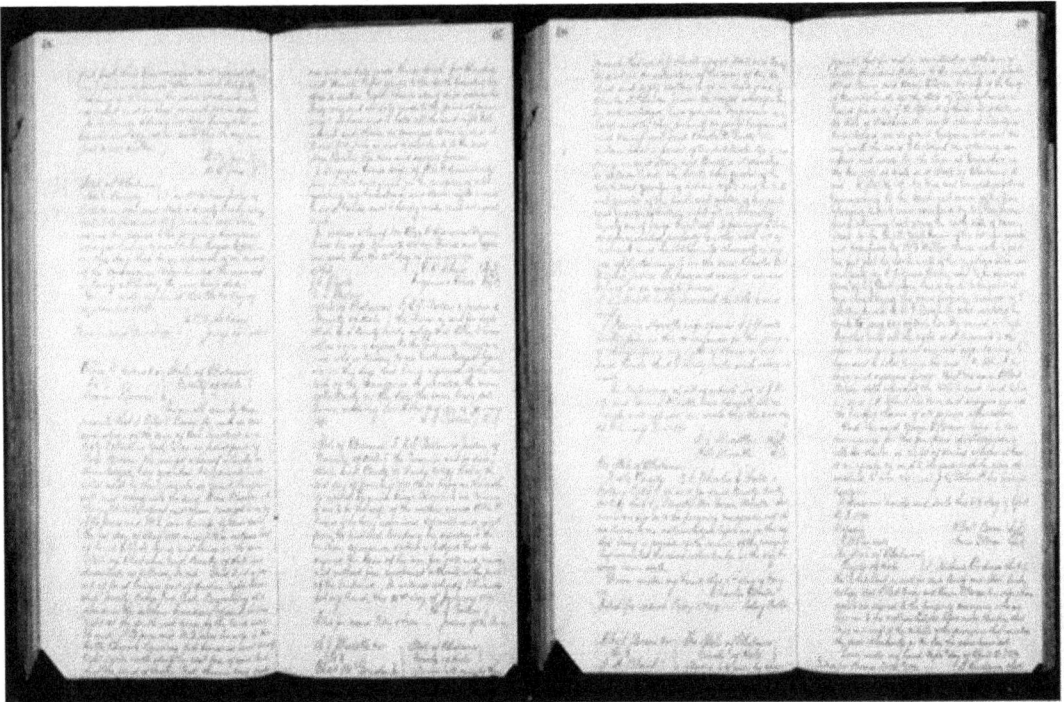

S.J. Monette & W

To Chas McGruder Jr.

State of Alabama, County of Hale

Know all men by these presents that we S.J. Monette of said State and County for and in consideration of the sum of One hundred and fifty dollars to me in hand paid by Charles McGruder Junior the receipt whereof is hereby acknowledged have granted bargained and sold, and by these presents do grant bargain sell and convey unto said Charles McGruder that certain tack or parcel of land situate lying and being in said state and County and described as follows to wit: the South East quarter of the South West quarter of section eight and the South East quarter of the South West quarter of the South West quarter of section eight all in Township Twenty one of range three east. To have and to hold the afore granted

---

[325] Hale County, Alabama, Probate Court General Index, 1867-1918, Deeds 1867-1902, Deed Book M p 497-498; digital images *Family Search* (https://www.familysearch.org/ark:/61903/3:1:3Q9M-C375-8SS9-Q?i=587&cat=487823 : accessed 30 Jan 2021); citing FHL#, 8586684, no image#.

property together with all the tenements and hereditaments thereunto in anywise appertaining to his, the said Charles McGruder Junior his heirs and assigns use and behoof in fee simple forever.

I, Fannie Monette, wife of said S.J. Monette, hereby join in this conveyance for the purpose of relinquishing my right of dower in and to said lands and I hereby make such relinquishment.

In this testimony of all of which we, S.J. Monette and Fannie Monette, have hereunto set our hands and affixed our seals this the 2nd day of February A.D. 1891

S.J. Monette

F.A. Monette[326]

The State of Alabama,

Hale County

I, Charles E. Walles, a Notary Public, in and for said County hereby certify that S.J. Monette & Mrs. Fannie Monette whose names are signed to the foregoing conveyance and who are known to me, acknowledged before me on this day that being informed of the contents of the conveyance, they executed the same voluntarily on the day the same bears date.

Given under my hand this 2nd day of Febr'y 1891.

Charles E. Walles

Notary Public

Filed for record Febr'y 2nd 1891

---

[326] On the 1856 Snedecor Map of Greene County landowners, several individuals surnamed Monette appear in the vicinity of the Wynne and Ferrell properties.

1895 Land Purchase of Charles McGruder Jr.[327]

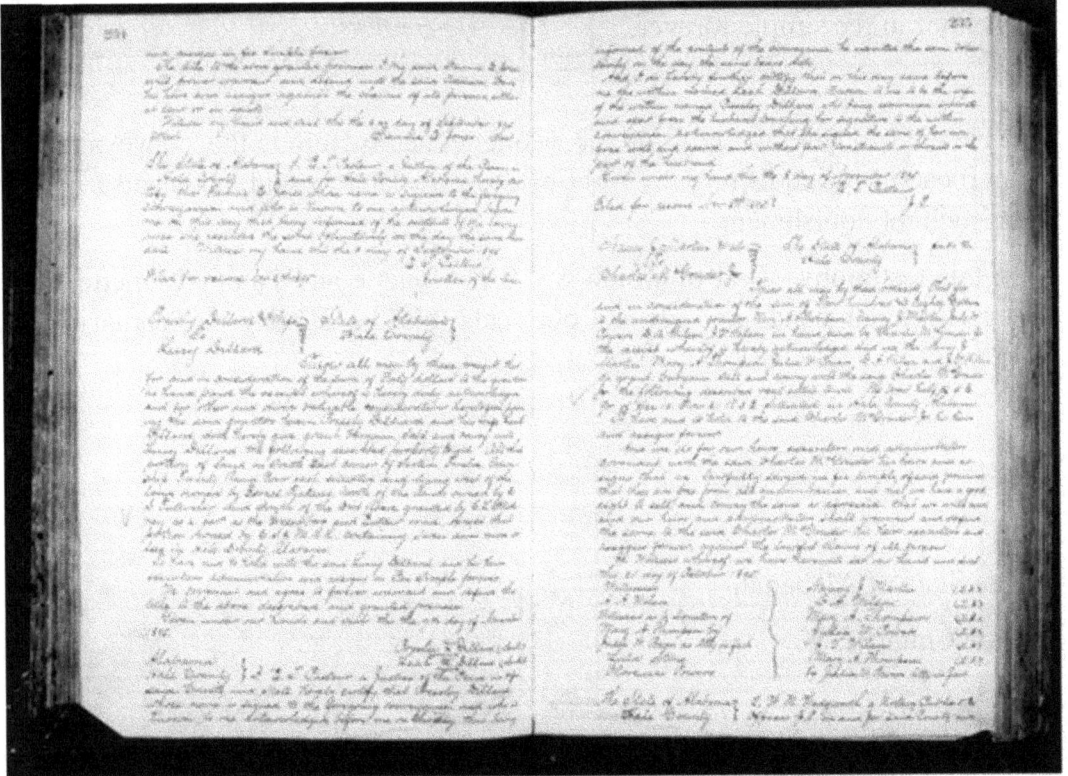

Nancy J. Martin et. Al.

To Charles McGruder

The State of Alabama,

Hale County ($480.00)

Know all men by these presents: That for and in consideration of the sum of Four hundred and Eighty Dollars to the undersigned grantors Mary A. Thompson, Nancy J. Martin, July W. Powers, D.A. Wilson, J.V. Wilson, in hand paid by

---

[327] Hale County, Alabama, Probate Court General Index, 1867-1918, Deeds 1867-1902, Deed Book O, p 235; digital images *Family Search* (https://www.familysearch.org/ark:/61903/3:1:3Q9M-C375-89BL-2?i=298&cat=487823 : accessed 30 Jan 2021); citing FHL#8586685, image# 299.

Charles McGruder the receipt whereof is hereby acknowledged that we Nancy J. Martin, Mary A. Thompson, Julia W. Powers, D.A. Wilson, and J.V. Wilson do grant, bargain, sell, and convey unto the said Charles McGruder Jr. the following described real estate to wit: The West half of S.E. qr of Sec10, Tow 21, R.2 E Situated in Hale County, Alabama.

To have and to hold to the said Charles McGruder in his heirs and assigns forever.

And we do for our heirs, executors and administrators covenant with the said Charles McGruder his heirs and assigns that we [are] lawfully seized in fee simple of said premises, that they are free from all encumbrances, and that we have a good right to sell and convey the same as aforesaid: that we will and our heirs and administrators shall warrant and defend the same to the said Charles McGruder his heirs executors and assigns forever, against the lawful claims of all persons.

In witness whereof, we have hereunto set our hand and seal
this 25 day of October 1890.

Witness

A.A. Wilson

Witness as to Signature of

Mary A. Thompson by

Julia W. Powers as Atty in fact

Lula Stine

Florence Powers

Nancy J. Martin (I.S.)

D.A. Wilson (I.S.)

Mary a. Thompson (I.S.)

Julia W. Powers (I.S.)

J.V. Wilson (I.S.)

Mary A. Thompson (I.S.)

By Julia W. Powers Atty in fact

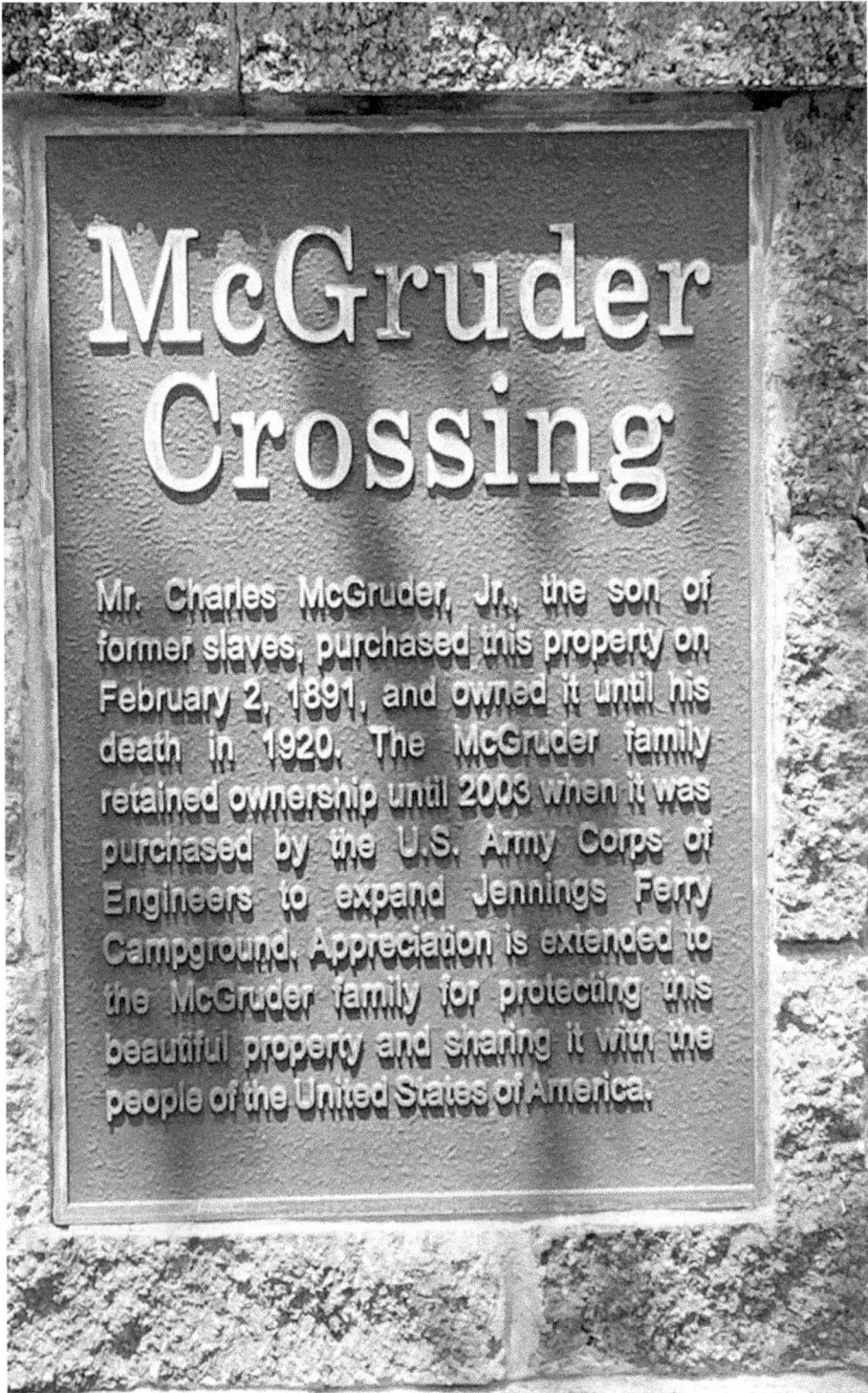

Courtesy of J.R. Rothstein. Sawyerville, Alabama, September 2020

Marriage Record of Charles McGruder Jr. & Emmaline Riddle[328]

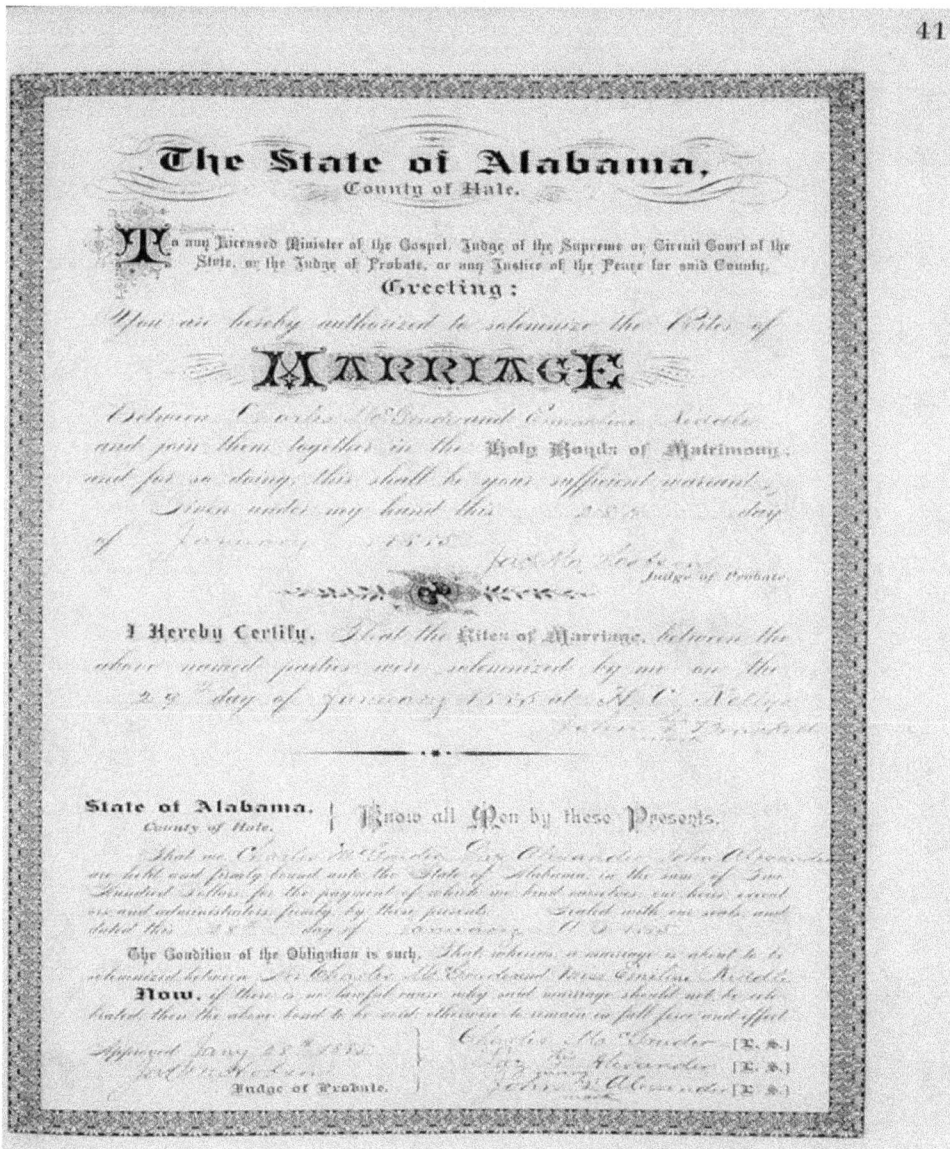

---

[328] Alabama County Marriages, 1809-1950, Marriage of Charles McGruder & Emmaline Riddle, file number 1289248, image 220; digital image FamilySearch.org (https://www.familysearch.org/ark:/61903/1:1:QKZS-TYN8 to : accessed 24 Jan 2021)

Some Children of Charles McGruder Jr.

The following photos and captions are courtesy of Marie McGruder and Sheryl Malone.

Ethew McGruder. Date and location unknown.

William Mack McGruder. Date and location unknown.

Marvin McGruder Sr. Date and location unknown.

Rosie Nell McGruder. Date and location unknown.

Zanny McGruder. Date and location unknown.

Alphonso McGruder. Date and location unknown.

rear: Isaiah, Payrene, Calvin, Alphonso; *front:* Zaney, Charles, Rosa Nell, Willie Mac.
(not pictured: Emmaline, Ethew, Marvin)

Drawing of the family of Charles McGruder Jr. Original is lost.
Date and location unknown.

According to a note about this drawing circulated at the 1992 McGruder Family Reunion: "The photo [sic] was probably taken around the early 1900's. The picture is of Charles McGruder and his children. Missing from this photo is Emmaline McGruder, his wife, and Ethew and Marvin McGruder, his two oldest sons. Rose Nell appears at his left shoulder, Willie Mac at her left, behind him probably Alphonso. The older male (standing) has been identified as Calvin. Standing next to him (the female) is Payreen who was born in 1891—and died in 1909 at age 18. The two male children to Papa Charles's right are probably Zannie, who was born in 1896 and died in 1928, and Isaiah, who was born in 1889 and died in 1942. We are not sure which is Zannie and which is Isaiah."

Calvin McGruder. Date and location unknown.

Documents & Photographs Pertaining to Chapter Ten

Liberty Colored Methodist Church History

The following is an excerpt from the official history of the Bass Tabernacle Christian Methodist Episcopal Church:[329]

> The Bass Tabernacle Christian Methodist Episcopal Church is composed of two former congregations, Flatwood Christian Methodist Episcopal Church and Liberty Christian Methodist Episcopal Church. The histories of both the Flatwood C.M.E. Church and the Liberty C.M.E. Church date back to the time of slavery.
>
> The Flatwood Church was semi-integrated. The blacks were permitted to attend church with their masters, having a white minister as their leader. As time passed, the whites no longer wanted the blacks to share their church. The blacks then worshiped in whatever old building they could find until Mr. B.S. Evans, a member of the white Flatwood Church, donated an acre of land for the purpose of building a church.
>
> In 1892, under the leadership of Rev. Joseph Brown, the first Flatwood C.M.E. Church for the black people was established. In 1910, a meeting with Mr. Evans, the chairman of the trustees, and the members of the church was held. It was [at this] meeting that the members decided to purchase this acre of land. On April 13, 1910, our ancestors bought this land for $40.00.
>
> In 1931, Flatwood's own, Rev. R.T. Williams, served as pastor. in 1932, the church burned under the pastorship of Rev. M.C. Thomas. In 1933, the church was rebuilt under the leadership of Rev. C.M. Hughes. Members of the Board of Trustees were Bro. S.J. Johnson, Chairman, Bro. J.D. McGruder, Bro. Luke Charles, Bro. Nick Jones, and Bro. L.A. Alexander. Members of the Board of Stewards were Bro. W.E. Williams, Chairman, Bro. S.J.

---

[329] The History of the Bass Tabernacle Christian Methodist Episcopal Church (Akron, AL), https://www.basstabernaclecme.com/church-history.html : accessed 2 Oct 2021.

Johnson, Bro. G. Williams, Bro. Joseph Johnson, and Bro. Luke Charles.

As time passed, the Flatwood C.M.E. Church prospered under the leadership of Rev. O.C. Watts, Rev. W.L. Tucker, Rev. W.B. Franks, Rev. W.O. Davis, Rev. C.M. Hughes, Rev. O'Neal Smith, Rev. J.A. Williams, Rev. P.J. Kirksey, Rev. L. McCleod, Rev. L.G. McWilson and Rev. L.M. Jefferson. Trustees and Stewards who served included Bro. Edward Williams, Bro. Robert L. Williams, Bro. Roosevelt Williams, Bro. Woodrow Harris, Sr. and Bro. Charlie Johnson.

Rev. Glen Jones became Flatwood's pastor in 1984. Under his leadership, the church building was raised, a foyer with classroom space was added to the front of the church, the church steps were rebuilt, the kitchen area was added, and central heat and air was installed.

The Liberty C.M.E. Church was established in the 1800's and at first the church was semi-integrated. The negroes were permitted to worship on the first and third Sundays, while the whites worshiped on the second and fourth Sundays in the same building. On November 12, 1877, an acre of land was given to the Liberty congregation as a place of worship for the Colored Methodist Episcopal Church of America by Mrs. Harriet Chapman.

In the 1890's, the Liberty Colored Methodist Church was further established and moved forward under the leadership of ministers, which included the Reverend K.T. Summerville. In 1912, the church was still growing under the pastorship of Rev. G.B. Ward, Presiding Elder E. Weir, and Bishop G.W. Steward. In the 1917, Liberty was blessed to have Rev. W.L. Amous as pastor. Some of the officers during that time were Bro. Tom Brownlow, Chairman of the Board of Trustees, Bro. Ben Wilson, Chairman of the Board of Stewards, and Sis. Odett Merriweather, President of the Missionary Society. From 1918 to 1931, the church was under the leadership of Rev. M.R. Smith, Rev. R.W. Bolden, and others. Rev. W.L. Amous was Presiding Elder. In 1931, Liberty was blessed to have its own, Rev. R.T. Williams, as pastor.

From 1932 to 1939, Liberty was served by Rev. C.M. Hughes and others. During this period, some of the officers were Bro. Ed Marks, Chairman of the Board of Stewards, Bro. Will Brownlow,

Secretary, and Bro. Elzie Cooper, Treasurer. Some of the class leaders were Bro. Alfred Cooper, Bro. Ky Kittrell, Bro. Tom Brownlow, Bro. Richard Hobsom, Bro. Marvin McGruder, and Bro. Walter Brownlow. Sunday School Superintendent was Bro. Isiah McGruder. The Epworth League President was Sis. Dora McGruder. Stewardess President was Sis. Fannie Johnson. Sis. Tennie Bell Alexander was Missionary President. Sis. Rosa Nell McGruder provided leadership of Rev. E.D. Dent [sic] for six years. Rev. L.G. McWilson followed.

In 1948, the members of Liberty embarked upon a course to build a new church. In May of that year, the church held its first rally and raised $135.70. With faith in God and determination in our hearts, the dream of a new church became a reality. In March 1949, the new Liberty church was dedicated by Rev. O.C. Watts, who was pastor at that time. The church continued prospering under the leadership of Rev. W.L. Tucker, Rev. W.B. Franks, Rev. W.O. Davis, Rev. O'Neal Smith, and Rev. C.M. Hughes.

In 1965, under the dynamic leadership of Rev. W.O. Davis, Liberty started raising funds to build a new structure. Dedicatory services were held that same year with the Rt. Rev. E.P. Murchinson, Bishop, presiding. Bishop Murchinson was assisted by Presiding Elder L.O. Robinson and Pastor J.A. Williams. The trustees at the time were Bro. Richard Hobson, Jr., Chairman, Bro. Clinton Brasfield, Bro. Henry Brasfield, Jr., Bro. Elzie L. Cooper, Bro. Willie Brownlow, Jr., Bro. Robert Brasfield, and Bro. Elijah Jackson. On July 12, 1970, Liberty's first Homecoming Day was held to help raise funds for its building. Over two thousand dollars was raised.

These churches are deeply intertwined with the history of the Alabama Black McGruders and it is likely that all of the family were members of one of these two churches in their first years.

The spring term of the Hale county circuit court adjourned last Tuesday The criminal docket was a light one. There were four convictions, as follows: Daniel Williams, grand larceny, sentenced to 2 years and 10 months hard labor for county; Johnnie Jeffries, burglary, sentenced to 18 months hard labor; Paul McGruder, assault with attempt to murder, twenty years in penitentiary; Rembert McGruder, assault with attempt to murder, twenty years in penitentiary. The McGruders are the negroes who resisted the sheriff and his deputies so viciously near Sawyerville a few months ago. They barricaded themselves in a house and defied arrest and shot at the officers numbers of times. Charlie Key, colored, who was with the sheriff's posse, aiding in the capture of the McGruders, was shot by one of them in the arm, and the limb had to be amputated.

330

330 Spring Term of the Hale County Circuit Court, *Greensboro (Alabama) Watchman*, 18 April 1907, p. 3, col. 1; digital image *Newspapers.com* (https://www.newspapers.com/image/308322111/?terms=McGruder&match=1 : accessed 2 Oct 2021).

The folowing were convicted at the recent term of the circuit court—

Daniel Williams, grand larceny sentenced to two years and ten mouths hrrd labor for the county

Johnnie Jeffries, burglary, 18 m hard labor

Paul McGruder, assault with attempt to murder, 20 years in the penitentiary.

Rembert McGruder same offense same sentence.

331

---

331 Convicted at Recent Term of the Circuit Court, *(Greensboro) Alabama Beacon*, 24 April 1907, p. 2, col. 5; digital image *Newspapers.com* (https://www.newspapers.com/image/253642080/?terms=Daniel%20Williams&match=1 : accessed 14 Jan 2022).

Undated picture of Roena "Aunt Tiss" McGruder, center, and Alfred Cooper, right. Man on the left is an unidentified relative. Courtesy of Ron Cooper Bey and Jeanie Cooper-Ahanotu.

Undated picture of Julia McGruder Edmonds Pippens.
Courtesy of Geneva Gibbs Wesley

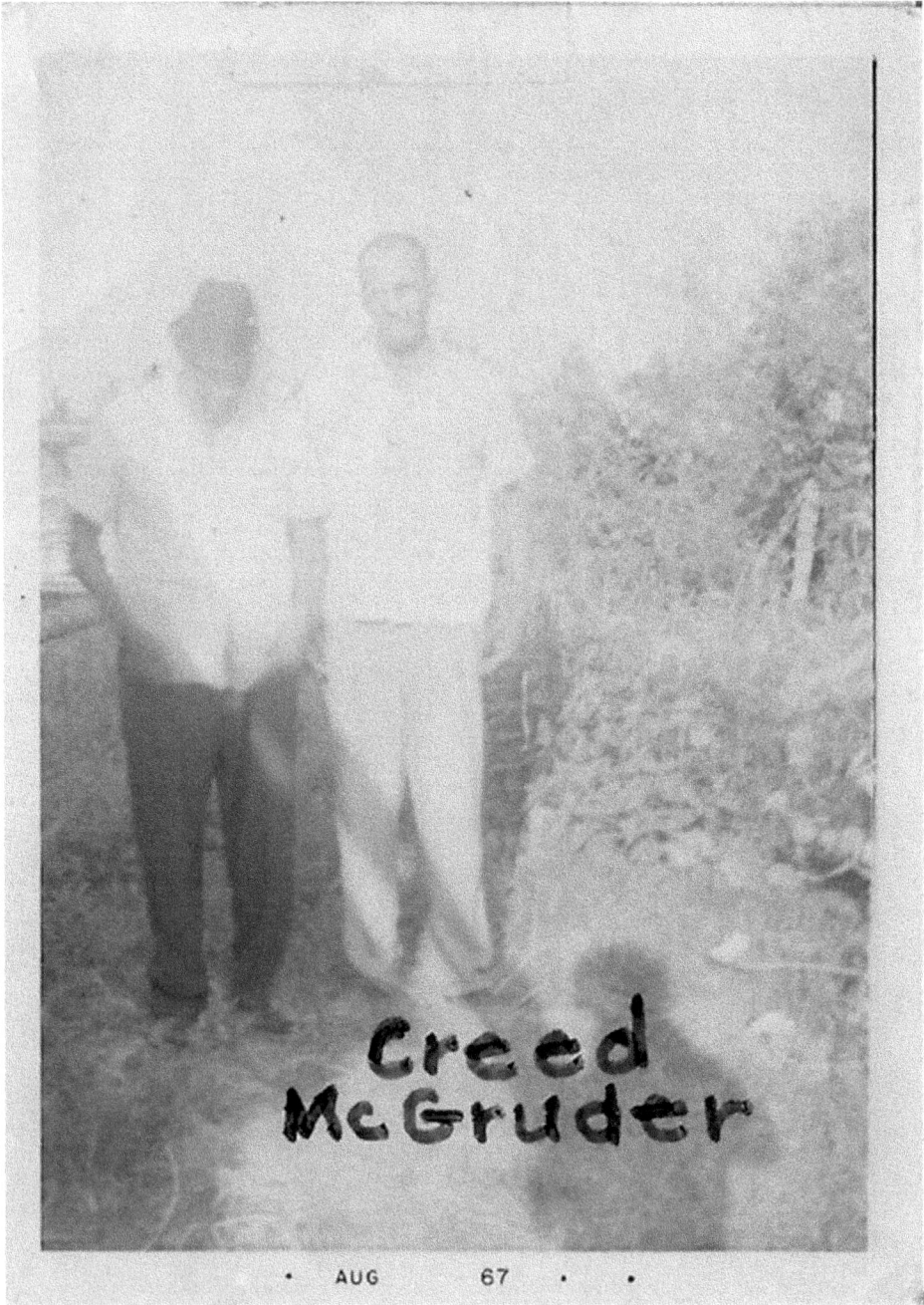

Creed McGruder. Wedgeworth, Alabama, August 1967.
Courtesy of Lucille B. Osborne.

McGruder-Hill Homestead Map

Below is a map of some of the compounds belonging to the McGruder-Hill family in Sawyerville, drawn from memory by Lucille Burden Osborne. The content of the map likely dates to the 1930s, when Lucille was a child.

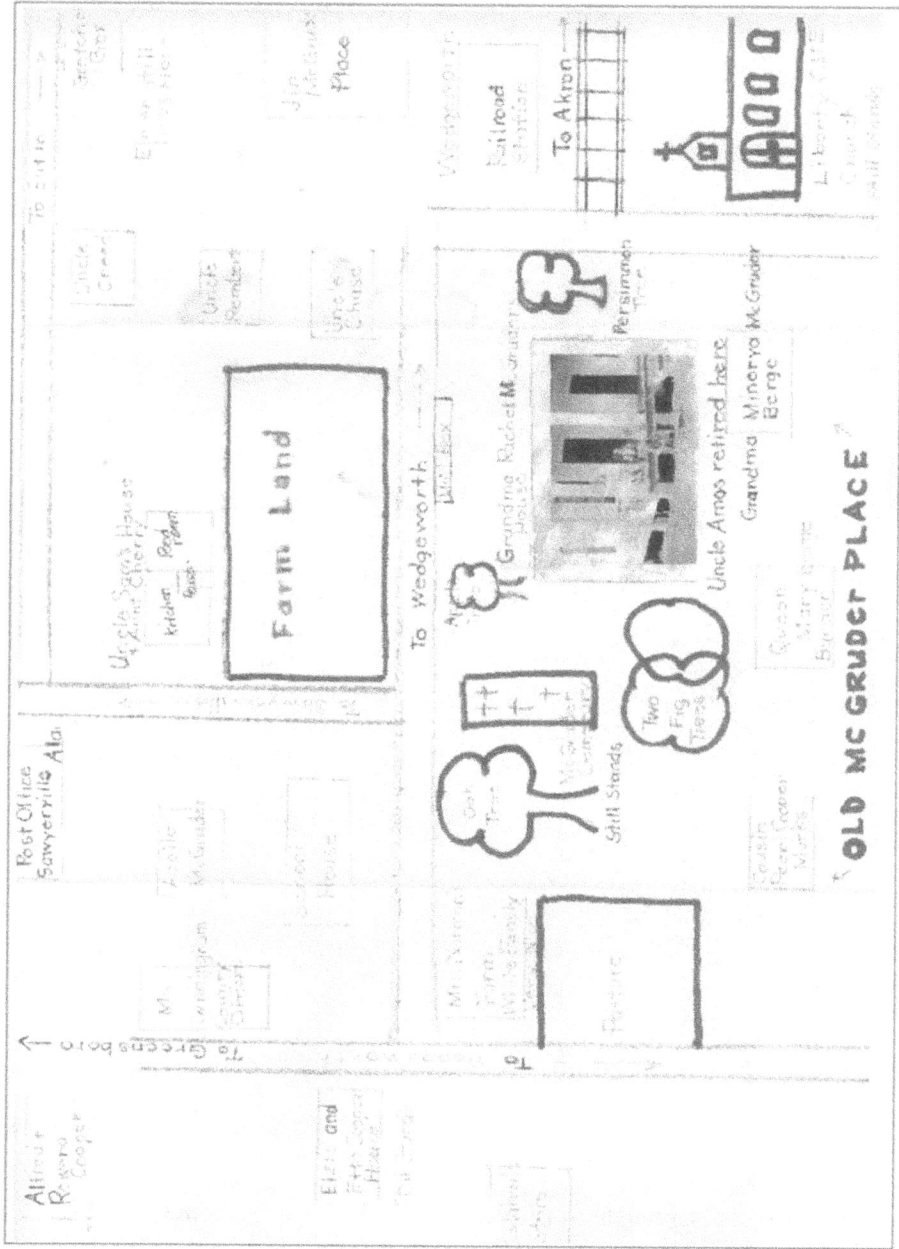

The following articles relate to the educational achievements of the Alabama Black McGruders during Jim Crow, and the formation of Wynne Academy. Included in this section are some articles which reference the character assasination of E.A. McGruder.

> The following persons passed the State teachers examination held in Greensboro several weeks ago:
>
> Whites: Misses Mary Carr, Rosalie Tutwiler Agnes Tutwiler, Vivian Anderson, Mary G. Dew, Lucy McCrary, Lillian Duncan, Alberta Overstreet, Messrs. Wm. J. Terry, Syd Dew, Miss Mae Stokes, Mrs. Fidelia Jones.
>
> Colored: Francis Agnew, E. A. McGruder, Ella Clarke, Robert Lynon, Webb Wilson, Geo. W. Edwards, Clem Lanier, Cornelia Tucker, Albert Taylor, Lenora Starkey, Grethen McGruder, Roxana McCrary, Lizzie Evans, Lelia Harris, Isaac Kennedy, Bina Agnew, Bernice Burks, Hattie Coleman, Emma Graham.

332

---

332 State Teachers Exam, *Greensboro (Alabama) Watchman*, 4 September 1913, p.5, col. 1; digital image Newspapers.com (https://www.newspapers.com/image/?clipping_id=14164140&fcfToken=eyJhbGciOiJIUzI1 NiIsInR5cCI6IkpXVCJ9.eyJmcmVlLXZpZXctaWQiOjMwODMyMTUwNiwiaWF0Ijox Nj MzODA1ODAxLCJleHAiOjE2MzM4OTIyMDF9.0ZKnr0GVHDtQq1NsNaFNIiuzO1xcwoi y_C-Gix4vHsU : accessed 9 Oct 2021.

Prof. S. C. Steinbrenner addressed the colored people of Greensboro Sunday afternoon on "The Aim of Life." The address should prove of great value to those who heard him. A very elaborate program was carried out. The meeting took place at Wynne Academy.

333

NOTICE.

The fall term of the Wynne Academy begins Monday Oct. 1st. Patrons and friends are asked to be present and witness the program, appropriate for opening. Under the new law pupils between the ages of 8 and 15 years must attend at least 80 days during the school year. The fees are the same as last term (from 15 cents to 50 cents per month.) We predict a most successful term under the able faculty, authorized by the State to teach, viz:

Mary Florence Toombs, The Primary Department 1st, 2nd, 3rd Grades.

Albert Taylor, Intermediate Department and Music, 4th, 5th and 6th Grades.

J. E. Toombs, Principal, Advanced Department, 7th, 8th and 9th Grades.

J. E. TOOMBS.

334

Address at Wynne Academy, *Greensboro (Alabama) Watchman*, 25 January 1917, p. 2, col. 3; digital image Newspapers.com (https://www.newspapers.com/image/308158219/?terms=Aim%20of%20Life&match=1 : accessed 9 Oct 2021).

334 Fall Term of Wynne Academy, *Greensboro (Alabama) Watchman*, 27 September 1917, p. 2, col. 3; digital image *Newspapers.com*

The Wynne Academy.

The Wynne Academy, colored school of Greensboro, Ala., closed April 19th, with the best Commencement in the history of the school. The whole school-term was unusually quiet and harmonious. Several pupils were promoted. The colored trustees, who had been absent all the term, called a meeting Thursday night, April 25th, to hear the annual report and to consider the subject: "A Principal for next term." The Board met at Wiley's drug store about 8.20 and adjourned about 11 o'clock. The following were present: L. O. Patton, chairman; B. F. Beverly, Jr., W. Wynne, F. W. Sykes, Josh Owens, E. Somerville, J. L. Stone and J. W. Wiley, Secretary. L. O. Patton stated the object of the meeting then spoke as follows: "It is true we sent the white Board a notice that we will make a change; get another principal for next term, thinking that a new principal would get the people together, raise money and pay off our school debts; but since I have talked with the chairman of the white Board and Prof. Toombs I myself, am willing to reconsider our actions and give Prof. Toombs another chance. We board members have nothing against his morals, ability or methods of teaching. He seems to have the people. Now let's hear from Prof. Toombs.

Toombs speaks—"Mr. Chairman and Members of this Honorable Body: I come to you to-night, as I've always come, for peace and good-will to all. When I announced over a year ago that I am here for ten years, I did so expecting your applause, but instead of applause I heard a few hisses. I took for granted that you then knew and now know I can get other schools to teach and other jobs that pay even better than teaching. I meant I was satisfied here and would perform my duty faithfully. I come to get you to agree with the patrons, rescind your petition and make the vote unanimous, your board and patrons. The white Board judges you as being the most intelligent citizens of Greensboro. If we differ the Trustees will have to take action. In this event it can't please both sides (you and patrons.) $1.2_ was raised by me this school-year. What is raised next year can go toward paying the debts. I think the board will pa_ three teachers next term."

Dr. J. W. Wiley then rose and said "__ am not willing to undo what we have don_ I want Toombs to know that he has been here three years and the school debts re main unpaid. He is getting the salary— I am getting nothing. Let me teach thi_ school next year. The power is in our hands to put Toombs out and that I am bound to do. Now if the white Board wants to elect him over us to please th_ patrons out of 62, let them do it. If we are to ever rule now is the time."

Next F. W. Sykes: "Why didn't Prof. Toombs come to us last term for our endorsement? He went right ahead, ignored us, put in his application and got the school. Now he knows we have the power which we must use, asking us to undo what we have done. I will never do it; and any rest of you that will is a fool. What will the white Board think of us? If we undo what we have done they will take the power out of our hands."

Next B. F. Beverly: "Gentlemen, I promised not to have anything to say, but seeing how far wrong you have gone, I am compelled to express my thought. If you have the power, there is no reason why you should use your powers unwisely. There may be one teacher out of a hundred that will come here, teach school, raise money to pay teachers and pay your debts. The school debts shouldn't be put on the teacher's shoulders any more than the debts of the church on the preacher's shoulder. The way to pay these debts is to get in behind them yourselves with the people. The white Board has a right to hear and to recognize you only when you act wisely. I have no kick to make. Any educated person can teach my children, Methodist, Baptist or what not."

Next John W. Wynne: "I think it the wrong time to even think of changing teachers. To get rid of Toombs would mean that your next teacher wouldn't be half as good as Toombs, to say nothing of his moral qualities. Remember, $30 per month for six month is no inducement for the man you seek. The six months are out, and Toombs has a little farm like most of us to make a living if he can. Toombs did what he could, you all did nothing. Now, who have you to offer as principal of Wynne Academy?"

Next J. L. Stone: "We will see after getting a principal. If we can't get one, why let the school stay locked up. The white Board must do as we say or there will be no school in the Wynne Academy. I have more children than anybody and I want them educated, but not by somebody my wife doesn't like."

Three members of the Board voted to enforce the petition; the others refused to vote either way.

Opinion 1st:—Some men have a fair knowledge of books and the trades yet they are wholly unprepared to serve the public.

Opinion 2nd:—The time has not yet come for the "Government Schools" to be placed in hands of "Negro Control." Were it not for white men on the board, Tuskegee would have been gone.

Opinion 3rd:—An educated teacher in the hands of "Negro-Control" is about as safe as an individual at the heels of a kicking mule in fly time.

INTERESTED PARTY.

335

---

335 The Wynne Academy, *Greensboro (Alabama) Watchman*, 2 May 1918, p. 3, col. 4; digital image *Newspapers.com*

William Reddick, Jr, colored, principal of Wynne Academy in Greensboro, died on the 23rd of influenza. He was a useful member of his race and will be missed.

336

Institute for Colored Teachers

The Hale County Institute for Colored teachers will be held in Greensboro at Wynne Academy on March 26th at 10 a. m. All teachers are required by law to attend.
Clarence Wilburn,
Superintendent.

337

(https://www.newspapers.com/image/308167785/?terms=Wynne%20Academy&match=1 : accessed 24 Jan 2022).

336 Death of William Reddick Jr., *Greensboro Watchman*, 26 Dec 1918, p. 3, col. 1; digital image Newspapers.com
(https://www.newspapers.com/image/308173308/?terms=Wynne&match=1 : accessed 8 Oct 2021).

337 Institute for Colored Teachers, *Greensboro (Alabama) Watchman*, 13 February 1919, p. 2, col. 3; digital image *Newspapers.com*
(https://www.newspapers.com/image/308174265/?terms=Wynne&match=1 : accessed 8 Oct 2021).

Last Sunday afternoon the colored people of Greensboro held a rally and raised $341 to pay off the debt on their school building. The Rally was under the direction of Prof. E. A. McGruder, Principal of the school.

338

---

338 School Fundraiser, *Greensboro (Alabama) Watchman*, 17 April 1919, p.3, col. 3; digital image *Newspapers.com* (https://www.newspapers.com/image/308175730/?terms=McGruder&match=1 : accessed 9 Oct 2021).

Like many others of the era—white and black—some of the McGruders were engaged in bootlegging. According to Marie McGruder, white offenders were left alone and the law was enforced only against black distillers[339]

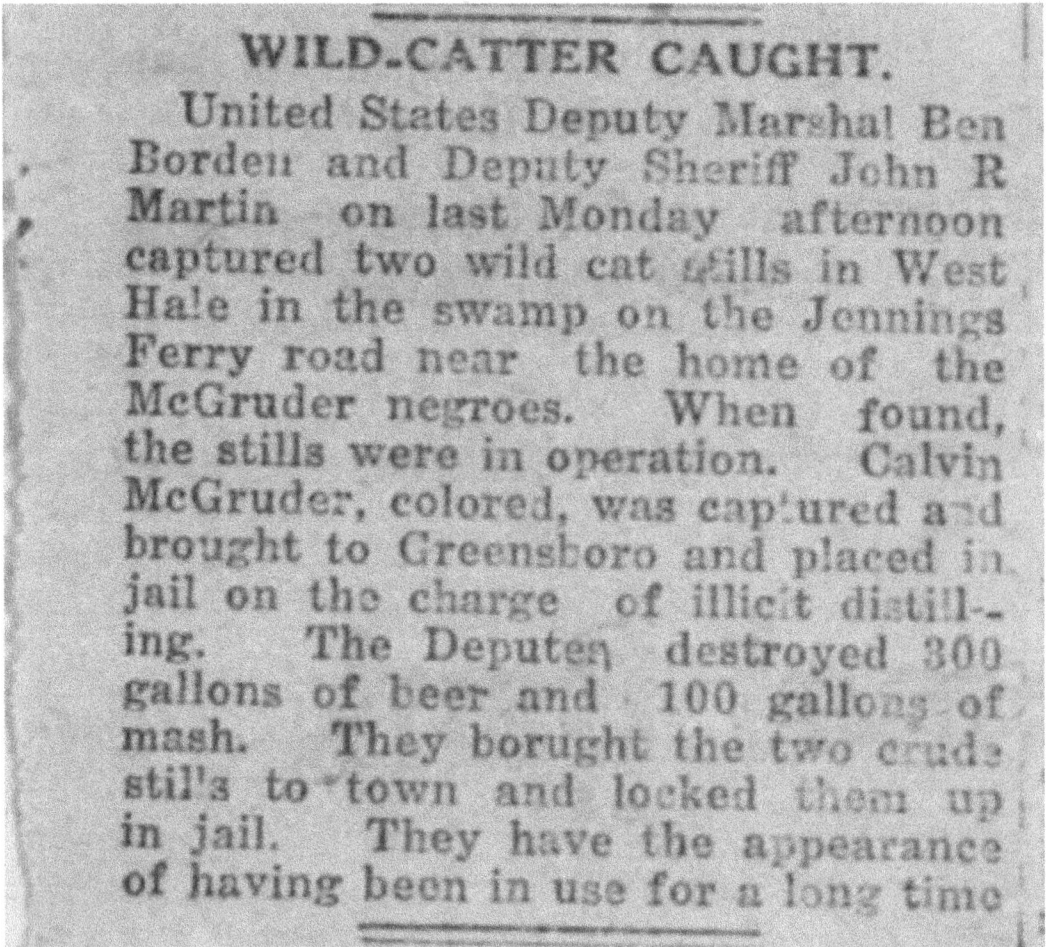

WILD-CATTER CAUGHT.

United States Deputy Marshal Ben Borden and Deputy Sheriff John R Martin on last Monday afternoon captured two wild cat stills in West Hale in the swamp on the Jennings Ferry road near the home of the McGruder negroes. When found, the stills were in operation. Calvin McGruder, colored, was captured and brought to Greensboro and placed in jail on the charge of illicit distilling. The Deputes destroyed 300 gallons of beer and 100 gallons of mash. They borught the two crude stil's to town and locked them up in jail. They have the appearance of having been in use for a long time

---

[339] Wild-Catter Caught, *Greensboro (Alabama) Watchman*, 13 May, 1920, p. 3, col. 1; digital image *Newspapers.com* (https://www.newspapers.com/image/308185934 : accessed 2 Oct 2021).

INDUSTRIAL EXHIBIT

An Industrial Exhibit of articles made by the pupils of the various colored public schools in Hale county was held at Wynne Academy in Greensboro last Friday and Saturday. A large number of people—both white and colored—visited the school building and inspected the work on exhibition. There were baskets, picture frames, horse collars, wicker work, chairs, fancy work, drawings, mattresses, plain and fancy sewing, cakes, bread, canned fruits and vegetables on display. The exhibit was most creditable to the teachers and pupils of the schools contributing to the display. This industrial branch of education is very valuable and should be encouraged.

340

---

340 Industrial Exhibit at Wynne Academy, *Greensboro (Alabama) Watchman*, 17 March 1921, p. 3, col. 1; digital image *Newspapers.com* (https://www.newspapers.com/image/308193742/?terms=Wynne&match=1 : accessed 9 Oct 2021).

MEETING OF COLORED TEACHERS.

The colored teachers in Hale county are requested to meet on Saturday morning, May 21st, at Wynne academy in Greensboro. An interesting progrom has been arranged for the occasion. Prof C J Calloway of Tuskegee, will be present and deliver an address.

Following are the colored teachers in Hale county:

Cato Pearson,	A B Rouser
Annie B Collins	M A Hamilton
Luvallie Young	Albert Taylor
Agnes Lewis	Ella B Jones
Lizzie Evans	Prince Ullman
Mattie Agnew	Mary Crecy
Lida Ruffin	Annie E Coleman
Louisa Pickens	Alice Hobson
Susie Stringer	Nathan Stringer
Mary L Stringer	Diana L Nixon
Minnie Thomas	Bina L Jackson
Addie V Burroughs	Blanche Hobson
Susie Lee	Matilda Harris
Lillie Ellis	Isaac L Kennedy
Gassenie Webb	E D Hobson
Mary MacGruder	Grethern Brox
Carrie Alexander	Pinkie Cephas
Lucy Hill	Eliza Washington
Willie N Wilson	Effie Watt
Carrie Richardson	J W Rice
Sarah L Gray	J A Holliday
A B Holliday	J H Saunders
Minnie Tabb	Sarah Taylor
Wiley Agnew	Lucile Taylor
R B Tabb	Izetta Cunegin
S G Jones	Prentice Jones
Dora Coleman	Lucy E Jones
Helen E Beverly	C C Lanier
E A MacGruder	Gertrude Deyampert
Lydia Martin	G W Fredd
Leola Martin	Hattie Reddick
Lelia Brown	Elnora Reddick.

341

---

341 Meeting of Colored Teachers, *Greensboro (Alabama) Watchman*, 19 May 1921, p. 2, col. 4; digital image *Newspapers.com* (https://www.newspapers.com/image/308195249/?terms=Wynne&match=1 : accessed 9 Oct 2021).

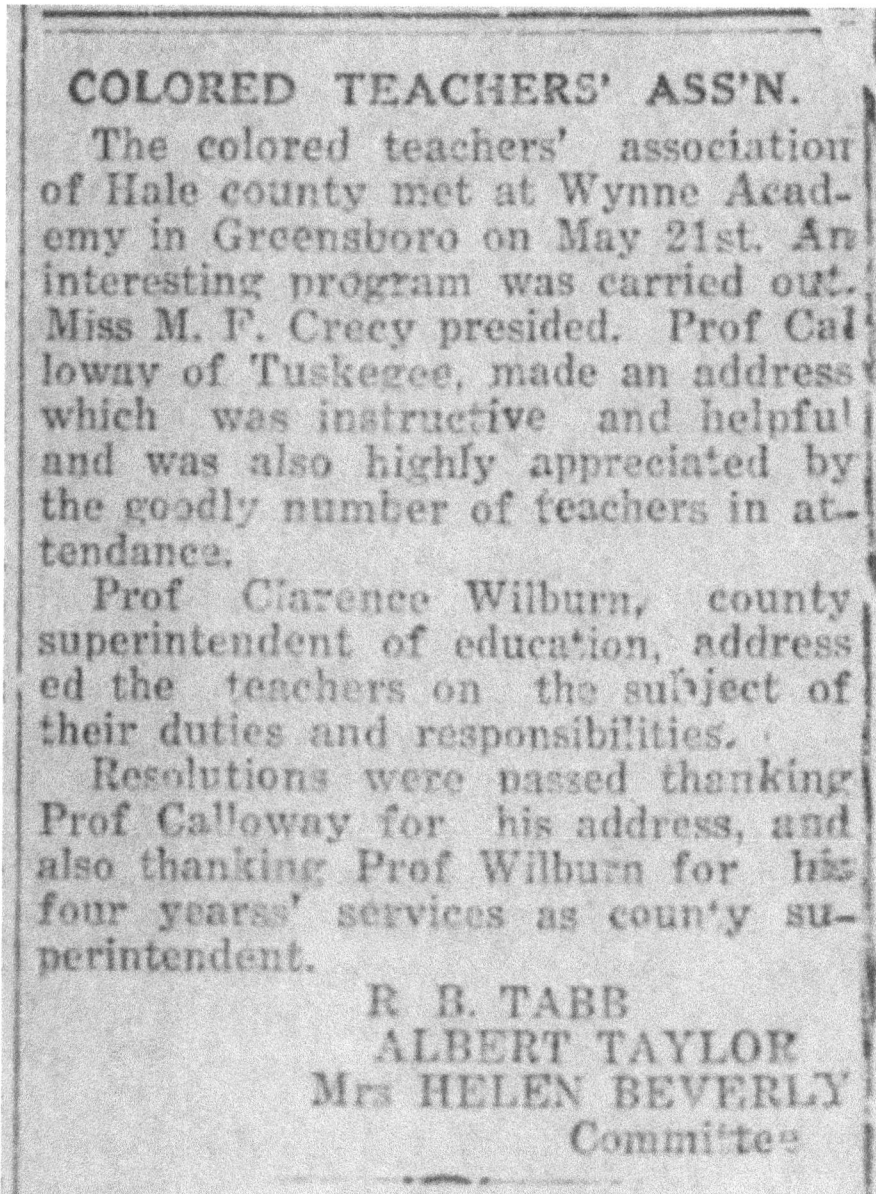

COLORED TEACHERS' ASS'N.

The colored teachers' association of Hale county met at Wynne Academy in Greensboro on May 21st. An interesting program was carried out. Miss M. F. Creey presided. Prof Calloway of Tuskegee, made an address which was instructive and helpful and was also highly appreciated by the goodly number of teachers in attendance.

Prof Clarence Wilburn, county superintendent of education, addressed the teachers on the subject of their duties and responsibilities.

Resolutions were passed thanking Prof Calloway for his address, and also thanking Prof Wilburn for his four years' services as county superintendent.

R. B. TABB
ALBERT TAYLOR
Mrs HELEN BEVERLY
Committee

342

---

342 Colored Teachers' Association, *Greensboro (Alabama) Watchman,* 26 May 1921, p. 3, col. 4; digital image *Newspapers.com* (https://www.newspapers.com/image/308195398/?terms=colored%20teachers&match=1 : accessed 9 Oct 2021).

TO THE PUBLIC:

You are hereby notified that the Wynne Academy will open Monday October 3rd, 1921. Parents are requested to see that children begin with school trrm. Incidental fees: 1st grade, 15c; other grades 25c per month.   E A McGruder, Prin. Mrs M W McGruder, Miss Christopher Hill, Miss Delina Jones, Ass'ts.

343

---

[343] Notification of Class Opening, Wynne Academy, *Greensboro (Alabama) Watchman*, 22 September 1921, p. 3, col. 3; digital image *Newspapers.com* (https://www.newspapers.com/image/308197777/?terms=wynne&match=1 : accessed 9 Oct 2021).

AN APPEAL TO THE COLORED PEOPLE.

Allow me to bring to your notice a mater which the three years that I have served Wynne Academy has caused me to consider very closely, why we cannot unite our forces to have a good modern public school in our city for colored children.

We have tried for three years to formulate a plan by which we might interest all of the people to give at least some support to this school; but each time our support has been sectional and by a limited number. Now, since we must speak frankly to all, of existing conditions in our school, we must also appeal to all to join us in adjusting these conditions.

There are always a few persons who can have private teachers to instruct their children—there are others who are able to send their children away to school while they are in the primary grade and keep them there till they graduate; but tpe masses of our children must receive their educational training in the public schools at home. For this reason it is each one's duty to give some amount now to aid in clearing the debt on our school building and making the buildings and grounds what they should be.

We have launched a "drive" for the purpose of raising all the money needed to pay off the indebtedness and make the necessary improvements. The final rally will end in April, but as an auxiliary to this rally we have organized a "Voting Contest" which ends February 16. In this contest the teachers of the primary and intermediate grades respectively are the contestants. The one receiving the highest number of votes will be crowned "Queen of the United Districts of Greensboro."

Let each person cast as many votes as he or she can purchase that through this drive we may raise $500.00.

Do not discuss what you have done nor what a family of many children has not done, but let us all resolve to do or best to raise the desired amount. Thank you.

A. M. McGRUDER, Prin.

344

---

344 An Appeal to the Colored People, *Greensboro (Alabama) Watchman*, 16 February, 1922, p. 2, col. 3; digital image *Newspapers.com* (https://www.newspapers.com/image/308320955/?terms=wynne&match=1 : accessed 9 Oct 2021).

Below is a list of the four colored adult school having the highest
attendance for the month of February:

Dora McGruder—76.

Maggie McGruder—47.

Ervene Odum—47.

George Washington Freed—43.

MRS CALVIN HOLLIS,

Visiting Teacher.

345

Colored Adults with the Highest Attendance, *Greensboro (Alabama) Watchman*, 7 March
1935, p. 4, col. 2; digital image *Newspapers.com*
(https://www.newspapers.com/image/538140380/?terms=%22colored%20adult%22&match=
1 : accessed 9 Oct 2021).

STRAYED — One black Jersey Steer about 2 years old, split in right ear, and cropped left ear. Reward. Left my place about 1 month ago. E A McGRUDER, Wedgworth, Ala.

346

346 Strayed Steer, *Greensboro (Alabama) Watchman*, 16 May 1935, p. 4, col. 2; digital image *Newspapers.com* (https://www.newspapers.com/image/538141193/?terms=strayed&match=1 : accessed 9 Oct 2021).

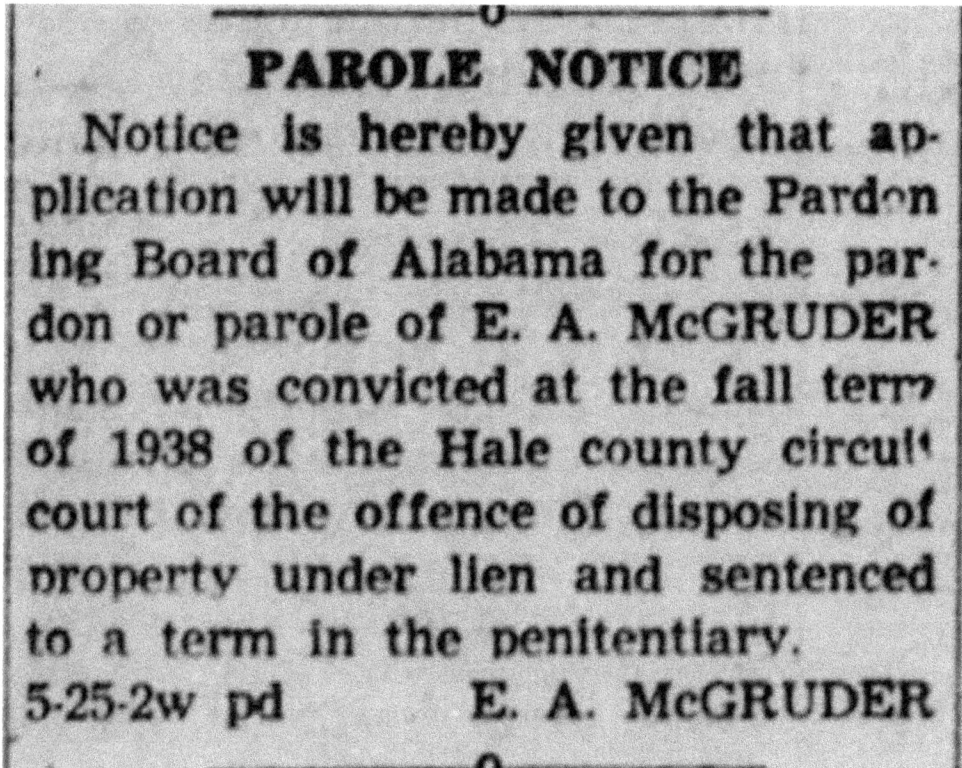

PAROLE NOTICE

Notice is hereby given that application will be made to the Pardon ing Board of Alabama for the pardon or parole of E. A. McGRUDER who was convicted at the fall term of 1938 of the Hale county circuit court of the offence of disposing of property under lien and sentenced to a term in the penitentiary.
5-25-2w pd   E. A. McGRUDER

347

347 Parole Application of E. A. McGruder, *Greensboro (Alabama) Watchman*, 1 June 1939, p. 4, col. 4; digital image *Newspapers.com* (https://www.newspapers.com/image/538113602/?terms=McGruder&match=1 : accessed 9 Oct 2021).

According to Betty Shaw, Ethew's wife Maggie also went to jail. Rumor has it that it was due to low quality materials being used in the construction of a white county high school. The author believes that Ethew may have been a victim of a campaign of racist forces and a victim of a legal lynching. This incident needs further research.

The following section contains selected references to mortgage sales and foreclosures involving family lands.[348]

MORTGAGE SALE

Under and by virtue of the power of sale contained in that certain mortgage executed on the 12th day of November, 1924, by Ethew A. McGruder and Maggie N. McGruder his wife, Calvin McGruder and Mattie McGruder, his wife, Fonsy McGruder and Dora McGruder, his wife, Zanie McGruder, unmarried, Isaiah McGruder, unmarried, Willie McGruder unmarried, Rosa Ann McGruder, unmarried, and Bettie McGruder to the undersigned, W.M. Wedgworth, which said mortgage is recorded in Book 119, pages 336 et seq. of the Mortgage Records of Hale county, Ala., I, the undersigned, will offer for sale in front of the court house of Hale county, Alabama, in Greensboro, at public outcry, within the legal hours of sale, to the highest bidder for cash on MONDAY, SEPTEMBER 23,1929 the following described real estate situated in Hale county, Ala., to-wit: The Southeast quarter of the Southwest quarter of Section eight, and the Southeast quarter of the Southwest quarter of the Southwest quarter of Section eight, and the West half of the Southeast quarter of Section ten, and five acres off the west side of the East half of the Northeast quarter of the Northwest quarter of Section nine, and the North half of the Southwest quarter of the Northeast quarter of Section nine, and the South half of the Southeast quarter of Section 9, and the South half of the North half of the Southeast quarter of Section nine, and the Northwest quarter of the Southeast quarter of Section nine, less five acres in the Northeast corner thereof and two acres off the West side of the Southwest quarter of the Southwest quarter of Section ten, all in Township twenty-one of Range three east, and containing three hundred and sixteen acres more or less, and being all the land owned by the above named mortgagors in Hale county, Alabama, and being the identical lands described in and conveyed by the said mortgage above described.

Default having been made in the payment of the debt secured by said mortgage and said default continuing said sale will be had for the purpose of enforcing the collection of the said debt secured by said mortgage together with the costs of collecting same including a reasonable attorney's fee.

W. M. WEDGWORTH
8-22-3w Mortgagee.

348 Mortgage Sale, default by Ethew A. McGruder et. al., on debt to W.M. Wedgeworth, *Greensboro (Alabama) Watchman*, 5 September 1929, p. 4, col. 5; digital image *Newspapers.com* (https://www.newspapers.com/image/538097662/?terms=McGruder&match=1 : accessed 9 Oct 2021).

NOTICE.

Default having been made in the payment of the debt secured by mortgage executed to the undersigned by Rembert McGruder, Will McGruder, Creede McGruder, J. D. McGruder and Roena Cooper, and which mortgage is recorded in Mortgage Book 93, page 572 of the Probate Records of Hale county, Alabama, I, the said undersigned will sell under the power of sale in said mortgage on SATURDAY, MARCH 20th, 1915, in front of the court house in the town of Greensboro, Alabama, during the legal hours of sale, at public auction, to the highest bidder for cash, the following described real estate, situate, lying and being in the County of Hale and the State of Alabama, to-wit: The west half of the southeast quarter of Section 13, all of our undivided interest in and to the following described lands: West half of the southeast quarter of Section 13, the east half of the southwest quarter of Section 13; the northwest quarter of the northeast quarter of Section 24; the northeast quarter of the northwest quarter of Section 24, all in Township 21, Range 3 east, containing two hundred and forty (240) acres more or less.

W. M. WEDGWORTH,
Mortgagee.

349

---

349 Sale Notice, default by Rembert McGruder et. al., *Greensboro Watchman*, 25 February 1915, p. 4, col. 3; digital image *Newspapers.com*

MORTGAGE FORECLOSURE SALE NOTICE

Default having been made in payment of the indebtedness secured by that certain mortgage executed by Marvin McGruder to E F Hildreth on October 8th, 1935, which is recorded in Probate Office of Hale County, Alabama, in Mortgage Book No. 147, page 515, the undersigned E F Hildreth, under the power and authority contained in said mortgage will sell to the highest bidder, for cash, before the courthouse door of Hale County, Alabama, during the legal hours of sale on

350

(https://www.newspapers.com/image/308321234/?terms=McGruder&match=2 : accessed 9 Oct 2021).

350 Mortgage Foreclosure Sale Notice, default by Marvin McGruder, *Greensboro (Alabama) Watchman*, 29 October 1936, p. 4. col. 4; digital image *Newspapers.com*

MORTGAGE FORECLOSURE SALE NOTICE

Default having been made in the payment of the indebtedness secured by that certain mortgage executed by E. A. McGruder and Maggie N. McGruder to E. F. Hildreth under date of October 23rd, 1935 which mortgage is recorded in Probate Office of Hale County, Alabama, in Mortgage Book No. 147, page 537 I will sell at public auction for cash, before the court house door of Hale County Alabama, on FRIDAY, DECEMBER 3rd, 1937, the following described real estate, lying and being situated in Hale County, Alabama, and being the same described in and conveyed by said mortgage, to wit:

Five acres in Northwest corner of Northeast quarter of Southeast quarter; Ten acres in Southwest corner of Southeast quarter of Northeast quarter; South Half of Southwest quarter of Northeast quarter Fifteen acres in Southeast corner of Southeast quarter of Northwest quarter; All in Section Nine, Township 21 North, Range Three East; less and except that portion of said lands belonging to Alabama State Bridge Corporation and Alabama State Highway Department.

The above sale is made for the purpose of collecting the indebtedness secured by said mortgage, together with the costs of sale, including a reasonable attorneys fee.

E. F. HILDRETH, mortgagee.
11-11-3w

351

(https://www.newspapers.com/image/538148321/?terms=McGruder&match=1 : accessed 9 Oct 2021).

[351] Mortgage Foreclosure Sale Notice, default by E.A. & Maggie N. McGruder, *Greensboro (Alabama) Watchman*, 11 November 1937, p. 4, col. 5; digital image *Newspapers.com* (https://www.newspapers.com/image/538141011/?terms=McGruder&match=1 : accessed 9 Oct 2021).

THURSDAY, JUNE 17, 1943

MORTGAGE FORECLOSURE SALE NOTICE

Default having been made in the payment of the indebtedness secured by that certain mortgage executed by Isaiah McGruder and Minnie Lee Mcgruder, his wife, to Mrs. Mamie S. Lanford under date of November 27th, 1935, and of record in the Probate Office of Hale County, Alabama, in Mortgage Book No. 147, page 567, which said mortgage, together with the indebtedness secured thereby, was transferred and assigned by the said Mrs. Mamie S. Lanford to E. F. Hildreth under date of March 25th, 1943, and of record in the Probate Office of Hale County, Alabama, in Mortgage Record No. 167, page 513; and said default continuing, the undersigned, E. F. Hildreth, as owner and holder of said mortgage and indebtedness secured thereby, will sell at public auction, for cash, to the highest bidder, before the courthouse door of Hale County, Alabama, on Friday, June 25th, 1943, the following described real estate, lying and being situated in Hale County, Alabama and being the same described in and conveyed by said mortgage, to-wit:

Seventeen acres in Southeast corner of East Half of West Half of Southwest quarter of Section 10; Eleven acres off Northeast quarter of Northeast quarter of Section 9; Twenty-two acres off East side of West Half of Southwest quarter of Section 9; All in Township 21, of Range 3 East; And also, an undivided one-seventh interest in and to the following described lands, viz: North Half of South Half of Northeast quarter of Section 9; Southeast quarter of Southeast quarter of Northeast quarter of Section 9; South Half of Southeast quarter of Section 9; Northwest quarter of Southeast quarter of Section 9; Northeast quarter of Southeast quarter of Section 9, less 5 acres in Northwest corner thereof; Five acres on West side of East Half of Northeast quarter of Northwest quarter of Section 9; West Half of Southeast quarter of Section 10, less two acres in Southwest corner thereof; Southeast quarter of Southwest quarter of Section 8; Southeast quarter of Southwest quarter of Southwest quarter of Section 8; All in Township 2 North, of Range 3 East, and containing 338 acres, more or less; and all real estate, or any interest therein, owned by the said Isaiah McGruder and Minnie Lee McGruder in Hale County, Alabama, on November 27th, 1935.

The above sale is made for the purpose of collecting the indebtedness secured by said mortgage, together with the costs and expense of said sale, including a reasonable attorneys fee.

  E. F. Hildreth, as owner and holder of said mortgage and the indebtedness secured thereby.

6-3-3c

According to Betty McGruder Shaw, Hildreth was a local judge who was well known for exploiting black people in the area, as well as the poor and uneducated of all backgrounds.

352

SALE NOTICE

Default having been made
n the payment of the indebt-
dness secured by that certain
mortgage executed by E. A.
McGruder and Maggie N. Mc-
Gruder to E. F. Hildreth under date of October 23rd, 1935
which mortgage is recorded
n Probate Office of Hale
County, Alabama, in Mortg-
ge Book No. 147, page 548,
will sell at public auction,
for cash, before the court-
ouse door of Hale County,
Alabama, on FRIDAY, DEC-
EMBER 3rd, 1937, the follow-
ng described real estate, ly-
ng and being situated in Hale
County, Alabama, and being
he same described in and con-
eyed by said mortgage, to-
vit:

North Half of South Half
f Northeast quarter of Sec-
on 9; Southeast quarter of
Southeast quarter of North-
ast quarter of Section 9;
South Half of Southeast quar-
r of Section 9; Northwest
uarter of Southeast quarter
f Section 9; Northeast quart-
r of Southeast quarter of Sec-
ion 9, less 5 acres in North-
vest corner thereof; Five acres
n West side of East Half of
Northeast quarter of North-
vest quarter of Section 9;
West Half of Southeast quart-
r of Section 10, less two acres
n Southwest corner thereof;
Southeast quarter of South-
vest quarter of section 8;
Southeast quarter of South-
vest quarter of Southwest
uarter of Section 8; All in
Township 21, Range 3 East.

The above lands are sub-
ect to first mortgage to J. B.
Stickney.

The above sale is made for
he purpose of collecting the
ndebtedness secured by said
mortgage, together with the
osts of sale, including a
easonable attorneys fee.

E. F. HILDRETH, mortgagee
11-11-3w

353

---

352 Mortgage Foreclosure Sale, default by Isaiah & Minnie McGruder, *Greensboro (Aoabama) Watchman*, 17 Jun 1943, p.8, col. 6; digital image *Newspapers.com* (https://www.newspapers.com/image/538125280/?terms=McGruder&match=1 : accessed 14 Jan 2022).

353 Mortgage Foreclosure Sale Notice, default by E.A. & Minnie McGruder, *Greensboro (Alabama) Watchman*, 25 Nov 1937, p.4, col. 6; digital image *Newspapers.com* (https://www.newspapers.com/image/538141167/?terms=McGruder&match=1 : accessed 14 Jan 2022).

www.ingramcontent.com/pod-product-compliance
Lightning Source LLC
Chambersburg PA
CBHW080555030426
42336CB00019B/3195